Additions and Corrections to the W.P.A. Inventory of Ross County, Ohio: CHILLICOTHE

Jana Sloan Broglin

HERITAGE BOOKS
2025

HERITAGE BOOKS

AN IMPRINT OF HERITAGE BOOKS, INC.

Books, CDs, and more—Worldwide

For our listing of thousands of titles see our website
at
www.HeritageBooks.com

Published 2025 by
HERITAGE BOOKS, INC.
Publishing Division
5810 Ruatan Street
Berwyn Heights, MD 20740

(Originally Titled)
INVENTORY OF THE COUNTY ARCHIVES OF OHIO

Prepared by
The Historical Records Survey
Division of Professional and Service Projects
Work Projects Administration

No. 71. ROSS COUNTY (CHILLICOTHE)

Columbus, Ohio
The Historical Records Survey
June 1939

International Standard Book Number
Paperbound: 978-0-7884-5220-8

The Historical Records Survey

Luther H. Evans, National Director
John O. Marsh, State Director

Division of Professional and Service Projects

Florence S. Kerr, Assistant Administrator
Mildred M. Thrasher, State Director

Works Progress Administration

F. C. Harrington, Administrator
Carl Watson, State Administrator

TABLE OF CONTENTS

The *Inventory of the County Archives of Ohio* is one of a number of bibliographies of historical materials prepared throughout the United States by workers on the Historical Records Survey of the Works Progress Administration. The publication herewith presented, an inventory of the archives of Ross County, is number 71 of the Ohio series.

The Historical Records Survey was undertaken in the winter of 1935-1936 for the purpose of providing useful employment to needy unemployed historians, lawyers, teachers, and research and clerical workers. In carrying out this objective, the project was organized to compile inventories of historical materials, particularly the unpublished government documents and records which are basic in the administration of local governments, and which provide invaluable data for students of political, economic, and social history. The archival guide herewith presented is intended to meet the requirements of day-to-day administration by the officials of the county, and also the needs of lawyers, businessmen, and other citizens who require facts from the public records for the proper conduct of their affairs. The volume is so designed that it can be used by the historian in his research in unprinted sources in the same way he uses the library card catalog for printed sources.

The inventories produced by the Historical Records Survey attempt to do more than give merely a list of records - they attempt further to sketch in the historical background of the county or other unit of government, and to describe precisely and in detail the organization and functions of the government agencies whose records they list. The county, town, and other local inventories for the entire country will, when completed, constitute an encyclopedia of local government as well as a bibliography of local archives.

The successful conclusion of the work of the Historical Records Survey, even in a single county, would not be possible without the support of public officials, historical and legal specialists, and many other groups in the community. Their co-operation is gratefully acknowledged.

The Survey was organized and has been directed by Luther H. Evans, and operates as a nationwide project in the Division of Professional and Service Projects, of which Mrs. Florence S. Kerr, Assistant Administrator, is in charge.

F. C. Harrington
Administrator

PREFACE
2nd edition

In 1929 after the stock market crash along with the Great Depression, drought of 1930, and crop failures which followed, President Herbert Hoover and his successor Franklin D. Roosevelt formulated relief projects, the most successful was the establishment of the Works Progress Administration (WPA).

Established as the Works Projects Administration in 1935, the WPA was the largest of the many programs developed during Roosevelt's "New Deal." In 1939, the agency's name was changed to Works Progress Administration, and continued as such until its demise in 1943.

The Federal Writers' Project, a division of the WPA (known as Federal Project Number One), created jobs for many unemployed librarians, clerks, researchers, editors, and historians. The workers went to courthouses, town halls, offices in large cities, vital statistics offices and inventoried records. Besides indexing works, many records were transcribed. One of these many projects was the *Inventory of the County Archives* which has benefitted genealogists and historians. The inventories listed the records, either by volumes or file boxes and years per record type, within the office. Although the WPA oversaw this project, the information for each volume of records may differ significantly by the information submitted.

Many of these volumes included in the *Inventory of the County Archives* contain listings of records initiated specifically for the depression era. Records may include volumes for the WPA, CCC (Civilian Conservation Corps) and NYA (National Youth Administration, as well as for tuberculosis hospitals. These listings may include the names of the workers.

The information herein is verbatim using the vernacular of the time. Obvious spelling errors have been corrected. Records listed may have met the requirement for retention and have been destroyed as per the records retention act, while other records are considered permanent records. Records once considered "open" to the public, such as lunacy, idiotic, and juvenile cases, or records involving children, such as children's homes, and school records may be "closed" due to a revision of state laws. (*See:* **https://codes.ohio.gov/ohio-revised-code**) Ohio Revised Code, sections 149.31 and 149.34). However, the records may be opened to family members with adequate proof of lineage.

PREFACE
2nd edition

Although this project was to encompass all of Ohio's 88 counties, approximately 30 of these inventories have been located while others may not have been done, lost, or are located in libraries and not known to the general public.

Volumes follow a general format listing the offices. Those for Fulton, Medina, Muskingum, and Wayne include either additional information or may be lacking segments found in other volumes as these were "missing" books.

The addresses and website section of this edition list an up-to-date location guide to each office mentioned. Non-governmental websites may list locations where documentation for the county may be found.

Jana Sloan Broglin
Fellow, Ohio Genealogical Society
Swanton, Ohio
2025

Preface
1st edition

The Historical Records Survey began operations in Ohio in February 1936. In the sixteen districts of the Works Progress Administration in Ohio, the project was organized and operated by district supervisors of the Writers' Project. In November 1936, the Survey became an independent part of the Federal Project No. 1. Russell S. Drum, Assistant State Director, has been in charge of the administrative details of the project.

The purpose of the Survey in Ohio has been the preparation of complete inventories of the records of the state and of each county, city, and other local governmental unit. The *Inventory of the County Archives of Ohio* will, when completed, consist of a set of eighty-eight volumes with a separate number for each county in the state. The units of the series are numbered according to the respective position of the county in an alphabetical list of the counties. Thus, the inventory herewith presented for Ross County is number 71. The inventory of the State Archives and of municipal and other local records will constitute separate publications.

The principle followed in the inventory of county records has been to place a record in the office of origin rather than in the office of deposit. The records are arranged with those of the executive branch of the county government first, followed by judicial, law-enforcement, fiscal, and miscellaneous agencies. Minor agencies are placed in the general arrangement according to function rather than according to constitutional or statutory responsibility to a major subdivision. The legal development of each office or agency has been treated in a prefatory section preceding the inventory of the records of the office. Although a condensed form of entry is used, information is given as to the limiting dates of all extant records, the contents of individual series, and the location of records in state house, county courthouse, or other depository.

The Historical Records Survey was inaugurated in Ross County in May 1936 and was under the supervision of William S. Davis. The final rechecking of the county records was completed by George Reichert in July 1938. The wholehearted co-operation of the county officials with the project workers has meant much in the thoroughness and completeness of the result. Members of the state editorial staff of the Historical Records Survey, under the supervision of Miss Winifred Smith, State Editor, compiled, arranged, indexed, edited, and reproduced the volume for distribution among public and semipublic institutions and organizations. The historical research was performed by Drs. Hilliard, Pross, and

Roadabaugh of the project.

The various units of the *Inventory of the County Archives of Ohio* will be issued in mimeographed or printed form for free distribution to state and local public officials and public libraries in Ohio, and to a limited number of libraries and government agencies outside the state. Requests for information concerning particular units of the *Inventory* should be addressed to the Historical Records Survey, Old Post Office Building, State and Third Streets, Columbus, Ohio.

John O. Marsh
State Director
The Historical Records Survey

Columbus, Ohio
June 28, 1939

LIST OF ABBREVIATIONS, SYMBOLS, AND EXPLANATORY NOTES

adm. .... administration
Arch. .... Archaeological
Art. .... Article
bull. .... bulletin
CCC. .... Civilian Conservation Corps
cf. .... (confer) compare
chap(s). .... chapter(s)
comp. .... compiler
Const. .... Constitution
ed(s). .... editor(s)
et al. .... (et alii), and others
(et) passim .... and here and there
ex *rel.* .... (*ex relations*) at the instance of
et seq. .... and following
G. C. .... General Code
ibid. .... the same reference
loc. cit. .... *(coco citato)*
N.P. .... The Ohio NISI PRIUS REPORTS
n.p. .... no place of publication shown
nolle prosequi .... decline to prosecute
n.s. .... new series
NYA .... National Youth Administration
O.L. .... *Laws of Ohio*
op. cit. .... (*opere citato*) In the work cited
R. .... River
rep. .... reporter
R.S. .... Revised Statutes
sic .... thus, following copy
U.S.C.A. .... United States Code Annotated
v. .... versus
vol(s). .... volume(s)
W.P.A.. .... Works Progress/Project Administration
x .... by
— .... current, to date
4-H .... (Four - H)

LIST OF ABBREVIATIONS, SYMBOLS, AND EXPLANATORY NOTES

Each chapter or section of County Offices and Their Records of this volume consists of (1) an essay describing the legal status and functions of one department of county government and (2) an inventory of the records of that department.

Each record constitutes a separate entry. Entries are arranged under topical headings and subheadings.

Every entry sets forth, insofar as applicable, the following:

Entry number. Entries are numbered consecutively throughout the inventory.

The exact title as it appears on the record or if the record has no title a supplied title in brackets. If the title of the record is non-descriptive, misleading, or incorrect an additional title (in capitals and lower-case letters), also enclosed in brackets, has been supplied.

Dates show inclusive years or parts of years covered by the record. Breaks in dates indicate that the record is missing or was not kept between dates shown. A dash in place of the final date indicates an open record. If no current entries have been made the date of the last entry is noted. Where no statement is made that the record was discontinued at the last date shown, it could not be definitely established that such was the case. Where no comment is made on the absence of prior and subsequent records, no definite information could be obtained.

Quantity, given in chronological order wherever possible.

Labeling. Numbers and letters within parentheses indicate labeling on volumes, file boxes, or other containers.

Variations in title. The current or most recent title is used but significant variations are shown with dates for which each was used.

Change of agency. Occasionally a record is discontinued as a county record and kept by some other agency.

Description. A statement of the nature and purpose of the record and of what the record shows. As the contents of a record may vary over a period of time the description may differ somewhat from the record at any one period. Wherever feasible, changes in content are shown with dates. In map and plat entries the names of author and publisher and the scale are omitted only when not available.

Arrangement. Records said to be alphabetically arranged are frequently alphabetized only as to initial letter of the surname. This is true especially where there is a secondary arrangement.

Indexing. Self-contained indexes are described in the entry. Separate indexes constitute separate entries with cross references to and from the record entry.

Nature of recording. Changes are indicated with dates.

Condition. No statement is made if good or excellent.

Number of pages. Averaged for the series.

Dimensions show size of volumes, maps, file boxes, or other containers and are expressed in inches in every instance. The dimensions of volumes are given in order of height, width, and thickness; of file boxes in order of height, width, and depth.

Location. Rooms referred to are in the county courthouse unless some other building is specified.

Title-line cross references are used to complete series where a record is kept separately for a period of time or in other records for different periods of time. They are also used in all artificial entries which are made to show, under their proper office, records kept in the same volume or file with records of another office. In both instances, the description of the master entry shows the title and entry number of the record from which the cross reference is made. Dates shown in the description of the master entry are for the part or parts of the record contained therein, and are shown only when they vary from those of the master entry. Artificial entries show only title, dates, and description.

Separate third-paragraph cross references from entry to entry, are used to show prior, subsequent, or related records which are not a part of the same series. If, however, both entries are under the same department which contain records logically belonging under that heading but which have been classified under an equally appropriate heading.

While Ohio was still a part of the Northwest Territory, Ross County was erected and organized on August 20, 1798, in accordance with a proclamation of Governor Arthur St. Clair.[1] It was named for the Federalist senator from Pennsylvania, James Ross, the "Territory's staunch defender in the Senate," and one of the leading speculators in Ohio lands.[2] At first the county's huge territory extended from the northern boundary of Adams County to Wayne's treaty line. In 1800, however, part of its area was lost to the newly-created Fairfield County and in 1803 more land was lost by the erection of Franklin and Greene Counties. Other changes were made until 1850, when Ross was reduced to its present boundaries by the formation of Vinton County.[3] Ross County is located in the south central part of the state where it is bounded by Pickaway County on the north, by Hocking, Vinton, and Jackson Counties on the east, by Pike on the south, and by Highland and Fayette on the west. In 1930 its area of 668 square miles, third largest in Ohio, contained a population of 45,181, of which 18,340 resided in Chillicothe, the county seat.[4]

Before the arrival of the white man, Ross County was one of the favorite habitats of Indian tribes of both the prehistoric and historic. It "comprises within its territory the most interesting archaeological area of its size in Ohio and probably in the United States and might be termed the center of highest culture of the mound building peoples."[5] It is remarkable not only for numbers, but also for size and variety of the earthworks. Representing the highest degree of culture is the Hopewell Group in Union Township, the enclosure of which includes more than 125 acres.[6] At Mound City, a rectangular enclosure containing 23 mounds, located a few miles north of Chillicothe, specimens of the highest sculptural art of the prehistoric race have been found.[7] Other important remains in the county include

---

1. Salmon P. Chase, comp., *The Statutes of Ohio and the Northwestern Territory, 1788-1833* (Cincinnati, 1835), III, 2097.
2. Henry Howe, comp., *Historical Collections of Ohio . . .* (Norwalk, 1896), II, 491; Randolph Chandler Downes, *Frontier Ohio, 1788-1803 (Ohio Historical Collections,* III, Columbus, 1935). 171.
3. Randolph Chandler Downes, "Evolution of Ohio County Boundaries," *Ohio State Archeological and Historical Quarterly*. XXVI (1927), 340-477.
4. Ohio Secretary of State, *Ohio Fifteenth Federal Census, 1930* (Columbus, 1931), 7, 11.
5. William C. Mills, *Archaeological Atlas of Ohio* (Columbus, 1914), 71.
6. Henry C. Shetrone "Exploration of the Hopewell Group of Prehistoric Earthworks," *Ohio State Archeological and Historical Quarterly,* XXV (1926), 5-227.
7. Mills, *op. cit.*, 71.

the Harness and High Banks works, the Seip group,[8] the Adena mound,[9] and the Baum works on Paint Creek in Twin Township, an example of a lower culture. Ross County, with 370 mounds and 49 enclosures, has the largest numbers of each of those remains in the state. In addition there are nine village sites and 27 burials recorded.[10]

In the historic Indian period Ross County was in the land of the Shawnees. The first historic mention of the Shawnees in the Ohio Country dates back to 1684, when the Iroquois attacked the Miamis on the grounds that they had invited the Shawnees into their country to make war on the Iroquois. About the middle of the eighteenth century the eastern division of the Shawnees joined their western brethren. During the following years this tribe sided with the French against the English in the international struggle for possession of the Ohio Valley. When the Americans began to settle the West, the Shawnees distinguished themselves as the most hostile to the whites. During a series of Indian wars this tribe was driven first from the Scioto Valley to the Miami and, by General Anthony Wayne's victory and the Treaty of 1795, from the latter region to the headwaters of the Auglaize.[11]

The colony, later the state of Virginia, claimed possession of the Northwest Territory on the basis of charters issued to the London Company by King James I in 1606 and 1609.[12] During the American Revolution the Continental Congress asked the states to cede their lands to the United States for the common benefit of the nation. In October 1783, Virginia complied, giving up her claims to the territory northwest of the Ohio River, reserving, however, the lands between the Scioto and Little Miami Rivers for military bounty purposes.[13] The Scioto cuts through present Ross County from north to southeast. Approximately two thirds of the county, that part west of the river, lay in the Virginia Military Tract. This area was surveyed and the land sold without any plans as to the shape of the various tracts. Instead of definitely sized and shaped townships, sections, and other tracts, there was irregularity in size and shape. Boundaries were marked by stones, trees, and other objects that were likely to disappear with the years. This led to considerable

---

8. See *Ohio State Archeological and Historical Quarterly*, SL (1931), 343-509.
9. See *Ibid.*, X (1901-192), 452-179; LXI (1932), 369-523.
10. Mills, *op. cit.*, 71.
11. Frederick Webb Hodge, ed., *Handbook of American Indians North of Mexico* (Bureau of American Ethnology, *Bulletin* XXX, pt. ii, Washington, 1912), 531-537.
12. W. E. Peters, *Ohio Lands and Their Subdivision*, 2nd edn. (Athens, 1918), 105-106.
13. *Ibid.*, 106-108.

confusion in establishing land titles at later dates. The part of the county east of the Scioto lay within the Congress Lands which were surveyed and marketed in accordance with the Ordinance of 1785 and the Act of 1796 which provided for six-mile townships, one-mile sections, and reservations for the United States and for educational purposes.[14]

In 1792 Nathaniel Massie and others from Kentucky explored the Scioto Valley and returned with glowing accounts. The Presbyterian congregations of Cane Ridge and Concord, Kentucky, opposed to slavery and troubled by the questioning of their land titles, decided to emigrate into the Scioto region. The Indian wars, however, restrained them. After Wayne's treaty in 1795, Massie, a noted land speculator, and the Kentuckians formed a company agreeing to make a settlement in the spring of 1796. About 40 assembled in April and proceeded to the junction of Paint Creek and the Scioto where they founded Chillicothe.[15] According to Henry Howe, many of Wayne's soldiers and camp women settled in the town.[16]

Massie, formerly a Virginian, probably interested some of his fellow Virginians in the lands of his speculation. In 1797 a small band of pioneers, in order to escape the institution of slavery, moved from Berkeley County, Virginia, to Chillicothe.[17] Other Virginians, enticed by the lands offered them as army bounties, also settled in Ross County. Chillicothe and Ross County, therefore, became a center of Kentucky and Virginia influence in the development of the new state of Ohio. Among the early Kentucky settlers were the Reverend J. B. Finley, Henry, Bazil, and Reuben Abrams, Joseph McCoy, Benjamin and William Rodgers, David Shelby, and James Harrod.[18] The Virginians numbered among them several men important in the pages of Ohio history, including Edward Tiffin and his brother-in-law, Thomas Worthington.

Within a few years Chillicothe became the leading frontier town in the Scioto Valley[19] and one of the important towns of the Northwest Territory.

---

14. C. E. Sherman, *Original Ohio Land Subdivisions* (Ohio Cooperative Topographical Survey, *Final Report*, III, Columbus, 1923), 20.
15. Howe, *op. cit.*, II, 492; Downes, *Frontier Ohio*, 81.
16. Howe, *op. cit.*, II, 492.
17. L. W. Renick et al, *Che-le-co-the, Glimpses of Yesterday*, (Chillicothe, 1896), 33; Downes, *Frontier Ohio*, 201.
18. Howe, *op. cit.*, II, 492.
19. Downes, *Frontier Ohio*, 201

County government began to function in 1798. In December the court of common pleas for the Territory met in Chillicothe presided over by "gentlemen justices" commissioned by Governor St. Clair. After statehood the first court met in Ross County in April 1803. Wyllys Silliman was president judge and Reuben Abrams, William Patton, and Felix Renick were associate judges.[20] Records for the early years of Ross County's government are incomplete and but few of the first officers seem to be known. Thomas Scott was clerk of courts and Jeremiah McLane was sheriff.[21] The first punishments for crimes included whipping, branding with a red-hot iron, binding out to labor for seven years or less, execution, and use of the stocks and pillory.[22] The first courthouse was a small hewed log cabin built by Reuben Abrams. It contained also the assembly hall for the Territorial legislature in 1800-1801, the office of the Auditor of Public Accounts of the Northwest Territory, gambling room, and living quarters for a family. In 1801 a stone courthouse was completed which probably held the sessions of the first state legislature. A new courthouse was finished in the 1850s and the old one was torn down.[23]

Chillicothe has an important place in Ohio history. In 1800 Congress made that town the capital of the Territory much to the disgust of the politicians of Cincinnati and Marietta.[24] The power and prestige thus acquired by the Chillicotheans gave them a real advantage in the fight for statehood which soon followed. This struggle was not only for the right of self-government, but also a political struggle between the Jeffersonian Republicans, i.e., the Chillicothe Kentuckians and Virginians, and the Federalists, led by Governor Arthur St. Clair. The real movement for statehood actually emanated from Chillicothe after St. Clair vetoed some legislative acts creating new counties.[25] Worthington won the support of Jefferson's administration for the movement. [26] The Constitutional Convention met at Chillicothe in November 1802. Jeffersonians (Republicans under the

---

20. Lyle S. Evans, *A Standard History of Ross County, Ohio* (Chicago and New York, 1917), I, 144, 150.
21. *Ibid.*, 151.
22. *Ibid.*, 152.
23. Evans, *op. cit.*, I, 126-130.
24. Downes, *Frontier Ohio*, 198.
25. *Ibid.*, 201.
26. *Ibid.*, 204.

leadership of the Chillicothe Junto) controlled the committees of the convention.[27] Tiffin was chosen presiding officer, while Worthington, Massie, and Micael Baldwin, all of Ross County, were leading figures in drawing up the constitution. Chillicothe became the new state's first capital, and Tiffin its first governor, Worthington one of its first United States senators, Baldwin, first speaker of the house, Massie, first speaker of the senate, and William Creighton, Jr., also of Ross County, first secretary of state.

Within a few years a rift developed in the Ohio Republican party, a number of the party trying to overthrow the Tiffin followers. In organizing against this threat the Chillicothe Junto espoused the cause of the Tammany Society. The first Tammany wigwam in Ohio was established at Chillicothe in 1810 by Thomas Lloyd. Governor Tiffin became the Grand Sachem and Worthington was a leading member.[28] Chillicothe remained the capital until 1810 when Zanesville became the state's seat of justice. Again from 1812-1816 Chillicothe served as the capital until the new state house at Columbus was ready for occupation. After the first decade of the nineteenth century the Chillicotheans began to lose that almost absolute control of state politics that had been theirs. However, Ross County still produced famous statesmen. Perhaps none reached higher office than William Allen, a Jacksonian Democrat who served Ohio as congressman, senator, and governor, and his nephew, Allen G. Thurman, who served as congressman, associate justice and chief justice of the Ohio supreme court, and senator. The latter was also Cleveland's candidate for vice president when the democrats went to defeat in 1888.

Ross County's population grew rapidly after Wayne had relieved the back country of the Indian menace. By 1800 its population had jumped to 8,540. After another decade the total was 15,514, and in 1820 it was 20,619. Steady increases from about three to five thousand each decade continued until 1880 when the figure of 40,307 was reached. The population remained steady at about 40,000 until the decade of the 1920s when it rose to the 45,000 mark. During all of these years the

---

27. Robert E. Chaddock, *Ohio Before 1850: A Study of the Early Influence of Pennsylvania and Southern Populations in Ohio* (Columbia University, *Studies*, XXXI, no. 2. New York, 1908), 63: Eugene Holloway Roseboom and Francis Phelps Weisenburger, *A History of Ohio* (New York, 1934), 108.

28. William T. Utter, *Saint Tammany in Ohio: A Study in Frontier Politics*, *Mississippi Valley Historical Review*, XV (1928-1929), 321-340; Samuel W. Williams "The Tammany Society in Ohio," *Ohio State Archaeological and Historical Quarterly*, XXII (1913). 349-370.

city of Chillicothe was slowly growing from 2,426 in 1820 to 7,100 in 1850, to 10,938 in 1880, and to 12,976 in 1900. During the decade of the twenties it increased in size from 15, 832 to its present figure.[29]

It has been pointed out that the first population of the county was composed largely of Kentuckians and Virginians. As the population increased and continued to include proportionately larger numbers of emigrants from Virginia than from other states. However the valley of the Scioto also attracted emigrants especially from Pennsylvania, Maryland, and Delaware. Foreign countries represented by considerable numbers were Ireland and Scotland.[30] It is quite probable that the earliest settlers of Ross County were predominantly of Scotch-Irish stock. The settlements of Cane Ridge and Concord in Bourbon County, Kentucky, were peopled by Scotch-Irish.[31] People from these congregations, we have said, followed Massie to Chillicothe in 1796.[32] Scotch-Irish also came from Berkeley County, Virginia (now West Virginia), and from western Pennsylvania, the center of Scotch-Irish settlements in the United States.[33] Emigrants from North Carolina settled Jefferson Township in 1798.[34] By 1799 there were at least three Scotch-Irish settlements in Ross County, namely, Chillicothe, Union, and Paint Creek.[35]

Another prominent group of pioneers in Ross County were the Germans. It is probable that a few Germans came with the early migrations from Kentucky and the back country of Pennsylvania.[36] The revolutionary period of the 1830s in Europe saw a great migration of Germans to the United States. A number came into Ross County at this time and again in the late 1840s. By 1851 the German population was sufficiently large to support the *Ohio Correspondent*, a German newspaper published in Chillicothe. After several years the Chillicothe *Anzeiger*

---

29. *Eleventh Census of the United States.* 1890, *Population.* I, pt. I, 35; Ohio Secretary of State, *Ohio Fifteenth Federal Census, 1930*, 7, 11.
30. Cf. biographies in Evans, *passim*; Isaac J. Finley and Rufus Putnam, *Pioneer Record and Reminiscences of the Early Settlers and Settlement of Ross County, Ohio* (Cincinnati, 1871), *passim.*
31. Charles A. Hanna, *The Scotch-Irish; or the Scot in North Britain, North Ireland and North America* (New York and London, 1902). II, 125; W. H. Hunter, "Influence of Pennsylvania on Ohio," *Ohio State Archeological and Historical Quarterly,* XII (1903), 287-309.
32. Strickland, W. P., ed., *Autobiography of Rev. James B. Finley; or Pioneer Life in the West* (Cincinnati, 1859).
33. Hannah, *op. cit.,* II, map opposite title p. 49, 61.
34. Evans, *op. cit.,* I, 476.
35. Hanna, *op. cit.,* II, 126.
36. Chaddock, *op. cit.,* 34-35.

became the German paper of the community, succeeded by *Unsere Zeit* in 1868.[37] In 1852 the Germans formed the *Gesang Verein Eintracht*, a singing society, which was virtually disbanded during the World War, although there were still a few active members as late as 1931.[38] In 1870 Ross County residents born out of the state of Ohio included 2,188 from Germany and 598 from Ireland, 2,241 from Virginia and West Virginia, 867 from Pennsylvania, and 337 and 328 from Maryland and Kentucky respectively.[39] Today the foreign-born population is less than one percent of the total, while the negroes [sic], numbering 2,469, account for nearly five and one half percent of the total.[40]

Ross County is primarily a rural county. At the last census 26,841 persons were classified as living in rural areas, of which 14,905 were rural-farm and 11,936 were rural-non-farm population.[41] Massie and his Kentucky followers had noted the richness of the soil of the Scioto Valley.[42] Ross County lies partly in the glaciated plateau, partly in the till plains, and partly in the un-glaciated plateau. The Scioto Valley, particularly, has rich bottom lands.[43] At first grains and other produce were raised for local consumption. On February 26, 1803, the *Scioto Gazette*, of Chillicothe, reported: "Thursday a large Orleans boat loaded with Pork for Messrs. James & McCoy, of this place, left it for New Orleans. This is the first boat of the kind ever built upon the waters of the Scioto." Flatboats loaded with corn and flour were sent to New Orleans the same year by merchants McLaughlin and John Carlisle.[44] In 1797 Zane's Trace was cut through the forest from Wheeling to Chillicothe, and soon extended to Limestone (Maysville), Kentucky. English-bred cattle, Shorthorns and Durhams, were imported at an early date into Ross County, and in 1804 George Renick drove the first western cattle over the mountains to an eastern market.[45]

---

37. Evans, *op. cit.,* I, 366-367
38. Chillicothe *News-Advertiser,* Nov. 16, 1931.
39. *Compendium of the United States Ninth Census.* 1870, 431.
40. *Fifteenth Census of the United States*, 1930, *Population*, III, pt. ii, 483.
41. *Ibid*, III, pt. ii, 483.
42. Strickland, *op. cit.,* 101, 105.
43. Roderick Peattie, *Geography of Ohio, Geological Survey of Ohio*, series iv, *Bulletin*, XXVII (Columbus, 1923), 3-5.
44. Evans, *op. cit.,* I, 79.
45. Howe, *op. cit.,* II, 512; William M. Gregory and William B. Guitteau, *History and Geography of Ohio* (Boston, 1922) 140.

The production of a surplus led to the rise of industry and to demands for better means of transportation. By 1831 the Ohio Canal was opened from Cleveland to Chillicothe, and in 1832 it was in operation the whole length of the state, down to Portsmouth. Chillicothe became an important shipping center for an extensive community.[46] In the 50s railroad lines began to enter the county. Agriculture still remains the most important industry in the county. It employs 4,693 persons, about 30 percent of those in all industries.[47] In 1930 the county's 2,404 farms, lands and buildings, were valued at 19,562,618, 41st in Ohio. The value per farm was 8,133 in contrast to the average of 7,720 for the state; the average value per acre in the county was but $56 in contrast to the average of $79 for the state.[48] The leading products of the county in 1930 were: corn (ranked third), fruit, and livestock. It ranked 14th in the production of swine in 1930, with 61,406; at the same time it recorded 19,185 cattle and 7,032 horses.[49] The values of crops in 1929 were reported as follows: field and orchard, $2,738,823, and domestic animals, $2,430,965.[50] The department of rural economics of Ohio State University reported that there were 23.4 percent more farms in 1935 than in 1930. Still the average income per farm was $1,334, which amounts to $106 more than the state average. At that time Ross County ranked 26th in Ohio in gross cash agricultural income.[51]

The development of agriculture and transportation and the increase in population led to the rise of the manufacturing industry. The raising of grain led to the construction of distilleries and flour mills. Other early important industrial institutions were tanneries, meat-packing houses, saw and planing mills, woolen mills, and paper mills.[52] By 1817 Chillicothe had become both the market town and the industrial center for the region.[53] The largest manufacturing establishment in Ross County today, the Mead Corporation, dates back to 1840. A paper mill had been established as early as 1812, and continued near the village of Kinnikinnick until 1870. In 1930 the various Mead interests were consolidated into a $30,000,000

---

46. Evans, *op. cit.,* I, 86-87.
47. *Fifteenth Census of the United States,* 1930, *Population*, III, pt. ii, 512.
48. *Ibid., Agriculture,* III, pt. I, 284-292.
49. *Ibid*, II, pt. I, 428, 436, 458.
50. *Ibid.*, 466.
51. Ohio Study of Local School Units, *A Study of the Public Schools of Ross County . . .* (mimeographed, Columbus, 1937), 5.
52. Evans, *op. cit.,* I, 368-369, 428.
53. Evans, *op. cit.,* I, 270.

concern. The Chillicothe plant employs around 1,600 men, and produces book and magazine paper, coated paper, corrugated board, and other paper products.[54] At the last census there were 34 manufacturing establishments in the county, annually employing nearly 2,000 wage earners at wages of $15,950,602.[55] Since 1900 the tax duplicate of Ross County rose from $18,283,117 to $68,291,860 in 1930 from which figure it declined to $49,807,092 in 1935. In the latter year the average of the tax duplicate per citizen of the county amounted to $1,512, whereas the average for the state was over $2,057.[56]

The Scotch-Irish pioneers brought with them their own church, the Presbyterian. Nearly all of the first settlers were of that faith.[57] Within a year after the founding of Chillicothe the Presbyterians organized under the Reverend William Speer, a Pennsylvanian. This sect prospered and numbered among its ministers, Robert G. Wilson, later president of Ohio University, and Thomas Woodrow, President Wilson's maternal grandfather.[58] The Methodists organized in 1798 with Tiffin as their minister.[59] The Baptists established themselves in Concord Township as early as 1800, and the Associate Reformed organized in 1806 at the county seat under the Reverend Samuel Crothers, later a famous anti-slavery leader in the Presbyterian church.[60] The Episcopal church saw its beginning in 1817 under the Reverend Roger Searle. The arrival of the Germans led to the formation of the Evangelical and Catholic churches in the 30s, and to the development of the Lutheran church in the 40s, although Lutheranism had begun in Colerain Township as early as 1810.[61] As early as 1821 the negro [sic] citizens, freed slaves, broke away from the Methodist Church, forming their own under the leadership of the Reverend Richard Allan, the first colored Methodist bishop in this country.[62]

---

54. Chillicothe *News-Advertiser*, Nov. 16, 1931; *Fifteenth Census of the United States,* 1930, *Population*, III, pt. ii, 512.
55. *Fifteenth Census of the United States,* 1930, *Manufacturers*, III, 398.
56. Ohio Auditor of State, *Annual Report*, 1935, 552.
57. Howe, *op. cit.*, II, 493.
58. Evans, *op. cit.*, I, 247-248, 316-317; Ray Stannard Baker, *Woodrow Wilson Life and Letters: Youth 1850-1890* (New York, 1927), 18-19.
59. Evans, *op. cit.*, I, 247, 315.
60. Evans, *op. cit.*, 323, 395.
61. Evans, *op. cit.*, I, 253, 325, 327.
62. Evans, *op. cit.*, I, 335.

At the last census of religious bodies were 13,751 members of all denominations in Ross County, including 5,412 Methodists, 2,068 Roman Catholics, 1,712 Presbyterians, 1,024 Baptists, 905 United Brethren, 817 Evangelicals, 410 Episcopalians, and 228 Lutherans.[63]

Ross County men were among the leaders in the early movement for public education in Ohio.[64] The educational history of the county seems to have begun in a small log cabin on the corner of Fourth and Paint Streets in the last years of the eighteenth century. An Irishman named Nathaniel Johnston was one of the first teachers. In 1802 he opened a school for boys in his own house. John Hutt and his wife opened a school for girls that same year, and a little later N. B. Smith announced the opening of his Chillicothe Academy and Boarding School for young women. Old Chillicothe Academy, built 1808, was the leading educational institution in the town for over 40 years. Meanwhile schools were opened elsewhere in the county; in Union Township about 1800 or 1801, another in the same township in 1805-1806, and one in Springfield Township in 1815. Salem Academy, a Presbyterian institution founded by the Reverend H. S. Fullerton in 1842, was an important and well-known institution in the West for at least 40 years. After the mid-century reorganization of the school system began in 1852, three school buildings were erected in Chillicothe. In 1874 a separate school for colored children was erected and the whole city system was reorganized, reducing cost and increasing the efficiency of the system.

During the World War a large cantonment, Camp Sherman, was constructed near Chillicothe. The men trained there constituted the Eighty-Third Division which arrived in France in June 1918.Two important federal institutions are located near Chillicothe today, namely, the United States Veterans Hospital No. 97 and a United States Industrial Reformatory.[66]

---

63. Bureau of Census, *Religious Bodies: 1926*, I, 657.
64. William McAlpine, "The Origin of Public Education in Ohio," *Ohio State Archeological and Historical Quarterly*, XXXVIII (1929), 409-447.
65. Evans, *op. cit.*, I, 255-256, 280-283; *A Study of the Public Schools of Ross County*, 2-3, 82-89.
66. Sanford Bates, *Prisons and Beyond* (New York, 1937), 136-137.

GOVERNMENTAL ORGANIZATION AND RECORDS SYSTEM

The county as a political institution and as a subdivision of the state for purposes of political and judicial administration is of ancient origin.[1] In a form substantially similar in all general features and functions it has existed in England since early times, and in America since settlement. As the tide of migration moved westward, following the American Revolution, the institutions of the seaboard states were transferred to the newer west, undergoing such alteration as best suited frontier conditions.[2]

The earliest provision for the organization of counties in what is now the state of Ohio was contained in the Ordinance of 1787, by which the government of the Northwest Territory was directed to "lay out the parts of the district in which the indian [sic] titles shall have been extinguished, into counties and townships, subject, however, to such alterations as may thereafter be made by the legislature."[3] The organization of county government, therefore, began before the organization of the state and before the adoption of a state constitution. Prior to statehood nine counties were organized. The first county lines were drawn in 1788.[4] The last county lines were altered in 1888, exactly 100 years later.[5]

The establishment of local government in the Northwest Territory was one of the first concerns of Governor St. Clair. The Ordinance of 1787 furnished the framework, but details of institutions had to be constructed. All county officials, under the provisions of the Ordinance, were made appointive by the governor. St. Clair, a former resident of Pennsylvania, in providing for local administration depended in a large part upon the Pennsylvania Code, which, in some instances, was altered to meet the needs of pioneer communities.[6]

---

1. Edward Channing, *A History of the United States* (New York, 1905), I, 425-426.
2. Beverley W. Bond, Jr., *The Civilization of the Old Northwest: A Study of Political, Social, and Economic Development, 1788-1812* (New York, 1934). 58-59.
3. Clarence Edwin Carter, ed. and comp., *The Territorial Papers of the United States* (Washington, 1934), II, 44.
4. *Ibid.*, III, 279.
5. *Laws of Ohio*, LXXXV, 418; Randolph Chandler Downes, "Evolution of Ohio County Boundaries," *Ohio State Archeological and Historical Quarterly*, XXXVI (1927), 449.
6. The governor and judges were given power to "adopt and publish in the district such laws of the original states" as they thought necessary and these laws were to remain in force unless disapproved by Congress. In many cases the governor and judges had not adopted laws of the original states, as the Ordinance stipulated, but had passed measures that conformed in spirit. Since there was some question of the legality of these laws St. Clair, in 1795, after the lower house of Congress disapproved of the

The provisions for local administration were, for the most part, simple and effective. In each county the court of general quarter sessions, composed of three or more justices of the peace, served as the fiscal and administrative board of the county, estimating county expenditures, appointing tax commissioners, and providing for highway and bridge construction.[7] By the end of the decade the court was authorized to enter into contracts for building or repairing the county jail and the courthouse.[8] Other county officials included a sheriff, a coroner, a recorder, a treasurer, a license commission, and justices and clerks of the various courts.[9]

Officers having been appointed, the next step in the organization of government was the establishment of a system of local courts. Evidence seems to indicate that the judicial system for the county had been carefully planned. The court of common pleas, composed of not less than three nor more than five appointive judges, was an inferior court having general common law jurisdiction, though concurrent jurisdiction in the various counties with that of the supreme court.[10] The court of general quarter sessions, besides serving as the fiscal and administrative board of the county, had jurisdiction in lesser criminal cases.[11] A probate court, composed of a single judge, was given jurisdiction in probate and testamentary matters.[12] In 1795, following St. Clair's revision of the territorial code, circuit courts were established and orphans' courts were instituted.[13]

In the meantime the local government was further developed by the organization of civil townships. The governor and judges adopted a law from the Pennsylvania Code requiring the justices of the court of quarter sessions to divide each county into townships and appoint in each a constable to act in townships and

---

laws passed at the legislative session of 1792, called a legislative session to revise the territorial code. The commission, after sitting for three months, completed Maxwell's Code, named in honor of the printer, W. Maxwell. Few changes were made in the Maxwell Code by the territorial assembly which was elected in 1798. Carter, II, 43. The minutes of the legislative assembly were reproduced in *The Ohio State Archaeological and Historical Quarterly*, XXX (1921), 13-53.

7. Theodore Calvin Pease, comp., *The Laws of the Northwest Territory, 1788-1800* (*Illinois State Bar Association Law Series*, Springfield, 1925), 4, 36, 337, 6970; 467-468; 74, 77, 453, 456, 485.

8. *Ibid.,* 485

9. *Ibid.,* 8, 24-25, 61, 68-69, 197.

10. *Ibid.,* 7.

11. *Ibid.,* 4-7.

12. *Ibid.,* 9.

13. *Ibid.,* 157, 181-188

the county, a clerk, and one or more overseers of the poor.[14]

The territory entered the second stage of administration when, in 1798, the population having reached the requisite 5,000, the governor ordered the election of a representative assembly.[15] The system of local government continued as established by the governor and judges, and the transition was achieved without a disturbance of local administration.

The admission of Ohio as a state did not, in the main, materially affect county organization and administration. The system of local government having been organized by the governor and judges and the legislature of the Northwest Territory, the basic offices were continued. Except for the provision for the election of a county sheriff and a county coroner in each county, two officials of utmost importance in pioneer communities, the constitution was silent on such matters as titles, number, and duties of officials.[16]

It devolved, therefore, upon the legislature to confer powers upon the county. In 1804 the legislature made provision for a board of county commissioners, composed of three members elected for a three-year term.[17] The board of county commissioners, supplanting the court of quarter sessions, became the administrative and fiscal board of the county. In 1803 the legislature, recognizing the need for a more adequate system of land records, provided for a recorder to be appointed by the court of common pleas for a seven-year term and for a surveyor to be appointed by the court of common pleas.[18] Another act authorized the appointment of a county treasurer by the associate judges - a later one provided for his appointment by the county commissioners.[19]

---

14. *Ibid.*, 37-41, 338. The system of local governmental administration was the result of sectional compromise, since it combined the county system of the southern and middle states with the elements of the New England town. Dwight G. McCarty, *The Territorial Governors of the Old Northwest: A Study in Territorial Administration* (Iowa City, 1910), 53-54.
15. Carter, *op. cit.*, III, 514-515.
16. *Ohio Const., 1802*, Art. VI, sec. 1.
17. *Laws of Ohio,* II, 150.
18. *Ibid.*, I, 136, 90-93.
19. *Ibid.*, I, 97-98; II, 154; XX, 264.

The legislature also provided during its first session for a prosecuting attorney to be appointed by the supreme court to prosecute cases on behalf of the state.[20] In 1805 the appointing power was transferred to the court of common pleas.[21]

A new office was created in 1820. The county auditor, first appointed by the legislature, had as his duty the preparation of the tax duplicate.[22] The county board of revision, the purpose of which was to correct some of the inequalities of assessments, was established in 1825. The first board of revision or equalization, as it was sometimes called, was composed of the commissioners, the auditor, and the assessors.[23]

The judicial power of the state in matters of law and equity was vested in the supreme court, the court of common pleas, and the justices' courts. The articles of the constitution provided for a court of common pleas to be composed of a president and associate justices. The members of the court, appointed by a joint ballot of both houses of the general assembly, were to hold court in three judicial circuits into which the state was to be divided by the legislature.[24] The court was assigned common law and chancery jurisdiction in all cases as provided by law.[25] To the court was assigned jurisdiction in probate and testamentary matters and in the appointment of guardians, functions performed during the territorial period by the probate court.[26] Finally, the court was authorized to appoint a clerk.[27]

The county offices created by the legislature were designed to transact the business of a state as yet unaffected by the transformations wrought by industrialism and the problems presented by large urban areas. Aside from the maintenance of county poorhouses, the county had no functions in the administration of public welfare.

---

20. *Ibid.,* I, 50.
21. *Ibid.,* III, 47.
22. *Ibid.,* XVIII, 70.
23. *Ibid.,* XXIII, 68-69.
24. *Ohio Const. 1802,* Art. III, secs., 3, 8.
25. *Ibid.,* Art. III, sec. 3.
26. *Ibid.,* Art. III, sec. 5; Pease, *op. cit.,* 9.
27. *Ibid.,* Art. III, sec. 9.

As the wave of democratic philosophy swept across the country in the 1820s and 1830s there arose a demand not only for an extension of the franchise but also for the election of public officials. Accordingly the auditor became an elective official in 1821, the treasurer in 1827, the recorder in 1829, and the prosecuting attorney in 1833.[28]

While the legislature responded to the general demand for the election of county officials, there arose a further demand for a revision of the constitution which failed to meet the needs of an expanding state. This movement came as a result of dissatisfaction with the judicial system which placed the burden of judicial administration upon four judges who had the task of holding court each year in all the counties.[29] Then, too, there arose a demand for the election of all public officials, for the prohibition of charters that granted special privileges, and for a limitation on the power of the legislature to create a state debt. In February 1850 the legislature, following a favorable popular vote on the proposition, called for the election of delegates to meet in convention in May. The constitution drafted by the delegates, was approved by a special election on June 17, 1851. The constitution of 1851, like the constitution of 1802, failed to provide a definite form of county government and administration. Aside from the constitutional provision for the election of a county treasurer, sheriff, and clerk of courts and recreating the probate court which had existed during the territorial period, the organic instrument was silent on the administrative duties of the county.[30] Again all matters pertaining to county government were entrusted to the legislature. While the legislature conferred certain powers upon the county, it was limited by constitutional provision which required all laws of a general major to be uniform throughout the state.[31]

The present administrative organization of Ohio county government presents a picture of extraordinary complexity. Each county quadrennially selects, besides the board of county commissioners, nine administrative officials the recorder, clerk of courts, probate judge, prosecuting attorney, coroner, sheriff,

---

28. *Laws of Ohio*, XIX, 116; XXV, 25-32; XXVII, 65; XXXI, 13-14.
29. J. V. Smith, rep., *Official Reports of the Debates and Proceedings of the Ohio State Convention. . .held at Columbus, Commencing May 6, 1850, and at Cincinnati, Commencing December 2, 1850* (Columbus, 1851), 597 *et seq.* [Jacob] Burnet, *Notes on the Early Settlement of the North-Western Territory*, Cincinnati, 1847), 356. See also *The Ohio State Journal,* December 11, 1840.
30. *Ohio Const. 1851,* Art. X, sec. 3; Art. IV, sec. 16; Art. IV, sec. 7.
31. *Ibid.,* Art. II, sec. 26.

treasurer, auditor, and the county engineer. While these officials conduct a major portion of the county's business, there is a variety of appointive officers and boards, as well as *ex officio* commissioners. For convenience the work of county government may be classified under the following general heads: administration, judicial system, law enforcement, finance and taxation, elections, health, public welfare, and public works.

Administration

The board of county commissioners is the central feature of the present structure of county government. The functions of this board touch either directly or indirectly every other branch and department. The board is the agency in whose name actions for and against the county are brought. This board is empowered to determine certain matters of policy for the conduct of county affairs such as adoption of the budget, establishment of services left optional by law, and the authorization of improvement.[32] Thus in a limited sense it constitutes the legislative branch of the county. The commissioners, however, have no ordinance-making powers. The board also functions as the central administrative body although much of the administration, centered in other elective offices, is beyond its immediate control. The county auditor was originally made secretary of the board and still functions as such in a majority of the counties.[33] Later provisions of the law permitted the board to appoint its own clerk, thus removing this duty from the auditor.

Judicial System

The constitution of 1851 made significant changes in the composition of the court of common pleas. The judges, heretofore appointed by the legislature, were made elective for a five-year term. For the purpose of electing judges the state was divided into nine districts. Each district was divided into three parts, in each of which one common pleas judge was to be elected. Court was to be held in every district or county with such jurisdiction as should be provided by law.[34]

---

32. *General Code*, sec. 2421.
33. *Ibid.,* 2566. See p. 11
34. *Ohio Const. 1851.* Art. IV, secs. 3, 4.

The legislature made provision for the districts but left the jurisdiction of the court much as it had been in the earlier years of its existence.[35] The constitutional amendment of 1912 abolished the divisions and subdivisions provided by the constitution of 1851, and authorized the election of one or more common pleas judges in each county.[36]

The judicial system was extended in 1851 by the creation of district courts composed of one supreme court justice and several common pleas judges in each district.[37] For administrative purposes the nine common pleas districts were apportioned into five judicial circuits.[38] The courts were assigned original jurisdiction in the same matters as the supreme court and such appellate jurisdiction as might be provided by law.[39] The district courts, abolished by the constitutional amendment of 1883, or superseded by the circuit courts which were given the same jurisdiction as their predecessors. The state was divided into seven circuits. In each circuit three judges were to be elected.[40] The judicial system was again altered in 1912 when, by constitutional amendment, the circuits were renamed courts of appeals.[41] The state is divided into nine appellate districts. There are three judges in each district elected by the people of the district for a six-year term.[42]

The constitution of 1851 re-created the probate court, which, existing during the territorial period, was abolished by the first constitution, its authority and jurisdiction being then vested in the courts of common pleas. Each county has one probate judge elected by the people for a four-year term.[43] By constitutional provision, the probate judge has original jurisdiction in probate and testamentary matters, the appointment of guardians, the settlement of the accounts of the executors, administrators, and guardians,[44] and the issuance of marriage licenses.

---

35. *Laws of Ohio*, LI, 145.
36. *Ohio Const. 1851.* (Amendment), Art. IV, sec. 3.
37. *Ohio Const. 1851*, Art. IV, sec. 5.
38. *Laws of Ohio,* L, 69.
39. *Ohio Const. 1851,* Art. IV, sec. 6.
40. *Ibid.,* Art. IV, sec. 6.
41. *Ibid.,* Art. IV, sec. 6.
42. G. C. sec. 1514.
43. *Laws of Ohio,* CXIV, 320.
44. *Ohio Const. 1851,* Art. IV, sec. 8.

An amendment to the constitution of 1912 authorized the common pleas judge, when petitioned by ten percent of the voters in the counties having a population of less than sixty thousand, to submit to the voters at any general election the question of combining the probate and common pleas courts[45] This combination exists in Adams, Henry, and Wyandot Counties.

Due to an increased amount of juvenile delinquency, the legislature, in 1904, authorized the judges of the court of common pleas, the probate court, and the insolvency courts where established to appoint one or more of their members as juvenile judges to hear cases involving neglected, dependent, and delinquent children.[46] In most Ohio counties, including Ross, the probate judge serves as judge of the juvenile court.

Law Enforcement

Closely related to the courts are the agencies of law enforcement in the county. Law enforcement is conducted by four officials: sheriff, prosecuting attorney, coroner, and the dog warden. These officials are concerned primarily with the enforcement of state laws, and leave the enforcement of municipal ordinances, and, in some instances, of state statutes in urban centers to municipal law-enforcing agencies.

The county sheriff, whose duties have been materially curbed by municipal law-enforcement agencies and the state highway patrol, has as his duty the enforcement of state laws.[47] He serves as custodian of the county jail,[48] and as an executive agent of the courts.[49] It has been estimated that approximately one half of his time is devoted to duties connected with the courts. The sheriff is restricted by

---

45. *Ibid.,* Art. IV, sec. 7.
46. *Laws of Ohio,* XCVII, 561-562.
47. G. C. sec. 2833. The sheriff's authority extends to all parts of the county although for obvious practical purposes he rarely makes an arrest in incorporated areas.
48. *Ibid.,* sec. 3157.
49. *Ibid.,* sec. 2834.

lack of scientific equipment which has become essential to law enforcement.[50]

The county prosecuting attorney, the most important agent in the enforcement of criminal law, is directed by law to "inquire into the commission" of crime within his county, and to prosecute on behalf of the state all complaints, suits, and controversies to which the state is a party.[51] In conjunction with the state attorney general, he prosecutes in the supreme court cases arising in his county.[52] He acts, also, in a civil capacity as legal counsel for the commissioners and other county officials.[53] The prosecuting attorney may institute proceedings against an individual, but as a rule charges must be filed against the offender before action is taken. The prosecuting attorney has certain administrative duties such as serving as a member of the county budget commission and on the board of sinking fund trustees.[54]

The county coroner has the ancient duty of determining the cause of death where death occurs under suspicious circumstances or by unlawful means,[55] the making of the proper distribution of property found on or about the deceased,[56] and the management of the county morgue.[57] It has been suggested, by authorities on county administration, that the office be abolished and the duties transferred to a medical examiner appointed by the prosecuting attorney.[58]

---

50. *The Reorganization of County Government in Ohio: Report of the Governor's Commission on County Government* (n.p. December 1934), 105. The sheriff system worked admirably in rural communities. From the standpoint of police administration, it is unsatisfactory in areas of dense population. In such areas there is need for a force of officers whose duty it is not merely to apprehend law violators but to prevent the infraction of the law by patrolling the territory. For an interesting discussion of some of the newer problems confronting law-enforcing agencies see Donald C. Stone, "The Police Attack Crime," *Nat. Mun. Review,* XXIV, (1935), 39-41.
51. G. C. sec. 2916.
52. *Ibid.,* sec. 2916.
53. *Ibid.,* sec. 2917.
54. *Laws of Ohio,* CXII, 399-400; CXV, pt. ii, 412; CXVI, 585; CVIII, pt. I, 700-702.
55. G. C. sec. 2856.
56. *Ibid.,* secs. 2863, 2864.
57. *Ibid.,* sec. 2856-1.
58. W.F. Willoughby, *Principles of Judicial Administration* (Washington, 1929), 165-173. According to a recent act, effective June 8, 1937, only a licensed physician or person who shall have previously served as coroner is eligible to fill the office. G. C. sec. 2856-3.

Another law enforcement agent existing within the county is the dog warden. This official is appointed by and is responsible to the county commissioners. No special qualifications are required for the office. The dog warden has as his duty the enforcement of the sections of the General Code relative to licensing of dogs, impounding and destruction of unlicensed dogs, and the payment of compensation for damages to livestock inflicted by dogs.[59]
The dog warden and his deputies, in the performance of their legal duties, have the same "police powers" as those conferred by statute upon sheriffs and police.[60] Prior to 1927, the duties now performed by the dog warden were performed by the county sheriff.

Law enforcement in the county is defective in two respects: first, there is little or no co-ordination between the four agencies of the law enforcement, and second, there is little or no responsibility for neglect of duty. Evidence seems to indicate that the present inefficient and antiquated system could be corrected by consolidating all law-enforcing agencies into a county department of law enforcement under the immediate supervision of the county prosecuting attorney.[61]

The administration of criminal justice in the county has grown up in more or less hit-or-miss fashion and is for the most part unsatisfactory and extremely cumbersome. Arrests are made by the sheriff, or other police officers, who are theoretically officers of the state, but who are under little or no supervision. The accused person is brought before a local magistrate for a preliminary hearing. In the event the accused is committed, it is necessary, in most cases, to receive an indictment before a grand jury.[62]

---

59. *Laws Of Ohio,* CVIII, pt. I, 535; CXII, 348.
60. G. C. sec. 5652-7.
61. *Report of Governor's Commission*, 117-122.
62. For a criticism of the administration of criminal justice, see Edwin H. Sutherland, *Principles of Criminology* (Chicago, 1934), chap. xiv; Willoughby, *op. cit.,* chaps. xi, xiv, xxxvi.

Finance and Taxation

There are three types of financial functions performed by county officers: tax administration, handling of fiscal affairs of the county, and the trusteeship of funds held for individuals in court procedure. The principal financial authorities are the board of commissioners, the auditor, and the treasurer. The commissioners levy taxes, appropriate funds, and authorize payments.[63] The auditor's primary duties are the keeping of accounts, the issuance of warrants, evaluation of real estate, and the preparation of the tax list.[64] The treasurer collects taxes, receives and has custody of county money, and disburses it upon warrant from the auditor.[65] Other functions related to the county finance are performed by the board of revision, budget commissioners, and board of sinking fund trustees.

During the early years of Ohio history, the principal sources of state and county revenue were the general property tax, the poll tax, and fees received from licenses and permits to engage in certain kinds of business.[66]

A tax law enacted by the first territorial legislature (1799) designated certain types of property as taxable for county purposes. All houses in towns, town lots, out-lots, all water and windmills, ferries, cattle and horses, were put on the county tax duplicate. A tax on land, subsequently used also for county purposes, was originally devoted exclusively to the needs of the territorial government. County officials were to assist in the administration of this tax as well as that of the county levy.[67]

---

63. G. C. secs. 5630, 5637, 7419.
64. *Ibid.,* secs. 2570, 2573, 2583-2589.
65. *Ibid.,* secs. 2649, 2649-1, 2656, 2674.
66. An act of 1825 levied a tax on the income of attorneys, physicians, and surgeons for state purposes. Amount of tax was determined by the court of the common pleas. Salmon P. Chase, comp., *The Statutes of Ohio and of the Northwestern Territory* (Cincinnati, 1833), 1471. This act was repealed in 1852. Maskell E. Curwen, comp., *Public Statutes at Large of the State of Ohio* (Cincinnati, 1853), 1755. The poll tax was perpetually abolished by constitutional authority in 1802. *Ohio Const. 1802,* Art. VIII, sec. 23.
67. Chase, *op. cit.,* 267-272; 272-279. Previous acts of 1792 and 1795 were temporary in nature.

In the course of time many additions were made to the original list of taxables. Taxable property came to include capital employed in merchandising (1826), and by exchange brokers (1825), pleasure carriages (1825), money loaned at interest (1831) and stock in steamboats.[68] In the latter year dividends of bank, insurance, and bridge companies were also made taxable.[69] The first act of a general nature directing the taxation of railroads was passed in 1851.[70] In 1862 a tax on the gross receipts of express and telegraph companies was enacted.[71] A levy on the capital stock of freight lines was authorized in 1896.[72] Subsequent enactments brought into the category of "general property" the possessions of public utilities in general. By such accumulations "property" by the end of the nineteenth century, had become a much more inclusive term than it had been one hundred years earlier.

County agencies became even more useful with the discovery of new tax sources. When, at the turn of the twentieth century, the general property tax lost its importance as a revenue source for the state, taxes on inheritance and cigarettes, then, later, on gasoline, liquid fuel, liquor, retail sales, malt and the like, took its place.[73] County officials continued to administer the general property tax, which was devoted henceforth to the uses of local governments, but they assisted in administration of a number of those newer taxes as well.

The assistance rendered by county officials has been equally extensive in the system of issuing licenses and permits. The issuance of marriage licenses began during the territorial period (1788).[74] An act to license merchants, traders, and tavern keepers was passed in 1792.[75] Ferry licenses were authorized in 1799.[76]

---

68. *Ibid.,* 1517; 1476; *Laws of Ohio,* XXIX, 272-280.
69. *Laws of Ohio,* XXIX, 302-303.
70. Curwen, *op. cit., 1647.*
71. J.R. Sayler, comp., *The Statutes of the State of Ohio* (Cincinnati, 1876), 301.
72. *Laws of Ohio,* XCII, 89-93.
73. Ohio Tax Commission, *Financing State and Local Government, in Ohio, 1900-1932,* (mimeographed, Columbus, 1934), 2.
74. Chase, *op. cit.,* 101.
75. Chase, *op. cit.,* 114-115.
76. Chase, *op. cit.,* 219.

With the passage of time one license after another has been required until unlicensed businesses have become something of an exception rather than the rule. Even with the increasing assumption of licensing authority by the state, county officials have continued to issue certain licenses assigned to their jurisdiction long ago.[77]

Under the early laws (1792) county commissioners, appointed to annual terms by the courts of common pleas, were to list the male inhabitants above the age of eighteen, stocks of cattle, yearly value of improved land, and other property. Valuation of this property was made by township and village assessors, appointed annually by the court of common pleas.[78] These local assessors, who became elective in 1795, were again appointed in 1799.[79] In 1825 property valuation was assigned to a new official, the county assessor, also appointed by the court of common pleas.[80] This official, became elective in 1827, was succeeded in turn, in 1841, by a township assessor to be elected annually.[81]

In conjunction with these administrators a system of real estate reappraisal was initiated. In 1846 county commissioners were directed to divide their counties into suitable districts and to appoint an assessor for each whose chief function should be to revise the valuation of real property.[82] An act of 1863 made these officers elective and provided for reappraisal every tenth year.[83] This was subsequently changed (1868) to every fifth year and in 1878 returned to the ten year interval.[84]

In 1913 the assistance of county officers in tax administration was temporarily dispensed with and their duties were given to state officials. The county was again made an entire assessment district but district (or county) assessors were now to be appointed by the governor. The tax commission (established in 1910) was

---

77. See pp. XL, 45.
78. *Laws of the Territory of the United States Northwest of the River Ohio* (Philadelphia and Cincinnati, 1792-1796), II, 17-18.
79. Chase *op. cit.,* 169, 273.
80. Chase, *op. cit.,* 1477.
81. Curwen, *op. cit.,* 775-779.
82. Curwen, *op. cit.,* 1269.
83. Sayler, *op. cit.,* 413.
84. Sayler, *op. cit.,* 1641; *Laws of Ohio,* LXXV, 459.

directed to supervise and direct the assessment of real and personal property.[85] This attempt at unification of authority in the state was partially abandoned, however, in 1915, when assessment was returned to the county auditor and to elected township, village, and ward assessors.[86] In 1925 the latter officers were discontinued and the duties of assessment developed upon the county auditor alone.[87]

The advent of the state tax commission brought no great alteration in the process of assessment. The county remains the basic unit and the county auditor continues to serve as an agent of the state. Though the state commission now assesses certain forms of property, certification is made to the county auditor. For example, public utilities are now assessed by the commission and proportional shares of the revenue are apportioned to the counties which contain such property.[88] Financial institutions report directly to the commission which certifies to each county auditor the assessment of each taxable deposit.[89] Intangible property (defined in 1931) owned by individuals and corporations, not otherwise excepted, is listed and valued by the county auditor. Returns showing more than $500 of taxable income are forwarded to the commission for appraisal and certified by it back to the county auditor.[90] From these certifications of the commission, the personal property lists returned to him by individuals, and the real estate assessment for which he is personally responsible, the auditor makes up the grand duplicate of real and personal property taxes.

The county continues to be the basic unit also in the matter of budgeting and the levying of taxes on property. In 1792 the courts of general quarter sessions were directed to estimate the sums needed to defray the costs of county government, specifying as nearly as possible the purposes for which such sums were necessary. This earliest of budgets was to be laid before the governor and judges and approved by the legislature. County commissioners were to apportion or levy the tax.[91]

---

85. *Laws of Ohio,* CIII, 786-787.
86. *Ibid.,* CVI, 246 *et seq.*
87. *Ibid.,* CXI, 486-487. Revaluation of real estate was required in 1925 and every sixth year thereafter.
88. G. C. sec. 5430.
89. *Ibid.,* sec. 5412, 5412-1.
90. *Report of the Governor's Commission,* 75.
91. Chase, *op. cit.,* 118-119.

In 1799 it became the duty of these commissioners to ascertain the probable expenses of the county as well as levy the tax - a duty which continued until refinements in administration were made necessary because of the increasing number of taxing authorities.[92]

In order to achieve some systematic arrangement in the county fiscal system, the function of estimating expenses, or budgeting, was consolidated in recent years in the hands of a county budget commission. Since the Ohio legislature, in 1911, established a tax rate limitation, it was necessary to establish a commission vested with authority to reduce the amounts set up in annual tax budgets when the overlapping districts required more than the aggregate maximum tax rate permits.[93] Organized in 1911 the county budget commission was composed, for a time, of the auditor, the mayor of the largest municipality, and the prosecuting attorney. Taxing authorities in the county were directed to submit their budgets to this body through the agency of the auditor.[94] The board was authorized to make adjustments to the budgets, alterations which the taxing authority might appeal to the tax commission. The budget commission, directed in 1911 to certify its action to the auditor, was subsequently instructed to make such certification to the various taxing units which should themselves authorize the necessary tax levies and certify them to the auditor.[95] In 1927 the composition of this board was altered when the treasurer replaced the mayor.[96]

Early appeals against unjust assessments (1792) were heard by judges of the general court, judges of the common pleas court, or justices of the general quarter sessions court.[97] After 1795 petitions for redress were directed to the county commissioners.[98]

---

92. Chase *op. cit.,* 276-277.

93. G. C. sec. 5625-3. Since 1934 there has been a limitation of ten mills on the dollar. *Ibid.,* sec. 5625-2.

94. *Laws of Ohio,* CII, 270-272.

95. G. C. sec. 5625-25.

96. *Laws of Ohio,* CXII, 399.

97. *Laws of the Territory. Northwest of the River Ohio,* II, 20-21.

98. Chase, *op. cit.,* 171.

This appeal agency was superseded in 1825 by the board of equalization, composed of the commissioners, assessor, and auditor.[99] This agency continued to function through the following years though with occasional changes in personnel.[100]

With the reorganization of property tax administration in 1913 the function of tax revision was taken away from county officers. In each district (county) the tax commission was directed to appoint three persons for the term of three years to form a district board of complaints.[101] An act of 1915 abolished this plan, however, and returned the function of revision to the care of county officials. A board composed of the treasurer, prosecuting attorney, probate judge, and president of the board of commissioners, was directed to appoint a county board of equalization.[102] This plan, too, was soon dispensed with. An act of 1917 constituted the county treasurer, auditor, and president of the board of commissioners as the county board of revision.[103]

The history of tax collection is equally intricate. The fiscal duties of the county treasurer, who now collects the property tax, comprised, in the very early period, only the receipt and custody of revenue funds. The actual collection was performed by other agencies. Due to the fact that in earlier years there were two district tax levies - one on land for the territory and later the state, and one on other property for county purposes - tax collection involved a double operation and duplicate officials.

---

99. Chase, *op. cit.,* 1476-92.
100. The county surveyor became a member at times, in 1868, for example, Sayler, *op. cit.,* 1642.
101. *Laws of Ohio,* CIII, 790-791.
102. *Ibid.,* CVI, 254-255.
103. *Ibid.*, CVII, 40; G. C. secs. 5580, 5596. Highest appellate jurisdiction, held originally by the general court and later (1805) by the associate judges of common pleas, was given, in 1825, to a state board of equalization composed of the state auditor and one member from each congressional district. Later, these boards were composed of the auditor and a member from each state senatorial district. With the establishment of the state tax commission that agency was made the final appeal. *Laws of Ohio*, III, 111; Chase, *op. cit.*, 1481; Curwen, *op. cit.* 1784; G. C. sec, 5625-28.

The collectors of the county levy assessed in 1792 were appointed by the judges of the court of common pleas who were empowered to designate the sheriff, constable, or any other suitable person to perform this function.[104] By an act of 1795 township collectors were appointed by the commissioners and assessors.[105] From 1799 to 1805 taxes for county purposes were collected by county collectors.[106] An act of 1805 designated the township listers as collectors of the county levy but, in 1806, the commissioners were permitted to appoint a county collector instead if they believed such a course to be expedient. This arrangement remained in force until 1825.[107]

The first statute of a general nature providing for a tax on land for territorial purposes was enacted in 1799. From 1799 to 1804 the collectors of the county tax were to collect the territorial tax also.[108] In 1804, however, the county sheriff was specifically designated as the collector of the state tax.[109] From 1806 to 1816 the county commissioners were again permitted to use their own discretion as to whether a county or township collector should be appointed.[110] The county collector of the land tax mentioned in the statutes from 1816 to 1825 was, in all probability, the same official who collected the county tax, though due to a lack of definite terminology it is impossible to be certain.[111]

In 1825 the arrangement for a separate tax duplicate for state and county purposes was abolished and levies for both were made on the same property. In 1827 the office of county collector, who had performed that function in the intervening two years, was abolished and the treasurer, henceforth to be an elective officer, was given the duty of tax collection.[112]

---

104. Chase, *op. cit.,* 119.
105. Chase, *op. cit.,* 171.
106. Chase, *op. cit.,* 277.
107. Chase, *op. cit.,* 471, 527, 771, 1384-5.
108. Chase, *op. cit.,* 270.
109. Chase, *op. cit.,* 415.
110. Chase, *op. cit.,* 537, 727, 973.
111. Chase, *op. cit.,* 973, 1370-71.
112. *Laws of Ohio,* XXV, 25.

The collection of certain taxes other than that on general property is performed by county agency. Thus, for example, inheritance taxes, authorized by the legislature in 1894, are computed by the county auditor, adjusted by the probate court, collected by the county treasurer, and distributed to the proper agency by the county auditor.[113] County auditors certify to the tax commission lists of persons licensed to engage in the business of selling cigarettes. County treasurers are the agents of the state treasurer for the sale of cigarettes tax stamps.[114] The tax on wines, cordials, and beer is collected by means of the sale of stamps by county treasurers in a manner similar to that employed in collecting the cigarette tax.[115] The tax on brewers' wort and malt is collected in an identical manner.[116]

The dispersal of administrative functions among county agencies is demonstrated more effectively, perhaps, in the issuance of licenses and permits which furnish a source of revenue for both the state and the county. The county auditor has issued, collected, and accounted for dog licenses from 1917 to the present;[117] he has issued and the treasurer has collected the fees from cigarette (1893—),[118] malt (1933—),[119] peddlers' (1862),[120] and show licenses (1827—).[121] Hunting and fishing licenses have been issued by the clerk of courts since 1904 and 1919 respectively.[122] In addition, the clerk has issued for the court of common pleas ferry licenses (1805—),[123] auctioneers' licenses (1818),[124] and peddlers' licenses (1810-1862).[125] Marriage licenses, issued from 1803 to 1851 by the clerk of courts, since the latter date, have been in the jurisdiction of the probate court.[126]

---

113. G. C. secs. 5338, 5341, 5348-11.
114. *Ibid.*, sec. 5894-1 *et seq.*
115. *Ibid.*, sec. 6064-42.
116. *Ibid.*, sec. 5545 *et seq.*
117. *Laws of Ohio,* CVII, 334.
118. Jay F. Laning, comp., *Revised Statutes of the State of Ohio* (Norwalk, 1905), 1513.
119. G. C. sec. 5545-5 *et seq.*
120. Sayler, *op. cit.*, 273; G. C. sec. 6349.
121. Chase, *op. cit.*, 1582; G. C. secs. 6374, 6375.
122. *Laws of Ohio,* XCVII, 474; G. C. (Page and Adams) sec. 1430.
123. *Laws of Ohio,* III, 96; VIII, 107; XXIX, 447. Ferry licenses were issued by the general assembly 1803-1805. *Ibid.*, I, 94.
124. Chase, *op. cit.*, 1040; G. C. secs. 5868, 5869.
125. Chase, *op. cit.*, 670.
126. Chase, *op. cit.*, 354; *Ohio Const. 1851,* Art. IV, sec. 8.

The establishment of a board of trustees of the sinking fund (1919) was a logical development in county fiscal administration. This board, composed of the auditor, treasurer, and prosecuting attorney, has as its principal function the payment of bonds issued by the county and the investment in bonds of moneys credited to the sinking fund. Bonds issued in the process of county borrowing must be recorded in the office of the sinking fund trustees and signed by the auditor, as secretary of the board. The trustees certified to the board of commissioners the rate of tax necessary to provide a sinking fund for the payment of the principal and interest of the bonded indebtedness. The trustees are required to keep a full and complete record of transactions and a complete record of the funded debt of the county.[127]

Elections

During the first nine decades of Ohio history the county sheriff was charged with the duty of announcing the time and place of holding elections, providing ballot boxes, ballots, and other supplies, and the township trustees were directed by law to serve as judges of the elections.[128] This system continued, with slight alterations designed to facilitate the conduct of elections in municipal centers until 1892. At that time there were created the offices of state supervisor of elections and deputy state supervisor of elections with the duties prescribed for the conduct and supervision of all elections in the state.[129] The secretary of state, designated as the state supervisor of elections, was authorized and instructed to appoint four deputy supervisors for each county, who, in turn, appointed in all precincts four judges and two clerks of elections.[130]

Under the present election laws, provision is made for a chief election officer, a board of elections in each county, and judges and clerks in each precinct. The board of elections in each county consists of four qualified electors in the county, the members of which are appointed by the secretary of state, two of such

---

127. G. C. sec. 2976-18 *et seq.*

128. *Laws of Ohio,* I, 76-77; III, 331-332; XXIX, 44; L, 312: LXVIII, 68.

129. *Ibid.,* LXXXIX, 455. This act, however, did not apply to the election of school directors.

130. In 1892 each township, exclusive of the territory embraced within the limits of a municipal corporation which was divided into wards, composed an election precinct. See *Laws of Ohio,* LXVII, 47.

members being appointed on the first day of March and in even-numbered years, to serve a four-year term.[131] In making appointments to the membership of the board, equal representation is given to the political party casting the highest and next highest number of votes for the office of governor in the last preceding state election. In this connection provision is made for party recommendations of persons for such appointments.[132]

Under the early election laws the canvassing board was composed of the clerk of court of common pleas and two justices of the peace called by him to his assistance.[133] This practice continued until 1892 when the board of state supervisors of elections succeeded to the duties normally performed by the clerk of the court of common pleas and the county sheriff. The sheriff, however, continued to announce the time and place of holding elections in the county until January 1, 1930 when the board of elections assumed this historic duty.[134] The duty of canvassing the returns, under the present statutes, is performed by the board of elections. The board in each county is required, within five days after each general or special election, to canvas the returns, and to prepare abstracts of the votes cast.[135] A certified copy of the abstract is to be transmitted to the secretary of state, and another copy filed in the office of the board.[136.] The board is required also to prepare and transmit to the president of the senate a separate abstract of the returns of election of governor, lieutenant governor, secretary of state, auditor of state, and attorney general.[137]

---

131. G. C. secs. 4785-6, 4785-8. See also p. 215.
132. G. C. sec. 4785-9. Under the Ohio election law, it is the duty of the secretary of state to appoint persons so recommended, unless he should have reason to believe that such a person would not be a competent member of the board.
133. *Laws of Ohio*, I, 83; III, 336-337; VII, 119-120; XXIX, 49; L, 316; LXI, 68; LXXXII, 30.
134. G. C. sec. 3785-5; *Laws of Ohio*, CXIII, 507; LXXXIX, 455. The election laws of Ohio were revised and re-codified by an act of the general assembly, passed April 5, 1929. *Laws of Ohio*, CXIII, 37-413.
135. G. C. secs. 4785-152, 4785-153.
136. *Ibid.*, sec. 4785-153.
137. *Ohio Const. 1851,* Art. III, sec. 3; G. C. sec. 4785-154.

Health

Prior to 1919 the county had few responsibilities regarding health administration. With the development of urban centers with congested areas the problem of health administration was brought to the attention of the legislature. Prior to the enactment of the present health code in 1919, jurisdiction in matters of health was vested in the cities, villages, and townships. Under the act of 1919 all villages and townships in the county were combined into a general health district under the supervision of a board appointed by the advisory council composed of the mayors of villages and chairman of township trustees. Each city in the district is organized as a separate health district. Two general health districts or a general health district and a city health district located within such a district may combine.[138] All physicians are required to report communicable diseases to the district health commissioners who impose quarantines.[139]

The legislature has placed on the county the burden of responsibility in the treatment of tuberculosis. Any county, regardless of size, may employ nurses, operate clinics, and care for patients in private, municipal, or county sanatoriums. Any county having a population of 50,000 or more inhabitants made with the consent of the state department of health erect and operate sanatoriums, and two or more counties may form districts for the same purpose. The sanatoriums are operated by special boards appointed by the county commissioners.[140]

Besides establishing sanatoriums for the treatment of tubercular patients, counties are authorized to operate general hospitals. The county hospital is operated by a board appointed by the county commissioners.[141] Evidence seems to indicate that the county is the proper unit for hospital administration.

---

138. *Laws of Ohio,* CVIII, pt. I, 238; CVIII, pt. ii, 1085-86. See also p. 223.
139. *Ibid.,* CVIII, pt. ii, 1088-89.
140. G. C . secs. 3148-1, 3148-3.
141. *Ibid.,* secs. 3127-3138-4.

Public Welfare

The administration of public welfare is one of the most complex and one of the most expensive functions of county government. The administration of institutional and outdoor relief is delegated to eight boards and commissions operating independently and with little regard for efficiency.

The administration of the county home is vested in the county commissioners and a superintendent, appointed from a list of names of persons eligible under civil service regulations.[142] Employees are appointed by the superintendent.

Although provision was made for the institutional care of the county's indigent as early as 1816, it was not until after the conclusion of the War between the States when hundreds of Ohio children were left homeless, that the legislature enacted measures for the care of dependent children.[143] Prior to the act of 1865, the trustees of the poorhouses were authorized to apprentice dependent children. The administration of the children's home is vested in a board of trustees, appointed by the commissioners, and a superintendent appointed by the board of trustees.[144]

The board of county visitors, an agency for the examination of county institutions, was created by the general assembly in 1882. Until 1913 the board was appointed by the court of common pleas and after that date by the probate judge.[145] The board consists of six persons appointed for terms of three years.

In 1886 counties were required by law to provide relief for indigent soldiers and sailors and their indigent wives, children, and parents.[146] Soldiers' relief is administered by a commission consisting of three persons appointed by the court of common pleas for terms of three years. This commission, in turn, selects township and ward committees.[147]

---

142. *Ibid.,* sec. 2523.
143. *Laws of Ohio,* III, 276; VIII, 223-224. See also p. 229.
144. G. C. secs. 3081, 3084.
145. *Laws of Ohio,* LXXIII, 174; G. C. secs. 3082-1, 3085.
146. *Ibid.,* LXXXIII, 232-234.
147. G. C. secs. 2930, 2933.

In 1884 the legislature made provision for a soldiers' burial commission in each county.[148] The administration of soldiers' burials is vested in a commission consisting of two persons in each township and ward appointed by the county commissioners.[149]

Counties maintain a system of pensions for the needy blind. Prior to 1936 blind relief was administered in the county by the probate judge (1904-1908), by a blind relief commission appointed by the probate judge (1908-1913), and by county commissioners (1913-1936).[150] The present system originated in 1936 when the legislature accepted the provisions of the federal social security act. Blind relief is financed by federal, state, and local funds and is administered in the state by the Ohio commission for the blind and in the county by the county commissioners, whose decisions are subject to review by the Ohio commission for the blind.[151]

Prior to 1932 the county confined its relief activities to the institutional care of the indigent. Outdoor relief, except for those persons lacking a legal settlement, was provided and administered by the townships and cities. With the coming of the economic depression the resources of the municipalities and townships proved inadequate for financing relief activities. Accordingly, in 1932, the legislature conferred on all counties the authority to care for the poor in their own homes. Funds for such purposes were provided by the issuance of bonds and by a diversion of gasoline taxes for financing such services. While the state relief commission, created for administering state relief, is required to pass upon local relief budgets, the county relief offices, administered by the county commissioners, provide relief services in the county.

Today old age pensions are relieving the counties of the increased burden of institutional relief. This system, originating in 1933, provides for persons 65 years of age. No person may be granted a pension if the net value of his property is in excess of $3,000 or his annual income is in excess of $300.[152] The old age pension system is financed by state and federal funds and is administered by a

---

148. *Laws of Ohio,* LXXXI, 146-147.
149. G. C. sec. 2950.
150. *Laws of Ohio,* XCVII, 392-394; XCIX, 56-58; CIII, 60.
151. *Ibid.,* CXVI, pt. ii, 195-200. See also p. 247.
152. *Ibid.,* CXV, pt. ii, 431-439.

division of the department of public welfare through county boards of aid for the aged.[153] Under the provision of the initial act the county commissioners served as *ex officio* members of the board of aid for the aged in the county. Since May 1, 1937 the chief of the division has been required by law to appoint an advisory board in each county consisting of five members. This board, appointed for a two-year term, succeeded to the duties formerly performed by the county commissioners.[154]

Aid to dependent children, although provided for by the legislature in 1913 in the form of mothers' pensions, assumed a new significance, when, in 1936, the legislature accepted the provisions of the federal social security act. Aid to dependent children is financed by federal, state, and local funds. The administration of the act is delegated to the department of public welfare and in Athens County to the juvenile judge.[155]

Public Works

The responsibility for administration of public works in the county rests with the board of county commissioners, the county engineer, and the sanitary engineer. The county commissioners, since the inauguration of county government, have had the responsibility for the authorization and financing of public works. With the immense development of highway improvement, occasioned by the introduction of automobiles and trucks as means of transportation, public works became one of the most important functions of the county commissioners and consequently the county engineer, who, during the first 120 years of his office, had as his principal duty the surveying of lands, received new duties and responsibilities with respect to the construction of roads, culverts, ditches, and in most cases bridges.[156] Within the last two decades the township roads, under the joint authority

153. *Ibid.*, CXV, pt. ii, 431-439.
154. G. C. sec. 1359-12. See also p. 240.
155. *Laws of Ohio,* CXVI, pt. ii, 188-196. See also pp. 148, 242.
156. *Laws of Ohio,* XCVIII, 245-247; CVIII, pt. I, 497.

of the county and township trustees, have been gradually absorbed by the county-state system of highways.[157]

The Ohio counties were formed to meet the needs of rural pioneer communities with a population spread relatively uniformly over the entire state. Recent decades have, of course, brought remarkable changes. Many sections of the state have become thoroughly industrialized, and, as a result of the change, have been forced to treat such problems as housing, health, sanitation, police administration, scientific transportation, and sewage disposal. These problems with which the county organization has been unable to cope are rapidly taking the form of city problems.

When it is considered that in 1930, of the 1,201,455 persons in Cuyahoga County, 900,429 were in Cleveland, that of the 361,055 people in Franklin County, 290,564 were in Columbus, that of the 589,356 people in Hamilton County, 541,160 were in Cincinnati, and that of the 347,709 people in Lucas County, 290,718 were in Toledo, it is not strange that demands were made for a reorganization of county government to eliminate the waste and confusion occasioned by overlapping jurisdiction of county and municipal functions.[158]

In view of the growth of large cities and the confusion occasioned by the conflict of county and municipal powers, there has been an attempt to work out a more satisfactory relationship between the two organs of local government. This took the form of a constitutional amendment, which, defeated in 1919, was placed on a ballot in 1933 by initiative petition and adopted by the electorate. The amendment provides:

> "The general assembly shall provide by general law for the organization and government of counties, and may provide by general law– alternative forms of county government. No alternative form shall become operative in any county until submitted to the electors thereof and approved by a majority of those voting thereon under regulations provided by law.

---

157. The centralization of highway construction was guaranteed under the road law of 1915. The township trustees, at one time one of the most important agencies in local highway construction, have become a local improvement board with powers to authorize but not to supervise road construction. *Laws of Ohio,* CVI, 589-594.

158. *Fifteenth Census of the United States,* 1930, *Population,* III, pt. ii, 518, 520, 521, 525. C. A. Dykstra "Cleveland's Effort for City-County Consolidation," *Nat. Mun. Review,* viii (1919), 551-556.

> Municipalities and townships shall have authority, with the consent of the county, to transfer to the county any of their powers or to revoke the transfer of any such power, under regulations provided by the general law, but the rights of initiative and referendum shall be secure to ... every measure ... giving or withdrawing such consent."[159]

The constitutional amendment of 1933 altered the status of the county. Where the status of the county was formerly fixed by statute, it is now subject to local determination in the same manner as municipalities.

The arguments advanced in favor of the system fall under three heads:

1. It makes possible a different form of government for urban centers where political, social, and economic conditions differ from those of rural counties.
2. It promotes efficiency and economy by the elimination of duplicate officers and employees.
3. It promotes efficiency by the centralization of power and responsibility.[160]

A commission on county government was appointed by Governor White in 1933 to formulate original plans of county government for submission to the legislature.[161] Accordingly, in 1935, the commission submitted to the legislature ten bills embodying its recommendation as to matters of county reorganization. The major bills authorize three optional forms of county government, subject to adoption by the local electorate: (1) a county manager plan, (2) the elective plan, (3) the appointive executive plan.[162] Of the ten bills presented, two became laws. One of these authorized the transfer to the county of any local governmental activity by voluntary agreements between the county and a local subdivision within the county. This measure, of course, opened the way for the consolidation of such

---

159. *Ohio Const. 1851* (Amendment, adopted November 7, 1933), Art. X, sec. 1.
160. *The Ohio State Journal,* October 9, 1933; C. A. Dykstra, *Loc. cit.*
161. R. C. Atkinson, "County Home Rule Developments in Ohio," *Nat. Mun. Review,* XXIII (1934), 235.
162. R. C. Atkins, "Ohio - Optional County Legislation," *Nat. Mun. Review,* XXIV, (1935), 228.

activities as welfare, police, and sewer construction which need unification in counties having a large urban population.[163] The other act authorized the charter county to take over health administration, noninstitutional relief, and park construction.[164]

While the amendment offers an opportunity for the improvement of local government and counties in which large municipalities have developed, no use has been made of the provision.[165] At present Franklin County with a population of 361,055 has essentially the same type of county government as Vinton County with a population of 10,287.[166]

While unsuccessful attempts have been made to correct some of the defects of the county administration in areas containing large urban populations, little consideration has been given to rural counties where, due to a constant decline in population, the old governmental organization has become unduly expensive and ill-suited to the needs of the population. This is particularly true in the counties located in the southeastern and northwestern portions of the state where the population has steadily declined since 1880. There is a question as to whether the services of modern government in such counties can continue to be maintained without the consolidation of contiguous territory for purposes of administration. The Ohio constitution, from its beginning in 1802, has contained a restriction upon the legislature regarding the minimum area of counties. None could be formed with less than 400 square miles – or reduced below that size.[167] With the development of modern means of transportation and communication this area is ridiculously small. The combination for administrative purposes of sparsely populated counties, having social and economic interests would eliminate waste, overhead, and duplication of personnel.

---

163. *Laws of Ohio*, CXVI, 102-104.
164. *Ibid.*, CXVI, 135.
165. Home rule charters were submitted to the voters in Hamilton, Cuyahoga, Lucas, and Franklin Counties. Advocates of home rule attributed the defeat of these measures to politicians who saw in the scheme the destruction of the spoils system. See R. C. Atkinson, "Ohio - County Charter Elections," *Nat. Mun. Review*, XXIV (1935), 702-703.
166. *Fifteenth Census of the United States,* 1930, *Population,* III, pt. ii, 520, 531.
167. *Ohio Const. 1851,* Art. II, sec. 30; *Ohio Const. 1802,* Art. VII, sec. 3.

Governmental service is constantly requiring the employment of better trained officials. Evidence seems to indicate that only by enlarging the size of administrative area to make possible the specialization in work can the requisite degree of training and skill be secured in the performance of public service.[168]

The relation of the county to the state is also a matter of importance. As a result of radical changes in economic life, matters which were at one time a purely local interest and concern have become of state-wide importance. During recent years the old type of county organization has proved inadequate to meet the needs of modern civilization. Recognition of this fact is found in the steady growth of state control of such matters as public accounting, health and welfare administration, and law enforcement.

At the same time the county has definitely supplanted the township as the administrative unit. This is particularly noticeable in the substitution of the general health district for the township district, and the transfer of tax assessment from township assessors to the county auditor. The county-state administration of highway maintenance and public welfare has been effected. Although many deplore the passing of the little red schoolhouse, the substitution of the county school district for the township area has resulted in better educational advantages for children residing in rural areas.

It is significant that modern invention has removed the necessity for the rural administrative units of such small proportions. The transfer of power from the smaller to the larger unit has arisen out of the desire for better service and economy. Little remains to justify the retention of the township.

Records System

It has been the duty of most officials since the beginning of county government to keep a record of the business of their offices. Differences in population between counties however, forced a wide variance in a recording as evidenced by the fact that several types of records were kept in the same book in some counties, and in others were kept in separate books. As indicated in detail in

---

168. Cf. H. Eliot Kaplan, "A personal Program for County Service," *Nat. Mun. Review,* XXV (1936), 596-600.

office essays, preceding the records of each office, the legislature eventually prescribed not only what records were to be kept but also the content. In this field there was a remarkable advance following the adoption of the constitution of 1851. Such legislation assured some uniformity in the county records system.

There are three strictly clerical officers who work consists mainly in the preparation and custody of records: recorder, clerk of courts, and the judge of the probate court. All three have some part in the recording of documents and instruments affecting the title of property and of other documents presented for record. The last two have as their principal duty the keeping of court records; the clerk of courts serving as clerk of both the court of common pleas and the court of appeals, and the probate court looking after its own records.

It is the duty of the county recorder to copy, index, and file documents authorized to be recorded in his office. The system of recording is prescribed in detail by law. In most counties recording is done by typewriter with considerable use of printed forms. The photographic method of copying is in use in Clark, Hamilton, Lucas, Montgomery, and Summit Counties. Deeds, mortgages, plats, and leases must be copied into separate books, and indexed by direct and reverse indexes.[169] The recorder is required, also, to prepare daily an alphabetical index to such instruments.[170]

The principal records of the clerk of courts are prescribed by statute. They include an appearance docket, trial docket, and execution docket, a journal, and a complete record of proceedings, a system of indexes, and a file of original papers.[171] The clerk is responsible for a variety of nonjudicial records work of which the filing and indexing of automobile bills of sale was the major item. The bill of sale law was repealed by an act effective January 1, 1938, requiring the clerk to issue certificates of title to motor vehicles in triplicate and to file a duplicate of the certificate.[172] At present the clerk of courts acts as the agent of the state for the sale of hunting, trapping, and fishing licenses,[173] and also issues auctioneers' and ferry licenses.[174]

---

169. G. C. secs. 2757, 2764.
170. *Ibid.*, secs. 2764, 2766.
171. *Ibid.*, secs. 2878, 2884, 2885.
172. *Ibid.*, sec. 6290-6.
173. G. C. sec. 1432.
174. *Ibid.*, secs. 5868-5869, 5947-5950.

The clerical office of the probate court performs the following services: the recording of miscellaneous instruments, including marriage license,[175] and certificates of physicians, surgeons, and nurses which authorize them to practice their professions in the county.[176] The court record system of the office, originating in 1853 and continued by the probate code of 1931, is prescribed by statute and involves the proper keeping of papers in each case and copying materials in appropriate record books.[177]

Few records are prescribed for the law-enforcement agencies. The county sheriff is required by law to keep at least three books: a foreign execution docket,[178] a cashbook,[179] and a jail register.[180] Indexes, direct and reverse, to the foreign execution docket were prescribed in 1925.[181] The system of recording is prescribed by statute. The county coroner's records consist of two: a report of findings in cases of unlawful death,[182] and an inventory of articles found on the person or about the deceased.[183] Such records are prescribed by law and the contents of the records minutely prescribed.

The number and type of records kept by county prosecuting attorneys vary widely. In Ross County, current probation and alimony records are kept, but in many counties in the state, no records or files are kept and individual memoranda are disposed of by the incumbent. In some of the counties, however, the records of the prosecuting attorney, kept on standard forms, include such records as a grand jury docket, a grand jury testimony record, and a criminal court docket. Since the prosecuting attorney is vested with large discretionary powers, there is need of

---

175. *Ohio Const. 1851,* Art. IV, sec. 8.
176. *Laws of Ohio,* XCII, 45-47; XCIX, 499; CVI, 193.
177. *Ibid.,* CXIV, 321-322. See p. 92.
178. G. C. sec. 2837.
179. *Ibid.,* sec. 2839.
180. *Laws of Ohio,* XLI, 74; G. C. sec. 3158.
181. *Laws of Ohio,* CXI, 31.
182. G. C. sec. 2857.
183. *Ibid.,* sec. 2859, See also p. 134.

special records and files. Such records, according to authorities on judicial administration, should include, among others, a permanent record of the names and addresses of witnesses, the deputy or division handling the case, and a reason for failure to prosecute, and the reason for which a *nolle prosequi* was asked and granted.

The records of the financial agencies of county government are prescribed by statute. Although records were kept in the earlier years, it was not until 1902 that the manner of keeping and the content of such records attracted the attention of the legislature. It was evident that accounts had not only been poorly kept but there had been little uniformity among the counties of the state. Accordingly, in 1902, the legislature enacted the most important and far-reaching laws on the subject. This act provided for a uniform system of accounting, auditing, and reporting, under the supervision of a newly-created bureau of inspection located in the office of the auditor of state. The act further provided for the annual examination of finances of all public offices.[184]

The governor's commission on the reorganization of county government, after studying the county records system and noting the illogical combination of administrative, judicial, and financial functions, made the following recommendations:[185]

1. County charters and optional forms of government should provide for a department of records and court service to take over the functions of the recorder and clerk of courts, the non judicial record work of the probate court, and the functions of the sheriff as a court officer.
2. The issuance of licenses should be transferred from the clerk of courts to the department of finance.
3. Wider use should be made of the photographic process of recording in large counties.
4. Legislation should be adopted permitting the destruction of chattel mortgages and automobile bills of sale after they have ceased to have effect.

---

184. *Laws of Ohio,* XCVI, 511-515.

185. *Report of Governor's Commission,* 186-187. See also, R. E. Heiges. *The Office of Sheriff in the Rural Counties of Ohio* (Findlay, 1933) 55-56, 60-61.

5. The requirement of three systems of indexes of cases in the clerk's office should be eliminated from the code and only the index of pending suits and living judgments should be required.

6. Provisions should be made in the rules of common pleas court for service of process by mail and that method should be brought into general use.

Concurrently with the development of the records system, steps were taken to assure the proper restoration of damaged or dilapidated records treating of lands and surveys. The county engineer, when directed by the county commissioners, is required by law to transcribe any and all dilapidated maps and records of plats and field notes of surveys from the records of the courts of common pleas, auditor, recorder, or other officer in the state where they may be procured.[186] Similarly, the county recorder, when authorized by the county commissioners, is required to transcribe from the record of the counties all deeds, mortgages, powers of attorney, and other instruments of writing, for the sale, conveyance, or encumbrance of lands, tenements, or hereditaments situated within his county.[187]

The large accumulation of county records, occasioned by increasing governmental services, presents a serious problem. It is important, on the one hand, that valuable space in county courthouses and other county depositories not be cluttered up with vast quantities of useless materials. On the other hand, it is important that every precaution be taken to prevent public officials from destroying valuable public records in order to make space for current business.

Within recent years photography has become an increasingly important aid in archival administration. The Ohio legislature, following the modern trends in recording, has enacted measures looking forward to the conservation of space in the county courthouses by permitting county officials to destroy records which have been reproduced photographically. Under this act, passed in 1937, any county official charged with keeping public records may, when the space requires it, have such records copied or reproduced by any photographic process and destroy the original papers. The original records, however, must be preserved until the time for filing legal proceedings based upon the document shall have elapsed.[188]

---

186. G. C. sec. 2804.
187. G. C. sec. 2763.
188. *Ibid.*, sec. 32-1.

While the legislature has attempted to enact legislation looking forward to conservation of much needed space in county courthouses a significant trend is to be observed and the increasing interest which is being displayed for a department of county archives where all noncurrent records may be properly housed, classified, listed, and made more readily accessible to those interested in consulting them. The arguments advanced in favor of such a system are: (1) that the preservation of county records should be viewed as a distinct function of county government, (2) that the administration of county archives should be under the direction of those qualified to serve efficiently and effectively both the needs of the administration and historians, (3) that the construction of county archives buildings for noncurrent records would make available more space for current business, which at present, is seriously curtailed.

In the field of archival administration the state, rather than the county, has been the experimental laboratory and the results have been eminently successful.[189]

---

189. For an interesting and informative article on the administration of state archives, see Charles M. Gates, "The Administration of State Archives," *The Pacific Northwest Quarterly,* XXIX, (January 1938), no. 1; also in *The American Archivist*, I (July 1938), 130-141.

The first court of Ross County (the court of quarter sessions) was held in a log building which stood at the corner of second and Walnut Streets, Chillicothe. It was built in 1798 by Bazil Abrams. It was a two-story building 24 by 36 feet with an ell 18 by 24 feet. The main room on the lower floor was the courtroom and in 1800, after Chillicothe became the capital of the Northwest Territory, the territorial legislature met in this room. The lower floor of the ell housed the clerk's offices. The upper floor of the main part of the building was a billiard room and gamblers' resort. This building was razed in 1870.[1] A plaque on the wall of a stone building which now occupies the site, reads: "Here stood the two story log-house, in which sat the first court of Ross County. Here met the legislature of the Northwest Territory in 1800, 1801, 1802."

In December 1798 the territorial court of quarter sessions ordered "That Thomas Worthington and Samuel Smith superintend the building of a courthouse, jail, jailer's house, stocks and pillory," and "That Thomas Worthington and William Patton apply to General Nathaniel Massie for a deed to the public ground on which the buildings are to be erected." In 1799 the court ordered that $1,200 be levied by the commissioners to finance the proposed building. In May 1800 the court ordered Thomas Worthington to advertise in Freeman's paper (*Scioto Gazette*) for contracts for building the courthouse. Contracts were let to William Rutledge for the stone work and to William Guthrie for the carpenter work. The building was completed in 1801. Ross County assumed the entire cost of the building. It was located at the corner of Main and Paint Streets on the site of the present county courthouse. It was a two-story stone structure, surmounted by a cupola, on which was mounted a gilded eagle standing on a ball. The building stood back about fifty feet from Paint Street, facing Main Street. Soon after the building was occupied, it was found that the space was inadequate to accommodate both branches of the state legislature which was located in Chillicothe at the time. A two-story brick building was built on the south side of the original building, with the front on a line with Main Street.

---

1. Howe, *op. cit.,* 168.

A covered walk connected the upper floors of the two buildings. The senate assembled in the upper floor of the brick edition and the house of representatives in the upper floor of the main building. After the state capital was moved to Columbus in 1816, the brick building was used for a town hall.[2]

The first courthouse and capitol was used until 1852 when it was torn down to make way for a new courthouse, since the old building was no longer adequate to house the county governmental departments, because of increased business due to the large increase in population. During the period of construction of the new building court was held on the third floor of the Waddell block. A Philadelphia architect was employed to design the building on which construction was begun in 1855. This building, which was finished and occupied in 1858, is still in use as the county courthouse.[3] The building has a two-story central portion, 64 by 120 feet, and a wing on each side. The front of the building is constructed of native freestone whereas the sides and rear are of brick. The main part of the building is of Renaissance type of architecture, with Ionic order used in the general lines, and it is surmounted by a clock tower. The total cost of the building was $100,000.00.

On the first floor of the courthouse are located the offices of commissioners, recorder, clerk of courts, probate court, juvenile court and aid to dependent children, auditor, treasurer, sheriff, board of election, and engineer. On the second floor are located the offices of court of appeals judge, common pleas judge, the common pleas courtroom, and the law library.

County Commissioners. The county commissioner's office, consisting of one room approximately 18 by 18 feet, adjoins the auditor's department. There are two entrances, one through the auditor's office and the other from the court at the rear of the courthouse. The room is well ventilated and has good facilities for both natural and artificial lighting. This office, which is used mainly as a conference and hearing room, has adequate space and equipment for the use of the commissioners. While the commissioners' journal and a few other records are filed here and a small percent of the commissioner's old records are in the middle and rear basement storerooms, most of their records are kept in the auditor's vault.

---

2. Henry Holcomb Bennett, *State Centennial History of Ohio and Ross County* (Madison, 1902), 61-63.
3. Simeon D. Fess, *Ohio Reference Library* (Chicago and New York, 1937), III, 304.

Relief Administration. The relief administration offices are located at 96 North Water Street. Three rooms are occupied by this department: the first is used as a waiting room, the adjoining room as an interviewing room, and the room in the rear as a record file room. The space and equipment are entirely adequate and conditions for housing the records quite satisfactory. All the records are unbound and are filed in steel cabinets.

Recorder. The recorder's department consists of an office and a vault or record file room. The office, which is approximately 30 by 30 feet, located on the north side of the main building and has its main entrance facing Paint Street and rear entrance from the court. The room is well ventilated, well lighted, and free from dampness. Only a small percent of the records of this office are located here; most of them are located in the vault adjoining the recorder's office in the north side of the main building, and occupies a space about 18 by 41 feet, and some are in the middle and rear store rooms in the basement. The vault is well equipped with shelving for bound volumes and has a sufficient number of steel cabinets for filing unbound records. Atmospheric conditions and lighting facilities are satisfactory. An ample number of tables and chairs are provided for the accommodation of clerks and the public.

Clerk of Courts. The clerk of courts' department occupies two rooms. The office is in the south wing adjoining the central portion of the building and has its main entrance from Paint Street and a rear entrance from the court. The office contains only one set of records. The vault or file room occupies a space approximately 15 by 41 feet in the central structure and adjoins the office through which it must be entered. The steel shelves for the bound volumes and the steel cabinets for the filing of unbound records are overcrowded and there is no space for additional equipment. There are adequate accommodations for the use of the records.

Court of Common Pleas. Records are kept by the clerk of courts.

Supreme Court. Records are kept by the clerk of courts.

Court of Appeals. Records are kept by the clerk of courts.

Probate Court. The probate court occupies four rooms, two of which contain records. The main office is located in the southeast corner of the south wing. Only a few current records are kept in the office. Back of the office is a large Z-shaped room, the vault, covering approximately 1,205 feet, which houses a large percent of the records of the probate court. The room is well lighted, well ventilated, and free from dampness. The equipment for filing records consists of steel roller shelves for bound volumes and steel file boxes for unbound records. The filing space and equipment will be adequate for the future needs of this department for a number of years.

Juvenile Court. The juvenile division and the office of aid to dependent children is located in a room approximately 14 by 15 feet adjoining the probate courtroom on the north side. This room is well ventilated, well lighted, and free from dampness. The office is equipped with necessary files and office furniture. Records of aid to dependent children, the probation department and current juvenile court records are filed in this room. There is an entrance to this room through the probate courtroom and an outside entrance from the court at the rear of the courthouse. Some of the older records are housed in the middle and rear basement storerooms.

Jury Commissioners. Records are kept by the clerk of courts.

Prosecuting Attorney. Records of this official are kept in the private office of the incumbent since no office is provided by the county. On the change of officials, active records pertaining to the office are turned over to the incoming official, so that only current records for this office are to be found. These records are in the office of the present prosecuting attorney, Mr. Lester Reid, Phillips Building, 10 East Main Street, Chillicothe.

Coroner. The bound records of this office are kept in the auditor's vault and the unbound records in the clerk of courts' vault.

Sheriff. The sheriff's department is located in the center of the south wing of the courthouse between the offices of clerk of courts and probate court. The main office, which houses most of the records, is well ventilated, well lighted, and free from dampness. The accommodations for filing records are limited with no room for installing more equipment which is badly needed. The office is well equipped, but overcrowded. To the rear of the main office is a small room used as a private office by the sheriff and which also contains a few records. The equipment and space provided meet the needs of this office.

Dog Warden. Records are deposited in the office of the county commissioners.

Auditor. The auditor's department consists of five rooms. The main office is in the northeast corner of the courthouse with the entrance facing Paint Street. This room is 16 by 24 feet, well ventilated, well lighted, and free from dampness. The space and equipment provided this office are ample for the needs of the department and accommodations of the public. No records are filed in this room. Adjacent to the auditor's office is the record vault which is approximately 16 by 24 feet. Artificial lighting is good and there is no dampness. The equipment for filing records consists of steel roller shelving for bound records and steel file boxes for unbound records. The filing space is much overcrowded and there is no space for much needed additional equipment. Owing to the crowded conditions, accommodations for the public are only fair.

Treasurer. This office is located in the center of the north wing of the county courthouse between the recorders and auditor's offices. Three rooms house this department, two of which contain records. The front or main office facing Paint Street, is well lighted and ventilated, and free from dampness. Space and accommodations provided are ample for the department workers and transaction of public business. Only a few current record books are kept in this room. To the rear of the main office is the record vault. This room is well ventilated, well lighted, and free from dampness. Steel roller shelving is provided for filing bound record volumes and steel file boxes for unbound records. A steel burglar-proof safe is located in this room. Space and filing equipment provided in this department are ample for the needs of the office for some time to come. Some of the treasurer's records are kept in the auditor's vault and many of the older records in the middle and rear basement storerooms.

Budget Commissioners. Records are kept by the county auditor, ex officio secretary of the budget commission.

Board of Revision. Records are kept by the county auditor, ex officio secretary of the budget commission.

Trustees of the Sinking Fund. Records are kept by the county auditor, ex officio secretary of the budget commission.

Board of Elections. The board of elections' office, consisting of two rooms, is located on the south side of the corridor in the main wing of the courthouse. No records are filed in the office, which is very crowded. Adjoining the office on the west is the record and supply room, measuring about 15 by 20 feet. Sufficient steel filing equipment and ample accommodations are provided.

Board of Education the offices of the board of education are located in the basement at 62 South Paint Street, Chillicothe. The board occupies four rooms but records are housed only in the main office, a room approximately 21 by 30 feet, located in the northeast corner of the building. Lighting and ventilation are fair and there's no dampness apparent. Most of the records are unbound and are filed and steel cabinets. Adequate equipment and accommodations for the public are provided.

Board of Health. The board of health office, which comprises two rooms, is located at 121 West Main Street, second floor of the Welfare Building. The records are housed in the main office, a well-lighted, well-ventilated, and damp-free room. The amount of space, the equipment, and accommodations are adequate. Most of the records are unbound and are filed in steel cabinets.

Mount Logan Tuberculosis Sanitorium. The Mount Logan Tuberculosis Sanatorium is situated on Carlisle Hill southwest of Chillicothe. The office, in which house all records of the institution, is located on the first floor, to the right of the entrance. Conditions for housing and using the records are favorable. Most of the records are unbound and steel cabinets are provided for housing them.

Superintendent of the County Home. The county home is situated on State Route 104, five miles north of Chillicothe. All records of the institution are kept in the superintendent's office, which is located on the first floor to the right of the main entrance. This room, being 12 by 18 feet, provides ample space and adequate accommodations for the public. It is well lighted, well ventilated, and free from dampness. Filing equipment is badly needed as none has been provided. Records are kept in desk drawers and on wooden shelves.

Board of Trustees of the Children's Home. The children's home is located on Western Avenue at Locust Street. The records are all found in the entrance lobby, which serves as the superintendent's office. Lighting and atmospheric conditions are satisfactory, but the space, being but 12 by 15 feet, is wholly inadequate. Owing to the crowded conditions, accommodations for the public are limited. Steel cabinets are provided for unbound records which constitute the greater part of the records of this department.

Board of County Visitors. No records kept.

Soldiers' Relief Commission. No records kept.

Soldiers' Burial Commission. No records kept.

Blind Relief Commission. Records are kept in the office of the county commissioners who administer blind relief.

Board of Aid for the Aged. This office, located at 63 West Second Street, occupies three rooms on the first floor of the building. Records are kept only in the main office, a room 12 by 30 feet, which furnishes ample space for the needs of the department. Conditions of ventilation and humidity are satisfactory. All records, being unbound, are filed in steel filing cabinets.

Visitor for Aid to Dependent Children. Records are in the juvenile court office.

County Engineer. The county Engineers Department occupies two rooms on the first floor in the west end of the main building of the courthouse. No records are filed in the office, but all are located in the engineers drafting and record room. This room is approximately 18 by 30 feet, well lighted, well ventilated, and free from dampness. A steel safe 4 by 6 x 7.5 feet is provided for filing bound records and steel file boxes for unbound records. Drafting and working equipment are ample as well as space and accommodations for the public.

Agricultural Society. No records located.

Agricultural Extension Agent. The agricultural extension agent occupies two rooms on the second floor of the United States Post Office Building, which is located on Paint Street at Fifth. Both rooms are commodious and are provided with steel cabinets to file the records, all of which are in unbound form.

There are three storerooms for county records in the basement of the courthouse, having a combined area of approximately 1,956 square feet. Lighting and ventilation are very poor, and much dust accumulates in these rooms, but there is little dampness. Wooden shelving is provided for bound records. Unbound records are filed in old type cardboard file boxes or placed in bundles in cardboard cartons. In spite of adverse conditions, the records are, in general, in good condition. Accommodations for research work in the store rooms are very poor.

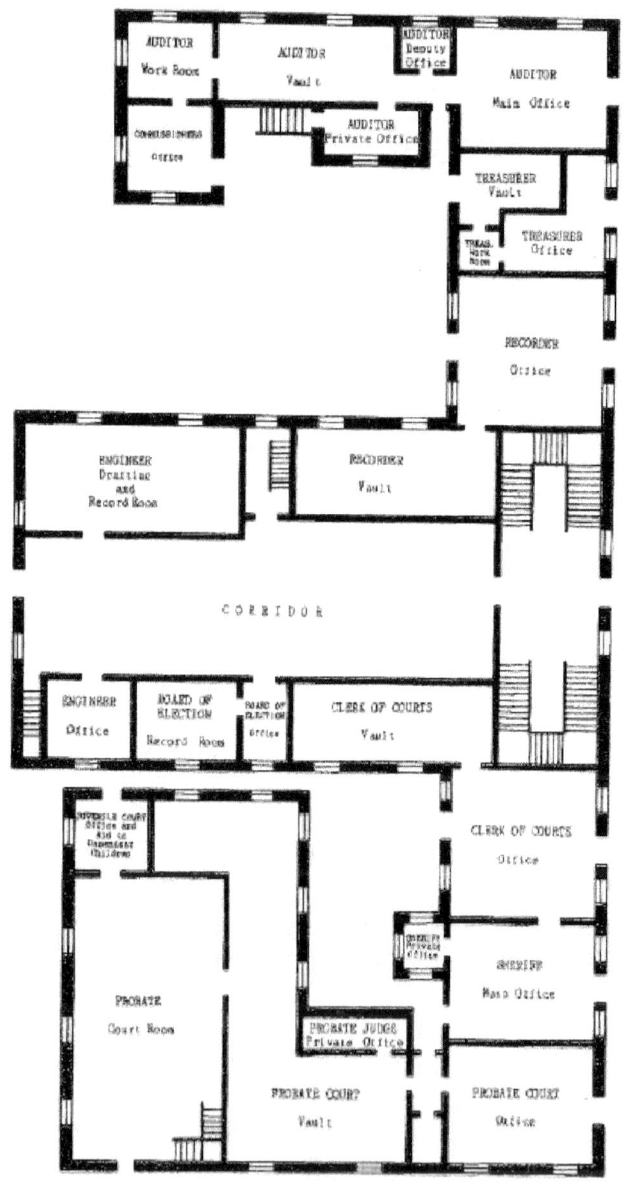
AUDITOR
Work Room
AUDITOR
Vault
AUDITOR
Deputy
Office
AUDITOR
Main Office
COMMISSIONERS
Office
AUDITOR
Private Office
TREASURER
Vault
TREASURER
Office
RECORDER
Office
ENGINEER
Drafting
and
Record Room
RECORDER
Vault
CORRIDOR
N
ENGINEER
Office
BOARD OF
ELECTION
Record Room
CLERK OF COURTS
Vault
CLERK OF COURTS
Office
SHERIFF
Main Office
PROBATE
Court Room
PROBATE JUDGE
Private Office
PROBATE COURT
Vault
PROBATE COURT
Office

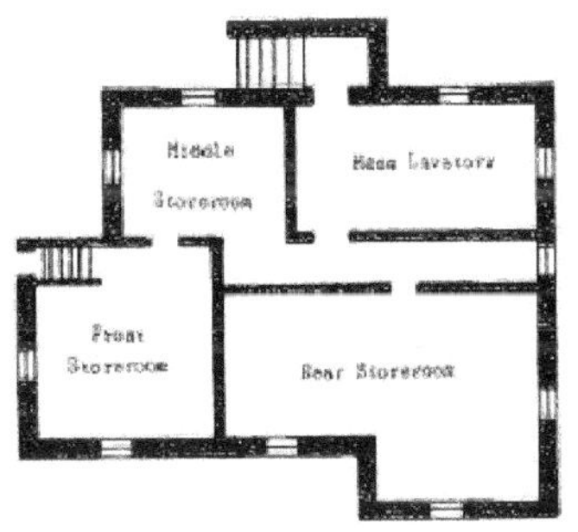
Middle Storeroom
Mens Lavatory
Front Storeroom
Rear Storeroom
BASEMENT FLOOR PLAN

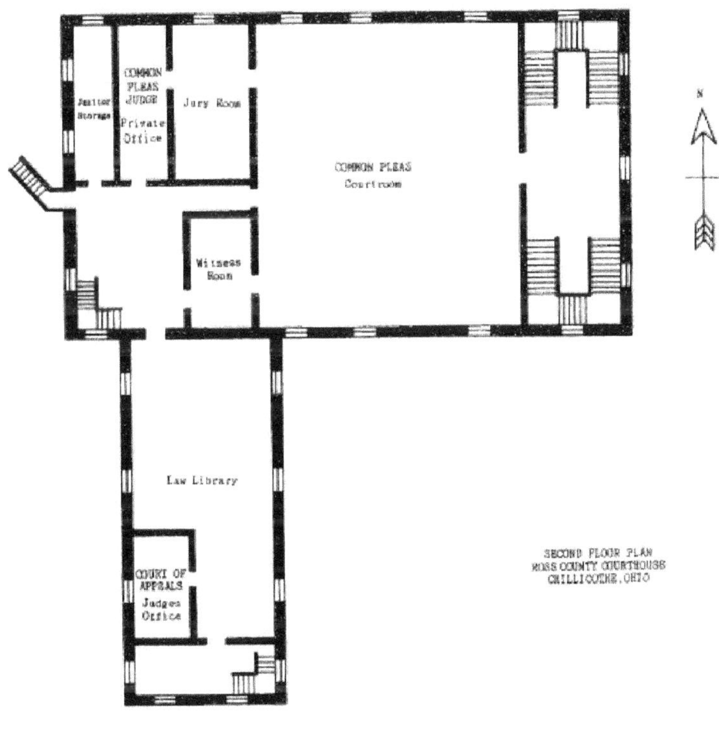
Janitor Storage
COMMON PLEAS JUDGE Private Office
Jury Room
COMMON PLEAS Courtroom
Witness Room
N
Law Library
COURT OF APPEALS Judges Office
SECOND FLOOR PLAN
ROSS COUNTY COURTHOUSE
CHILLICOTHE, OHIO

The governmental system established in 1802, under the first constitution of Ohio, made no provision for the office of county commissioners and its existence is due entirely to statutory enactment. The board, created in 1804, was the successor of the courts of general quarter sessions, which, during the territorial period, served as the representative agent of the county. The board of county commissioners consisted of three members elected for a three-year term.[1] In 1807 the commissioners were made a corporate body vested with the power to sue and be sued.[2] They were required to keep a record of their proceedings, to levy taxes for the support of the county, appoint a county treasurer and to supervise the construction of bridges.[3] They were paid on a per diem basis. Moreover, during the same period (1804) they were given the task of constructing courthouses, jails, and offices for the clerk of courts, court of common pleas, sheriff, auditor, and the treasurer.[4] From 1805 to 1820 the commissioners were required to fix the amounts of tavern and ferry licenses and the rates of transportation by ferry.[5] Of these earlier duties the commissioners retain all but those of fixing the amounts of tavern and ferry licenses and ferriage rates and that of appointing a county treasurer. However, since 1831 they have been authorized to examine and compare the accounts of the county treasurer and to examine the condition of county finances.[6]

Besides the duties regarding county building construction and finance, the commissioners were given the task of constructing local highways when so authorized by the legislature. During the first thirty years of Ohio history the duties of the commissioners in this respect were local in nature. But as the system of road construction expanded they were given the additional duty of converting free turnpikes into state roads.[7] During the forties and fifties private companies were authorized by the legislature to construct plank roads.[8] When those companies were caught in the stringency of a financial depression in 1857, the commissioners were authorized to purchase their holdings.

---

1. *Laws of Ohio,* II, 150.
2. *Ibid.,* V, 97.
3. *Ibid.,* VIII, 48.
4. *Ibid.,* II, 154-157; XXIX, 316.
5. *Ibid.,* III, 96; VIII, 107; XVIII, 170.
6. *Ibid.,* XXIX, 291. See also G. C, sec, 2644.
7. *Laws of Ohio,* XLVI, 74.
8. *Ibid.,* XLIV, 126-127; XLVI, 36, 42; XLIX, 424.

If such transaction was made, the transfer signed by the president of the company was to be deposited with the county auditor.[9] In 1871 the commissioners, although earlier subjected to regulatory measures by the legislature, were prohibited from limiting taxes for roads to exceed three and a half mills on the dollar on the taxable property in the county.[10] Later, in 1885, they were authorized to levy taxes not to exceed five mills on the dollar on all taxable property in the county for the maintenance of roads which have been damaged by excessive wear or were damaged from other causes.[11]

With the development of modern means of transportation, scientific principles were applied to road construction and maintenance. Although the county surveyor, now the county engineer, had in earlier years furnished the commissioners with estimates for bridge construction, it was not until the latter part of the nineteenth century that they were authorized to utilize his scientific knowledge in road construction.[12] At the beginning of the present century the surveyor was directed to appoint a maintenance engineer, with the consent of the commissioners, to supervise repairing of improved roads in the county.[13]

Although the county commissioners have never been closely associated with the administration of criminal justice, their earlier duties regarding the construction of county jails qualified them, in the earlier period, for additional duties in this respect. During the middle of the nineteenth century the commissioners of Cuyahoga County were authorized to employ persons on construction work who were confined in the county jails.[14] While this provision was repealed by the criminal code, adopted in 1853, other earlier functions applicable to all counties were continued. Since 1843 the commissioners have provided equipment and fixtures for places of incarceration, food and clothing for prisoners, and appointed a jail physician.[15] Since 1869 they have been authorized to offer a reward for the detection or apprehension of any person charged with a felony in the county.[16]

---

9. *Ibid.,* LIV, 198.
10. *Ibid.,* LXVIII, 117.
11. G. C., sec. 7419.
12. *Laws of Ohio,* LXXVIII, 285; XCVIII, 245-247. See also p. 258.
13. *Laws of Ohio,* CVIII, pt. i, 497.
14. *Ibid.,* XXXVII, 54.
15. *Ibid.,* XLI, 74; LXXXVII, 186.
16. *Ibid.,* LXVI, 321.

Since 1892 the commissioners in any county where there is no workhouse may, under certain conditions, release or parole an indigent person confined in the jail.[17] With the extension of modern crime into the rural areas in the form of small-town bank robbing, the commissioners were given the duty of furnishing motorcycles to the sheriff and his deputies in an attempt to compete with the high-powered equipment used by modern gangs. One of the latest functions in this respect is the contracting with radio stations for the broadcasting of descriptions of fleeing criminals.[18]

Besides providing for those who have violated the laws, the commissioners were given the duty of caring for persons who, because of poverty or physical or mental defects, became public charges. Thus, county relief for the indigent, one of the most pressing problems of the twentieth century, was met in frontier Ohio. As early as 1805 an act, modeled from the territorial law, was passed which was similar in all respects to the poor laws of the seventeenth century England.[19] Under the early enactments the township trustees were authorized to appoint overseers of the poor. In 1816 the county commissioners were authorized to construct "poor houses" for the care of the county's indigent. As the system developed in succeeding decades the county was made responsible for those who had become permanently disabled, and for paupers who could not be satisfactory cared for except at the county infirmary, now called the county home.

The township trustees and officials of municipal corporations were made responsible for providing temporary relief to needy residents of the state, or the county, township, or city. In the event any person became chargeable to a township in which he had not gained legal residence, it was the duty of the overseers, later the township trustees, to remove him to the township where he was legally settled. With slight alterations, the principles of this system continued until the twentieth century.[20]

Since 1908 the commissioners have been authorized to issue warrants for the relief of the blind in sums varying from $100 to $400 per year.[21]

---

17. *Ibid.,* LXXXIX, 408; CXIII, 203.
18. G. C. sec. 1341-1.
19. *Laws of Ohio,* III, 272.
20. For an excellent study, but biting criticism, of the administration of relief in Ohio prior to 1934 see Aileen Elizabeth Kennedy, *The Ohio Poor Law and its Administration* (Sophonisba P. Breckinridge, ed., *Social Service Monographs,* no. 22, University of Chicago Press, 1934).
21. See p. 248.

Since 1913 they have been authorized, in any county containing a city which has an infirmary, to contract with the director of public safety for the care of the county's indigent.[22]

In addition to furnishing financial aid to the civilian population the commissioners were authorized, in 1886, to levy a tax for the relief of indigent Union soldiers, sailors, or marines of the Civil War, or if such veterans were deceased, for their dependents.[23] In 1919 the provision of the original act was amended to include all indigent veterans of the World War.[24] The commissioners were authorized also, in 1884, to defray the funeral expenses of any honorably discharged soldier, sailor, or marine who died indigent. Ten years later the provision of the act were extended to include the mother, wife, or widow of any soldier, sailor, or marine, and war nurses.[25]

The humanitarian duty of caring for the county's dependent and neglected children were delegated to the county commissioners. Since 1865 they have been authorized to establish and maintain a children's home. At the beginning of the present century, when the treatment of children was undergoing a remarkable change, they were authorized to place dependent and neglected children in private homes or institutions where they would receive food, clothing, and medical and dental treatment.[26] The development of the juvenile court system added new responsibilities. In order to segregate completely juvenile offenders from adults being tried in a regular criminal court, the commissioners were authorized to provide a separate building, to be known as the "juvenile court."[27]

The unprecedented depression in the third decade of the twentieth century proved the antiquated, uncentralized system of relief administration entirely inadequate. As a result of the abnormal employment conditions and the crop failures following the drought of 1930, many local subdivisions of the county charged by law to administer support and medical relief for the indigent were unable to discharge their obligations.

---

22. G. C. sec. 2419-1.
23. *Laws of Ohio,* LXXXIII, 232. See also p. 244.
24. *Laws of Ohio,* CVIII, pt. i, 633.
25. *Ibid.,* XC, 177. See also p. 245.
26. *Laws of Ohio,* CIX, 533.
27. *Ibid.,* CXIII, 470.

Accordingly, in 1931, the legislature passed an emergency act authorizing the county, township, and municipal taxing authorities to borrow money and issue bonds for poor relief, providing the state commission found that no other funds were available.[28]

During the early months of 1932 the governor, aware of the widespread suffering in the state, called the legislature into special session.[29] At this session the legislature authorized him to appoint a state relief commission composed of five members to study the relief situation. This commission was permitted to co-operate with the national, state, or local relief commission, which, in many counties, had been established and was already functioning. Since the county and township treasuries were depleted, on account of the excessive drain caused by the county relief load and the study decline of tax collections, the legislature authorized an excise tax on utilities, for the years 1932-1937, to be used for relief purposes. This state tax was to be allocated to the counties on the basis of population, the tax duplicate, and the value of utilities property in the county as of 1930. The funds allocated to each county under this act were to be credited to the "county poor relief excise fund."[30]

The county commissioners were authorized to borrow money for emergency relief and evidence such as indebtedness by the issuance of negotiable bonds and notes. Upon submission of such resolution to the state tax commission, the commissioners were directed to estimate the amount which would probably be allocated to the county from the public utility excise taxes and was directed to calculate the total amount of bonds, the principal and interest on which might be paid out of such estimated allocation. The date of maximum maturity of such bonds was to be on or before March 15, 1938. If, in the year 1932, additional funds were needed for poor relief, the county commissioners were authorized, after the state tax commission found that no other funds were available, to issue additional bonds in the amount not exceeding one tenth of one percent of the general tax list and duplicate of the county. The maturity date of such additional bonds was to be on or before September 15, 1940.[31]

---

28. *Ibid.,* CXIV, 11-12.
29. See message of the governor to the eighty-ninth general assembly in *Laws of Ohio,* CXIV, pt. ii, 5-8.
30. *Laws of Ohio,* CXIV, pt. ii, 19-20.
31. *Laws of Ohio,* CXIV, pt. ii, 18-21.

The proceeds of the sale of such bonds were to be placed in a special fund, denominated the "emergency relief fund." No expenditures were to be made from this fund except in accordance with the method and under the uniform regulations prescribed by the state relief commission, and in no case after December 31, 1933. The county commissioners were authorized to distribute, prior to the first of March 1933, portions of the fund to the political subdivisions of the county, according to the needs for poor relief determined by the county and set forth in such an approved budget. The money distributed to the subdivisions was to be expended in them for poor relief, including the renting of lands and the purchase of seeds for gardening by the unemployed.[32] County poor relief included mothers' pensions, soldiers' relief, temporary assistance to nonresidents, maintenance of a county and a children's home, and work and direct relief. In the townships and municipalities relief was interpreted to be the support of the poor and the burial of persons who died indigent. Each subdivision administering funds under the act was expected to require labor in exchange for relief given to any family in which resided and able-bodied wage earner.[33]

In the same year the county commissioners were designated as a board to administer the state law providing aid for the aged.[34] In February 1933 the tenure of the state relief commission was extended to March 1, 1935.[35] In the same year the legislature levied an additional stamp tax on the sale of bottled and bulk beer, malt, cosmetics, and toilet preparations to furnish additional funds for emergency relief.[36] The state treasurer was authorized to appoint the county treasurer as his deputy for the purpose of selling tax stamps to be fixed to such articles.[37]

The commissioners' duties regarding poor relief were further extended in 1935. They were authorized to provide noninstitutional support, care, assistance, or relief for the indigent in the county.[38] In 1935 the state relief commission ceased to exist by reason of the terms of the act creating it.

---

32. *Ibid.,* CXIV, pt. ii, 21, 22.
33. *Ibid.,* CXIV, pt. ii, 17.
34. *Ibid.,* CXV, pt. ii, 431-439. See also p. 252.
35. *Laws of Ohio,* CXV, 22.
36. *Ibid.,* CXV, 642, 649; CXV, pt. ii, 5, 33, 83, 177, 200, 247, 256.
37. *Ibid.,* CXV, 642.
38. *Ibid.,* CXVI, 571.

The legislature however, passed a measure designed to co-operate and correlate all emergency poor relief work, activities, and administration with the federal emergency relief administration which was authorized to administer and direct the distribution and expenditure of federal funds for relief in the state. Accordingly, all powers previously vested in the state relief commission were transferred to the county commissioners. Whenever in their discretion such action was necessary in order to continue the co-ordination and correlation of state, local, and federal funds they were authorized to appoint, with the approval of the director of finance of the state of Ohio, a representative or representatives of such emergency poor relief.[39] If such an officer were appointed, the representative succeeded to all powers and functions, which, under the act, were delegated to the county commissioners. This representative, however, was subject to such terms and conditions in respect to auditing, examinations, and reports as were directed by the county commissioners and such federal agency. The county commissioners were directed to conduct relief activities in so far as practicable, and were to be guided by the recommendations of the township trustees with respect to relief need in such political subdivisions. Again, as in 1932, the commissioners were authorized, if the state tax commission found that no other means existed to provide funds, to borrow money and issue bonds in the year 1935-1936. The maximum maturity date of such bonds was to be on or before March 1, 1944.[40] Other bonds, in addition to those secured by the county's share of the excise tax, might be issued not to exceed one fifth of one percent of the general tax list of the county.[41] If the county was unable to issue bonds by reason of limitations imposed by the constitution,[42] the taxing authority of each subdivision was authorized to submit the question of issuing bonds to the electorate either at a general or special election.[43]

The year 1936 saw the recreation of the state tax relief commission. Consisting of four members appointed by the governor, this body was authorized to serve until January 31, 1937.

---

39. *Ibid.,* CXVI, 571; Although such action was not authorized by law until 1935, the commissioners of Ross County appointed a relief director in 1933. Ohio Attorney General, *Opinions,* 1933, volume I, 770, Commissioners' Journal [Ross County], volume, S, p. 241.
40. *Laws of Ohio,* CXVI, 571.
41. *Ibid.,* CXVI, 575.
42. *Ohio Const. 1851,* Art. , sec. 2.
43. *Laws of Ohio,* CXIV, 578.

Again, as in 1932 the commission was directed to study problems of relief, to receive advice from federal, state, and local governmental departments, to co-operate with agencies of the national and local governments and private agencies engaged in the administration or financial support of direct or indirect relief, to administer moneys appropriated to the commission for poor relief, to examine the conduct of local governmental agencies in administering relief, and to order the distribution and payment of moneys from state treasury.

The county commissioners were authorized to administer all advances by the state to the relief commission and were directed to operate through duly authorized agencies of townships, municipalities, and school districts. Within the appropriations made by the commissioners and subject to the rules and regulations of the state relief commission, the commissioners were instructed to appoint assistants and such other employees as were necessary.[44]

The county commissioners, like the state relief commission, were directed to co-operate with all agencies of the federal, state, and county governments, and with private agencies which were engaged in administering relief or financial support to the needy. It was made the duty of all county, township, and municipal governments administering relief or assistance to dependents to report to county commissioners, at their request, the names and addresses of all persons to whom they were providing aid and the amount and character of aid given.[45]

The principle of issuing bonds and securing them by the county's share of the utility taxes was continued. Moreover, there was appropriated to the state relief commission for the general revenue fund the sum of $3,000,000 which was designated as the "state tax relief rotary fund." The various counties of the state which had not issued bonds and were not authorized to do so without the consent of the people, were empowered to obtain an advance from the state relief rotary fund in an amount equal to that of bonds which were permitted to be issued under the provisions of this act. If the county failed to repay the total of all advances and interest at two percent before June 1936, the state relief commission was directed to refuse to make further allocations or distributions to the county.[46]

---

44. *Laws of Ohio,* CXVI, pt. ii, 133-148.
45. *Ibid.,* CXVI, pt. ii, 133-148, 240.
46. *Ibid.,* CXVI, pt. ii, 133-148.

In the early months of 1937 the legislature authorized the state relief commission to serve until April 1937. Under this act the county commissioners are authorized to give temporary support and medical relief to nonresidents and to all needy persons possessing legal residents in the county. Funds may be expended for both direct and work relief. However, all persons on relief able and competent to perform labor who refuse to accept private employment of under prevailing conditions and prevailing wages, maybe dropped from the relief rolls. This ruling does not apply, however, to areas where strikes are prevalent. On the other hand, any person receiving relief in the county is permitted to engage in any business without losing his relief status. During the period of such employment, he is required to forfeit the *pro rata* amount of relief received by him, and is eligible to his former release status upon the conclusion of such employment.

The county commissioners are required to file with the state relief commission a budget and a detailed statement and plan showing how the funds to be received are to be expended, the purpose for which they are to be used, the nature and kind of work to be carried on, and the number of persons to be aided by such relief. Besides this, the county commissioners must file a complete analysis of their proposed expenditures, together with the estimate of all available resources, including the unencumbered proceeds of any bonds heretofore issued and the amount of bonds which the county commissioners have a right to issue without a vote of the people on the approval of the state tax commission of Ohio as authorized in 1935.

Of the funds allocated to the county by the state relief commission for district relief, the commissioners may, when they believe that the cost of administration may be reduced, reallocate the funds on a percentage basis of requirements of the various subdivisions.[47]

The emergency relief measures passed during the period 1932-1937 gave the counties for the first time a centralized relief administration. All records of this work are located in the relief administration office.

While control over relief work has become one of the most important phases of the commissioners' work, particularly in recent years, many other responsibilities have been assigned to them.

---

47. George C. Trautwein, ed., *Page's Ohio Cumulative Code Service* (Cincinnati, 1937), No. 20, 65-67.

The commissioners, by the authority conferred upon them to construct public buildings, were given duties regarding educational advancement. Since 1871 they have been authorized to accept requests for the construction of county libraries, and since 1923 to issue bonds, after receiving the approval of the voters, for the construction of libraries, or to contract with existing libraries for the use of people in the county.[48] Moreover, during the same period, they were authorized to provide and maintain civic centers in the county and to employ an expert director to supervise and administer them.[49]

Other duties not closely related to the original ones and have been added from decade to decade. For example, in 1850 the commissioners were authorized to subscribe for one leading newspaper of each political party in the county and caused them to be bound and deposited with the county auditor as public archives.[50] The newspapers on file in the auditor's office have not been listed in this inventory as they are to be the subject of a separate publication. An amendment to the original act, passed in 1923, provided for the preservation of such newspapers for a period of ten years, after which they may be removed to the Ohio State Archaeological and Historical Society library.[51] They have been authorized also to promote historical research by appropriating annually a sum not to exceed $100 to defray the expenses of compiling and publishing historical data for historical societies not incorporated for profit.[52]

During the early years of the twentieth century the commissioners were given the duty of providing facilities for county sanitation, which, in previous years had been sadly neglected. In 1917 they were authorized to lay out, establish, and maintain one or more sewer districts within the county. Since 1917 no sewer or sewage treatment works may be constructed outside of any incorporated municipality by any person, persons, firms, or corporations until the plans have been approved by the commissioners.[53]

---

48. G. C. secs. 2454, 2455; *Laws of Ohio,* CX, 242.
49. G. C. sec. 2457-4.
50. *Laws of Ohio,* XLVIII, 65.
51. *Ibid.,* CX, 4.
52. G. C. sec. 2457-1.
53. G. C. sec. 6602-1; *Laws of Ohio,* CVII, 440.

Then, too, during the same period the commissioners were authorized to provide facilities for the treatment of tuberculosis. In 1908 they were authorized to establish a county tuberculosis hospital and in 1909 to co-operate with the commissioners of other counties for the establishment of a district tuberculosis hospital.[54] Ross County is one of a group of counties maintaining such district hospital.[55] In counties not served by a county or district hospital the commissioners were empowered in 1913 to appoint, with the approval of the state department of health, one or more instructing and visiting nurses to visit homes or places housing tubercular patients.[56] Since 1917 they have been authorized to establish tuberculosis dispensaries and provide by tax levies the necessary funds for their establishment and maintenance.[57]

Finally the county commissioners have acted in a supervisory capacity over other county officials. Since 1850 they have been authorized to compare the annual reports and statements made to them by the prosecuting attorney, clerk of courts, sheriff, and the treasurer; take measures to ratify errors, correct discrepancies, and record in their journal the results of such examinations. Prior to the transfer of the duties as secretary to the board of county commissioners to a full-time commissioner' clerk, appointed in 1933[58] under the provisions of the act of 1904,[59] these reports were required to be filed with the county auditor, who had custody of the commissioners official acts and proceedings.[60] In 1896 the commissioners were given their present duty of visiting hospitals, detention homes, private asylums, and any other institution exercising a reformatory or correctional influence over individuals, and reporting on the sanitary conditions and the treatment of inmates.[61] Although these reports are required to be filed with the county prosecuting attorney and kept open to the inspection and examination of the public, they were not located in the inventory of Ross County records.

---

54. *Laws of Ohio,* XCIX, 62; C, 87.
55. See p. 238.
56. G. C. sec. 3153-1.
57. *Ibid.,* secs. 3148-1, 3153-4, 3153-5.
58. Commissioners' Journal, volume S, p. 3.
59. *Laws of Ohio,* XCVII, 304.
60. G. C. Sec. 2504; *Revised Statutes,* 886; *Laws of Ohio,* XLVIII, 66.
61. *Laws of Ohio,* XCII, 212.

The board of county commissioners offers a typical example of an office, which, designed primarily for an agricultural society, has expanded to meet the needs and requirements of modern society.[62]

---

62. *Ibid.,* CVIII, pt. ii, 1300

Journals

1. ORDER BOOKS
1809-1841. 5 volumes.

Minutes of meetings of the board of county commissioners showing date, names of members present, notations of petitions filed to establish, change route, or vacate public roads, petitions to change township lines, and resolutions pertaining to public affairs; also record of orders issued by commissioners for payment of bills and claims filed, showing date, order number, name of payee, and for what amount. Arranged chronologically by dates of meetings. No index. Handwritten. Average 480 pages. 12 x 8 x 3. Auditor's vault.

For subsequent minutes, see entry 2.

2. [Commissioners'] JOURNAL
1841—. 22 volumes. (A-V).

Minutes of meetings and proceedings of board of county commissioners, showing date and complete record of all business transacted by the board. Records for the following dates also shown: 1850—, approval of reports of treasurer, sheriff, prosecuting attorney, and clerk of courts; 1884—, record of grants for soldiers' burials; 1886—, record of grants for soldiers' relief. Also contains: Commissioners' Infirmary Journal, 1933—, entry 4; Soldiers' Burial Record, 1925—, entry 13; Ditch Record, 1841-1915, 1926—, entry 16; Sheep Claim Record, 1926—, entry 22. Arranged chronologically by dates of entry. 1841-1860, indexed alphabetically by subjects; for separate index, 1861—, see entry 3. 1841-1916 handwritten, 1917—, typed. Average 580 pages. 18 x 12 x 4. 18 volumes, 1841-1929, Auditor's vault; 4 volumes, 1930—, Commissioners' office.

For order books, 1809-1841, see entry 1.

3. INDEX TO COMMISSIONERS' JOURNAL

1861—. 10 volumes. (1-10).

Index to [Commissioners'] Journal, entry 2, showing names of creditors, petitioners, contractors, roads, bridges, and county departments, date, for what, and volume letter and page number of journal. Also contains index to Commissioners' Infirmary Journal, entry 5. Arranged alphabetically by names of principals. Handwritten. Average 700 pages. 16 x 11 x 4. 9 volumes, 1861-1927, Auditor's vault; 1 volume, 1928—, Commissioners' office.

4. COMMISSIONERS' INFIRMARY JOURNAL

1913-1932. 1 volume. Initiated 1913. 1933— in [Commissioners'] Journal, entry 2.

Minutes of meetings of county commissioners, sitting as board of infirmary directors, showing date and itemized account of infirmary expenses approved and ordered paid; also copies of semi-annual reports to commissioners by infirmary superintendent. Arranged chronologically by dates of entry. For index, see entry 5. 1913-March 1916, Handwritten; April 1916-1932, typed. 640 pages. 18 x 12 x 4.5. Basement, middle storeroom.

For other records, see entries 25, 559.

5. INDEX TO COMMISSIONERS' INFIRMARY JOURNAL

1913-1932. 1 volume. 1933— in Index to Commissioners' Journal, entry 3.

Index to Commissioners' Infirmary Journal, entry 4, showing names of creditors or principals, for what, date, and volume and page numbers of journal. Arranged alphabetically by names of creditors and chronologically thereunder. Handwritten. 550 pages. 18 x 12 x 4.5. Basement, middle storeroom.

Reports and Statements

6. FINANCIAL RECORD

1813-1841. 3 volumes.

Commissioners statements of semi-annual examination of county treasurer's accounts, showing date, total receipts, total disbursements, amount of delinquent tax, and balance. Arranged chronologically by dates of examinations. No index. Handwritten. Average 180 pages. 12 x 8 x 1.25. Auditor's vault.

7. [Financial] REPORTS

1901—. 5 file boxes. (183, 315, 478, 621, 980).

Copies of commissioners' annual financial statements to common pleas court, showing dates, total revenue from all sources, appropriations to each fund, total expenditures, and balance. Arranged chronologically by dates of reports. For index, see entry 330. 1901-1915, handwritten on printed forms; 1916—, typed on printed forms. 10 x 5 x 14. Auditor's office.

For earlier reports, see entry 463.

8. [Infirmary Directors'] REPORTS

1872-1912. 3 file boxes. (232, 374, 497).

Original annual reports of infirmary directors to county commissioners, showing date, funds appropriated, receipts, expenditures, and balance; also number of indigents cared for, number admitted, number discharged, and number of deaths. Arranged chronologically by dates of reports. For index, see entry 330. Handwritten on printed forms. 10 x 5 x 14. Auditor's vault.

For subsequent superintendent's reports, see entry 9.

9. [Infirmary Superintendent's] REPORTS

1913—. 3 file boxes. (567, 749, 931).

Original monthly reports of county infirmary superintendent to county commissioners, showing date, receipts and expenditures for operation of the institution; also number of indigents cared for, number admitted, number discharged, and number of deaths. Arranged chronologically by dates of reports. For index, see entry 330. Handwritten on printed forms. 10 x 5 x 14. Auditor's office.

For infirmary directors' reports, 1872-1912, see entry 8.

10. REPORTS [County Officials]

1871—. 9 file boxes. (9, 141, 205, 272, 382, 401, 559, 716, 929).

Original annual reports to commissioners from county officials including those other clerk of courts, sheriff, prosecuting attorney, treasurer, and infirmary directors, showing date, office or department, amount of funds appropriated, itemized account of expenditures, balance or overdraft, detailed account of routine business transaction, and date filed. Arranged chronologically by dates of filing. For index, see entry 330. 1871-1914, handwritten on printed forms; 1915—, typed on printed forms. 10 x 5 x 14. Auditor's vault. For earlier reports, see entry 462.

11. [Dog Pound] RECORD
1929—. 1 volume.

Complete copies of dog warden's reports to the commissioners of unlicensed dogs picked up in Ross County and impounded, showing date, where found, description of dog, and notations as to final disposition of dog. Arranged chronologically by dates of entry. No index. Handwritten. 410 pages. 18 x 14 x 3. Commissioners' office.

For notices of impounded dogs, see entry 327.

12. DOG WARDEN'S REPORTS
1930—. 1 file box.

Dog warden's reports to county commissioners on animal claims investigated, showing name of claimant, date and number of animals, amount of compensation recommended, and date. Arranged chronologically by dates of reports. No index. Handwritten on printed forms. 10 x 5 x 14. Commissioners' office.

13. SOLDIERS' BURIAL RECORD
1884-1924. 6 volumes. (1-6). 1925— in [Commissioners'] Journal, entry 2.

Record of burial of indigent soldiers, sailors, and marines, or their wives or widows, showing date, name of decedent, company, regiment, rank, itemized statement of burial expense, and commissioners' approval; also list of committees appointed in each township and city ward to investigate burial claims. Arranged chronologically by dates of entry. Indexed alphabetically by names of decedents. Handwritten on printed forms. Average 280 pages. 16 x 11 x 2.25. Auditor's vault.

Improvements
(See also entries 589-595)

14. ROAD RECORD
1799-1821. 1 volume.

Record of road surveys and resolutions to establish public roads. Last half of volume is a record of miscellaneous bonds issued, showing dates, for what issued, amount, and interest rate, record of township lines, and copy of resolutions authorizing building an office for the clerk of courts.

Arranged chronologically by dates of entry. No index. Handwritten. 140 pages. 15 x 10 x 1. Auditor's vault.

For subsequent records, see entry 589; for road papers, see entry 15.

15. [Road] RECORDS

1844—. 29 file boxes. (130, 164, 165, 236-238, 240, 250, 251, 298, 390, 394, 420, 464, 467, 468, 481, 503, 511, 521, 604, 681, 739, 792, 844, 873, 893, 923).

Commissioners' road records consisting of petitions by freeholders for establishment of roads and turnpikes, resolutions of commissioners approving establishment of roads, turnpike, and county highways and co-operation with the state highway department; also reports by county engineer of road and highway surveys made. Arranged to chronologically by dates of papers. Typed on printeed forms. 10 x 5 x 15. Auditor's vault.

For records of roads, see entries 14, 589.

16. DITCH RECORD

1916-1925. 1 volume. 1841-1915, 1926— in [Commissioners'] Journal, entry 2.

Record of county commissioners' proceedings on ditch petitions, showing dates, list of petitioners, and resolutions. Arranged chronologically by dates of entry. No index. Typed. 480 pages. 18 x 12 x 3.5. Auditor's vault.

17. CONTRACTS

1892—. 12 file boxes. (179, 180, 263, 313, 348, 419, 473, 537, 573, 733, 779, 861).

Copies of contracts entered into with various individuals and companies by county commissioners to perform specific work or furnish materials for road and county buildings, showing date and term. Arranged chronologically by dates of contracts. For index, see entry 330. 1892-1917, handwritten on printed forms; 1918—, typed on printed forms. 10 x 5 x 14. Auditor's vault.

18. BIDS

1901—. 7 file boxes. (374, 470, 571, 632, 681, 769, 877).

Copies of bids submitted to commissioners on construction projects for labor and material and bids on supplies for county offices, showing name of contractor or vendor, date, and amount of bid. Arranged chronologically by dates of bids. For index, see entry 330. Typed on printed forms. 10 x 5 x 14. Auditor's vault.

19. ESTIMATES AND SPECIFICATIONS

1924—. 14 file boxes. (462, 465, 466, 470, 472, 531, 541, 561, 572, 603, 613, 750 824, 893).

Copies of specifications and estimates on proposed construction or repairs of roads and bridges, showing date, name of project, itemized specifications, and estimated cost. Arranged chronologically by dates of estimates. For index, see entry 330. Typed on printed forms. 10 x 5 x 14. Auditor's vault.

Fiscal Accounts

20. COMMISSIONERS' BLOTTER

1909-1910. 1 volume.

Record of bills filed with commissioners and approved, showing to whom due, for what amount, from what fund, date allowed, and date paid. Arranged under tabs by code numbers and alphabetically thereunder by names of payees. Code index (for use of clerk). Handwritten. 264 pages. 16 x 20 x 2. Basement, middle storeroom.

21. DOCKET OF BILLS FILED

1904-1913. 1 volume. 1923— in Auditor's Docket, Commissioners' Bills, entry 412.

Record of commissioners' bills filed, showing date, consecutive number, name of creditor, for what, amount, date approved, date paid, and warrant number. Arranged numerically by bill numbers and chronologically thereunder. No index. Handwritten. 600 pages. 18 x 12 x 4.5. Auditor's vault.

22. SHEEP CLAIM RECORD

1892-1925. 3 volumes. 1926— in [Commissioners'] Journal, entry 2.

Record of claims for compensation for sheep killed and injured by dogs, as filed with township trustees, and certified to the county commissioners, showing date, number of animals killed or injured, grade, value, amount of claim, and amount allowed. Arranged chronologically by dates of entry. No index. Handwritten on printed forms. Average 480 pages. 16 x 11 x 3.5. Auditor's vault.

23. [Animal] CLAIMS

1893—. 7 file boxes. (175, 201, 202, 364, 463, 464, 5030.

Original copies of claims for compensation for loss of animals injured or killed by dogs, showing name of claimant, township, date, number and kind of animals injured or killed, value, and amount of claim. Arranged chronologically by dates or claims. For index, see entry 330. Handwritten on printed forms. 10 x 5 x 14. Auditor's vault.

For dog warden's record, see entry 326.

24. ORDERS, INFIRMARY FUND

1876-1886. 3 volumes. Discontinued.

Copies of orders issued by infirmary directors for payment of bills and claims allowed, showing amount, to whom issued, for what issued, date, and signature of creditor. Arranged chronologically by dates of orders. No index. Handwritten on printed forms. Average 200 pages. 12 x 10 x 1.5. Auditor's vault.

25. RECEIPTS AND EXPENDITURES

1927-1932. 1 volume.

Record of receipts and expenditures of the county home, showing date, from what source received, to whom paid, and for what paid. Arranged to chronologically. No index. Handwritten. 215 pages. 17 x 14 x 1.5. Basement, rear storeroom.

Miscellaneous

26. BLIND RELIEF RECORDS

1906—. 4 file boxes. (347, 396, 475, 729).

Blind relief records including applications for relief, physicians' certificates, and record of blind fund receipts and expenditures. Arranged chronologically. For index, see entry 329. Handwritten on printed forms. 10 x 5 x 14. Auditor's vault.

For records of payments, see entry 262; for other records, see entry 573-575.

27. ANNUAL INVENTORY

1926—. 1 volume.

Itemized inventory of county property of each office, department, or institution, as of January 1 each year. Arranged chronologically by years, thereunder by departments, and alphabetically thereunder by items. Indexed alphabetically by names of the departments, offices, or institutions. Typed. 180 pages. 12 x 16 x 1.25. Auditor's vault.

28. MISCELLANEOUS RECORDS

1839-1858. 1 volume.

Record of miscellaneous items such as scrip issued by county commissioners, 1839-1853, showing date issued, to whom payable, date due, interest rate, serial number, and amount; courthouse bonds issued, 1855, showing date, bond number, amount, date due, and interest payments; abstracts of personal property in Ross County as listed for taxation, 1853-1857; receipts and expenditures of Ross County 1854-1857; surplus revenue of Ross County, 1855-1858; record of levies, 1842-1857; record of railroads bonds (Marietta and Cincinnati railroad and Belpre and Cincinnati railroad) for 1851, showing date of issue, bond number, amount, to whom delivered, and redemption date; outstanding turnpike scrip, 1839-1844; copy of sheriff's, treasurer's, coroner's, and recorder's surety bonds, 1842-1857. Also contains [Report to School Commissioner], 1850-1854, entry 443. Arranged chronologically by years. No index. Handwritten. 422 pages. 16 x 11 x 3.5. Auditor's vault.

Relief Administration

Case Records

29. CASE RECORDS

1933—. 16 file boxes.

Complete records of relief cases including application, case or family history, and report and recommendation of case worker; also record of aid given. Papers of each case filed together in a folder, showing name of client in case number. Folders arrange numerically by case numbers; papers within folder, arranged chronologically. Typed on printed forms. 11 x 13 x 27. Relief administration office, 96 North Water Street.

30. MASTER FILE [Ross County Relief Records]

4 file boxes. (3 file boxes labeled active, 1 file box labeled closed). Card index to Case Records, entry 29, showing name of client, case number, and date of application. Arranged alphabetically by names of clients. Typed. 3 x 6 x 14. Relief administration office, 96 North Water Street.

31. [OLD RELIEF RECORDS]

1933-1935. 1 file box.
Old records of relief cases, under FERA, of clients who have either moved from Ross County or died. Arranged alphabetically by names of clients. No index. Typed on printed forms. 11 x 13 x 27. Relief administration office, 96 North Water Street.

32. INDEX, MOTHERS' PENSION CASES

1936—. 2 file boxes. (1 file box labeled active, 1 file box labeled closed). Current record of relief cases which were transferred to aid to dependent children department, showing name of mother, number of children, and date of transfer. Arranged alphabetically by names of clients. No index. Typed. 6 x 8 x 14. Relief administration office, 96 North Water Street.

33. INDEX, BLIND PENSION CASES

1935—. 1 file box.
Card record of relief cases which were transferred to blind relief department, showing name and address of client and date of transfer. Arranged alphabetically by names of clients. No index. Typed. 6 x 8 x 14. Relief administration office, 96 North Water Street.

34. INDEX, OLD AGE PENSION CASES
1935—. 1 file box.
Card record of relief cases which were transferred to old age pension department, showing name and address of client and date of transfer. Arrange alphabetically by names of clients. No index. Typed. 6 x 8 x 14. Relief administration office, 96 North Water Street.

WPA Records

35. CERTIFICATE AND ASSIGNMENT RECORDS
November 1935—. 4 file boxes.
Certifications of relief clients for WPA employment; also record of assignments of persons certified to WPA employment. Arranged alphabetically by names of persons certified and chronologically thereunder by dates of certifications or assignments. For index, see entry 336. Typed on printed forms. 8 x 10 x 24. Relief administration office, 96 North Water Street.

36. INDEX TO WPA RECORDS
1935—. 1 file box.
Card index to Certification and Assignment records, entry 35, showing name and address of person certified, case number, and date. Arranged alphabetically by names of persons certified. Typed. 4 x 6 x 20. Relief administration office, 96 North Water Street.

37. IDENTIFICATION CARDS
1935—. 1 file box.
Applicants' identification cards, United States Employment Service form No. 350, showing name and address of client, date registered, case number, and type of work. Alphabetically arranged by names of clients. No index. Typed on printed forms. 4 x 6 x 10. Relief administration office, 96 North Water Street.

CCC Records

38. CCC CASES
1933—. 4 file boxes.

Complete record of CCC cases including application, case history, copy of report of medical examination, and enrollment record. Papers of each case are filed together in a separate folder, showing name of client and case number. Folders, arranged numerically by case numbers; papers within each folder, arranged chronologically by dates of papers. For index, see entry 39. Typed on printed forms. 11 x 13 x 27. Relief administration office, 96 North Water Street.

39. MASTER FILE, CCC ENROLLEES, ACTIVE AND INACTIVE
1933—. 1 file box.

Card index to CCC Cases, entry 38, showing name and case number of enrollee, date of application, and date enrolled. Active cases are in the front of the file and inactive cases are in the back of the file. Arranged alphabetically by names of enrollees. Typed. 4 x 6 x 20. Relief administration office, 96 North Water Street.

40. CORRESPONDENCE AND REJECTED APPLICATIONS
1933—. 1 file box.

Applications for CCC enrollment which have been rejected with notations of reasons for rejection; also interoffice and departmental correspondence concerning CCC activities. Correspondence is filed in front of the file and rejected applications are filed in the back of the file. Correspondence, arranged chronologically; applications, arranged alphabetically by names of applicants. No index. Correspondence, typed; applications, typed on printed forms. 11 x 13 x 27. Relief administration office, 96 North Water Street.

Fiscal Accounts

41. FINANCIAL STATEMENTS
1935—. 1 file box.

Relief director's statements of appropriations and expenditures, showing date, source of receipts and account of all expenditures, showing total spent for each item such as food, fuel, clothing, and shelter. Arranged chronologically by months. No index. Typed on printed forms. 11 x 13 x 27. Relief administration office, 96 North Water Street.

42. EXPENDITURES
1935—. 2 file boxes.
Record of expenditures for each relief case. Papers of each case are filed in separate folder, showing name of client, date of expenditure, for what, amount, and total each month. Arranged alphabetically by names of clients. No index. Typed on printed forms. 11 x 13 x 27. Relief administration office, 96 North Water Street.

Miscellaneous

43. SURPLUS COMMODITIES
1935—. 2 file boxes.
Record of the distribution of Federal surplus commodities, showing name of client, number in family, amount of each commodity allowed, and total for each month. Papers of each case filed together in a separate folder. Arranged alphabetically by names of clients. No index. Typed on printed forms. 11 x 13 x 27. Relief administration office, 96 North Water Street.

The office of county recorder, although not unknown as an early English institution for the registration of land titles, developed in colonial America, where, because of the mobility of the restless pioneers, changes in land titles were frequent and some system was needed to protect purchasers against previous encumbrances. Public land registers, established in most of the colonies during the colonial period and continued by the states following independence, served as a model of land registration for the territory of which the present state of Ohio was then a part. Thus the office of county recorder was established by an act of the Northwest Territory, effective August 1, 1795. This act, adopted from the Pennsylvania Code, provided for the appointment by the governor of a recorder in each county whose principal duty was the recording of the deeds.[1]

When Ohio entered the union in 1803 no constitutional provision was made for the continuance of the office, but the legislature during its first session passed an act providing for a recorder in each county to be appointed by the judge of the court of common pleas for a seven-year term.[2] The recorder continued to be an appointive officer until 1829, when, by an act of the legislature, the office became elective for a three-year term.[3] The tenure of the office remained at three years until the constitutional amendment on November 7, 1905, which provided for the election of all county officers in the even-numbered years.[4] The term of office was fixed at two years, and so continued until the amendment of 1933, which extended the tenure of the incumbent until January 1937, at which time the recorder, elected at the regular election in November 1936, began to serve a four-year term.[5]

The first county recorder was directed by statute to record "all deeds, mortgages and conveyances of lands and tenements," lying within his county, and also all instruments and writings required by law to be recorded.[6] In 1806 he was directed to record all plats and maps of newly laid-out villages.[7]

---

1. Theodore Calvin Pease, comp., *The Laws of the Northwest Territory, 1788-1800* (*Illinois State Bar Association Law Series*, Springfield, 1925, I). 197-199.
2. *Laws of Ohio,* I, 136.
3. *Ibid.,* XXVII, 56.
4. *Ohio Const. 1851* (Amendment, 1905), Art. XVII, sec. 2.
5. *Laws of Ohio,* XCVIII, 271; CXV, 191.
6. *Ibid.,* I, 137.
7. *Ibid.,* III, 213-215.

In 1835 he was permitted, when authorized by the county commissioners, to transcribe from the records of other counties all deeds, mortgages, and other instruments of writing for the sale or conveyance of lands, tenements, or hereditaments affecting land titles in his county.[8]

Since the establishment of the office many duties besides those of recording land titles have been added. The present practice of recording powers of attorney had its beginning in 1819.[9] Although the mechanics of Cincinnati were authorized to file mechanics' liens with the recorder as early as 1823, it was not until 1843 that the privilege was extended to the laborers of Ross County.[10] Successive acts in 1865, 1872, 1881, 1884, 1888, 1904, and 1923 added new duties to the office in the recording of soldiers' discharges,[11] copies of certificates of compliance authorizing insurance companies not incorporated under the laws of Ohio to transact business in the state, and certified copies of renewal as granted by such companies to their agents,[12] limited partnership agreements,[13] stallion keepers' liens,[14] oil and gas leases,[15] partition fence records,[16] and federal tax liens.[17] The recording of chattel mortgages and conditional sales began in 1846. Such instruments were to be deposited with the township clerk where the mortgagor was a resident. In all townships, however, in which the recorded maintain his office such instruments were to be deposited with him.[18] Since 1906 chattel mortgages have been filed with the county recorder exclusively.[19] It is provided that in order to be valid against subsequent mortgages, the chattel mortgage must be deposited with the county recorder of the county where the mortgagor resides at the time of its execution, and to retain its validity the mortgage must be renewed every three years.[20]

---

8. *Ibid.,* XXXIII, 8; XXXV, 10-11.
9. *Laws of Ohio,* XVI, 155-156.
10. *Ibid.,* XXI, 8-10; XLI, 66.
11. *Ibid.,* LXII, 59.
12. *Ibid.,* LXIX, 32, 148; XCVII, 405.
13. *Ibid.,* LXXVIII, 248.
14. *Ibid.,* LXXXI, 43.
15. *Ibid.,* LXXXV, 179.
16. *Ibid.,* XCVII, 140.
17. *Ibid.,* CX, 252.
18. *Ibid.,* XLIV, 61.
19. G. C. sec. 8561.
20. *Ibid.,* sec. 8565.

In 1936 the legislature passed an act authorizing the recorder to destroy such instruments six years after the time of refiling has expired.[21]

An important extension of the method of recording land titles known as the "Torrens System," was provided by an act of the general assembly in 1896.[22] In 1897 this act was declared unconstitutional by the supreme court of Ohio as being contrary to section 16 of the bill of rights of the state constitution.[23] The act of 1913, amended in 1913 and 1915, provides for the examination of land title by the recorder and the issuance, if the title proved to be held in free simple, of a certificate of title by the court of common pleas or probate court. The official certificate becomes a title of ownership and is indefeasible. However, in the event an interest is found in the land, after the issuance of the certificate, a claim is allowed to the legal claimant from a fund created for that purpose at the time of registration.[24] This system, although adopted by a few counties, exclusive of Ross County is not used as widely as it might be because of the difficulty of replacing the traditional complicated system.

The recorder, like other county officials, had been required in earlier years to keep records of the business of his office, but it was not until the middle of the nineteenth century that the legislature, looking forward to some uniformity in land registration, enacted measures prescribing the form and content of such records. Since 1850 the recorder has been required to keep a record of deeds in which is recorded all deeds, powers of attorney, and other instruments of writing for the unconditional sale of land, tenements, or hereditaments.[25] The same year saw the beginning of a record of mortgages in which was recorded all mortgages, powers of attorney, and other instruments of writing by which land, tenements, or hereditaments "shall or may be mortgaged" or otherwise conditionally sold; and a record of plats in which was to be recorded all plats and maps of town lots and of the subdivisions thereof, and other divisions of surveyed lands, in like regular succession according to the priority of their presentation.[26]

---

21. *Laws of Ohio,* CXVI, 324.
22. *Ibid.,* XCII, 220.
23. *Ohio State Reports* (Cincinnati, 1852—), LVI, 575.
24. G. C. secs. 8572-34 - 8572-56; *Laws of Ohio,* CIII, 914-960; CVI, 27; CXV, 443
25. *Laws of Ohio,* XLVIII, 64.
26. *Ibid.,* XLVIII, 64.

Since 1851 the recorder has been required to keep a separate record of deeds and mortgages denominated respectfully as "Record of Deeds" and "Record of Mortgages."[27] Since 1865 the recorder has been required to keep a separate record of leases.[28] The present practice at keeping a daily register of deeds and a daily register of mortgages had its beginning in Ross County in 1886 although not required by statute until 1896.[29]

Although indexes had been prepared in earlier years, the present system of indexing had its beginning in 1851 and took practically its present form in 1896.[30] At present the recorder, at the beginning of each day's business, is required to make and maintain a general alphabetical index, direct and reverse, of all names of both parties of all instruments recorded by him. The indexes show the kind of instruments, the date, range, township and section, survey number and the number of acres or the lot and sublot numbers and the part thereof, of each tract or lot of land describe it any such instrument of writing; the names of each grantor is entered on the direct index under the appropriate letter and followed on the same line by the name of the grantee; the name of each grantee is entered in a reverse index under the appropriate letter and followed on the same line by the name of the grantor.[31]

Since 1859 the county commissioners have been authorized to provide sectional indexes to the records of all real estate in the county, beginning with the designated year and continuing through a period of years as may be specified.[32]

The present duties of the recorder do not differ, in the main, from those prescribed in the middle of the nineteenth century. His records, bound in large bulky volumes, are open to the inspection of the public and are transferred to his successor.

All records are located in the recorder's vault, unless otherwise specified.

---

27. *Ibid.,* XLIX. 103.
28. *Ibid.,* XLII, 170.
29. *Ibid.,* XCII, 268.
30. *Ibid.,* XLIX, 103; XCII, 268; CII, 288.
31. G. C. sec. 2764.
32. *Ibid.,* sec. 2766; *Laws of Ohio,* 256; LXXVI, 49; CII, 289.

Real Property Transfers
(She also entries 328, 329, 331)

Deeds

44. DEED RECORD

[Original Adams County, Northwest Territory]. 1797-1903. 7 volumes. (1-7).

Copies of original deeds to land in Chillicothe district, showing names of grantor and grantee, date filed, valuation, and amount of real estate. These records have been transcribed into Deed Record, entry 49. Arranged chronologically by date of filing. For index, see entry 45. Handwritten. Condition fair. Average 400 pages. 14 x 8 x 2.5.

For other deed records, see entry 49.

45. RECORD OF INSTRUMENTS FILED AND INDEXED TO DEED BOOKS

[Original Adams County, Northwest Territory], 1797-1803. 1 volume.

Daily record of instruments filed for record and index to Deed Record, entry 44, showing date filed, name of grantor and grantee, location of land, volume and page numbers of record, and amount of fee. Arranged chronologically by dates of filing. Handwritten. Condition fair. 300 pages. 14 x 8.5 x 1.5.

46. GENERAL INDEX TO DEEDS AND LEASES

1803-1900. 8 volumes. (labeled by contained letters of the alphabet).

Index to Deed Record, entry 49, and Lease Record, entry 60, showing date, names of grantor and grantee, kind of instrument, survey or section number, town or township, quantity of land, lot number, consideration, and volume and page numbers of record. Arranged alphabetically by names of grantors. Handwritten. Average 400 pages. 18 x 15 x 3.

For subsequent records, see entries 47, 48.

47. GENERAL INDEX TO DEEDS AND LEASES

[Direct], 1901—. 10 volumes. (1-10).

Direct index to Deed Record, entry 49, and Lease Record, entry 60, showing file number, date, names of grantor and grantee, kind of instrument, volume and page numbers of record, survey or section number, town or township, quantity of land, lot number, auditions or subdivision, and consideration. There are 2 volumes for Chillicothe, 2 for towns and villages, 4 for Virginia Military Lands, and 2 for sectional lands. Arranged alphabetically by names of grantors and chronologically thereunder. Handwritten. Average 600 pages. 18 x 15 x 4.5.

For prior records, see entry 46.

48. GENERAL INDEX TO DEEDS AND LEASES

[Reverse], 1901—. 10 volumes. ((1-10).

Reverse index to Deed Record, entry 49, and Lease Record, entry 60, showing file number, date, names of grantee and grandor, kind of instrument, volume and page numbers of record, survey or section number, town or township, quantity of land, lot number, addition or subdivision, and consideration. There are 2 volumes for Chillicothe, 2 for towns and villages, 4 for Virginia Military Lands, and 2 for sectional lands. Arranged alphabetically by names of grantees and chronologically thereunder. Handwritten. Average 600 pages. 18 x 15 x 4.5.

For records, see entry 46.

49. DEED RECORD

1797—. 230 volumes. (1-230).

Copies of deeds conveying title to real estate, showing names of grantor and grantee, date of instrument, description of property, time of filing, and date of transfer; and record of power of attorney for real property transfers. Also contains; Lease Record, 1797-1864, entry 60; Mortgage Records, 1797-1849, entry 63. Arranged chronologically by dates of filing. Indexed alphabetically by name of grantors; also separate indexes, entries 46-48. 1797-1910, handwritten; 1910—, typed. Average 550 pages. 18 x 12 x 3.5.

For transcribed deeds from Adams County, see entry 44; for power of attorney, personal property, see entry 91.

50. RECORDER'S JOURNAL [Deeds]

1881-1886. 1 volume.

Record of conveyance by deed, showing date, names of township, grantor, and grantee, description of tract, consideration, and volume and page numbers of deed record, entry 49. Arrange chronologically by dates of entry. No index. Handwritten.

500 pages. 18 x 12 x 3. Basement, rear storeroom.

For subsequent records, see entries 51, 52.

51. RECORDER'S JOURNAL OF DEEDS AND MORTGAGES

1886-1900. 4 volumes. (1-4).

Daily record of deeds and mortgages filed, showing date and hour of filing, names of grantor and grantee, quantity of land, survey or section number, location, fee, consideration or amount of mortgage, and volume and page numbers of Deeds Record, entry 49, and Mortgage Record, entry 63. Deed entries are in first half of each volume and mortgage entries in last half of each volume. Arranged chronologically by dates of filing. No index. Handwritten. Average 350 pages. 18 x 12 x 2.5. Basement, middle storeroom.

For prior register of deeds, see entry 50; for subsequent records, entry 52.

52. DAILY REGISTER of CONVEYANCE

1901—. 10 volumes. (1-10).

Daily record of instruments conveying title to real estate filed for record, showing names the grantor and grantee, kind of instrument, date filed, and amount of fee. Arranged chronologically by dates of filing. No index. Handwritten. Average 300 pages. 16 x 11 x 2.25.

For prior register of deeds, see entries 50, 51.

53. DEEDS AND MORTGAGES

1850-1900. 16 volumes. (1-16). Subtitled by names of townships.

Record of transfers of real estate by deeds or mortgages, showing date, names of grantor and grantee or mortgagor and mortgagee, acreage, description of tract, consideration or amount of mortgage, cancellation date of mortgage, and volume and page numbers of Deed Records, entry 49, or Mortgage Record, entry 63. Arranged chronologically by dates of entry. Indexed numerically by section numbers for townships, east of Scioto River; numerically by survey numbers for townships west of Scioto River. Handwritten. Average 600 pages. 16 x 11 x 4.

Abstracts and Registers of Titles

54. ABSTRACT OF TITLES
1797—. 19 volumes. Subtitled by names of townships and city of Chillicothe.

Record of real property transfers: deeds and leases, showing names of grantor and grantee, volume and page numbers of Deed Record, entry 49, acreage, consideration, kind of instrument, description of tract, and date recorded; mortgages or liens, showing names of mortgage or mortgagee, volume and page numbers of mortgage record, entry 63, amount of mortgage or lien, acreage, date recorded, and description of tract. There is 1 volume for each township and 3 volumes for city of Chillicothe. Arranged chronologically by dates of recording. Indexed numerically by section numbers for Congressional Lands, by survey numbers for Virginia Military Lands, and by lot numbers for Chillicothe. Typed. Average 500 pages. 18 x 15 x 4. Recorder's office.

55. ADDITIONS, CITY OF CHILLICOTHE
1812—. 3 volumes. (1-3).

Abstract of title to lots and tracts: conveyance by deed, showing dates, name of subdivision or addition, names of grantor and grantee, volume and page numbers of Deed Record, entry 49, and description of lot or tract; conveyance by mortgage, showing date, names of mortgagor and mortgagee, volume and page numbers of Mortgage Record, entry 63, amount of mortgage, date cancelled, and description of lots or tract. Arranged alphabetically by names of additions and subdivisions and chronologically thereunder by dates of entry. No index. Handwritten. Average 600 pages. 16 x 11 x 4.5.

56. GENERAL INDEX TO LOTS
1803—. 2 volumes. (1, 2).

Record of abstract of title to lots of Ross County outside of city of Chillicothe: transfer by deeds, showing date, names of grantor and grantee, volume and page numbers of Deed Record, entry 49, and description of lot; transfer by mortgage, showing dates, names of mortgagor and mortgagee, volume and page numbers of Mortgage Record, enter 63, amount of mortgage, date cancelled, and description of lot. Arranged alphabetically by names of towns and villages, numerically thereunder by lot numbers and chronologically thereunder by dates of entry. No index. Handwritten. Average 640 pages. 16 x 11 x 4.5.

57. IN-LOTS, CITY OF CHILLICOTHE
1798—. 2 volumes. (1, 2).
Record of abstract of title to ln-lots: transfer by deed, showing date, names of grantor and grantee, volume and page numbers of Deed Record, entry 49, and number and description of lot; transfer by mortgage, showing names of mortgagor and mortgagee, volume and page numbers of Mortgage Record, entry 63, amount of mortgage, date cancelled, and number and description of lot. Arranged numerically by lot numbers and chronologically thereunder. No index. Handwritten. 700 pages. 16 x 11 x 5.

58. OUT-LOTS, CITY OF CHILLICOTHE
1798—. 1 volume.
Record of abstract of title to out-lots: transfer by deed, showing date, names of grantor and grantee, volume and page numbers of Deed Record, entry 49, and number and description of lot; transfer by mortgage, showing names of mortgagor mortgagee, volume and page numbers of Mortgage Record, entry 63, amount of mortgage, date cancelled, and number and description of lot. Arranged numerically by lot numbers and chronologically thereunder. No index. Handwritten. 700 pages. 16 x 11 x 5.

59. REGISTRY OF TITLES RECORD
1915—. 1 volume.
Record of registration of title of ownership of real estate, showing dates, description of tract with sketch including boundaries. Prepared by county engineer. Arranged chronologically by dates of entry. No index. Typed and hand drawn. Scales vary. 302 pages. 18 x 12 x 2.5.

Leases

60. LEASE RECORD
1865—. 10 volumes. (1-10). 1797-1864 in Deed Record, entry 49.
Copies of leases and agreements for the use of real estate and equipment, showing

date, names of lessor and lessee, and terms of agreement. Arranged chronologically by dates of entry. Indexed alphabetically by names of lessors; also separate index, entries 46-48. 1865-1917, handwritten; 1917—, typed. Average 550 pages. 16 x 11 x 4.5.

61. RIGHT OF WAY GRANTS

1926—. 3 volumes. (1-3).

Record of rights of way to real estate granted by owners, trustees, guardians, executors, and others, to public utility companies and individuals, granting access to property to construct and maintain lines of communication, power, transportation, and private roads, showing date and terms of agreement. Arranged chronologically by dates of entry. Indexed alphabetically by names of grantors. Typed on printed forms. Average 300 pages. 16 x 11 x 2.5.

62. EASEMENT

1928—. 2 volumes. (1, 2).

Record of easements for right of way grants for highway purposes which were given to owners, trustees, guardians, and executors, showing date recorded, names of grantor and grantee, date, and term of agreement. Arranged chronologically by dates of entry. Indexed alphabetically by names of grantors. Typed. Average 680 pages. 18 x 12 x 4.5.

Mortgages

63. MORTGAGE RECORD

1850—. 149 volumes. (1-149). 1797-1849 in Deed Record, entry 49.

Copies of mortgages secured by real estate in Ross County, showing date, names of mortgagor and mortgagee, description of real estate, amount of mortgage, and date of release. Arranged chronologically by dates of entry. Indexed alphabetically by names of grantors; also separate indexes, entry 64-66. 1850-1911, handwritten; 1911—, typed. Average 600 pages. 18 x 12 x 4.5.

64. INDEX TO MORTGAGES

1850-1907, 1913-1920. 3 volumes. (1 unnumbered, 1, 3).

Index to Mortgage Record, showing date and hour of filing, filing number, names of mortgagor and mortgagee, acreage, survey or section number, amount, kind of conveyance, date cancelled, and volume and page numbers of record. Alphabetically arranged by names of mortgagors and chronologically thereunder by time of filing. Handwritten. Average 580 pages. 19 x 12 x 4.5. 2 volumes, 1850-1907, Recorder's vault; 1 volume, 1913-1920, Basement, middle storeroom.

For mortgage indexes, 1907—, see also entries 65, 66.

65. GENERAL INDEX TO MORTGAGE AND LIENS [Direct]
1907—. 12 volumes.

Direct index to Mortgage Record, entry 63, and Mechanics' Lien Record, entry 69, showing date, names of grantor and grantee, survey and section numbers, name of town or township, acreage, lot number, amount of mortgage or lien, dates released, and volume and page numbers of record. Arranged alphabetically by names of grantors and chronologically thereunder by dates of entry. Handwritten. Average 360 pages. 18 x 15 x 2.5.

66. GENERAL INDEX TO MORTGAGE AND LIENS [Reverse]
1907—. 12 volumes.

Reverse index to Mortgage Record, entry 63, and Mechanics' Lien Record, entry 69, showing date, names of grantee and grantor, survey and section numbers, name of town or township, acreage, lot number, amount of mortgage or lien, date released, and volume and page numbers of record. Arranged alphabetically by names of grantees and chronologically thereunder by dates of entry. Handwritten. Average 360 pages. 18 x 15 x 2.5.

67. CERTIFICATE OF DISCHARGE OF MORTGAGE
1891—. 2 volumes. (1, 2).

Copies of certificates of cancellation of mortgages secured by real estate, showing names of mortgagor and mortgagee, volume and page number of Mortgage Record, entry 63 and date. Arranged chronologically by dates of entry. Indexed alphabetically by names of mortgagors. 1891-1926, handwritten; 1926—, typed. Average 320 pages. 20 x 12 x 2.5.

For records of releases, see entry 68.

68. RECORD OF MORTGAGES RELEASED BY CERTIFICATES FROM COURTS

1902—. 1 volume.

Copies of certificates of cancellation of real estate mortgages issued by courts, showing names of parties to action, kind of cause, date, and volume and page numbers of Mortgage Record, entry 63, and Order Books, entry 172. Arranged chronologically by dates of entry. Indexed alphabetically by names of plaintiffs. Handwritten on printed forms. 320 pages. 19 x 12 x 2.5.

For record of discharges, see entry 67.

Liens

69. MECHANICS' LIEN RECORD

1845-1872, 1883—. 5 volumes. (1, 3-6).

Record of liens taken by workmen for wages due and by mechanics for materials supplied, showing names of persons involved, date, and amount of lien. Also contains Laborers' Liens, 1903—, entry 70. Arranged chronologically by dates of entry. Indexed alphabetically by names of claimants; also separate indexes, 1907—, entries 65, 66. 1845-1972, 1883-1922, handwritten; 1923—, typed. Average 500 pages. 16 x 11 x 3.5.

70. LABORERS' LIENS

1888-1902. 1 volume. 1903— in Mechanics' Lien Record, entry 69.

Record of liens taken by employees against employers for wages due, showing name, date, and itemized copy of claim. Arranged chronologically by dates of entry. Indexed alphabetically by names of claimants. Handwritten. 420 pages. 16 x 11 x 3.25.

71. INDEX OF LIEN NOTICES AND DISCHARGES

1929—. 1 volume.

Record of securities of recognizance (bail) bonds, showing recorder's filing number, from what court, names of surety and defendant, and date of cancellation. Arranged alphabetically under tabs by names of sureties and chronologically thereunder. Handwritten. 400 pages. 17 x 11 x 3.

72. CORPORATION RECORD
1933—. 1 volume.

Copies of notices of payments of franchise or excise taxes and discharges of liens thereof, showing name of public utility or corporation, amount of tax, penalty, date of payment, and filing number. Arranged chronologically by dates of payment. For index, see entry 73. Typed on printed forms. 500 pages. 16 x 11 x 3.5.

73. EXCISE AND FRANCHISE TAX LIEN INDEX AND INDEX TO CORPORATE RECORD
1930—. 1 volume.

Record of excise and franchise taxes assessed and due, showing recorders filing number, name of public utility or corporation, date and hour of filing, amount of tax, penalty, date paid, date and hour of filing notice of payment and discharge of lien, and volume and page numbers of Corporate Record, entry 72. Arranged alphabetically under tabs by names of public utilities or corporations and chronologically thereunder. Handwritten. 480 pages. 16 x 11 x 3.5.

74. RECORD OF LIENS, RAILROAD
1937—. 1 volume.

Copies of liens held against railroad property by creditors, showing name of railroad, name of claimant, date and amount of lien, and date filed. Arranged alphabetically under tabs by names of railroads and chronologically thereunder by dates of filing. No index. Handwritten. 480 pages. 16 x 11 x 3.5

75. PERSONAL TAX LIEN RECORD
1937—. 1 volume.

Copies of liens filed by county treasurer against taxpayers for delinquent taxes other than real property taxes, showing taxing district, date filed, name of debtor, years delinquent, volume and page numbers of Personal and Classified Duplicate, entry 468, date filed, amount of tax, penalty, total amount due, and date paid. Arranged alphabetically by names of debtors and chronologically thereunder by dates of filing. No index. Handwritten on printed forms. 210 pages. 14 x 11 x 1.5. Recorder's office.

76. INDEX OF LIENS FOR PROTECTION AND BENEFIT OF STALLION OWNERS

1884-1892. 1 volume.

Record of liens, showing name of stallion owner filing lien, date, name of contracting party, terms of agreement, and amount of lien. Arranged alphabetically under tabs by names of stallion owners and chronologically thereunder by dates of entry. No index. Handwritten. 250 pages. 15 x 8.5 x 2.

Surveys and Plats (See also entries 332-334, 583-588)

77. RECORD OF PLATS AND SURVEYS

1821—. 3 volumes. (1-3).

Record of village and town plats and surveys, showing name of village or town, date, survey data, and name of surveyor; also sketch of plats, showing streets, alleys, lots, watercourses, and boundaries. Prepared by county engineer. Arranged chronologically by dates of recording. Indexed alphabetically by names of towns and villages. Hand drawn. Scales vary. Average 300 pages. 19 x 12 x 2.5.

78. SURVEY BOOK, VIRGINIA MILITARY DISTRICT

1793-1857. 1 volume.

Record of original and subsequent surveys of Virginia Military Lands in Ross County (all territory west of Scioto River), showing date, description of each survey including sketch of tract, showing watercourses and landmarks, acreage, names of grantees, survey number, and date recorded. Prepared by county surveyor. Arranged chronologically by dates are recording. Indexed numerically by survey numbers in front of volume and indexed alphabetically by names of grantees in back of volume. Handwritten and hand drawn. Scales vary. 308 pages. 16 x 11 x 2.5.

79. RECORD OF SURVEYS

1797-1859. 1 volume.

Record of original and subsequent surveys of Ross County east of Scioto River (Congressional Lands), showing description of survey, section lines, tract boundary lines, watercourses, landmarks, and acreage. Arranged chronologically by dates of entry. Indexed alphabetically by names of applicants for surveys. Handwritten. 330 pages. 19 x 12 x 2.5.

80. ADDITIONS, CHILLICOTHE

1852—. 3 volumes. (1-3).

Plats and surveys of additions and allotments of the city of Chillicothe, showing streets, alleys, and lots with thoroughfare widths and lots numbers and dimensions. Prepared by county engineer. Arranged numerically by lot numbers. No index. Handwritten and hand drawn. No scale shown. Average 310 pages. 18.5 x 14. x2.5.

81. PARTITION FENCE RECORD

1905—. 1 volume.

Record of petitions to township trustees or fence viewers by landowners regarding line or partition fences, showing date of petition, names of petitioners, and terms of agreement. Arranged chronologically by dates of entry. Indexed alphabetically by names of petitioners. 1905-1920, handwritten; 1921—, typed. 480 pages. 18 x 12 x 2.5.

Personal Property Transfers

82. CHATTEL MORTGAGE RECORD

1877—. 2 volumes. (1, 2).

Record copies of chattel mortgages, showing instrument number, names of mortgagor and mortgagee, date, amount secured, itemized list of chattels, conditions of mortgage, dates filed and recorded, and date cancelled. Arranged chronologically by dates of recording. Index alphabetically by names of mortgagors showing names of mortgagees. Handwritten. Average 620 pages. 20 x 12 x 4.

83. CHATTEL MORTGAGES

1894—. 729 bundles, 60 file boxes. (labeled by contained instrument numbers).

Original or duplicate copies of chattel mortgages filed, showing instrument number, date of mortgage, names of mortgagor mortgagee, amount secured, itemized list of chattels, conditions of mortgage, signature of mortgagor, date filed, date refiled, and date recorded if recorded.

84. INDEX TO CHATTEL MORTGAGES

1877-1897. 4 volumes. (1-4).

Index to Chattel Mortgages, entry 83, showing names of mortgagor and mortgagee, instrument number, date of mortgage, amount, and dates of filing, refiling, and cancellation. Arranged alphabetically under marginal indentations by names of mortgagors and chronologically thereunder. Handwritten. Average 250 pages. 14 x 8.5 x 1.5.

For subsequent indexes, see entries 85-87.

85. CHATTEL MORTGAGE INDEX [Direct and Reverse]
1903-1907. 16 volumes. (1-16).

Index to Chattel Mortgages, entry 83, showing instrument number, names of mortgagor mortgagee, date of instrument, amount of mortgage, date of filing, and date of cancellation or renewal. Direct index in front half of volume and reverse index in back half of volume. Arranged alphabetically, direct, by names of mortgagors and reverse, by names of mortgagees. Handwritten. Average 250 pages. 16 x 11 x 1.5. Basement, rear storeroom.

For prior index, see entry 84; For subsequent indexes, see entries 86, 87.

86. INDEX TO CHATTEL MORTGAGES, GRANTOR
1907—. 10 volumes. (2 unnumbered, 1-8). Title varies: Chattel Mortgage Index, Direct, 1907-1925, 2 volumes.

Index to Chattel Mortgages, entry 83, showing instrument number, names of mortgagor and mortgagee, date of mortgage, amount of mortgage, and dates of filing, refiling, or cancellation. Arranged alphabetically by names of mortgagors and chronologically thereunder. Typed. Average 400 pages. 19 x 15 x 3.25. 2 volumes, 1907-1925, Basement, middle storeroom; 8 volumes, 1926—, Recorder's vault.

For prior records, see entry 84, 85

87. INDEX TO CHATTEL MORTGAGES, GRANTEE
1907—. 10 volumes. (2 unnumbered, 1-8). Title varies: Chattel Mortgage Index, Reverse, 1907-1925. 2 volumes.

Index to Chattel Mortgages, entry 83, showing instrument number, names of mortgagees and mortgagor, date of mortgage, amount of mortgage, and dates of filing, refiling, or cancellation. Arranged alphabetically by names of mortgagees and chronologically thereunder. Typed. Average 400 pages. 19 x 15 x 3.25. 2 volumes, 1907-1925, Basement. middle storeroom; 8 volumes, 1926—, Recorder's vault.

For prior records, see entry 84, 85.

Incorporations and Partnerships

88. INCORPORATIONS

1845—. 1 volume.

Copies of articles of incorporation and agreements of churches, societies, and business and manufacturing concerns, showing date, names of incorporators, and names of corporations. Arranged chronologically by dates of entry. Indexed alphabetically by names of corporations. Handwritten. 280 pages. 14 x 8.5 x 2.

89. RECORD OF LIMITED PARTNERSHIPS

1845-1900. 2 volumes. (1, 2).

Copies of limited partnership agreements, showing date, names of partners or members, number of shares of stock, total amount of stock, names of company officials, and titles of officials. Arranged chronologically by dates of entry. Indexed alphabetically by names of companies. Handwritten. Average 300 pages. 16 x 11 x 2.25.

For register of partnerships, see entry 137.

90. INDIVIDUAL AND PARTNERSHIP TRADE RECORDS

1884-1886. 1 volume. Discontinued; law repealed.

Record of tradesmen filing names of business establishments, as required by statute, showing date, name under which each business operated, and location and kind of business. Arranged chronologically by dates of entry. Indexed alphabetically by names of business establishments. Handwritten. 478 pages. 17 x 11 x 3.5.

Licenses and Grants of Authority

91. POWER OF ATTORNEY

1895—. 2 volumes. (1, 2).

Record of power of attorney granted to perform acts of conveyance of personal property as directed by grantors, showing date, name of grantor and grantee, date, and term of agreement. Arranged chronologically by dates of entry. Indexed alphabetically by names of grantors. 1895-1931—, typed. Average 420 pages. 16 x 11 x 3.5.

For power of attorney, real property transfers, see entry 49.

92. INSURANCE AGENTS' LICENSES

1926—. 2 file boxes.

Certified copies of licenses which were issued by state superintendent of insurance to agents to sell insurance in Ross County, showing date, names of licensee and insurance company represented, and name of employer. Arranged chronologically by dates are filing. No index. Typed on printed forms. 7 x 6 x 18. Recorder's office.

93. CERTIFICATES OF COMPLIANCE

1920—. 3 file boxes.

Copies of certificates, which were issued by state superintendent of insurance to insurance companies, certifying that insurance regulations have been complied with by the company, showing date, name of company, and signature of state superintendent. Arranged chronologically by dates of filing. No index. Typed on printed forms. 7 x 6 x 17. Recorder's office.

Fiscal Accounts

94. RECORDER'S FEE RECORD

1911—. 13 volumes. (1-13).

Daily record of fees, showing date, instrument number, by whom paid, kind of instrument, and amount of fee. Arranged chronologically by dates of entry. No index. Handwritten. Average 154 pages. 15 x 9.5 x 1. 8 volumes, 1911-1928, Basement, rear storeroom; 5 volumes, 1928—, Recorder's office.

95. CASH BOOK

1914—. 7 volumes. (1-7).

Daily record of cash receipts, showing date, consecutive instrument number, chattel mortgage number, by whom paid, kind of instrument, kind of service, and total fee. Arranged chronologically by dates of entry. No index. Handwritten. Average 400 pages. 18 x 12 x 3. 1 volume, 1914-1919, Basement, rear storeroom; 6 volumes, 1919—, Recorder's office.

Miscellaneous

96. SOLDIERS' DISCHARGE RECORD, CIVIL WAR
1832-1868. 1 volume.

Copies of official discharges of Union soldiers, Civil War, showing name of soldier, company, regiment, service record, and dates of filing, enlistment, and discharge; also, in back of volume is a record of discharge of 8 soldiers (regular army or marines) 1905-1918. Arranged chronologically by dates of filing. Indexed alphabetically by names of soldiers. Handwritten. 500 pages. 16 x 11 x 4.5.

For other discharge records, see entry 97, 98.

97. RECORD OF SOLDIERS' DISCHARGES
1898—. 1 volume.

Copies of official discharges, which were filed in Ross County of United States soldiers, Spanish-American War, and subsequent regular army enlistments, showing name of soldier, company, regiment, service record, and dates of filing, enlistment, and discharge. Arranged chronologically by dates of filing. Indexed alphabetically by names of soldiers. 1898-1933, handwritten on printed forms; 1933—, typed on printed forms. 314 pages. 18 x 12 x 2.5.

For other discharge records, see entries 96, 98.

98. SOLDIERS' DISCHARGE RECORD
1918—. 2 volumes. (1, 2).

Copies of official discharges which were filed in Ross County, of United States soldiers and sailors in World War and subsequent regular army and navy enlistments, showing name of soldier or sailor, company, regiment or ship, service record, and dates of enlistment, filing, and discharge. Arranged chronologically by dates of filing. Indexed alphabetically by names of soldiers or sailors. Handwritten on printed forms. Average 480 pages. 18 x 12 x 3.5.

For other discharge records, see entry 96, 97.

99. NOTARY PROTEST DOCKET
1845-1954. 1 volume. Discontinued.

Record of protests on promissory notes, which were filed by James McLain, notary public, showing names of debtor and creditor, amount of note, and date of protest.

Arranged chronologically by dates of protest. No index. Handwritten. 100 pages. 13 x 8 x 1.

100. MISCELLANEOUS RECORDS
1896—. 4 volumes. (3-6).

Record of miscellaneous instruments filed including contracts and agreements of all kinds, options, and miscellaneous papers not coming under regular record titles, showing date, kind of instrument, name of contracting parties, and term of agreement. Arranged chronologically by dates of entry. Indexed alphabetically by names that grantors or principals. 1896-1923, handwritten; 1923—, typed. Average 450 pages. 16 x 11 x 3.5.

The office of clerk of courts, an ancient English institution originating before the time of Edward I[1] was transplanted to America during the colonial period. The American Revolution made no radical change in the political heritage derived from England, and the office was continued by the states. The duties of the office were modified in the newer states, however, because of a separation of administrative and judicial functions, which under the English system had been combined.

The sections of the Ohio Constitution of 1802 creating the judicial system for the state provided for the appointment of a clerk of courts by the judges of the court of common pleas. He was to serve a seven-year term, but was subject to removal by the appointing power for a breach of good behavior.[2] The constitution of 1851 made the office of clerk elective with a three-year term.[3] A constitutional amendment in 1905 provided that the terms of all elective offices should be for an even number of years not exceeding four. In compliance with this amendment, the general assembly passed an act fixing the term of office of the clerk at two years.[4] The term remained at two years until 1936 when it was extended to four years.[5] The remuneration of the office was by fees until 1906 when the legislature prescribed a definite salary based on the population of his county.[6]

The duties of the clerk of courts, like those of other county officers, are prescribed by statute. In 1853 a code of civil procedure was adopted summarizing the earlier duties and forming the basis for the present ones which are in most respects similar to those prescribed during the earlier years of the office. The clerk of courts was directed to issue all writs and orders for provisional remedies; endorse the date upon all papers filed in his office; keep the journal, record books, and papers appertaining to the court of common pleas and record its proceedings, and keep five books to be called the appearance docket, the trial docket and a printed duplicate of the trial docket, the journal, the record, and the execution docket.[7]

---

1. Sir Frederick Pollock and Frederic William Maitland, *The History of English Law Before the Time of Edward I* (Cambridge, 1895), I, 184.
2. *Ohio Const. 1802,* Art. III sec. 9.
3. *Ohio Const. 1851,* Art. IV, sec. 16.
4. *Laws of Ohio,* XCVIII, 273.
5. *Ibid.,* CXVI, pt. ii, 184.
6. *Ibid.,* XCVIII, 94, 117. The salary in Ross County for 1937 was $2,925. Ohio Auditor of State, *Annual Report, 1937,* 369.
7. *Laws of Ohio*, LI, 107, 158-159; LXXVIII, 88; LXXXII, 33; LXXXVI, 26.

The present practice of keeping an index, direct and reverse, to judgments began in 1866.[8] In 1871, the clerk was made official custodian of the law reports and books furnished by the state for the use of the court and bar, and was made liable in the event of their destruction.[9]

Some of the duties of the clerk as defined by the civil code of 1853 are still effective, others have been added by subsequent legislation. Thus, for example, in 1858 the clerk was directed to receive notary commissions for record.[10] He was required, also, to receive for record special police commissions (1867), timber trade-marks (1883), partnership agreements (1894), copies of judgments of federal courts (1898), marks of ownership [trademarks] (1911), motor vehicle bills of sale (1921), and certificates of judgments to operate as a lien (1935).[11] Since January 1, 1938 he has issued certificates of title to motor vehicles.[12] On the other hand, many of the earlier duties of the clerk have been transferred to other departments of local government or have been abolished. The clerk issued marriage licenses and recorded ministers' licenses until 1852, after that date they have been issued by the probate court,[13] to which court the records have been transferred. Moreover the clerk issued peddlers' licenses until the decade of the sixties, since that time they have been issued by the auditor.[14] These records were not found in the inventory. The clerk has been authorized to act as an agent of the state in the sale of hunting and trapping licenses to nonresidents of the state since 1904 and to residents since 1919.[15] He has been authorized also to serve as an agent in the sale of fishing licenses to nonresidents since 1919 and to residents since 1925.[16] The practice of recording in the office of the clerk, the names of black or mulatto persons to be used as certificates of freedom was, of course, discontinued after the close of the War between the States in 1865.

---

8. *Ibid.,* LXIII, 10; LXXV, 103; LXXVIII, 88; LXXXII, 33; LXXXVI, 26.
9. *Ibid.,* LXVIII, 109.
10. *Laws of Ohio,* LV, 13; XCIII, 406.
11. *Ibid.,* LXIV, 60; LXXX, 195; XCI, 3571 XCII, 25; XCIII, 285; CII, 513-514; CIX, 333; CXVI, 274.
12. G. C. sec. 6290-6. See also p. LII.
13. *Laws of Ohio,* I, 31; XXIX, 429; L, 84; *Ohio Const. 1851,* Sec. IV, sec. 8.
14. *Laws of Ohio,* LIX, 67.
15. *Ibid.,* XCVII, 474; CVIII, pt. i, 595. For additional licenses, see pages 27, 31, 32, 109.
16. G. C. sec. 1430.

In 1856 the clerk was directed by the legislature to preserve a list of births, marriages, and deaths as returned to his office by the assessors, and to transmit annually, on or before the first day of June, a copy of such statistics to the secretary of state. These lists are no longer preserved. From these county lists, the secretary of state prepared tabular statements showing the vital statistics in each county. The clerk received ten copies of the report, one of which he was required to preserve in his office.[17] The clerk was relieved of the task of collecting and preserving vital statistics, when, in 1867, such powers and duties were vested in the probate judge.[18]

The clerk of courts was given other duties in addition to those of serving the court of common pleas and receiving documents for record. Since 1850 he has been required to report each year to the county commissioners all fines assessed by the courts in criminal cases, together with the names of parties to each case, and the amount of money he has paid to the county treasurer.[19] Duplicate copies of these reports have not been preserved in the clerks office but the commissioners' copies are listed in entry 10. Moreover since 1867 he has been required to report annually to the secretary of state the number of crimes committed in his county, the number of pending cases, and the amount of fines collected.[20] An act of 1927, amending the act of 1867, directed the clerk to report on any matters which the secretary of state might require, and to forward a duplicate copy of his report on crime in his county to the state board of clemency [board of pardons and parole].[21] The state board of clemency was abolished in 1921 and its duties were assigned to a board of pardons and parole within the department of public welfare.[22]

The county clerk of courts, like the county prosecuting attorney, is one of the most important persons in the judicial system. His significance and influence, however, was not recognized until recent years.

All records are located in the clerk of courts vault, unless otherwise specified.

---

17. *Laws of Ohio,* LIII, 73-75.
18. *Ibid.,* LXIV, 63-64.
19. *Ibid.,* XLVIII, 66; LVIII, 69; LXXXVVI, 239.
20. *Ibid.,* LXIV, 17.
21. *Ibid.,* CXII, 203.
22. *Ibid.,* CIX, 111, 124.

Calendars and Dockets
(See also entries 165-169)

101. COURT CALENDAR
1892-1909. 15 volumes. (labeled by years).
Calendar of all cases filed in common pleas court, showing court term, date of hearing, case number, names of litigants and attorneys, and kind of action. Arranged chronologically by dates of court terms. No index. Handwritten. Average 80 pages. 20 x 14 x .5. 5 volumes, 1892-1898, Basement, rear storeroom; 10 volumes, 1899-1909, Clerk of courts' vault.

102. EXECUTION DOCKET
1802—. 27 volumes. (1-27).
Record of executions ordered to satisfy judgments of the court of common pleas and other courts, showing names of litigants, kind of action, amount of judgment, date entered, sheriff's returns, description of property levied on, date of appraised, amount of appraisement, date of sale, amount of sale, to whom sold, date sale confirmed, and date deed executed. Arranged chronologically by dates of entry. Index alphabetically by names of plaintiffs. Handwritten. Average 450 pages. 18 x 14 x 3.5.

103. BAR DOCKET
1900-1909. 14 volumes. (labeled by court terms).
Docket of all actions before court of common pleas, showing term of court, date of hearing, case number, names of litigants and attorneys, kind of action, and court order. Arranged chronologically by dates of court terms. No index. Handwritten. Average 140 pages. 20 x 12 x 1.

104. MOTION AND DEMURRER DOCKET
1913—. 3 volumes. (1-3).
Copies of motions and demurrers filed in court of common pleas, showing case number, names of litigants and attorneys, text of motion, and date of filing. Arranged chronologically by dates of filing. No index. Handwritten. Average 300 pages. 10 x 12 x 3.

105. PRAECIPE DOCKET
1903—. 8 volumes.

Record of praecipes issued to the clerk of courts, showing names of litigants and attorneys, case number, kind of action, kind of writ, date issued, and sheriff's returns. Arranged chronologically by dates of issue. No index. Handwritten. Average 200 pages. 14 x 10 x 1.5.

106. RULE DOCKET
1810-1921, 1828-1836. 3 volumes.

Docket of rules established by court of common pleas governing the duties of sheriff, constables, prosecuting attorney, clerk, and attorneys, showing term of court, and office for which rule was made. Arranged chronologically by dates a court terms. No index. Handwritten. Condition fair. Average 400 pages. 16 x 10 x 3.

Records of Trials
(See also entries 170-176)

107. JUDGMENT INDEX
1850—. 21 volumes. (1-21).

Index record of judgments of court of common pleas, showing names of litigants, term of court, case number, kind of cause, amount of judgment, and volume and page numbers of Execution Docket, entry 102, Order Books, entry 171, and complete record, entry 174. Arranged alphabetically, direct, by names of plaintiffs, and reverse, by names of defendants. Handwritten. Average 640 pages. 18 x 12 x 4.5.

108. INDEX TO PENDING SUITS AND LIVING JUDGMENTS
1885—. 5 volumes. (1-5).

Index record of pending suits and living judgments of court of common pleas, showing names of litigants, living judgment of pending suit case number, volume and page numbers of appearance docket, entry 165, date of judgment, and date of execution. Arranged alphabetically under tabs by names of plaintiffs. Handwritten on printed forms. Average 575 pages. 20 x 12 x 4.

109.ORIGINAL [Court] PAPERS

1799—. 711 file boxes. (1-711).

Original case papers in court of common pleas cases, papers of each case filed together in a jacket, showing names of litigants, title of case, case number, date filed, file box number, and volume and page numbers of Appearance Docket, entry 165, and Order Books, entry 171. Also contains: Transcripts, 1923—, entry 111; Judgments, State Causes, 1860—, entry 112; Executions and Orders of Sales, 1910—, entry 113; Executions Returnable, 1858—, entry 114; Demurrers and Petitions, 1799-1921, entry 115; [Original Court Papers, Court of Appeals]. 1913—, entry 197. Arranged numerically by case numbers. 1799-1913, no index; for index, 1914—, see entry 110. 1799-1844, handwritten; 1845-1909, handwritten on printed forms; 1910—, typed on printed forms. 10 x 5 x 14.

For volume record of cost bills, 1864-1906, see entry 153; motions, 1854-1870, entry 116.

110. INDEX TO PENDING SUITS

1914—. 3 volumes.

Index to original [Court] Papers, entry 109, showing file box number, name of plaintiff, case number, title of case, and date filed. Arranged alphabetically under tabs by names of plaintiffs. Handwritten. Average 240 pages. 18 x 14 x 2.

111. TRANSCRIPTS

1855-1922. 8 file boxes. 1923— in Original [Court] Papers, entry 109.

Original transcripts to court of common pleas from magistrates' courts in criminal cases, showing case number, what court, name of accused, offence charged, itemize account of magistrates' and marshall's or constable's fees, and date filed. Arranged chronologically by dates of filing. No index. Handwritten. 10 x 5 x 14.

112. JUDGMENTS, STATE CAUSES

1804-1959. 13 file boxes. (labeled by years). 1860— Original [Court] Papers, entry 109.

Original papers in state cases in court of common pleas consisting of writs of executions, records of sales, and sheriff's returns, showing case number, name of defendant, offence, amount of judgment, date filed, and volume and page numbers of Execution Docket, entry 102, Appearance Docket, entry 165, and Order Books, entry 171. Arranged chronologically by dates of filing. No index. Handwritten. 10 x 5 x 14.

113. EXECUTION AND ORDERS OF SALES
1856-1909. 18 file boxes. (labeled by years). 1910— in Original [Court] Papers, entry 109.

Executions issued on judgment decrees of court of common pleas and sales ordered to satisfy judgments, showing case number, names of litigants, title of case, amount of judgment, date filed, and volume and page numbers of Execution Docket, entry 102, Appearance Docket, entry 165, and Order Books, entry 171. Arranged chronologically by dates of filing. No index. Handwritten on printed forms. 10 x 5 x 14.

114. EXECUTIONS RETURNABLE
1799-1857. 6 file boxes. (labeled by years). 1858— in Original [Court] Papers, entry 109.

Original papers in executions ordered, showing date, names of litigants, case number, and sheriff's returns and date of filing. Arranged chronologically by dates of filing. No index. Handwritten. 10 x 5 x 4.

115. DEMURRERS AND PETITIONS
1922. 4 file boxes. (labeled by years). 1799-1921 in Original [Court] Papers, entry 109.

Original papers of demurrers and petitions to common pleas court on all cases filed, showing case number, names of the litigants, and data filing. Arranged chronologically by dates of filing. No index. Handwritten and typed printed forms. 10 x 5 x 14.

116. MOTIONS
1854-1870. 1 volume.

Copies of motions to common pleas court in civil cases, showing names of litigants and attorneys, title of case, date, and case number. Arranged chronologically by dates of filing. No index. Handwritten. 290 pages. 12 x 8 x 1.25.

For original papers, 1871—, see entry 109.

117. BILLS OF EXCEPTIONS

1892-1902, 1908, 1914—. 170 volumes.

Original bills of exceptions to verdicts and orders of courts as basis of appeals to higher courts, and orders for new trials, showing case number, names of litigants, title of case, name of appellant, names of attorneys, court of origin, court of appeal, and date filed. Each case is bounded separately. Arranged chronologically by dates of filing. No index. Typed. Average 50 pages. 10 x 18 x .5.

Witnesses and Jury Records
(See also entries 303, 323)

118. [Witnesses'] ATTENDANCE RECORD

1806-1879. 1 volume.

Record of witnesses called in common pleas court cases, showing name, term of court, and number of days attended. Arranged chronologically. No index. Handwritten. Condition poor. 500 pages. 12 x 8 x 3.5.

For complete witness record, see entry 121.

119. TALESMAN BOOK

1888-1910. 1 volume.

Register of persons drawn for jury duty in county courts, showing names and term of court. Arranged alphabetically by names of jurors. No index. Handwritten. 225 pages. 12 x 8 x 2.

For jury books, 1885—, see entry 122.

120. GRAND JURY SUBPOENAS

1911—. 1 file box.

Duplicates of subpoenas for grand jury, of person subpoenaed, showing name and term of court. Arranged alphabetically by names of persons subpoenaed. No index. 1911-1925, handwritten; 1925—, typed. 10 x 5 x 14.

121. WITNESS BOOKS

1803-1838, 1852-1859, 1895-1904, 1912—. 16 volumes.

Record of witnesses called to testify in court of common pleas and county appellate court cases and of grand jury witnesses. Trial cases show date, names of litigants, kind of action, number of days in court, milage due and total fees due. Arranged chronologically by dates of entry. Indexed alphabetically by names of witnesses. 1803-1925, handwritten, 1925—, typed. 1803-1898, average 200 pages. 12 x 8 x 1.25; 1898—, average 400 pages. 18 x 12 x 3.

For attendance record, 1806-1879, see entry 118.

122. JURY BOOKS

1885—. 8 volumes.

Record of venires drawn for grand and petit jurors, showing term of court, names of jurors, number of days served, mileage due, total fees due, excused or discharged, and reason. Arranged chronologically by dates of court terms. Indexed alphabetically by names of jurors. 1885-1926, handwritten; 1926—, typed. Average 300 pages. 16.5 x 12 x 2.

For jury register, 1888-1910, see entry 119; for original venires, see entry 123.

123. JURY VENIRES

1910—. 2 file boxes.

Original venires drawn for jury duty in Ross County courts, showing names of jurors and court term. Arranged chronologically by dates of court terms. No index. 1910-1918, handwritten; 1918—, typed. 10 x 5 x 14.

For jury books, 1885—, see entry 122.

Motor Vehicles

(See also entry 431)

124. BILLS OF SALE AND SWORN STATEMENTS OF OWNERSHIP

1921- December 31, 1937. 72 file boxes. (labeled by years and contained bill of sale numbers).

Bills of sale or sworn statements of ownership of motor vehicles filed with the clerk of courts, showing document number, date, names of grantor and grantee, make of vehicle, model, type, name of manufacturer, motor number, serial number, and date filed. Arranged numerically by document numbers. For index, see entries 125-127. Typed on printed forms. 10 x 5 x 14.

125. MOTOR VEHICLE BILL OF SALE AND TRANSFER INDEX
1921-1923. 2 volumes.

Direct and reverse index to Bills of Sale and Sworn Statements of Ownership, entry 124, showing names of grantor and grantee and number of instrument. Direct index in front of each volume; reverse index in back of each volume. Arranged alphabetically, direct, by names of grantors, and reverse, by names of grantees. Handwritten on printed forms. Average 640 pages. 16 x 12 x 4.

For subsequent indexes, see entries 126, 127.

126. MOTOR VEHICLE BILL OF SALE AND TRANSFER INDEX [DIRECT]
1924-1937. 12 volumes.

Direct index of Bills of Sale and Sworn Statements of Ownership, entry 124, showing names of grantor and grantee, document number, make and type of car, motor number, serial number, and date of filing. Arranged alphabetically by names of grantors. Handwritten on printed forms. Average 350 pages. 14 x 18 x 3.

For index, 1921-1923, see entry 125.

127. MOTOR VEHICLE BILL OF SALE AND TRANSFER INDEX [REVERSE]
1924-1937. 12 volumes.

Reverse index of Bills of Sale and Sworn Statements of Ownership, entry 124, showing names of grantee and grantor, document number, make and type of car, motor number, serial number, and date of filing. Arranged alphabetically by names of grantees. Handwritten on printed forms. Average 350 pages. 14 x 18 x 3.

For index, 1921-1923, see entry 125.

128. CERTIFICATE OF TITLE
January 1, 1938—. 4 file drawers. (labeled by contain certificate numbers).

Duplicate certificates of title to motor vehicles, showing certificate number, date, names of purchaser and vendor, make, type, model, motor and serial numbers, date of purchase, notation of all liens and terms thereof, and cancellation of liens. Arranged numerically by certificate numbers. For index, see entry 129. Typed on printed forms. 10 x 16 x 25. Clerk of courts' office.

129. INDEX CERTIFICATES OF TITLE

January 1, 1938—. 2 file drawers.

Index to Certificate of Title, entry 128, showing name and address of owner, make of vehicle, and certificate number. Arranged alphabetically by names of owners. Typed on printed forms. 8 x 16 x 26. Clerk of courts' office.

Licenses and Commissions

130. NOTARIES' COMMISSIONS

1858—. 8 volumes. (one unnumbered, 1-7).

Copies of notaries public commissions granted by the governor, showing name of notary, date of commission, length of commission, and oath of notary. Arranged chronologically. Indexed alphabetically by names of notaries. Handwritten on printed forms. Average 250 pages. 15 x 10 x 1.5.

131. JUSTICES' COMMISSIONS

1830-1855, 1869-1895, 1892—. 6 volumes.

Copies of justices of peace commissions and oaths of office, showing name of justice, length of term, date of commission, and date filed. Arranged chronologically by dates of filing. Indexed alphabetically by names of justices. 1830-1855, handwritten; 1869-1885, 1892—, handwritten on printed forms. Average 175 pages. 14 x 10 x 1.

132. HUNTING AND FISHING LICENSES

1929—. 3 volumes.

Record of resident fishing licenses, showing license number, name, address, and description of licensee. Also contains Hunters' Licenses, entry 133. Fishing license records are in front of volume and hunting licenses are in back of volume. Arranged alphabetically under tabs by names of licensees. No index. Handwritten. Average 500 pages. 18 x 12 x 4.

133. HUNTERS'[LICENSES

1913-1920, 1925-1928. 3 volumes. 1929— in Hunting and Fishing Licenses, entry 132.

Record of resident hunting licenses issued, showing license number, date, and name, age, occupation, description, and address of licensee. Arranged alphabetically by names of the licensees. No index. Handwritten. Average 180 pages. 18 x 12 x 1.5.

134. OPTOMETRY RECORD
1920—. 1 volume.
Record of persons licensed to practice optometry in Ross County, showing name of licensee, date of license, and date recorded. Arranged chronologically by dates of recording. Indexed alphabetically by names of licensees. Handwritten on printed forms. 159 pages. 10 x 8 x 1.

135. RAILROAD POLICE COMMISSIONS
1916—. 1 volume.
Record of persons authorized to act as police officers for railroads in Ross County, showing name, date of commission, and date recorded. Arranged chronologically by dates of recording. Indexed alphabetically by names of policemen. Handwritten on printed forms. 159 pages. 15 x 10 x 1.

136. REAL ESTATE BROKERS' REGISTER
1925—. 1 volume.
Record of licenses granted to brokers to buy, sell, and trade real estate for others, showing name of licensee and date. Arranged chronologically by dates of entry. Indexed alphabetically by names of the licensees. Handwritten on printed forms. 100 pages. 14 x 9 x 1.

Partnership Record

137. REGISTER OF PARTNERSHIP
1894—. 1 volume.
Record of partnerships formed to engage in business, showing name of company, names of partners, business location, and date certificate was filed. Arranged chronologically by dates of filing. Indexed alphabetically by names of companies. Handwritten. 481 pages. 20 x 14 x 3.5.

For limited partnership records, see entry 89.

Elections
(See also entries 531-533)

138. RECORD OF APPOINTED AND ELECTED OFFICIALS
1855-1884. 21 volumes.

List of names of persons serving in the various county, township, and corporation offices, showing date elected, name of official, what office, name of township or corporation, term of office, and date assuming duties of the office. Arranged chronologically by dates of election. Indexed by names of offices. Handwritten. Average 500 pages. 16 x 9 x 3.5.

139. POLL BOOKS AND TALLY SHEETS
1911. 51 volumes.

Record showing names of electors casting ballots on the proposal for a state constitutional convention to revise the state constitution, election of November 1911. Tally sheets record the results of the votes on proposals. Arranged alphabetically by names of electors. No index. Handwritten. Average 30 pages. 26 x 14 x .25.

140. REPUBLICAN POLL BOOKS AND TALLY SHEETS, PRIMARY ELECTIONS
1916, 1924, 1928, 1932, 1936—. 155 volumes. (labeled by years and precinct numbers).

Poll books of primary elections, showing name and address of voter and signature. Tally sheets show number of votes received by each candidate for each proposal or issue. Poll books, arranged alphabetically by names of voters; tally sheets, no orderly arrangement. No index. Handwritten on printed forms. Average 30 pages. 26 x 14 x .25.

For poll books and tally sheets, general elections, see entry 142.

141. DEMOCRAT POLL BOOKS AND TALLY SHEETS, PRIMARY ELECTIONS
1916, 1924, 1928, 1932, 1936—. 150 volumes. (labeled by years and precinct numbers).

Poll books of primary elections, showing name and address of voter and signature. Tally sheets showe number of votes received by each candidate and for each proposal or issue. Poll books, arranged alphabetically by names of voters; tally sheets, no orderly arrangement. No index. Handwritten on printed forms. Average 30 pages. 26 x 14 x .25.

For poll books and tally sheets, general elections, see entry 142.

142. POLL BOOKS AND TALLY SHEETS, REGULAR ELECTIONS
1908, 1916, 1918, 1921, 1922, 1928, 1929, 1931—. 622 volumes. (labeled by years and precinct numbers).

Poll books of regular elections, showing name and address of voter, and signature. Tally sheets show number of votes received by each candidate and for each proposal or issue. Poll books, arranged alphabetically by names of voters; tally sheets, no orderly arrangement. No index. Handwritten on printed forms. Average 30 pages. 26 x 14 x .25.

For poll books and tally sheets, primary elections, see entries 140, 141.

Naturalization Records
(See also entries 263, 264)

143. PETITIONS FOR NATURALIZATION [Military]
1919. 6 volumes. (1-6).

Petitions of aliens for naturalization as United States citizens for military duty in World War. These are regular petition forms as prescribed by the United States Department of Labor, showing date, name of alien, nativity, date of arrival in the United States, port of entry, and name of sovereign from whom he renounces allegiance. Arranged chronologically by dates of entry. Indexed numerically by petition numbers. Handwritten on printed forms. Average 250 pages. 12 x 22 x 2.

For stubs of certificates, 1919-1920, See entry 144.

144. CERTIFICATES OF NATURALIZATION
1919-1920. 34 volumes. (labeled by container certificate numbers).

Record stubs of certificates of naturalization (military) granted by common pleas court, showing certificate number, date, name of naturalized citizen, and nationality. Arranged numerically by certificate numbers. No index. Handwritten on printed forms. Average 50 stubs. 10 x 4 x .25.

For petitions (military), 1919, see entry 143.

145. DECLARATION OF INTENTION
1908—. 1 volume.
Record of declarations by aliens of intention to become citizens of the United States by naturalization, showing name of declarant, date of arrival in United States, port of entry, nativity, age, physical description, and date filed. Arranged chronologically by dates of filing. Indexed alphabetically by names of applicants. Handwritten on printed forms. 100 pages. 14 x 9 x 1.

146. PETITION AND RECORD
1908—. 2 volumes.
Copies of petitions of aliens for naturalization as citizens of the United States with record of citizenship granted by common pleas court, showing name of petitioner, date filed, length of residence in United States, nativity, age, affidavit of two freeholders as to length of residence and character, date final papers granted, and copy of certificate of citizenship. Arranged chronologically by dates of filing. Indexed alphabetically by names of applicants. Handwritten on printed forms. Average 100 pages. 22 x 12 x 1.

Fiscal Accounts

147. CLERK'S FEE BOOK
1802-1924, 1857-1863. 10 volumes.
Clerk of courts' record of fees due from various sources, showing name of payer, date, and amount. Arranged chronologically by dates of entry. No index. Handwritten. Average 200 pages. 14 x 8 x 1.25.

148. ACCRUED FEES
1907-1918. 2 volumes.
Clerk of courts' record of fees, showing by whom paid, amount, for what service, and date accrued. Arranged chronologically by dates of accrual. No index. Handwritten. Average 250 pages. 18 x 12 x 1.25.

149. RECORD OF FEES
January 1, 1938—. 1 volume.
Clerk's record of fees for issuing or notarizing motor vehicles certificates of title, showing total daily fees for each document title issued or notarized, monthly total,

amount to state, county, and department clerks each thirty day period, and annual recapitulation of monthly totals. Arranged chronologically by daily, monthly, and annual entries. No index. Handwritten on printed forms. 15 pages (loose leaf binder), 16 x 20 x .25. Clerk of courts' office.

150. CASH BOOKS
1859-1867, 1872—. 22 volumes.
Record of money received by clerk of courts including payment of fees, judgments, and court cost, showing name of payer, date, amount, and source; also record of disbursements, showing date, name of payee, amount, and for what. Arranged chronologically by dates of entry. No index. Handwritten. 1859-1967, average 550 pages. 20 x 12 x 4; 1872—, average 200 pages. 18 x 18 x 1.5.

151. RECORD OF UNCLAIMED MONEY
1887—. 2 volumes.
Record of unclaimed money, witnesses and jury fees, paid into the county treasury, showing to whom money is due, amount, date money paid in, and date certificate for recovery was issued. Arranged alphabetically by names of owners. No index. Handwritten. Average 300 pages. 14 x 8 x 2.

152. CLERK'S RECEIPTS
1925—. 31 volumes. (labeled by contained receipt numbers).
Carbon copies of receipts given by the clerk of courts for money received including court costs and fees, showing name of payer, date, purpose, amount, and receipt number. Arranged numerically by receipt numbers. No index. Handwritten on printed forms. Average 350 pages. 16 x 10 x 2.5.

153. RECORD OF COST BILLS
1864-1906. 9 volumes.
Record of cost and fees due from court cases, showing date, names of litigants, case number, term of court, and itemized bill of cost and fees. Arranged chronologically by dates of entry. Indexed alphabetically by names of debeters. Handwritten. Average 450 pages. 18 x 12 x 3.5.

For original cost bills, see entry 109.

Miscellaneous

154. MISCELLANEOUS COURT PAPERS

1880-1918. 6 file boxes. (labeled by years).

Original papers of cases of no record or case numbers with miscellaneous titles, as appointments of court attendants and officers, appointments to soldiers' relief commission, orders to summon grand jury, and other court orders of no record, showing date, name of principals, nature of document, and date filed. Arranged chronologically by dates of filing. No index. Handwritten and handwritten on printed forms. 10 x 5 x 14.

155. CORONER'S INQUESTS

1803—. 22 file boxes. (labeled by years).

Copies of coroner's reports to clerk of courts on inquest and cases investigated, showing date, name of decedent, cause of death, and remarks. Arranged chronologically by dates of reports. No index. 1803-1861, handwritten; 1862—, handwritten and typed on printed forms. 10 x 5 x 14.

For coroner's records, see entry 307, 308

156. RECORD OF ESTRAYS

1800-1823, 1862-1918. 4 volumes.

Clerk of courts' record of reported estrays, showing date, name of person holding stray to be claimed by owner, and kind in description of stray; also record of sale where no claim of ownership was made. Arranged chronologically by dates of entry. Indexed alphabetically by names of persons reporting strays. Handwritten. 1 volume, 1800-1805, 125 pages, 6 x 5 x 1; 3 volumes, 1805-1918, average 335 pages. 12 x 8 x 2.5.

157. QUADRENNIAL ENUMERATION

1891, 1899, 1903, 1907. 69 volumes.

Enumeration for years specified of male residents of Ross County who were twenty-one years of age and over, showing name, address, and age. Arranged alphabetically by names of male residents. No index. Handwritten. Average 50 pages. 7 x 12 x .25.

158. CLERK'S RECORD BOOK [Papers Removed from Files]
1886-1897, 1910-1914. 2 volumes.

Clerk of courts' record of original papers and documents removed from files by attorneys or others, showing what record, case number, date removed, date returned, by whom removed, and by whom returned. Arranged chronologically by dates of removal. No index. Handwritten. Average 350 pages. 15 x 11 x 2.

159. RECORD OF MANUMISSION
1804-1855. 2 volumes. Discontinued.

Record of slaves being freed by their owners on settling in Ohio, showing date and names of owner and slave. Arranged chronologically by dates of entry. No index. Handwritten. Average 150 pages. 12 x 8 x 1.25.

The court of common pleas, like many other county institutions, originated in England during the reign of Henry II.[1] Established in America during the colonial period, the office was continued by the states following the War of American Independence.

The Northwest Ordinance of 1787 established a government consisting of a governor, a secretary, and three judges all appointed by Congress. The judges were to form a court, known as the general court, which had common law jurisdiction and together with the governor was authorized to draw up a code of civil and criminal law. The territorial act of 1788, establishing the American colonial policy in the newer west in respect to judiciary, contained sections authorizing the establishment in each county of a common pleas court to be composed of not less than three nor more than five members. These members, appointed and commissioned by the territorial governor, were given jurisdiction in all civil matters.[2] The same act established in each county a primary court called the court general quarter sessions of the peace to be composed of no more than five nor less than three justices of the peace, appointed and commissioned by the governor.[3] This court, which has limited jurisdiction in criminal matters, was not reestablished by the constitution of 1802 and the jurisdiction which had been exercised by this court was conferred upon the justices of the peace and the court of common pleas.[4] A complete set of the records of the court of general quarter sessions of the peace for Ross County is extant.[5]

When a constitution was drafted for Ohio in 1802, preparatory to the entrance of the state into the Union, provision was made for a continuation of the territorial court of common pleas.[6] The articles of the Ohio constitution, regarding the judiciary, provided for a court of common pleas in each county to be composed of a president and associate judges. For each county[7] not more than three nor less than two associate judges were to be appointed, with one president for each of the three judicial districts into which the counties were grouped.

---

1. George Burton Adams, *Constitutional History of England* (New York, 1921), 109, 134.
2. Pease, *op. cit.,* 7.
3. Pease, *op. cit.,* 4.
4. Pease, *op. cit.,* 5; *Laws of Ohio,* I, 40; II, 235.
5. See entries 160-164.
6. *Ohio Const, 1802,* Art. III, sec. 1.
7. At this time there were nine counties in the state.

The associate judges were not as a rule men who had a legal education.[8] The members of the court, appointed by joint ballot of both houses of the general assembly, were to hold court in three judicial districts into which the state was to be divided by legislating action. Their term of office was seven years "if so long they behaved well."[9]

It was almost half a century before any significant changes were made in the structure of the court. The constitution of 1851 provided that judges of the common pleas court were to be elected for a five-year term. For the purpose of their election the state was divided into nine districts composed of three or more counties. Each district, in turn, was to be subdivided into three parts, and each of which one common pleas judge was to be elected. The court of common pleas was to be held by one or more of these judges in each county in the district.[10] Power was given to the general assembly to increase or diminish the number of districts of the court of common pleas, the number of judges in any district and to change the districts or the subdivisions thereof, whenever two thirds of the legislature concurred therein.[11] Provision was also made for the removal of judges by a concurrent resolution of two thirds of the members elected to each house of the legislature.[12] An appellate court known as the district court was created, and was to be composed of one supreme court judge and several common pleas judges of the district. This court was to be held in each county of the district at least once in each year or at least three annual sessions in not less than three places.[13] The district courts were not a success, and after many attempts at revision the circuit courts, staffed by a separate group of elected judges, were adopted by vote of the people in 1883, thus relieving the common pleas judges of this appellate work.[14]

---

8. Francis J. Amer, *The Development of the Judicial System in Ohio the 1787 to 1932* (Johns Hopkins University, Baltimore, 1932. *Institute of Law Bulletin* no. 8), 17.
9. *Ohio Const. 1802,* Art. III, sec. 8.
10. *Ohio Const. 1851,* Art. IV, secs. 3, 4.
11. *Ibid.,* Art. IV, sec. 15.
12. *Ibid.,* Art. IV, sec. 17.
13. *Ohio Const. 1851,* Art. IV, secs, 5, 6.
14. Amer, *op. cit.,* 1-33; *Laws of Ohio,* LXXXI, 168.

The juvenile court was created in 1904 with jurisdiction in special matters relating to minors and was to be held by a judge of the court of common pleas, court of insolvency, or probate court who should be designated by the judges to hold such court.[15]

At the opening of the twentieth century sweeping changes in the organization of the courts were made. Constitutional amendments adopted in 1912 abolished the divisions and subdivisions of the common pleas provided by the constitution of 1851, and authorized the election of one or more common pleas judges in each county.[16] The chief justice of the supreme court was given authority to determine the disability or disqualification of any judge of the court of common pleas and also to assist any judge to hold court in any county.[17] Eleven years later the selection of a chief justice of the court of common pleas was authorized. Under an act of March 13, 1923, in certain counties more populous than Ross, where there were two or more common pleas judges, a chief justice was designated by vote of the judges. The justice so designated by his colleagues was to serve in such capacity until the expiration of his term, after which time the office was to be an elective one. The elective section of the act was nullified in effect in 1924 by the supreme court on the grounds that the creation of a new elective office was unconstitutional. Accordingly, in 1927 an amendment was passed eliminating the elective provision of the act.[18]

In recent years attempts have been made to improve the efficiency of the court by imposing stricter qualifications upon those who seek election to the bench. In 1917 an act was passed providing that a common pleas judge shall have been admitted to practice as an attorney at law for a period of six years preceding his election.[19] The salary of the office was also increased to $3,000 per year plus an amount based on the population of the county[20] thus making the position financially attractive, especially as the term of office is six years.[21]

---

15. *Laws of Ohio,* XCVII, 562. See also pp. 118-120.
16. *Ohio Const., 1851,* Art. IV, sec. 3.
17. *Ibid.,* Art. IV, secs. 3, 6.
18. *State ex rel.,* v. *Powell, Ohio State Reports,* CIX, 383; *Laws of Ohio,* CX, 52; CXII, 5; G. C. secs. 1532, 1558.
19. *Laws of Ohio,* CVII, 164.
20. G. C. sec. 2251-52.
21. G. C. sec. 1532.

in addition to the regular salaries, common pleas judges may be paid a per diem and expenses when assigned to special duty by the chief justice of the supreme court in a district not their own. When dockets become crowded or judges are incapacitated or disqualified, such assignments may be made.[22] In a few large counties judicial efficiency is promoted by assigning to certain common pleas judges specialized duties such as the hearing of domestic relations and juvenile court cases.

The jurisdiction of the court of common pleas has also been the product of a long period of historical development. The territorial law of 1788 which created the court provided that "The judges so appointed and commissioned . . . shall hold pleas of *assizes, scire facias, replevins,* and hear and determine all matters of pleas, actions, suits, and causes of a civil nature, real, personal, and mixed, according to the constitution and laws of the territory."[23] Individually, each judge of the common pleas was given jurisdiction over contract actions not exceeding five dollars.[24] The probate court was established by an act adopted August 30, 1788, and two of the judges of the court of common pleas sat with this judge in ruling on contested points, definitive sentences, and final judgments. There was no provision for an appeal from one court to another except from the probate court to the general court of the territory.[25]

In 1795 the judicial system underwent the first general revision and this increased the duties of the court of common pleas. A single justice of the peace or judge of the common pleas was given jurisdiction to hear certain civil actions up to $12.00. Actions under $5.00 were exclusive with the judges or justices and there was no appeal from their judgment. Actions between $5.00 and $12 .00 could be appealed to the court of common pleas. In 1799 this jurisdiction was raised to $20.00 and appeals could be taken to the common pleas if the judgment was over $2.00. If the judgment was for plaintiff, he could appeal only if the original demand was $4.00 more than the sum received.[26] Appeal from the common pleas to the general court was provided for in 1795, and could not be taken unless the title to the land was in question or when the amount of controversy exceeded $50.00.[27]

---

22. *Ohio Const. 1851* (Amendment, 1912), Art. IV, sec. 3.
23. G. C. sec. 1532.
24. Salmon P. Chase, *The Statutes of Ohio and of the Northwest Territory, 1788-1833* (Cincinnati, 1833), I, 94.
25. *Ibid.,* I, 96.
26. *Ibid.,* I, 143, 233, 307.
27. *Ibid.,* I, 306.

The constitution of 1802 gave the court of common pleas jurisdiction in such common law and chancery cases as shall be directed by law. In addition it was given jurisdiction of all probate and testamentary matters, and the appointment and supervision of guardians.[28] Moreover the court of common pleas and supreme court were assigned original cognizance of criminal cases as might be provided by law.[29] Appeals in civil cases might be made to the court of common pleas from the county commissioners, justices of the peace and other inferior courts.[30]

An act of the first general assembly in 1803 provided for the organization of the courts and defined their jurisdiction. The court of common pleas was given original jurisdiction in all cases, both in law and in equity, when the matter in dispute exceeded the jurisdiction of the justice of peace; of all probate, testamentary, and guardianship matters; and of all criminal matters exceeding the jurisdiction of the justice of peace, except when the punishment of the crime was capital. It was allowed to review certain cases from the justices of peace and also to review the decisions of the county commissioners in highway matters. In addition, the court had the same power to issue remedial and other process, writs of error and *mandamus* excepted, as had the supreme court.[31] In 1804 the courts jurisdiction in chancery cases was limited to cases involving less than $500.00,[32] and in 1805 it was given appellate jurisdiction from the justice of peace in all cases regardless of the amount involved.[33] In 1806 crimes wherein the punishment was capital could be tried in the common pleas court if the accused so elected.[34] In 1807 it was given jurisdiction in all chancery cases and concurrent jurisdiction with the supreme court in cases involving over $500.00.[35] In 1810 all cases in which the common pleas had original jurisdiction were committed to be appealed to the supreme court.[36]

---

28. *Ohio Const. 1802,* Art. III, secs. 3, 5.
29. *Ibid.,* Art. III, sec. 4.
30. *Ibid.,* Art. III, sec. 3.
31. Chase, *op. cit.,* I, 355.
32. *Laws of Ohio,* II, 261.
33. *Ibid.,* III, 14.
34. *Ibid.,* IV, 57.
35. *Ibid.,* V, 117.
36. *Ibid.,* VIII, 259.

By this act the right to appeal was established in Ohio in all civil cases. However the business of the supreme court increased so rapidly that in 1845 the right to appeal from a judgment of the common pleas court to the supreme court in actions at law was abolished. Instead, new trials were allowed "when law and justice required it."[37] Even earlier, appeals to the common pleas from inferior courts had been limited.[38] The chancery act, adopted in 1824, conferred general chancery powers on the court,[39] and in 1843 it was given concurrent jurisdiction with the supreme court in cases of divorce and alimony.[40]

The constitution of 1851 left the jurisdiction of the common pleas court to be fixed by law.[41] The jurisdiction conferred on this court by subsequent legislation was essentially the same as that exercised since 1810, with the exception of the jurisdiction which was transferred to the probate court,[42] and the addition, in 1853, of exclusive jurisdiction in divorce and alimony cases.[43] The court of common pleas was denied jurisdiction in cases of probate, testamentary, and guardianships matters, but final orders, judgments, and decrees of the probate court could be reviewed in common pleas on appeal or by writ of *certiorari*.[44] In 1853 the court of common pleas was given original jurisdiction of all crimes and offenses except minor criminal cases, the exclusive jurisdiction of which was vested in the justice of peace or other minor courts.[45]

The creation of criminal, mayors', and police courts also made certain changes in the powers and duties of the common pleas court.[46] The right to appeal from common pleas to the district court was restored in all civil actions in which the common pleas had the original jurisdiction,[47] but by an act of 1858 appeals were allowed to the immediate court only in nonjury cases.

---

37. *Ibid.*, XLIII, 80.
38. *Ibid.*, XXXVIII, 27.
39. *Ibid.*, XXII, 75.
40. *Ibid.*, XLI, 94.
41. *Ohio Const. 1851,* Art. IV, secs. 2, 4.
42. *Laws of Ohio,* L, 67. Records pertaining to probate matters were to be transferred to the probate court wherever it was possible to separate them from common pleas records. *Ibid.,* L, 88.
43. *Ibid.*, LI, 377. See also p. 77.
44. *Ibid.*, L, 84; LI, 145.
45. G. C. sec. 13422-5; *Law of Ohio,* LI, 474; LII, 73.
46. *Ibid.*, L, 90, 240, 246, 251, 253.
47. *Ibid.*, L, 93.

However, the same act provided for a second jury trial in common pleas as a matter of right in jury cases. This was granted upon demand made by either party at the close of the first trial on condition of his giving bond.[48] The abuse of this privilege led to its abolition in 1875.[49]

This period witnessed the re-establishment of superior courts in the state which were given the same jurisdiction as the courts of common pleas with certain exceptions.[50] At the same time as the superior court was established in Cincinnati, the legislature abolished the criminal court and transferred its jurisdiction to the common pleas court.[51] The criminal jurisdiction of the probate court was transferred to the common pleas court in 1857.[52] A limitation was placed on the right to appeal of probate court to common pleas in 1854.[53] This limitation was repealed, however, in 1856.[54]

For many years there were few changes in the powers of the court of common pleas except in the forms of appeal to higher courts,[55] and such added powers as resulted from the decline in the number of superior courts.[56] In 1894 the probate court in certain counties, exclusive of Ross, was given concurrent jurisdiction with the common pleas court in divorce, alimony, foreclosure, and partition cases,[57] and in 1906 it was given concurrent jurisdiction with common pleas in all counties in the trial of misdemeanors and all proceedings to prevent crime.[58] Certain other special courts, as insolvency courts, shared certain powers with the common pleas.[59]

Since 1906 the court of common pleas has had jurisdiction in naturalization proceedings.

---

48. *Ibid.,* LX, 81.
49. *Ibid.,* LXXII, 34.
50. *Ibid.,* LII, 34; LIII, 38; LIV, 37.
51. *Ibid.,* LII, 107.
52. *Ibid.,* LIV, 97.
53. *Ibid.,* LII, 104.
54. *Ibid.,* LIII, 8.
55. *Laws of Ohio,* LXII, 359; LXXXII, 230.
56. LXII, 58; LXXII, 89, 105; LXXXII, 85.
57. *Ibid.,* XCI, 799. For a full discussion, see p. 88.
58. *Laws of Ohio,* XCVIII, 49.
59. *Ibid.,* XCI, 844; XCII, 475; XCIV, 353.

In that year the federal statute was amended to limit jurisdiction in the granting of naturalization to the United States district courts and state courts having a clerk, a seal, and jurisdiction in matters of law and equity in which the amount of controversy is unlimited.[60]

Constitutional amendments adopted in 1912 had little effect upon the jurisdiction of the court of common pleas; this power being determined by law.[61] However the establishment of municipal courts, beginning in 1910, relieved common pleas courts in many counties, exclusive of Ross, of certain civil jurisdictions,[62] but this was balanced in 1911 by the abolition of the jurisdiction of the probate court in certain counties, likewise exclusive of Ross, in divorce, alimony, foreclosure, and partition cases.[63] In the same year the juvenile courts were given jurisdiction of all misdemeanors against minors and certain other offenses.[64] Provision was also made for error proceedings from juvenile courts to the court of common pleas.[65] The jurisdiction of the common pleas court of today is essentially the same as that of 1913. The few changes that had been made in the judicial system are found in a local, special courts, particularly in the rapidly developing municipal courts.

The common pleas court has never possessed extensive appointed powers. The constitution of 1802 authorized each court to appoint a clerk,[66] and in 1805 it was directed to appoint a county prosecuting attorney.[67] During the first three decades of Ohio history, the movement for the extension of the popular election of public officers deprived the court of common pleas of the privilege of appointing the county recorder (1829), county surveyor (1831), and county prosecuting attorney (1838).[68] The court continued to appoint a clerk of courts until 1851. In recent years, however, as new functions have been added to the county government, the court has again been given a limited appointive power.

---

60. *United States Statutes at Large,* XXXIV, pt. i, 596.
61. *Ohio Const. 1851,* Art. IV, sec. 6.
62. *Laws of Ohio,* CI, 364; CIII, 279.
63. *Ibid.,* CII, 100.
64. *Ibid.,* CII, 425.
65. *Ibid.,* CIII, 875.
66. *Ohio Const. 1802,* Art. III, sec. 9.
67. *Laws of Ohio,* III, 47.
68. *Ibid.,* XXVII, 65; XXIX, 399; Chase, *op. cit.,* III, 1935.

Successive acts in 1886, 1891, 1913, 1914, and 1925 authorized the court to appoint a soldiers' relief commission, a jury commission, an assignment commissioner, a conservancy district board, and a probation officer.[69] Other appointments authorized in 1911 are those of court interpreter and criminal bailiff.[70]

The court may also appoint a court reporter (or reporters),[71] and may co-operate with the county commissioners for the establishment of a department of probation, in which case the court appoints certain probation officers and supervisors their work.[72] In case the sheriff is absent, disabled, or disqualified from serving the court's warrant, the judge may appoint temporarily an official for this service.[73] By and large, however, the patronage power of the court of common pleas is a negotiable factor in county government. The court of common pleas has shared with other governmental agencies the function of issuing various licenses.[74] Since 1805 the court has been authorized to issue ferry licenses[75] and tavern keeper licenses.[76] Both ferry and tavern licenses may now be issued by municipal corporations also and the latter by the state of marshal.[77] From 1803 to 1852 this court also issued licenses to ministers to solemnize marriage ceremonies; since the latter year this function has been exercised by the probate court.[78]

The keeping of the records of the common pleas court presented no particular difficulties for decades. However, with the increased number of issues presented to the court in recent years the problem of judicial administration has become greater. This problem was solved in part by the creation of the office of chief justice of the court of common pleas who has been given the duties of superintending the business of the court, classifying it, and distributing it among the judges. Besides the duties enumerated, the chief justice annually makes a report to the clerk of courts showing the work performed by the court and by each judge in the proceeding calendar year.

---

69. *Laws of Ohio,* LXXXIII, 232; LXXXVIII, 200; CIII, 512; CIV, 13-64; CXI, 423.
70. G. C. sec. 1541.
71. *Ibid.,* secs. 1546-1554.
72. *Ibid.,* secs. 1551-1 - 1554-6.
73. *Ibid.,* sec. 2828.
74. See pp. XXXV, XL, 45.
75. *Laws of Ohio,* III, 96; G. C. secs. 5947, 5949.
76. *Laws of Ohio,* III, 96; XXIX, 310.
77. G. C. secs. 3641, 3672, 843-3.
78. *Laws of Ohio,* I, 31; L, 84. See also p. 89.

Moreover, he reports such other data as the chief justice of the supreme court may require.[79]

Judges of the common pleas court are also required to issue an annual order as to the exact time of sessions. The clerk of courts is required to make this information public and also send a copy to the secretary of state. The law sets certain requirements as to the sessions of the court and the power of the judge to call special sessions.[80] The records of the court are deposited for safekeeping with the clerk of courts. The clerk is custodian also of all law reports and books furnished by the state for the use of the court and the bar and is made liable in the event of their destruction.[81]

All records are located in the clerk of courts' vault.

---

79. G. C. Sec. 1558. See p. 64.
80. G. C. secs. 1533-1539.
81. *Laws of Ohio,* LXVIII, 109.

Court of Quarter Sessions of the Peace

160. SESSIONS DOCKET

1799-1803. 1 volume.

Appearance docket of territorial court of quarter sessions of the peace, showing names of litigants, date of filing, kind of action, court orders, and reading of will. Arranged chronologically by dates of filing. No index. Handwritten. Condition fair. 120 pages. 6 x 5 x 1.

161. EXECUTION DOCKET

1799-1803. 1 volume.

Execution docket of territorial court of quarter sessions, showing date, names of litigants, kind of action, amount of judgment, and sheriff's returns. Arranged chronologically by dates of entry. No index. Handwritten. Condition fair. 120 pages. 6 x 5 x 1.

162. ISSUE DOCKET

1799-1803. 1 volume.

Record of actions heard by territorial court of quarter sessions, showing dates, case number, names the litigants, cause, verdict rendered, and court cost. Arranged chronologically by dates of entry. No index. Handwritten. Condition fair. 125 pages. 6 x 5 x 1.

163. ORDER BOOK

1798-1803. 1 volume.

Journal entries of orders and decrees of the territorial court of quarter sessions in all cases coming before the court including wills, showing date, case number, names of litigants, title of case, and date filed. Arranged chronologically by dates of entry. No index. Handwritten. Condition fair. 200 pages. 14 x 5 x 1.5.

164. RECORD [Quarter Sessions]

1798-1803. 1 volume.

Record of territorial court of quarter sessions including a complete record of all matters heard and disposed of by this court, showing date case filed, date of trial, names of judges on case, names of litigants, title of case, brief of testimony and evidence introduced, verdict, and judgment or sentence. Arranged chronologically by dates of filing. No index. Handwritten. Condition fair. 200 pages. 18 x 8 x 1.5.

Dockets

(See also entries 101-106)

165. APPEARANCE DOCKET

1803—. 48 volumes. (1-48).

Appearance record of civil cases brought in common pleas court, showing date, case number, names of litigants and attorneys, trial date, and court orders. Also contains Criminal Appearance Docket, 1803-1864, entry 166. Arranged chronologically by dates of entry. Indexed alphabetically by names of plaintiffs. Handwritten. Average 400 pages. 19 x 13 x 3.

166. CRIMINAL APPEARANCE DOCKET

1865—. 10 volumes. (1-10). 1803-1834 in Appearance Docket, entry 165.

Appearance record of criminal cases in common pleas court, showing date, case number, names of defendant and attorneys, trail date, and court orders. Arranged chronologically by dates of entry. Indexed alphabetically by names of defendants. Handwritten. Average 500 pages. 18 x 12 x 3.5.

167. COURT DOCKET

1892-1900, 1906-1908. 11 volumes. (labeled by dates of court terms).

Docket of all cases to be heard by common pleas court, showing date, names of the litigants and attorneys, kind of action, last steps, and order of court. Arranged chronologically by dates of entry. Indexed alphabetically by names of plaintiffs. Handwritten. Average 80 pages. 18 x 12 x .5.

168. CIVIL DOCKET

1910—. 15 volumes. (labeled by dates of court terms).

Docket of civil cases heard by common pleas court, showing date, names of litigants, kind of action, orders of court, and date original papers were filed. Arranged chronologically by dates of entry. No index. Handwritten. Average 500 pages, (loose-leaf). 12 x 9 x 5.

169. ISSUE DOCKET

1803-1816. 3 volumes.

Record of all cases at issue before the common pleas court, showing date, names of litigants, kind of action, and date of court order. Arranged chronologically by dates of entry. No index. Handwritten. Condition fair. Average 175 pages. 9 x 7 x 1.25.

Record of Trials

(See also entries 107-117)

170. MINUTE BOOK

1798-1817. 2 volumes.

Record of calling sessions of court, adjournment motions, cases to be heard, record of fines imposed, licenses and permits to operate taverns, and various petitions. Arranged chronologically by dates of entry. No index. Handwritten. Condition fair. Average 275 pages. 13 x 9 x 2.

171. ORDER BOOKS

1803-1809, 1814—. 81 the volumes. (1, 2, 4-82).

Copies of journal entries in common pleas court actions, showing date, case number, names of litigants, title of case, titles and dates of filing of all entries. Arranged chronologically by dates of entry. Indexed alphabetically by names of plaintiffs. 1803-1809, 1814-1912, handwritten; 1913—, typed. Average 500 pages. 18 x 14 x 3.5.

172. DAY BOOK
1808-1811. 1 volume.

Condensed daily record of common pleas court, showing term of court, day of week and date, case number, names of litigants, title of case, brief history of daily proceedings, and copies of court orders and writs. Arranged chronologically by dates of entry. No index. Handwritten. 500 pages. 16 x 11 x 3.5.

173. CRIMINAL RECORD
1882-1908. 4 volumes. (1-4). 1803-1881, 1909— in Complete Record, entry 174.

Complete record of criminal cases prosecuted in common pleas court, showing term of court, case number, name of defendant, offense charged, copies of transcripts from magistrates' courts, grand jury indictment, plea, petitions, motions, brief of trial testimony and evidence, verdict of jury, and sentence. Arranged chronologically by dates of entry. Indexed alphabetically by names of defendants. Handwritten. Average 800 pages. 18 x 12 x 4.5.

174. COMPLETE RECORD
1803—. 116 volumes. (1-116).

Complete record of civil cases and petitions heard by common pleas court, showing term of court, case number, names of litigants, title of case, date filed, date of trial, copies of affidavits, petitions, answers, motions, briefs of trial proceedings, verdict of jury or court, and judgment or sentence. Also contains Criminal Record, 1803-1881, 1909—, entry 173. Arranged chronologically by dates of filing. Indexed alphabetically by names of plaintiffs. 1803-1809, handwritten; 1910—, typed. Average 500 pages. 18 x 14 x 3.5.

175. CHANCERY AND PARTITION
1824—. 38 volumes. (1-38).

Record of all chancery, partition, and equity cases, showing term of court, case number, names of litigants, title of case, date filed, date of hearing, copies of affidavits, petitions, answers, waivers, brief of hearing, and court decision.

Arranged chronologically by dates of filing. Indexed alphabetically by names of plaintiffs. 1824-1909, handwritten; 1910—, typed. Average 500 pages. 18 x 16 x 3.5.

176. MASTER COMMISSIONER'S RECORD
1865. 1 volume.
Record of report of master commissioner to common pleas court in various cases concerning distribution of assets in assignment and other cases, showing dates, names of litigants, case number, and title of case. Chronologically arranged by dates of entry. No index. Handwritten. 100 pages. 18 x 12 x 1.

Assignment Commissioners

In order to secure an even distribution of work among judges the legislature, in 1913, authorized the court of common pleas to designate the members of the jury commission to serve in the capacity of assignment commissioners. It was their duty, when serving in this capacity, to assign cases for trial and to perform such other duties as the court might require.[1] Eight years later, in 1921, the court of common pleas in any county having not more than one common pleas judge and having a population of 80,000 or more, with the consent of the county commissioners, was authorized to appoint such assignment commissioners.[2]

In 1931 the legislature passed an act relieving the jury commissioners of such tasks by making provisions for a separate and distinct body of assignment commissioners. Under this act, the provisions of which are still in force, the judges of the court of common pleas in any county, where two or more judges held court at the same time, were authorized to appoint assignment commissioners. These officials, serving at the pleasure of the court were to receive such compensation as the court might direct, not to exceed $4,900 for each commissioner per year. In the event such appointments were made the names of the appointees, together with their salaries, were to be recorded in the court journal.[3]

---

1. *Laws of Ohio,* CIII, 512; CVI, 534; CVIII, pt. ii, 1114; CIX, 281.
2. *Ibid.,* CIX, 152.
3. G. C. sec. 3007; *Law of Ohio,* CXIV, 212.

At the same time, the court of common pleas in any county having not more than one common pleas judge was authorized, when the business of the court required it, to appoint an assignment commissioner.[4] The maximum annual salary of the assignment commissioner in such counties was set at $1,800.[5] This official, serving at the pleasure of the court, could also be appointed court constable.[6]

Although Ross County has no regularly appointed assignment commissioner, the common pleas judge, the prosecuting attorney, and the attorney representing the litigants make assignments of cases for hearing.

---

4. G. C. sec. 3007-1; *Laws of Ohio,* CXIV, 213.
5. G. C. sec. 3007-1.
6. *Ibid.,* sec. 1692-3; Ohio Attorney General, *Opinions,* 1924, 60.

177. RECORD OF ASSIGNMENTS
1932—. 2 volumes.

Record of dates set for trial of causes filed in the Ross County court of common pleas, showing names of litigants, kind of action, names of attorneys, and trial dated. Arranged chronologically by dates of entry. Indexed alphabetically by names of plaintiffs. Handwritten. Average $280 pages. 18 x 24 x 2.25. Common Pleas Judge, private office.

The first constitution of Ohio provided for a supreme court consisting of three judges appointed by a joint ballot of the legislature for a seven-year term. The court was required to hold sessions at least once a year in each county.[1] The number of judges, according to constitutional provisions, might be increased to four after a period of five years, in which case the judges were committed to divide the state into two circuits. Accordingly, in 1808 the membership of the court was increased to four and the state was divided into the requisite number of circuits.[2] Two years later, in 1810, the membership of the court was reduced to three;[3] in 1824 it was again increased to four.[4]

By constitutional provision, this court was given original and appellate jurisdiction "both in common law and chancery," in such cases that should be provided by law.[5] Accordingly, by statutory provision, the court was assigned exclusive cognizance of all cases of divorce and alimony and concurrent jurisdiction of all civil cases both of law and equity where the title to land was in question, or the matter in dispute exceeded $1,000; and appellate jurisdiction from the court of common pleas "in all cases respecting the title of lands or where the matter in controversy exceeds the value of one thousand dollars, and all cases were proof of validity of wills or the right of administration shall be in question."[6] During the first half century of Ohio history the legislature granted decrees of divorce. Although the constitution of 1802 did not prohibit the legislature from exercising such jurisdiction, the supreme court prohibited the practice in 1848.[7] The constitution of 1851, Article II, section 32, contained a prohibiting clause. Moreover, the court was given original cognizance in the trial of capital offense.[8] All cases in which the title to land or freehold was in question were to be tried in the county where the land was situated. Furthermore, the court was given appellate jurisdiction from the court of common pleas in all cases in which the court of common pleas had the original jurisdiction.[9]

---

1. *Ohio Const. 1802,* Art. III. secs. 2, 8, 10.
2. *Laws of Ohio,* VI, 32.
3. *Ibid.,* VIII, 259.
4. *Ibid.,* XXII, 50.
5. *Ohio Const. 1802,* Art. III, sec. 2.
6. *Laws of Ohio,* I, 36-37; XIV, 310.
7. *Bingham* v. *Miller, Ohio Reports,* XVII, 445.
8. *Laws of Ohio,* I, 36-37.
9. *Ibid.,* XIV, 310-354.

In 1831 the supreme court was directed to meet annually in the town of Columbus for the final adjudication of all such questions of law as they have been reserved in any county or decision. This session of the court, known as the court in bank, was required to have its decisions in each case reduced to writing, and transmitted to the clerk of the supreme court in each county in which such question was reserved. The clerk was directed to enter such decisions "on the journal of the said court" and such proceedings were to be taken as if such decisions had been made in the county.[10] Six years later, in 1837, an act was passed providing that the final judgments in the supreme court, held within any county within the state, could be re-examined and reversed or affirmed in the court in bank upon a writ of error.[11]

This judicial arrangement continued until the adoption of the constitution of 1851, which provided a judicial system modeled upon the federal system existing at the time. The supreme court, as established in 1851, became for the first time in Ohio history, a reviewing court of last resort in the state. At the same time the jurisdiction of the supreme court was restricted. In 1853 the court of common pleas, rather than the supreme court, was given original cognizance of all crimes and offenses, except minor criminal cases, the exclusive jurisdiction at which was vested in the justice of the peace and other minor courts.[12] The supreme court, which, between the years 1803 and 1843, had had exclusive original cognizance in divorce and alimony cases and from 1843 to 1853 had concurrent jurisdiction to the court of common pleas in such cases, was denied such jurisdiction in 1853 when the latter court was granted exclusive jurisdiction in these cases.[13]

The opinions of the supreme court on circuit and the decisions of the court in bank, as transmitted to the clerk of the supreme court in each county, are in the offices of the respecting courts.

All records of the supreme court are in the clerk of courts' vault.

---

10. *Ibid.,* XXIX, 93-94.
11. *Ibid.,* XXXV, 60-62.
12. G. C. sec. 13422-5; *Laws of Ohio,* LI, 474; LII, 72.
13. *Laws of Ohio,* XLI, 94; LI, 377.

178. ISSUE DOCKET

1805-1841. 2 volumes.

Record of cases appealed to supreme court, showing date entered, names of litigants, grounds of appeal, and decision of court; also record of original jurisdiction causes such as divorce, injunction, and *habeas corpus.* Arranged chronologically by dates of entry. No index. Handwritten. Condition fair. Average 200 pages. 12 x 8 x 1.5.

179. MINUTE BOOK

1803-1847. 2 volumes.

Condensed record of the meetings of the supreme court, showing term of court, day of week and date, names of judges in attendance, title of case, names of litigants, notation of action, and orders or decrees issued in each case. Arranged chronologically by dates of entry. No index. Handwritten. Condition fair. Average 400 pages. 14 x 8 x 3.

180. JOURNAL

1803-1804, 1807-1813, 1816-1843. 6 volumes. (1, 3, 5-8).

Copies of journal entries in causes filed in or appealed to supreme court consisting of affidavits, petitions, answers, warrants, summonses and other writs , court orders, and decrees, showing case number, date filed, names of litigants, and title of case. Arranged chronologically by dates of filing. 1803-1804, 1807-1813, 1823-1843, no index; 1 volume, 1816-1822, indexed alphabetically by names of plaintiffs. Handwritten. Average 350 pages. 14 x 10 x 2.

181. COMPLETE RECORD

1805 -1808, 1810-1852. 16 volumes. (B-E, G-R).

Complete record of all cases heard by the supreme court in both appeals and original jurisdiction cases, showing case number, date, names of litigants, title of case, date filed, date of trial, copies of petitions, answers, affidavits, trial proceedings, and verdict. Arranged chronologically by dates of entry. Indexed alphabetically by names of plaintiffs. Handwritten. Condition fair. Average 400 pages. 18 x 12 x 2.5.

182. JUDGMENTS

1803-1852. 32 file boxes. (labeled by years).

Original papers of judgments handed down by the supreme court, showing case number, names of judgment creditor and debtor, amount of judgment, date decree issued, and date filed. Arranged chronologically by dates of filing. No index. Handwritten. 10 x 5 x 14.

183. MANDATES

1808-1843. 3 file boxes. (labeled by years).

Original mandates issued by the supreme court to the court of common pleas, showing term of court, case number, names of litigants, title of case, and date filed. Arranged chronologically by dates of filing. No index. Handwritten. 10 x 5 x 14.

Until 1851 the judicial power of the state of Ohio in matters of both law and equity was vested in the supreme court, the court of common pleas, and the justices' courts.[1] During the first fifty years of Ohio history the supreme court served as a court of appeals, holding court in each county annually.[2] When a new constitution was adopted in 1851 the judicial system was extended by the creation of district courts composed of one supreme court justice and several common pleas judges in the district. These courts were assigned original jurisdiction in the same matter as a supreme court, and such "appellate jurisdiction" as might be provided by law.[3] Thus by constitutional provision the courts were assigned original cognizance in *quo warranto, mandamus, habeas corpus,* and *procedendo.*[4] In addition to this, in 1852 the legislature authorized the courts to issue writs of error, *certiorari, supersedeas, ne exeat,* and all other writs not specifically provided by statute, whenever such writs were necessary for the exercise of its jurisdiction. The same act gave the courts appellate jurisdiction from the court of common pleas in civil cases wherein the latter court had original jurisdiction.[5]

For the purposes of the district courts the nine common pleas districts were apportioned into five judicial districts. A judge of the supreme court was designated to preside at the sessions of the district courts; in the event that no judge of the supreme court were present, as often was the case, the judge of the court of common pleas in whose subdivision court was being held was directed to preside.[6]

The district courts failed to function properly. Evidence seems to indicate that the increasing number of cases coming before the supreme court made it difficult for the justices to attend the meetings of the district courts. The supreme court dockets were overcrowded. In 1845 the legislature found it necessary to afford temporary relief by prohibiting appeals from the court of common pleas to the supreme court.[7] A similar condition of overcrowding existed in the sixties; so that, in 1865, the supreme court justices were relieved of the duty of attending the meetings of district courts for that particular year.[8]

---

1. *Ohio Const. 1802,* Art. III, sec. 1.
2. See p. 77.
3. *Ohio Const. 1851,* Art. IV, secs. 5, 6.
4. *Ibid.,* Art. IV, sec. 2.
5. *Laws of Ohio,* L, 69.
6. *Ibid.,* L, 69.
7. *Ibid.,* XLIII, 80.
8. *Ibid.,* LXII, 72.

The judicial system had become slow and cumbersome. The courts declined rapidly after 1865 and were finally abolished.

Following the complete collapse of the district courts an amendment to the constitution, adopted in 1883, made provision for circuit courts. "The circuit courts," stated the amendment, "shall be the successor of the district courts, and all cases, judgments, records, and proceedings pertaining to said district courts, in the several counties, of any district, shall be transferred to the circuit courts." The district courts, however, were to continue in existence until the election and qualification of the judges of the circuit court.[9] The circuit courts were assigned the same "original jurisdiction with the supreme court, and such appellet jurisdiction as may be provided by law." The compensation of the courts and the number of circuits were left to the discretion of the legislature. Accordingly, in 1884, an act was passed dividing the state into seven circuits, and providing for the election of three judges in each circuit.[10]

The circuit courts, in addition to the jurisdiction conferred upon them by the constitution,[11] were authorized by the legislature to issue writs of *supersedeas* in any case, and all other writs not specifically provided by statute when they were necessary for the exercise of their jurisdiction.[12] Moreover, the courts were authorized to make and publish, as they deemed expedient, rules of procedure in their respective circuits, not in conflict with the law or rules of the supreme court. The legislature directed that all cases taken to the circuit courts were to be entered on the docket in the order in which they were commenced, received, or filed, and "to be taken up and disposed of in the same order." However, cases in which persons seeking relief were imprisoned or were convicted of a felony; cases involving the validity of any tax levy or assessment; cases involving the constitutionality of a statute; and cases involving public right and proceedings in *quo warranto, mandamus, procedendo,* or *habeas corpus,* be taken up in advance of their assignment or order on the docket.[13]

---

9. *Ohio Const. 1851*, Art. IV, sec. 6.
10. *Laws of Ohio*, LXXXI, 168.
11. *Ohio Const. 1851*, Art. IV, sec. 6.
12. *Laws of Ohio*, LXXXI, 168.
13. *Laws of Ohio*, LXXXI, 168.

The judicial system of Ohio was again slightly changed in 1912 when, by constitutional amendment, the circuit courts were renamed courts of appeals. "The court of appeals shall continue the work of the respective circuit courts and all pending cases and proceedings in the circuit courts shall proceed to judgment and be determined by the respected courts of appeals." The judges of the several circuit courts were designated as judges of the courts of appeals, and were directed to perform the duties thereof until the expiration of their term of office. Vacancies caused by the expiration of terms of office of the judges were to be filled by the electors of the respective appellate districts. The term of office was fixed at six years.[14]

The jurisdiction of the court of appeals remained much the same as that of the district court in 1851. However, the court was assigned original cognizance in writs of prohibition and appellate jurisdiction in the trial of chancery cases.[15] Certain restrictions were imposed upon the court: "No judgment of a court of common pleas, a superior court or other court of record" shall be reversed except by "the concurrence of all judges of the court of appeals."[16]

At present the court consists of three judges in each of the nine districts into which the state is divided, each of whom shall have been admitted to practice as an attorney at law in the state for a period of six years immediately preceding his election. One court of appeals judge is chosen every two years, and he holds office for six years beginning on the ninth day of February next after his election. The salary of the court of appeals judge, fixed at $6,000 per year in 1913, was increased to $8,000 in 1920 and so continued.[17] The judges hold at least one session of court annually in each county in the district.[18]

All records of court of appeals are located in the clerk of courts' vault, unless otherwise specified.

---

14. *Ohio Const. 1851* (Amendment, 1912), Art. IV, sec. 6.
15. *Ibid.,* Art. IV, sec. 6.
16. *Ibid.,* Art. IV, sec. 6.
17. *Laws of Ohio,* CIII, 418; CVIII, pt. ii, 1301.
18. G. C. sec. 1517.

District Court

184. APPEARANCE DOCKET, DISTRICT COURT
1867-1884. 1 volume.
General record of cases filed in district court, showing case number, date filed, names of litigants, title of case, dates of filing various writs and court orders, and itemized bill of clerk of courts' and sheriff's fees. Arranged chronologically by dates of filing. Indexed alphabetically by names of plaintiffs. Handwritten. 800 pages. 18 x 13 x 4.

185. DIRECT COURT ISSUE DOCKET
1852-1884. 1 volume.
Docket of cases heard in district court, showing term of courts, date, name of litigants and attorneys, kind of action, last steps, and remarks. Arranged chronologically by dates of entry. No index. Handwritten. 200 pages. 17 x 12 x 1.5.

186. DISTRICT COURT COMPLETE RECORD
1852-1884. 3 volumes.
Complete record of cases heard by district court on appeal, showing term of court, date, case number, names of litigants, title of case, copies of bill of exceptions, affidavits, motions, petitions, decisions, and opinions of court. Arranged chronologically by dates of entry. Indexed alphabetically by names of plaintiffs. Handwritten. 600 pages. 18 x 12 x 3.5.

187. JUDGMENTS
1854-1883. 12 file boxes. (labeled by years).
Original papers of judgment decrees handed down by district courts, showing case number, names of judgment creditor and debtor, amount of judgment, and dates issued and filed. Arranged chronologically by dates of filing. No index. Handwritten on printed forms. 10 x 5 x 14.

Circuit Court

188. COURT CALENDAR
1895-1913. 2 volumes.

Docket of cases assigned for hearing, showing court term, case number, names of attorneys, names of litigants, style of case, statute of case, date of hearing, and orders of court. Arranged chronologically by dates of courts terms. No index. Handwritten on printed forms. Average 130 pages. 12 x 12 x 1. 1 volume, 1895-1901, Clerk of courts' vault; 1 volume; 1901-1913, Basement, rear storeroom.

189. APPEARANCE DOCKET, CIRCUIT COURT
1885-1912. 1 volume.

Docket of cases filed in circuit court, showing date filed, case number, names of litigants, title of case, dates of filing various writs and journal entries, and itemized bill of clerk's and sheriff's fees. Arranged chronologically by dates of filing. Indexed alphabetically by names of plaintiffs. Handwritten on printed forms. 480 pages. 18 x 12 x 2.5.

190. CIRCUIT COURT ORDER BOOK
1885-1912. 2 volumes.

Copies of journal entries, showing term of court, case number, names of litigants, title of case, and date filed. Arranged chronologically by dates of filing. Indexed alphabetically by names of plaintiffs. Handwritten. Average 600 pages. 18 x 13 x 3.5.

191. CIRCUIT COURT RECORD
1885-1912. 3 volumes.

Complete record of all cases heard by circuit court, showing court term, case number, names of litigants, title of case, dates filed, copies of bills of exception, petitions, motions, affidavits, answers, and court decisions and opinions. Arranged chronologically by dates of court terms. Indexed alphabetically by names of plaintiffs. Handwritten. Average 600 pages. 18 x 13 x 3.5.

192. COURT RECORDS [Original Papers]

1885-1912. 7 file boxes. (labeled by years).

Original papers issued by circuit court, (except bills of exceptions) consisting of affidavits, dispositions, summonses, petitions, and other writs, court orders, and decrees, showing case number, names of litigants and attorneys, title of case, and date filed. Arranged chronologically by dates of filing. No index. Handwritten on printed forms. 10 x 5 x 14.

Court of Appeals

193. COURT OF APPEALS CALENDAR

1913—. 1 volume.

Calendar of cases assigned for hearing, showing term of court, case number, names of litigants and attorneys, style of case, date of hearing, status of case, and court orders. Arranged chronologically by dates of court terms and thereunder by dates of hearings. No index. Handwritten on printed forms. 160 pages. 16 x 12 x 1.25.

194. APPEARANCE DOCKET

1913—. 1 volume.

Docket of cases filed in the court of appeals, showing date filed, case number, names of litigants, title of case, dates are filing various journal entries, and itemized bill of clerk's and sheriff's fees. Arranged chronologically by dates of filing. Itemized alphabetically by names of plaintiffs. Handwritten on printed forms. 500 pages. 18 x 13 x 2.5.

195. COURT OF APPEALS ORDER BOOK

1913—. 1 volume.

Copies of journal entries consisting of petitions, affidavits, writs, court orders, and decrees, showing term of court, names of litigants, case number, title of case, and date filed. Arranged chronologically by dates of court terms. Indexed alphabetically by names of plaintiffs. Typed. 600 pages. 18 x 13 x 3.

196. RECORD

1913—. 1 volume.

Complete record of proceedings in case heard by court of appeals, showing term of court, case number, names of litigants, title of case, copies of bills of exceptions, petitions, motions, answers, brief of hearing, and decisions and opinions of court. Arranged chronologically by dates of court terms. Indexed alphabetically by names of plaintiffs. Typed. 600 pages. 18 x 13 x 3.

197. [ORIGINAL COURT PAPERS, COURT OF APPEALS]

1913—. In original [Court] Papers, entry 109.

Original case papers of court of appeals. Papers of each case filed together in a jacket, showing names of litigants, and attorneys, case number, title of case, file box number, and volume and page numbers of Appearance Docket, entry 194 and Court of Appeals Order Book, entry 195.

198. MANDATES

1909—. 5 file boxes. (labeled by years).

Original mandates issued to common pleas court in cases disposed of, showing date, names of litigants, case number, title of case, and dates issued and filed. Arranged by dates of filing. No index. Handwritten and typed on printed forms. 10 x 5 x 14.

The probate court, established by an act of the Northwest Territory on August 30, 1788, consisted of a probate judge with jurisdiction in probate, testamentary, and guardianship matters, and two judges of the court of common pleas, who sat with him and ruled on contested points, definitive sentences, and final judgments.[1]

The judicial system established under the first constitution of Ohio in 1802 did not provide for a probate court but vested the court of common pleas with such powers as had been exercised by the court in the territorial period. The constitution of 1851 re-created the probate court and gave it original jurisdiction in "probate and testamentary matters, the appointment of administrators and guardians, the settlement of the accounts of executors, administrators and guardians, and such jurisdiction in *habeas corpus,* . . . and for the sale of land by executors, administrators and guardians, and such other jurisdiction, . . . as may be provided by law."[2] An amendment to the constitution adopted in 1912, authorized the common pleas judge, when petitioned by ten percent of the qualified voters in the counties having a population less than 60,000 to submit to the voters at any general election the question of combining the probate court and court of common pleas.[3]

One of the primary functions of the court since its inception has been the settlement of estates. The civil code adopted in 1853 gave the court original jurisdiction in taking proof of wills, granting letters testimentary, and in settling accounts of executors and administrators.[4] Until 1854 the court had jurisdiction in enforcing the payment of debts and legacies of deceased persons. While the court retains the original jurisdiction regarding estates, new duties have been added in recent years. With the development of inheritance tax laws in 1919 as a new means of taxation the probate court has been required to determine and assess the tax after the county auditor has appraised the decedent's estate.[5]

By constitutional provision the probate court has original jurisdiction in granting marriage licenses.[6]

---

1. Pease, *op. cit.,* 9.
2. *Ohio Const., 1851,* Art. IV, secs. 7, 8. See also p. 65.
3. *Ohio Const. 1851,* Art. IV, sec. 7. See also p. XXX
4. *Laws of Ohio,* LI, 167.
5. *Ibid.,* CVIII, pt. i, 561. See also p. XLII
6. *Ohio Const. 1851,* Art. IV, sec. 8.

The court also issues licenses to ministers to solemnize marriages.[7] The former provision was modified by an act adopted in 1931, which requires an elapse of at least five days between the time of application and that of the issuance of marriage licenses. However, power to suspend the operation of the act is vested in the probate judge.[8] Moreover, the probate courts in certain counties, exclusive of Ross, were given concurrent jurisdiction with the court of common pleas in "divorce, alimony, foreclosure, and partition" cases. Thus, in 1894 the legislature conferred such jurisdiction upon the probate court in Allen, Butler, Defiance, Perry, Richland, and Wood Counties.[9] The original act, subject to amendments in 1896, 1900, and 1904, which granted and denied such jurisdiction to the probate courts in certain counties, was repealed in 1911.[10] In 1919 concurrent jurisdiction in such matters was re-established in Coshocton, Defiance, Henry, Licking, Perry, Pickaway, and Richland, Counties, and established in Fayette County.[11] This jurisdiction was abolished in 1931.[12]

The jurisdiction of the court extends to the state's unfortunates. By the probate code of 1853, re-enacted in 1854, exclusive jurisdiction was granted to the court to make inquests respecting lunatics, insane persons, idiots, and deaf and dumb persons, subject by law to guardianships.[13] In 1856 the court was authorized to commit mentally incompetent persons to state institutions maintained for the care of such persons.[14] Two years later the court was given power to appoint and remove guardians over minors.[15] The act of 1859 authorized the court to render adoption decrees.[16] In recent years the court has been given jurisdiction in trial cases involving neglected, dependent, and delinquent children.[17]

---

7. *Laws of Ohio,* L. 84.
8. *Ibid.,* CXIV, 93.
9. *Ibid.,* XCI, 791, 799-800.
10. *Ibid.,* XCII, 643; XCIV, 137-138; XCVII, 113-114; CII, 100.
11. *Ibid.,* CVIII, pt. i, 625.
12. *Ibid.,* CXIV, 320.
13. *Ibid.,* LI, 167; LII, 103.
14. *Ibid.,* LIII, 81-86.
15. *Ibid.,* LV, 54.
16. *Ibid.,* LVI, 82; LXVII, 14.
17. See p. 118.

Since the middle of the nineteenth century the probate judge has been required to keep a record of vital statistics. In 1867 the duty of keeping a permanent record of births and deaths, which, in 1856, had been conferred upon the clerk of courts, was transferred to the probate judge.[18] When, in 1908, a bureau of vital statistics under the direction of the secretary of state was created the probate judge was relieved temporarily of this task.[19] In 1921 the act of 1908 was amended so as to require the local registrars to transmit to the district health commissioner, who was directed to serve as a state deputy registrar of vital statistics, all certificates of birth and deaths received during the preceding month, and a copy of all such certificates to the probate court. Although the General Code still requires the probate judge to keep a permanent record of birth and deaths and an index to such records,[20] neither has been kept in Ross County since 1908.

Jurisdiction in naturalization proceedings was exercised by the probate court until 1906 when an amendment to the federal statute vested exclusive jurisdiction in naturalization matters in the United States district courts and all state courts of record having a seal, a clerk, and jurisdiction in actions at law and equity in which the amount in controversy was unlimited.[21] The General Code still requires the probate judge to keep a naturalization record and an index to the records,[22] but jurisdiction was transferred to the courts of common pleas. No naturalization records have been kept since 1906.

During the early years of its existence the court was given limited criminal jurisdiction in cases in which the sentence did not impose capital punishment or punishment by imprisonment. By the code of civil procedure adopted in 1853 the judgments and final decrees of the probate court could be reviewed by the court of common pleas on error.[23] In 1857 the criminal jurisdiction of the probate court was transferred to the court of common pleas,[24] but later acts retain it in certain counties only.

---

18. *Laws of Ohio,* LXIV, 63-64.
19. *Ibid.,* XCIX, 296-307.
20. G. C. sec. 10501-15.
21. *United States Statutes at Large,* XXXIV, pt. I, 596; See also *State of Ohio* v. *George G. Metzger and Albert L. Irish,* 10 N. P., n. s., 97 *et seq.*
22. G. C. secs. 10501-15, 10501-16.
23. *Laws of Ohio,* LI, 145.
24. *Ibid.,* LIV, 97.

Thus, in 1858 the probate courts of certain counties, exclusive of Ross, were granted jurisdiction in all crimes in which the sentence did not impose capital punishment or imprisonment in a penitentiary.[25] This act was repealed in 1878 and the probate courts of certain counties, exclusive of Ross, were granted concurrent jurisdiction with the court of common pleas in all misdemeanors proceedings to prevent crime and in 1888 such jurisdiction was extended to the Ross County probate court[26] which continued to exercise such jurisdiction until 1931 when the last vestige of criminal jurisdiction disappeared with the adoption of the probate code.[27]

Miscellaneous duties remotely related to probate and testamentary matters, have been added by legislative action. Since 1888 the court has been required to file a certified list of all unknown depositors as furnished by institutions or persons engage in lending money for profit.[28] In 1896 the probate court was given concurrent jurisdiction with the court of common pleas in the matter of changing the names of persons who desired it[29] a matter in which the court of common pleas had exclusive cognizance from 1842 to 1896.[30] Since 1896 the probate court has been required to record certificates of doctors and surgeons, and since 1916 the certificates of registered nurses which authorize them to practice their profession in the state.[31] Since 1913 the court has been vested with the power to grant injunctions,[32] and since 1915 has had concurrent jurisdiction with the court of common pleas in condemnation proceedings for roads.[33]

---

25. *Ibid.*, LV, 186.
26. *Ibid.*, LXXV, 960; LXXXVI, 22.
27. *Ibid.*, CXIV, 475.
28. *Ibid.*, LXXXV, 56; G. C. sec. 9864.
29. *Laws of Ohio,* XCII, 28.
30. *Laws of Ohio,* XL, 28-29.
31. *Ibid.*, XCII, 46; XCIX, 499; CVI, 193.
32. *Ibid.*, CIII, 427.
33. *Ibid.*, CVI, 583.

In like manner the appointive powers of the probate judge have been expanded. In addition to the authority to appoint administrators and guardians he was authorized by the act of 1891 to appoint the members of the county board of elections; this appointed power was abrogated by the act of 1892.[34] Then, too, from 1908 to 1913 the probate judge was authorized to appoint a county blind relief commission[35] comprised of three members of each whom served a three-year term.[36] Since 1913 he has had authority to appoint members of the board of county visitors.[37]

The probate judge, like other county officials, has been required by statute to keep a record of the business of his office. The present system of records, originating for the most part in 1853 and continued by the probate code of 1931, includes a criminal record, an administrative docket, a guardians' docket, a marriage record, a record of bonds, and naturalization record, and a permanent record of birth and deaths.[38]

The probate judge has the care and custody of the files, papers, books, and records belonging to the probate office and is *ex officio* clerk of the court. The probate code, adopted in 1931, directed the probate judge to preserve for future reference and examination all pleadings, accounts, vouchers, and other papers in each estate, trust, assignment, guardianship, or other proceedings, such papers to be properly jacketed and tied together; he is required also to make proper entries and indexes omitted by his predecessors. Certificates of marriages, reports of birth, and similar papers not a part of a case or proceeding or to be arranged and preserved separately in the order of dates in which they are filed.[39]

At present the probate judge is elected for a four-year term.[40] In recent years there has been an attempt to raise the qualifications of those seeking election to the office. Accordingly, an amendment to the probate code in 1931 restricted eligibility to the office to a practicing attorney or to a person who "shall had previously served as probate judge immediately prior to his election."[41]

All records are in the probate court vault unless otherwise specified.

---

34. *Ibid.*, LXXXVIII, 449; LXXXIX, 455.
35. See p. 247.
36. *Laws of Ohio,* XCIX, 56; CIII, 60.
37. *Ibid.*, CIII, 173-174, 853.
38. *Ibid.*, LI, 167; LII, 103; CXIV, 324.
39. *Ibid.*, CXIV, 321-322.
40. *Ibid.*, CXIV, 320.
41. *Ibid.*, CXVI, 481.

Calendars and Dockets

199. COURT CALENDAR
1876—. 58 volumes. (labeled by years).

Calendar of cases filed in probate court, showing names of principals, date filed, and style of case. Arranged chronologically by dates of filing. Indexed alphabetically by names of decedents, wards, or petitioners. Handwritten. Average 450 pages. 15 x 9 x 3.25.

200. APPEARANCE DOCKET
1852—. 9 volumes. (1-9).

Records of actions filed in probate court, showing names of principals, date filed, and remarks such as notations of court orders and decrees. Arranged chronologically by dates of filing. Indexed alphabetically by names of principals. Handwritten. Average 550 pages. 18 x 12 x 1.5.

201. EXECUTION DOCKET
1884—. 4 volumes. (1-4).

Record of executions ordered by probate court, showing names of the litigants, kind of case, amount of judgment, date of execution, date returned by sheriff, and remarks. Arranged alphabetically by names of defendants and chronologically thereunder by dates of executions. No index. Handwritten. Average 420 pages. 18 x 12 x 3.5.

202. JUDGMENT INDEX
1882-1888. 1 volume.

Index to judgments awarded, showing names of litigants, amount and date of judgment, date of satisfaction of judgment, and volume and page numbers of Execution Docket, entry 201, Journal, entry 210, Cash Book, entry 279. Arranged alphabetically by names of plaintiffs and chronologically thereunder by dates of judgments. Handwritten. 490 pages. 18 x 12 x 4.

203. TRAIL DOCKET
1882-1889. 2 volumes.

Docket of cases set for trial and probate court, showing names that live against, data hearing, and remarks. Arranged chronologically by dates of hearings. Indexed alphabetically by names of defendants. Handwritten. Average 320 pages. 14 x 9 x 2.

204. CRIMINAL APPEARANCE AND EXECUTION DOCKET
1888-1912. 2 volumes.

Front half of each volume contains record of criminal actions filed in probate court, showing name of defendant, date filed, offense, and remarks such as notations of court orders. Last half of each volume contains record of executions to satisfy judgments ordered by probate court, showing name of defendant, in what matter, date, sheriff's returns, and remarks. Arranged alphabetically by names of defendants and chronologically thereunder by dates of filing. No index. Handwritten. Average 600 pages. 18 x 12 x 4.5.

205. CRIMINAL DOCKET
1888-1930. 2 volumes. (1, 2). Discontinued.

Docket of criminal cases filed in probate court, showing name of defendant, offense, date filed, date of hearing, and remarks. Arranged chronologically by dates of filing. Indexed alphabetically by names the defendants. Handwritten. Average 320 pages. 16 x 11 x 2.5.

206. TESTAMENTARY DOCKET
1810-1852. 9 volumes. (1-9).

Administration record of probate division of common pleas court including appointments of administrators, executors, guardians, and trustees, inventory and sale bill records, record of accounts, record of settlements, and record of petitions, showing date entered, names the principals, and date pertinent to each type of record. Arranged chronologically by dates of entry. Indexed alphabetically by names of descendants, wards or assignors. Handwritten. Average 375 pages. 15.5 x 10 x 2.5. For subsequent records, see entries 207, 209.

207. ADMINISTRATION DOCKET
1853—. 14 volumes. (1-14).

Docket of administration of estates showing name of descendant, name of administrator or executor appointed, names of sureties and appraisers, dates letters of administration were issued, date inventory filed, date account filed, date final account filed, date of settlement, discharge, and cost. Arranged chronologically by dates of appointments. Indexed alphabetically by names of descendants; also separate index, entry 208. Handwritten. Average 525 pages. 17 x 11 x 3.5.

For prior records, see entry 206.

208. GENERAL INDEX
1801—. 8 volumes. (1-8).

Index to Administration Docket, entry 207, Journal, entry 210, Criminal Record, entry 213, Court Papers, entry 215, Appointment of Administrator record, entry 223, Appointment of Executors Records, entry 225, Inventory and Appraisement Record, entry 234, Account Record, entry 248, Lunacy Record, entry 256, Epileptic record, entry 259, and Juvenile Record, entry 295, showing date, names of decedent, ward, assignors, and defendants, year, case number, and volume and page numbers of record. Arranged alphabetically under tabs by names of the decedents, wards, assignors, or defendants and chronologically thereunder by dates of entry. Handwritten. Average 600 pages. 18 x 14 x 4.5.

209. GUARDIANS' AND TRUSTEES' DOCKET
1879—. 6 volumes. (1-6).

Docket of guardians and trustees, showing name of ward, guardian, or trustee, names of sureties, date appointed, amount of bond, date inventory file, amount of inventory, date of settlement, amount of settlement, names of persons to whom settlements are made, volume and page numbers of Journal, entry 210, General Record, entry 212, and cost. Arranged chronologically by dates of appointments. Indexed alphabetically by names of wards. Average 600 pages. 18 x 12 x 4.5.

For prior records, see entry 206.

Court Proceedings

210. JOURNAL

1810—. 83 volumes. (1810-1852, A-I; 74 volumes, 1-74).

Copies of all journal entries such as appointments, petitions, affidavits, pleas, motions, orders, and decrees of probate court, showing case number, title of case, names of principals, and date filed. Arranged chronologically by dates of filing. For index, see entry 208. 1810-1916, handwritten; 1916—, typed. Average 600 pages. 18 x 12 x 4.5.

211. CRIMINAL JOURNAL

1853-1857, 1888-1931. 3 volumes. Discontinued.

Journal entries of all court orders and decrees in criminal cases tried in probate court, showing date, name of defendant, case number, charge, and court orders. Arranged chronologically by dates of entry. Indexed alphabetically by names of defendants. 1853-1917, handwritten; 1917-1931, typed. Average 600 pages. 18 x 12 x 4.

212. GENERAL RECORD

1878—. 22 volumes. (1-22).

Complete record of all proceedings and causes filed in probate court, showing case number, names of principals, title of case, date filed, dates of various proceedings, and date case disposed of. Arranged chronologically by dates of filing. Indexed alphabetically by names of decedents, wards, assignors, or defendants. 1878-1914, handwritten; 1914—, typed. Average 550 pages. 18 x 12 x 3.5.

213. CRIMINAL RECORD

1852-1957, 1888-1931. 3 volumes. Discontinued.

Complete record of all proceedings in criminal cases heard in probate court, showing case number, name of defendant, date filed, and dates of various proceedings on court orders. Arranged chronologically by dates of filing. Indexed alphabetically by names of defendants; also separate index, entry 208. 1852-1916, handwritten; 1916-1931, typed. Average 600 pages. 18 x 12 x 4.

214. WITNESS AND JURY BOOK

1889-1893. 1 volume.

Record of witnesses called and testifying in probate court cases and of jurors in probate court cases, showing date of hearing, case number, names of litigants, kind of action, number of days in court, mileage, and total fees due. Arranged chronologically by dates of hearing. Indexed alphabetically by names of defendants. Handwritten on printed forms. 600 pages. 18 x 12 x 4.5.

215. COURT PAPERS

1801—. 1,387 file boxes. (labeled by contain case numbers).

Court papers in all probate court cases, except criminal cases. Papers of each case filed together in a jacket, showing case number, names of principals, title of case, volume and page numbers of Administration Docket, entry 207, Journal, entry 210, and General Record, entry 212, date issued, and date filed.

Also contains:

a. Original wills, 1801-1851, entry 221.
b. Appointment of Administrators, 1801-1878, 1897—, entry 224.
c. Appointment of Executors, 1801-1874, 1898—, entry 226.
d. Appointment of Guardians, 1801-1890, 1902—, entry 228.
e. Petitions to sell Real Estate, 1801-1887, 1901—, entry 237.
f. Order of Sale, 1801-1878, 1894—, entry 238.
g. Cost Bills, 1801-1977, 1910, entry 246.
h. Lunacy Inquest, 1852-1891, 1897-1902, 1912—, entry 257.
i. Miscellaneous [Original Papers], 1852-1887, 1892-1893, 1897-1898, 1904—, entry 292.
j. Cost Bills [Juvenile Cases], 1916—, entry 299.
k. Adoption Record and Cost bills, 1852-1897, 1915—, entry 302.

Arranged numerically by case numbers. For index, see entry 2048. 1801-1914, handwritten on printed forms; 1915—, typed on printed forms. 10 x 5 x 14.

For other cost bill records, see entry 216, 241-246, 283, 284, 298.

216. COST BILLS [Criminal Cases]

1888-1890. 3 file boxes.

Itemized statements of fees taxed by probate court in state (criminal) cases, showing case number, name of defendant, offense, itemize account of court and sheriff's fees, total fees, and date filed. Arranged chronologically by dates of filing. No

index. Handwritten on printed forms. 10 x 4.5 x 14. Basement, rear storeroom.
For other cost bill records, see entries 215, 241-246, 283, 284.

217. STATE CASES
1887-1905. 8 file boxes. (labeled by years).
Original papers issued and filed in state (criminal) cases consisting of affidavits of information, warrants to arrest, warrants to convey to penal institution, pleas, motions, and all journal entries, showing case number, date filed, name of defendant, crime charged, date, and volume and page numbers of Criminal Journal, entry 211, and Criminal Record, entry 213. All papers of each case banded together. Arranged chronologically by date so filing. No index. Handwritten on printed forms. 10 x 4.5 x 14. Basement, rear storeroom.

218. CRIMINAL CASES DISMISSED
1888-1902. 3 file boxes. (labeled by years).
Original papers issued and filed in criminal cases which were dismissed without record, consisting of affidavits of information, citations to appear in court, and court orders, showing name of accused, nature of offense, and date filed. All papers of each case banded together. Arranged chronologically by dates of filing. No index. Handwritten on printed forms. 10 x 4.5 x 14. Basement, rear storeroom.

219. TRANSCRIPTS
1894-1899. 1 file box.
Copies of transcripts from magistrates' courts in criminal cases, which have been taken to probate court, showing date, case number, from what court, name of defendant, offense, and date filed. Arranged chronologically by dates of filing. No index. Handwritten on printed forms. 10 x 4.5 x 14. Basement, rear storeroom.

Wills

220. RECORD OF WILLS
1798—. 39 volumes. (21 volumes, 1798-1890, A-Z, some volumes bearing more than one letter; 1891—, 1-18).
Records for 1798-1802 are of wills filed and probated under the territorial courts; 1802-1952 are records of wills filed and probated in the probate division of common pleas court. Copies of wills filed for probate directing the distribution of

the testator's property, showing name of testator, date of will, names of witnesses, legatees and devisees, conditions and terms, date filed for probate, and date probated. Arranged chronologically by dates probated. Indexed alphabetically by names of testators. 1798-1916, handwritten; 1916—, typed. Average 500 pages. 15 x 10.5 x 3.5.

221. ORIGINAL WILLS
1852—. 31 file boxes. (labeled by years). 1801-1851 in Court Papers, entry 215-a.

Original wills filed and probated, showing date of will, name of testator, names of devisees or legatees, conditions and terms, usually name of person the testator desires to execute the provisions of the will, signatures of witnesses and testator, notarization, date filed for probate, and volume and page numbers were recorded. Arranged chronologically by dates for filing. No index. Handwritten and typed, some on printed forms. 10 x 4.5 x 14.

Estates

Appointments, Bonds, and Letters of Fiduciaries

222. APPOINTMENT JOURNAL
1860-1876. 1 volume.

Probate judge's record of appointments of administrators, executors, or guardians, showing name of appointee, name of decedent or ward, dates of appointment and inventory, amount of bond, and remarks. Arranged chronologically by dates of appointments. No index. Handwritten. Condition poor. 240 pages. 16 x 11 x 2. Basement, middle storeroom.

For subsequent records, see entries 223, 225, 227.

223. APPOINTMENT OF ADMINISTRATOR RECORD
1882—. 13 volumes. (A-M).

Record of appointments of administrators including copies of applications for appointments, showing date, names of applicant, decedent, and heirs, degree at kinship of heirs-at-law, and estimated value of estate; also copies of journal entries, showing names of decedent and administrator, and date of appointment. Also contains Administrator's Bonds and Letters, entry 230. Arranged chronologically by dates of appointment. Indexed alphabetically by names of decedents; also separate index, entry 208. 1882-1914, handwritten on printed forms; 1914—, Typed on printed forms. Average 500 pages. 18 x 12 x 4.5.

For records of appointments, 1860-1876, see entry 222.

224. APPOINTMENT OF ADMINISTRATOR

1879-1896. 4 file boxes. 1801-1878, 1897—, in Court Papers, entry 215-b. Original papers issued in appointments of administrators of estates, showing case number, names of decedent and appointee, date of appointment, and volume and page numbers where recorded. Arranged chronologically by dates of appointments. No index. Handwritten on printed forms. 10 x 4.5 x 14. Basement, rear storeroom.

225. APPOINTMENT OF EXECUTORS RECORD

1882—. 9 volumes. (A-I).

Record of appointments of executors, showing case number, names of decedent and appointee, names and degree of kinship of heirs-at-law, and estimated value of estate; also copies of journal entries, showing names of decedent and executor, and date of appointment. Also contains Executors' Bonds and Letters, entry 231. Arranged chronologically by dates of appointments. Indexed alphabetically by names of decedents; also separate index, entry 208. 1882-1914, handwritten on printed forms; 1914—, typed on printed forms. Average 600 pages. 18 x 12 x 4.5.

For record of appointments, 1860-1876, see entry 22.

226. APPOINTMENT OF EXECUTOR

1875-1897. 5 file boxes. 1801-1874, 1898— in Court Papers, entry 215-c. Original papers issued on appointments of executors of estates, showing case number, names of decedents and appointee, date of appointment, and volume and page numbers where recorded. Arranged chronologically by dates of appointments. No index. Handwritten on printed forms. 10 x 4.5 x 14. Basement, rear storeroom.

227. GUARDIANS' APPOINTMENTS

1876—. 8 volumes. (A-H).

Record of appointments of guardians for minors, imbeciles, lunatics, and other incompetents including copies of applications for appointments, showing names of incompetent and applicant, and estimated value of property; copies of letters of guardianship, showing names of ward and appointee, and date of appointment; and copies of journal entries. Also contains Guardian' Bonds, entry 232. Arranged chronologically by dates of appointments. Indexed alphabetically by names of wards. 1876-1914, handwritten on printed forms; 1914—, typed on printed forms. Average 500 pages. 18 x 12 x 3.5.

For records of appointments, 1860-1876, see entry 222.

228. APPOINTMENT OF GUARDIANS

1891-1901. 1 file box. 1801-1890, 1902— in Court Papers, entry 215-d.

Original papers issued in appointments of guardians for minors, imbeciles, and other incompetents, showing names of ward and appointee, date of appointment, and volume and page numbers where recorded. Arranged chronologically by dates of appointments. No index. Handwritten on printed forms. 10 4.5 14. Basement, rear storeroom.

229. APPOINTMENT OF TRUSTEE RECORD

1883—. 2 volumes.

Record of appointments of trustees of estates left in trust, showing application for appointment, copy of bond, amount of estate in trust, and copy of trustee's letter of appointment; copies of journal entries, showing names of decedent and appointee, date, names of sureties, and amount of bond. Arranged chronologically by dates of appointments. Indexed alphabetically by names of decedents. 1883-1916, handwritten on printed forms; 1916—, typed on printed forms. Average 300 pages. 18 x 12 x 2.25.

230. ADMINISTRATORS' BONDS AND LETTERS

1849-1882. 4 volumes. 1882— in Appointment of Administrator Records, entry 223.

Copies of administrators' bonds and letters of appointment, showing date of appointment, names of decedent and appointee, amount of bond, names of sureties, and copies of letters of administration. Arranged chronologically by dates of appointment. Index alphabetically by names of decedents. Handwritten on printed forms. Average 400 pages. 14 x 8 x 2.5.

231. EXECUTORS' BONDS AND LETTERS

1849-1882. 2 volumes. 1882— in Appointment of Executors Record, entry 225.

Records of executors' bonds, showing name of decedent and appointee, amount of bond, and names of sureties; and copies of letter of appointment, showing names of decedent and appointee and date of appointment. Arranged chronologically by dates of appointments. Indexed alphabetically by names of decedents. Handwritten on printed forms. Average 400 pages. 14 x 8 x 2.5.

232. GUARDIANS' BONDS

1849-1876. 2 volumes. 1876— in Guardians' Appointments, entry 227.

Copies of guardians' bonds, showing date, name of guardian appointed, amount of bond, names of sureties, name of ward, and copy of oath of guardian. Arranged chronologically by dates of bonds. Indexed alphabetically by names of wards. Handwritten on printed forms. Every 600 pages. 12 x 8 x 3.5.

233. RELEASE OF ESTATE FROM ADMINISTRATION

1932—. 1 volume. Record initiated 1932.

Record of estates released from administration through probate court action, showing date, name of decedent and administrator, and reason for withdrawal. Arranged chronologically by dates of entry. Alphabetical index by names of decedents. Handwritten on forms. 360 pages. 18 x 12 x 2.5. Probate court's office.

Inventories and Sale Bills

234. INVENTORY AND APPRAISEMENT RECORD

1802-1913, 1817—. 65 volumes. (12 unnumbered, 1841-1902, A-Z, 1-27).

Record of inventories and appraisements of assets of estates settled in court, showing order to make inventory and appraisement, names of appraisers appointed, itemized list of property with value as fixed by appraisers, and date filed. Records for 1802-1813, 1817-1852 are of probate division of common pleas court. Arranged chronologically by dates of filing. 1806-1813, 1817—, indexed alphabetically by names of decedents; also separate index, entry 208. 1802-1814, 1817-1902, handwritten; 1902-1913, handwritten on printed forms; 1913—, typed on printed forms. Average 530 pages. 15 x 10.5 x 3.5.

For other inventories, see entry 235.

235. JUDGE'S INVENTORY AND SALE RECORD

1887-1889. 1 volume.

Record of inventories and sale bills in administrations and guardianships, showing name of decedent or ward, volume and page numbers of Administration Docket, entry 207, and Guardians' and Trustees' Docket, entry 209, name of administrator, executor, guardian, or trustee, date inventory due, and date of filing. Alphabetically arranged by names of decedents and wards and chronologically thereunder by dates of filing. No index. Handwritten. 208 pages. 16 x 11 x 1.5.

For prior and subsequent records of inventory, see entry 234.

236. PETITIONS TO SELL REAL ESTATE

1852—. 43 volumes. (A-z, 1-17).

Copies of petitions filed by administrator, executors, trustees, or guardians to sell real estate to pay debts, showing case number, name of decedent or ward, name of administrator, executor, trustee, or guardian, estimated value of real estate, itemized schedule of debts and cost, total debts, and date filed. Arranged chronologically by dates of filing. Indexed alphabetically by names of decedents or wards. 1852-1915, handwritten; 1915—, typed. Average 450 pages. 16 x 11 x 2.5.

237. PETITIONS TO SELL REAL ESTATE

1888-1900. 3 file boxes. 1801-1887, 1901— in Court Papers, entry 215-e.

Original copies of petitions by administrators or executors to sell real estate to pay debt of decedents, showing date of petition, case number, names of decedent, administrator, and executor, date to filed, and volume and page numbers where recorded. Arranged chronologically by dates are filing. No index. Handwritten on printed forms. 10 x 4.5 x 14. Basement, rear storeroom.

238. ORDER OF SALE

1879-1893. 1 file box. -1801-1878, 1894— in Court papers, entry 215-f.

Original papers issued ordering sale of property in settlement of estates, showing date of issue, type of writ issued, and volume and page numbers where recorded. Arranged chronologically by dates of issue. No index. Handwritten on printed forms. 10 x 4.5 x 14. Basement, rear storeroom.

Schedule of Debts and Determination of Heirship

239. SCHEDULE OF DEBTS
1932—. 2 volumes. (1, 2).
Record of debts of decedents, showing case number, name of decedent, names of creditors, amount of claim, date filed, interest allowed, affidavit of administrator or executor, and copy of journal entry. Arranged chronologically by dates of filing. Indexed alphabetically by names of decedents. Typed on printed forms. Average 600 pages. 18 x 12 x 4.

240. [HEIRS-AT-LAW]
1909-1916. In Blind Records, entry 262.
List of heirs-at-law, in the settlement of estates, showing names of heirs, name of the decedent, and degree of kinship.

Cost Bills (For original cost bills, see entries 215, 216)

241. COST BILLS, APPOINTMENT ADMINISTRATOR
1871-1878. 2 volumes.
Cost bills of fees taxed on appointments of administrators, showing name of administrator, name of decedent, date, and itemized cost. Arranged chronologically by dates of entry. Indexed alphabetically by names of decedents. Handwritten on printed forms. Average 200 pages. 16 x 10 x 1.5.

242. COST BILLS, APPOINTMENT OF GUARDIAN
1869-1877. 2 volumes.
Cost bills of fees taxed on appointments of guardians, showing name of guardian, name of ward, date, and itemized cost. Arranged chronologically by dates of entry. Indexed alphabetically by names of wards. Handwritten on printed forms. Average 160 pages. 14 x 8 x 1.5. Basement, middle storeroom.

243. COST BILLS, INVENTORY AND SALE BILL
1874-1877. 1 volume.
Costs bills of fees taxed on filing inventories and sale bills, showing name of decedent, name of administrator or executor, date, and itemized cost. Arranged chronologically by dates of entry. Indexed alphabetically by names of decedents.

Handwritten on printed forms. 170 pages. 16 x 10 x 1.5. Basement, middle storeroom.

244. COST BILLS, FILING ACCOUNTS
1871-1875. 2 volumes.
Itemized cost bills of fees taxed on filing accounts by administrators, executors, or guardians, showing name of administrator, executive, or guardian, name of decedent or ward, date, and itemized cost. Arranged chronologically by dates of entry. Index alphabetically by names of decedents or wards. Handwritten on printed forms. Average 260 pages. 16 x 8 x 1.5. Basement, middle storeroom.

245. COST BILL RECORD, ESTATES
1879-1911. 9 volumes.
Record of costs in settlement of estates, showing date, itemized account for appointment of administrator or executor, probation of will, election of widow, inventory and appraisement, sale of personal property, petition to sell real estate, and filing account. Arranged chronologically by dates of entry. Indexed alphabetically by names of decedents. Handwritten on printed forms. Average 600 pages. 18 x 12 x 4.5.

246. COST BILLS
1878-1909. 17 file boxes. 1801-1877, 1910 in Court Papers, entry 215-g.
Itemized statement of fees taxed by probate court on filing of accounts and inventories in settlement of estates, showing names of administrator, executor, or guardian, and decedent or ward, date, amount of fee, and volume and page numbers where recorded. Arranged chronologically by dates of filing. No index. Handwritten on printed forms. 10 x 4.5 x 14. Basement, rear storeroom.

Accounts and Settlements

247. SETTLEMENT CALENDAR
1878-1913. 3 volumes.
Calendar of settlements of accounts by administrators, executors, guardians, and assignees, showing date of settlement, names of decedent, ward, or assignor, and administrator, executor, guardian, or assignee, volume and page numbers of Administration Docket, entry 194, or Guardians' and Trustees' Docket, entry 195,

date account due, date notice issued, and date of filing. Arranged alphabetically under tabs by names of decedents and chronologically thereunder by dates of filing. No index. Handwritten. Average 180 pages. 16 x 14 x 1.25.

For roster of settlements, see entry 249.

248. ACCOUNT RECORD

1852—. 74 volumes. (1852-1884, A-Z; 1884—, 1-48).

Record of administrators', executors', guardians', trustees', and assignees' accounts filed with probate court, showing date, copy of appointment, order of filing account, assets, liabilities, total charges, total credits, and copy of journal entry. Arranged chronologically by dates of entry. Indexed alphabetically by names of decedents, wards, or assignees; also separate index, entry 208. 1852-1914, handwritten; 1914—, typed. Average 600 pages. 18 x 12 x 4.5.

For other records of real estate settlements, 1889-1893, see entry 250.

249. ROSTER OF SETTLEMENTS

1894-1899. 1 volume.

Record of settlements by administrators, executors, or guardians, showing name of appointee, capacity, name of decedent or ward, volume and page numbers of Administration Docket, entry 194, or Guardians' and Trustees' Docket, entry 195, what account, date due, date notice issued, date of filing, and remarks. Arranged chronologically by dates of filing. No index. Handwritten. 210 pages. 16 x 14 x 1.5.

For settlement calendar, see entry 247.

250. REAL ESTATE (Settlement) RECORD

1889-1893. 1 volume.

Record of settlement of estates involving real estate, showing date, inventory, administrators' or executors' petition to sell, sales account, and schedule of debts. Arranged chronologically by dates of entry. Indexed alphabetically by names of decedents. Handwritten. 600 pages. 18 x 12 x 4.5.

For complete record of settlements, see entry 248.

Inheritance Tax
(See also entries 365, 384, 496)

251. DIRECT INHERITANCE TAX RECORD
1895. 1 volume.
Record of inheritance tax proceedings in probate court, showing name of decedent, name of executor or administrator, appraisement schedule, and amount subject to tax as determined by court. There is only one case recorded in the volume. No index. Handwritten on printed forms. 608 pages. 18 x 12 x 4.5.

252. INHERITANCE TAX RECORD
1904—. 11 volumes. (1904-1923, 1-5; 1923—, 1-6).
Records of estates subject to inheritance tax, showing date, name of decedent, name of executor or administrator, itemized statement of assets and liabilities, copy of journal entry to determine tax without county auditor's appraisal and findings of court, waiver of notice of and time within which to file exceptions, and copy of journal entry certifying tax to county auditor. Arranged chronologically by dates of entry. Indexed alphabetically by names of decedents. Copies of journal entries, typed; other entries, handwritten on printed forms. Average 400 pages. 18 x 12 x 3.

253. INHERITANCE TAX RECORD (No Tax)
1933—. 2 volumes. (1, 2).
Record of estates not subject to tax, showing date, itemized statements of assets and liabilities for determination of inheritance tax, and copy of journal entry. Arranged chronologically by dates of entry. Indexed alphabetically by names of decedents. Copies of journal entries, typed; other entries, handwritten on printed forms. Average 600 pages. 18 x 12 x 4.

Assignments

254. RECORD OF APPOINTMENT OF ASSIGNEES
1885—. 1 volume. Last entry 1932.
Appointment record of assignees including copies of letters of appointment, journal entries of appointments, bonds, letters, authority to assignees, and deed of assignment, showing date of appointment, name of assignor, assignee, and sureties, amount of bond, and other data. Arranged chronologically by dates of appointments.

Indexed alphabetically by names of assignors. Handwritten or printed forms. 600 pages. 18 x 12 x 4.5.

265. ASSIGNMENT RECORD
1859—. 15 volumes. (1-15).

Complete record of assignments by insolvents made through probate court, showing name of corporation, company, or individual making assignment, record of appointment of assignee, itemized list and value of assets and liabilities by appraisement, order of sale, and settlement account of assignee, showing dates of appointment and filing, names of assignor and assignee, and other data pertinent to each type of record. Arranged chronologically by dates of filing. Indexed alphabetically by names of assignors. 1859-1914, handwritten; 1914—, typed. Average 500 pages. 18 x 12 x 3.5.

Dependents

256. LUNACY RECORD
1877—. 9 volumes. (1-9).

Record of lunacy cases including dates affidavits filed, copies of affidavits, warrants to arrest, inquest proceedings, medical certificates, applications for admission to state institution, warrants to convey, and sheriff's returns, showing date of entry, and name of incompetent. Also contains cost bills, lunacy, entry 258. Arranged chronologically by dates of filing affidavits. Indexed alphabetically by names of persons brought before the court; also separate index, entry 208. Handwritten on printed forms. Average 500 pages. 18 x 12 x 3.5.

257. LUNACY INQUEST
1892-1896, 1903-1911. 2 file boxes. 1852-1891, 1897-1902, 1912— in Court Papers, entry 215-h.

Original papers filed in lunacy proceedings, showing affidavit of information, order to arrest, date of hearing, and volume and page numbers where recorded. Arranged chronologically by dates of hearing. No index. Handwritten on printed forms. 10 x 4.5 x 14. Basement, rear storeroom.

258. COST BILL, LUNACY

1873-1877. 1 volume. 1877— in Lunacy Record, entry 256.

Itemized cost bills of fees taxed in lunacy proceedings, showing date filed, case number, name of patient, and itemized account of court and sheriff's fees. Arranged chronologically by dates of filing. Indexed alphabetically by names of persons brought before court. Handwritten on printed forms. 140 pages. 14 x 8 x 1. Basement, middle storeroom.

259. EPILEPTIC RECORD

1893—. 2 volumes. (1, 2).

Record of epileptic cases brought before probate court, showing copy of complaint filed, date filed, order to arrest, record of hearing, application for admission to state institution, warrant to convey, and sheriff's return. Arranged chronologically by dates of filing. Indexed alphabetically by names of person brought before court; also separate index, entry 208. Handwritten on printed forms. Average 290 pages. 18 x 12 x 2.5.

260. RECORD OF FEEBLE-MINDED YOUTH

1905—. 2 volumes. (1, 2).

Complete record of proceedings in feeble-minded cases brought before probate court, showing date filed, name of youth, record of inquest, names of relatives, medical certificate, application for admission to state institution, warrant to convey, and sheriff's return. Arranged chronologically by dates of filing. Indexed alphabetically by names of youths. Handwritten on printed forms. Average 300 pages. 18 x 12 x 2.25.

261. DEAF AND DUMB RECORDS

1854-1876. 1 volume.

Record of cases of deaf and dumb children brought before probate court to be sent to special institutions or schools, showing date filed, names of child and parents, medical certificate, and copy of journal entry. Arranged chronologically by dates of filing. Indexed alphabetically by names of children. Handwritten. 260 pages. 18 x 12 x 1.5.

262. BLIND RECORDS

1909-1916. 1 volume.

Record of blind relief payments, showing name of recipient, date, and amount. Also contains" [Heirs-at-law], entry 240; Adoption Records, entry 301. Arranged chronologically by dates of payments. No index. Handwritten. 260 pages. 18 x 12 x 1.5.

For records of applications and proceedings, see entry 26, 573-575.

Naturalization

(See also entries 143-146)

263. NATURALIZATION RECORD (Short Form)

1851-1880. 2 volumes. (1, 2).

Record of declaration of intention by aliens to become citizens of the United States, showing name of alien, physical description, nativity, date, port of entry, and date recorded. Arranged chronologically by dates of recording. Indexed alphabetically by names of declarants. 1851-1866, handwritten; 1867-1880, handwritten on printed forms. Average 630 pages. 14 x 8.5 x 4.

For naturalization record (Long Form), see entry 264.

264. NATURALIZATION RECORD (Long Form)

1872-1906. 2 volumes. (1, 2).

Record of application for naturalization and declaration of intention by aliens become citizens of the United States, showing name of applicant, nativity, date entering United States, age, sex, copies of affidavits by citizens obtaining declaration of alien, copy of certificate of naturalization, and date recorded; also record of naturalization of minors, showing name of applicant, date, age, date entered United States, date and age when application was made, and date recorded. Arranged chronologically by dates are recording. Indexed alphabetically by names of applicants. Handwritten on printed forms. Average 460 pages. 18 x 12 x 3.5.

For naturalization record (Short Form), See entry 263.

Vital Statistics

Births and Deaths (See also entries 549-115)

265. RECORD OF BIRTH
1867-1908. 5 volumes. (1-5).
Record of births as reported by township and ward assessors, showing date of birth, names of child and parents, residents, color, sex, and date recorded. Arranged chronologically by dates of recording. Indexed alphabetically by surnames of infants. Handwritten on printed forms. Average 500 pages. 18 x 16 x 3.5.

266. RECORD OF DEATHS
1867-1908. 4 volumes. (1-4).
Record of deaths, as reported by township and ward assessors, showing name, residence, age, and color of decedent, date and cause of death, names of parents, and date recorded. Arranged chronologically by dates of recording. Indexed alphabetically by names of decedents. Handwritten on printed forms. Average 500 pages. 18 x 16 x 3.5.

267. BIRTH AND DEATH REPORTS
1883-1906. 305 reports.
Annual reports by township and ward assessors to probate court of birth and deaths. Front pages of reports are births, showing names of parents, residence, date of birth, and name and color of child; back of pages of reports are deaths, showing name, residents, age of decedent, date and cause of death, and names of parents. Arranged alphabetically, birth records, by names of infants, and death records, by names of decedents. No index. Handwritten. Average 35 pages, sizes vary from 4 x 12 x .25 to 12 x 12 x .25.Basement, middle storeroom.

Marriages

268. MARRIAGE LICENSE RECORD
1798—. 24 volumes. (1798-1874. 11 volumes, A-K, rebound in 5 volumes; 1875—, 1-19).
Record of licenses issued to marry, showing date issued, names and addresses of applicants, and names of officiating minister. Also contains: Marriage Register,

1877—, entry 269: Affidavits [Marriage Licenses], 1877—, entry 272. 1798-1875, Arranged alphabetically by names of grooms and chronologically thereunder by dates of filing certificates; 1875—, arranged chronologically by dates of licenses. 1798-1875, no index; 1875—, indexed alphabetically by names of applicants. 1798-1852, handwritten; 1852—, handwritten on printed forms. Average 600 pages. 16 x 11 x 1.5. 23 volumes, 1797-1937, Probate court's vault; 1 volume, 1937—, Probate court's office.

269. MARRIAGE REGISTER

1803-1876. 9 volumes. (1803-1840, A-D; 1840-1876, 1-5). 1877— in Marriage License Record, entry 268.

Copies of certificates of marriage, showing names of contracting parties, name of minister or magistrate performing marriage ceremony, and date filed. Arranged chronologically by dates of certificates. 1852-1876, indexed alphabetically by names of contracting parties; for separate index, 1803-1852, see entry 270. 1803-1852, handwritten; 1852-1876, handwritten or printed forms. Average 440 pages. 13.5 x 8 x 3.

270. INDEX, MARRIAGE REGISTER

1803-1852. 6 volumes. (1-6).

Index to marriage register, entry 269, showing names of contracting parties and volume and page numbers of register. Arranged alphabetically by names of contracting parties. Handwritten. Average 120 pages. 14 x 7.5 x 1.

271. MARRIAGE RETURNS AND CONSENTS

1800—. 26 file boxes. One subtitled: Certificates, 1908-1911.

Original marriage returns or certificates of marriage by ministers or magistrates performing ceremonies, showing date, names of contracting parties, and signature of person officiating; also original copies of written consent by parents or guardians for issuance of marriage licenses to minors, showing date, name of minor, and signature of parent or guardian. 1 file box, 1908-1911, contains only certificates. Arranged chronologically by dates of papers. No index. 1800-1839, handwritten; 1940—, returns, handwritten on printed forms, consents, handwritten 10 x 5 x 14. 25 file boxes, 1800—, Probate court's vault; 1 file box, 1908-1911, Basement, rear storeroom.

272. AFFIDAVITS [Marriage Licenses]

1852-1876. 4 volumes. 1877— in Marriage License Record, entry 268.

Copies of affidavits made by persons knowing applicants as to the ages of applicants, showing date, name and age applicant, and signature of affiant. Handwritten on printed forms. Average 600 pages. 14 x 8 x 3.5.

273. [Marriage License] APPLICATIONS

1910-1911. 1 file box. Prior and subsequent records destroyed.

Marriage license applications, showing names of applicant, date of application, and date license issued. Arranged chronologically by dates of applications. No index. Handwritten on printed forms. 10 x 4.5 x 14. Basement, rear storeroom.

Licenses and Permits

274. MINISTERS' LICENSE RECORD

1874—. 2 volumes.

Record of licenses issued to ordained ministers by Ross County probate court to perform marriage ceremonies, showing name of minister, denomination, and date issued. Arranged chronologically by dates of issue. Indexed alphabetically by names of ministers. Handwritten on printed forms. Average 400 pages. 15 x 10 x 2.5. Probate court's office.

275. RECORD OF MEDICAL CERTIFICATES

1897—. 2 volumes.

Copies of physicians' certificates on college diplomas and certificates on examinations, and midwives', and limited practitioners' certificates, showing name of licensee, and date issued. Arranged chronologically by dates of issue. Indexed alphabetically by names of the licensees. Handwritten on printed forms. Average 360 pages. 16 x 11 x 2.5.

276. CERTIFICATE REGISTER FOR NURSES AND LIMITED PRACTITIONERS

1916—. 1 volume.

Copies of certificates issued by state medical board to graduate nurses, showing certificate number, name of licensee, date of diploma, name of school awarding, and date of recording; also copies of certificates awarded to practitioners of limited branches of medical and surgery, showing certificate number, name of licensee, kind of certificate, date issued, and date recorded. Arranged chronologically by dates of recording. Indexed alphabetically by names the licensees. Handwritten on printed forms. Average 360 pages. 16 x 11 x 3.

277. PERMIT RECORDS
1925—. 1 volume.
Record of permits granted to conduct public dance halls and other places of entertainment, showing name of person receiving permit, kind of permit, location of place for which permit was granted, date granted, and names of references. Arranged chronologically by dates granted. No index. Handwritten on printed forms. 180 pages. 10 x 7 x 1.25.

278. RECORD OF REVOCATION OF PERMITS
1927—. 1 volume.
Record of entertainment permits revoked for violation of laws and regulations governing such, showing name of permit holder, reason for cancellation, date revoked, and location. Arranged chronologically by dates of revocation. No index. Handwritten on printed forms. 160 pages. 10 x 7 x 1.25.

Fiscal Accounts

279. CASH BOOK
20 volumes.
Record of cash entries, showing date, from whom received, for what, to whom paid, and what account. Also contains daily record of fees, showing from whom received, for what service, and case number. Arranged chronologically by dates of entry. No index. Handwritten. Average 300 pages. 20 x 14 x 2.25. 1 volume, 1896-1899, Basement, rear storeroom. 1 volume, 1900-1902, Basement, middle storeroom; 16 volumes, 1882-1896, 1905-1935, Probate court's vault; 2 volumes, 1935—, Probate court's office.

For other records of fees, see entry 280-282.

280. PROBATE JUDGE'S JOURNAL
1921-1929. 10 volumes. (labeled by years).
Probate judge's daily record of fees and cost received, showing date, by whom paid,

for what, amount, and daily total. Arranged chronologically by dates of entry. No index. Handwritten. Average 280 pages. 9 x 7 x 1.25.

For other records of fees, see entry 279, 281, 282.

281. RECORD OF FEES COLLECTED AND UNCOLLECTED

1876-1884. 1 volume.

Record of miscellaneous fees, showing date, to whom charged, for what, amount, and date paid, if paid. Arranged chronologically by dates of entry. No index. Handwritten. 300 pages. 18 x 12 x 2.5.

For other records, see entry 280, 282, 283.

282. RECORD OF ACCRUED FEES

1877-1881, 1909—. 11 volumes.

Record of accrued fees, showing dates, to whom charged, for what, in what matter, date paid, and by whom paid. Arranged chronologically by dates of entry. No index. Handwritten. Average 360 pages. 18 x 12 x 2.5. 9 volumes, 1877-1881, 1909-1932, Probate court's vault; 2 volumes, 1932—, Probate court's office.

For other records of fees, see entry 279-281.

283. COST BILL RECORD, MISCELLANEOUS

1884-1907. 6 volumes.

Record of cost (miscellaneous items) including bill of costs in filing claims of administrators or executors, inquest of lunacy, commitments to boys' and girls' industrial schools, proceedings in aid of execution, adoption, appropriation, and other jury cases, criminal cases, and appointment for trustees or assignees, showing names of principals, date, and itemized cost. Arranged chronologically by dates of entry. Indexed alphabetically by names of principals. Handwritten on printed forms. Average 600 pages. 18 x 12 x 1.5.

For other cost bill records, see entries, 215, 216, 241-246.

284. COST BILLS, CITATION

no date, 1 volume.

Itemized cost bill of fees taxed in citations, showing name of litigants, date, Plaintiff's and defendant's cost, and total fees. Arranged chronologically by dates of entry. Indexed alphabetically by names of plaintiffs. Handwritten on printed forms. 110 pages. 12 x 8 x 1. Basement, middle storeroom.

For other cost bill records, see entries 215, 216, 241-246.

Miscellaneous

285. EXAMINERS' REPORTS

1890-1904. 1 file box.

Copies of examiners' reports on condition of county treasury, showing date of report, receipts into treasury, disbursements, and balance or deficit. Arranged chronologically by dates or reports. No index. Handwritten on printed forms. 10 x 5 x 14.

For prior records, see entry 464; subsequent records, 436.

286. RECORD OF UNCLAIMED DEPOSITS

1889-1929. 2 volumes.

Record of unclaimed bank deposits as reported to probate court by banks, showing date of report, name of bank, sworn statement of bank official, name of depositor, account number, amount of account, interest, dividend, total amount, and date of last credit or debit to account. Arranged chronologically by dates of reports. Indexed alphabetically by names of banks. Handwritten. Average 350 pages. 18 x 12 x 3.

287. ROAD RECORD

1877-1880. 1 volume.

Record of court proceedings in petitions, injunctions, and appeals to the probate court in controversies concerning roads and highways, showing names of principals, date, findings, and court orders. Arranged chronologically by dates of entry. Indexed alphabetically by names of plaintiffs. Handwritten. 492 pages. 16 x 11 x 3.5.

288. PATENT RECORD

1868-1869. 1 volume.

Copies of affidavits filed as to patent rights, showing invention or improvement covered, oath of patentee or agent, date patent granted, to whom issued, and date filed. Arranged chronologically by dates of filing. Indexed alphabetically by names of patentees or agents. Handwritten on printed forms. 400 pages. 14 x 9 x 2.5.

289. RECORD OF PRINTERS' AFFIDAVITS
1876—. 12 volumes. (1-12).

Copies of affidavits by newspaper publisher as to publication of legal notices, showing dates, name of paper, clipped copy of notice or advertisement, and publication fee. Arranged chronologically by dates of notices. Indexed alphabetically by names of decedents, wards, or assignors. 1876-1914, handwritten; 1914—, typed. Average 400 pages. 18 x 12 x 3.

290. PROOFS OF PUBLICATION
1876-1884, 1892-1899, 1906—. 17 file boxes.

Affidavits of publication of legal advertisements and notices by newspaper publishers, showing date of publication, amount of fee, and clipped copy of advertisement or notice. Arranged chronologically by dates of publication. No index. Handwritten on printed forms. 10 x 4.5 x 14. 8 file boxes, 1876-1884, 1892-1899, Basement, rear storeroom; 9 file boxes, 1906—, Probate court's vault.

291. RECEIPTS FOR PAPERS
1905—. 2 volumes.

Record of papers removed from files, showing date, what record, case number, by whom removed, date returned, and by whom returned. Arranged chronologically by dates of removal. No index. Handwritten. Average 210 pages. 14 x 9 x 1.5. Probate court's office.

292. MISCELLANEOUS [Original Papers]
1888-1891, 1894-1896, 1899-1903. 3 file boxes, 1852-1887, 1892-1893, 1897-1898, 1904— in Court Papers, entry 215-i.

Original papers issued in various actions filed in probate court of which no entry was made on record books, showing names of principals, nature of action, and date filed. Causes included are *habeas corpus,* imbecile proceedings, lunacy inquest, miscellaneous motions, miscellaneous affidavits, and miscellaneous petitions. Arranged chronologically by dates of filing. No index. Handwritten on printed forms. 10 x 4.5 x 14. Basement, rear storeroom.

The juvenile court, though of uncertain origin, has been generally recognized as an American contribution to the administration of social justice. The establishment of such courts was a logical outcome of the practical philosophy of enlightened public men that child offenders against the law, or conventional social standards, should not be treated as criminals, but as unfortunates needing the help, supervision, and protection of the state.[1] Although the first separate court in the United States for the trial of juvenile offenders was established in 1899, in Cook County, Chicago, Illinois, by an act of the legislature of that state, the juvenile court was an institution of gradual growth. The Illinois experiment gave impetus to the children's movement in the middle west.[2]

The Ohio legislature was not slow in seeing the advantage of the Illinois experiment, and accordingly, in 1902, an act was passed creating the juvenile court in Cuyahoga County. Under this act all counties having a population of over 380,000 and an insolvency court were authorized, under an extension of jurisdiction of this court to establish children's courts. The stipulations of this act excluded Ross County. It gave the court jurisdiction of the trial of cases involving delinquent and neglected children; defined the terms "delinquent, dependent, and neglected;" authorized the appointment of a probation officer, and made it his duty to investigate the facts of cases coming before the court, and to take charge of the offender before and after trial. The clerk of the juvenile court was directed to keep a journal in which were to be recorded the minutes of the cases.[3] The judge of the insolvency court serving as juvenile judge served for a period of five years, and from 1935, the common pleas judge serving in such a capacity was to serve for six years.[4]

Two years after the establishment of the Cuyahoga County juvenile court, the general assembly provided by statute for the establishment of juvenile courts in the rural counties of the state which, because of their lack of population, were unable to create the newer agencies under the provisions of the act of 1902. Under the act of 1904 the judges of the court of common pleas, probate court, and where established, the insolvency courts, wherein three or more judges held court concurrently, were authorized to appoint one of their members as "juvenile judge."

---

1. Miriam Van Waters, *Youth in Conflict* (New York, 1925), 147, 159, 161.
2. Edwin H. Sutherland, *Principles of Criminology* (Chicago 1934), 270-272.
3. *Laws of Ohio,* XCV, 785.
4. *Ibid.,* XCI, 845; CXVI, pt. ii, 157.

The court was given original jurisdiction in all cases involving neglected, dependent, and delinquent children under the age of sixteen years; and all children, who had been scheduled in the past for a trial in a justice of the peace or police court were in the future to be tried before a juvenile judge. As under the act of 1902, the judge was authorized to appoint a probation officer, and the clerk of courts was directed to keep a journal of the minutes of each case.[5] In 1908 the court was given jurisdiction in cases involving minors under seventeen years of age, and such children as were brought before the juvenile judge were to become wards of the court until they had attained the age of twenty-one years. The county commissioners were authorized to provide by lease or purchase, a "detention home" where neglected or dependent children might be detained pending the final disposition of their case. The clerk of courts was directed to keep not only a journal, but also an appearance docket containing all orders, judgments, and findings of the court. It provided also for case studies to be made by the probation officer.[6] Since 1937 a cash book has been required to be kept. Records of the juvenile court are open only by order of the court to persons having a legitimate interest in them.[7] The age jurisdiction of the court was increased to eighteen years in 1913.[8]

While provisions were being made for the establishment of juvenile courts, the legislature gave the court jurisdiction in cases involving adults who committed crimes against children or contributed to the delinquency of dependent children. Thus in 1906 it was made a misdemeanor to contribute to the delinquency of a child under seventeen years of age.[9] Two years later the "lack of parental care" was defined and it was made a misdemeanor to fail to support a minor, or to cause him to engage in begging.[10] In 1913 "proper parental care" was defined by statute.[11]

---

5. *Ibid.,* XXCVII, 561.
6. *Ibid.,*XCIX, 192.
7. *Ibid.,*CXVII, 520.
8. *Ibid.,*CIII, 869.
9. *Laws of Ohio,* XCVIII, 314.
10. *Ibid.,*XCIX, 193.
11. *Ibid.,*CIII, 870.

Marked progress has been made in the medical treatment of juveniles. While the act of 1913 authorized the juvenile judge to submit any child sentenced to an institution for correction to a mental test, the act of 1929 authorized him to submit any child coming before the court to a mental and physical test to be made by a physician or psychiatrist.[12] To further the scientific handling of children, the county commissioners were authorized, in the same year, to lease or construct a separate building to be known as the "juvenile court" which should be appropriately constructed, arranged, furnished, and maintained for the convenient and effective transaction of the business of the court, including adequate facilities to be used as laboratories, dispensaries, or clinics for scientific use of specialist attached to the court.[13]

One of the guiding principles of the court has been to make its "custody and discipline" of children approximate nearly as possible that which should be given by their parents. In the cases involving neglected or dependent children not sentenced to state institutions, it has been the policy of judges to assign children to private homes, and make arrangements for their adoption. In 1913 the juvenile court was given the duty of administering mothers' pensions.[14] When the sections of the General Code governing mothers' pensions were repealed in 1936 with the acceptance of title IV of the federal social security act providing for aid to dependent children the juvenile judge was designated as "county administrator."[15]

The juvenile court of Cuyahoga County is the only independent juvenile court in the state. There are seven other juvenile courts in Ohio attached to the court of domestic relations. In Ross County, as in other counties where there is neither an independent juvenile court nor a court of domestic relations, the probate judge serves as *ex officio* judge of the juvenile court under the provisions of the act of April 29, 1937 which repealed the act of 1904 providing for the appointment of a juvenile judge.[16]

---

12. *Ibid.,* CIII, 872; CXIII, 471.
13. *Ibid.,* CXIII, 470.
14. *Ibid.,* CIII, 877.
15. G. C. sec. 1359-31. See also p. 255.
16. G. C. sec. 1639-7.

293. JUVENILE CALENDAR

1935— 1 volume.

Calendar of cases filed in juvenile court, showing name of offender, cause, date, name of complainant, and order of citation. Arranged chronologically by dates of entry. Indexed alphabetically by names of offenders. Handwritten on printed forms. 400 pages. 14 x 11 x 3. Juvenile court office.

294. JUVENILE JOURNAL

1924—. 5 volumes. (1-5). Record initiated in 1924.

Record entries of all orders and findings issued by juvenile court in juvenile cases, showing case number, date, name of offender, offence charged, and date filed. Arranged chronologically by dates of entry. Indexed alphabetically by names of principals. Typed. Average 520 pages. 18 x 12 x 4. Probate court's vault.

295. JUVENILE RECORD

1906—. 14 volumes. (1-14).

Complete record of all juvenile causes filed in juvenile court, showing case number, date, name of offender, offense, copies of affidavit or complaint, family history, medical certificate, and disposition of case. Arranged chronologically by dates of entry. Indexed alphabetically by names of principals; also separate index, entry 208. 1906-1915, handwritten; 1916—, typed. Average 640 pages. 18 x 12 x 4.5. Probate court's vault.

296. [Commitments to] REFORM SCHOOL

1878-1887, 1920-1921. 2 volumes.

Record of commitments to juvenile reform institutions, showing name of offender, date of commitment, and nature of offense. Arranged chronologically by dates of commitments. Indexed alphabetically by names of offenders. Handwritten on printed forms. Average 270 pages. 16 x 10 x 2. Probate court's vault.

297. COMMITMENTS [To Industrial Schools]

1897-1906. 1 file box.

Original papers issued in juvenile cases ordering commitments to boys' or girls' industrial school, showing institution to which committed, and date of commitment. Arranged chronologically by dates of commitments. No index. Handwritten on printed forms. 10 x 4.5 x 14. Basement, rear storeroom.

298. JUVENILE COST RECORD

1910. 1 volume.

Itemized account of cost taxed in juvenile cases, showing case number, name of defendant, offense, itemized bill of court and sheriff's fees, and date filed. Arranged chronologically by dates of filing. Indexed alphabetically by names of defendants. Handwritten on printed forms. 140 pages. 18 x 12 x 1. Probate court's vault.

For original cost bills, see entries 215, 299.

299. COST BILLS [Juvenile Cases]

1907-1915. 2 file boxes. 1916— in Court Papers, entry 215-j.

Itemized statements of fees tax by juvenile judge in juvenile cases, showing case number, name of defendant, offence, itemized bill of court and sheriff's fees, date filed, and volume and page numbers where recorded. Arranged chronologically by dates of filing. No index. Handwritten on printed forms. 10 x 4.5 x 14. Basement, rear storeroom.

For record of cost, see entry 298.

300. MOTHERS' PENSION RECORD

1915-June 1936. 3 volumes. (1-3).

Record of mothers' pensions, showing copy of application, date of hearing, journal entry, findings, and report of examination of home. Arranged chronologically by dates of hearings. Indexed alphabetically by names of applicants. 1915-1920, handwritten on printed forms; 1921-1936, typed on printed forms. Average 600 pages. 18 x 12 x 4.5. 1 volume, 1915-1920, Probate courts vault; 2 volumes, 1921-1936, Juvenile court office.

For subsequent records, see entry 582.

301. ADOPTION RECORDS

1921—. 2 volumes. (1, 2). 1909-1916, in Blind Records entry 262.

Record of adoption of orphans or dependent children, showing date, names of principals, and all proceedings of each case. Arranged chronologically by dates of entry. Indexed alphabetically by names of children. Typed. Average 360 pages. 16 x 11 x 3. Probate court's vault.

302. ADOPTION RECORD AND COST BILLS

1898-1914. 1 file box. 1852-1897, 1915— in Court Papers, entry 215-k. Original papers issued in adoption proceedings and an itemized statement of fees taxed in adoption cases, showing names of principals, date, amount of fees, date of filing, and volume and page numbers where recorded. Arranged chronologically by dates of filing. No index. Handwritten on printed forms. 10 x 4.5 x 14. Basement, rear storeroom.

In 1891 the judges of the court of common pleas in counties having a population of not less than 33,000 nor more than 50,000 were authorized to appoint four residents of the county to serve as a jury commission for a term of one year. The limitations of this act excluded Ross County. It was the duty of this commission to determine the qualifications and fitness of persons to be selected as jurors.[1] Three years later, in 1894, the provision of the act was extended to Ross County in all other counties in the state except Cuyahoga, Franklin, Hamilton, Lucas, Montgomery, and Mahoning.[2] In 1902 the statute was amended to include all counties.[3] In 1913 the number of jury commissioners in each county was reduced to two.[4]

The jury code, which became effective August 2, 1931, provided for a jury commission of the same number and same qualifications previously specified, to hold office at the pleasure of the court, and to meet and select prospective jurors, both grand and petit, for the ensuing year from the list provided by the board of elections.[5] At the beginning of each jury year the commissioners are required to make up a new and complete jury list, known as the annual jury list arranged alphabetically by precincts, districts, and township, recording the name, occupation, business address, and resident of each perspective jury, and to prepare an index to this list. A duplicate list is certified by the commissioners and filed in the office of the clerk of court of common pleas.[6]

The jury commissioners select prospective jurors for civil and criminal cases as well as for the grand jury. It selects jurors for the probate court, juvenile court, and other minor courts.

---

1. *Laws of Ohio,* LXXXVIII, 200.
2. *Ibid.,* XCI, 176.
3. *Ibid.,* XCVI, 3.
4. *Ibid.,* CII, 513; CVI. 106.
5. *Ibid.,* CXIV, 193-213.
6. *Laws of Ohio,* CXIV, 205.

303. RECORD A PROCEDURES AND EXEMPTION, JURY COMMISSION

1931—. 1 volume.

Minutes of the meetings of the jury commissioners, showing date and names of jurors selected. Also contains record of certificates of exemption from jury duty. Arranged chronologically by dates of entry. No index. Typed. 400 pages. 18.5 x 12.5 x 2.5. Clerk of courts' office.

For records of jurors, see entries 119-123,

The grand jury, sometimes called the palladium of English liberty, has as its function the preliminary examination of persons charged with a capital or other infamous crime. The right, guaranteed by the federal constitution, to an examination by a grand jury, is recognized in the provisions of the Ohio Constitution of 1802 and 1851 and in the amendments of 1912.[1]

Under the present system, which does not differ in detail from that inaugurated in the early days of the state's history, the grand jury is composed of fifteen members, resident electors of the county having "the qualifications of jurors."[2] It is the duty of the grand jury "to inquire and to present all offenses committed in the county in and for which it was empaneled and sworn."[3.] The proceedings of the grand jury are secret and each juror is required to take an oath to preserve such secrecy. Moreover, no grand juror may be required to reveal the way he or other grand jurors voted.[4]

The grand jurors are aided in their investigations by the county prosecuting attorney, who, since 1869, has been authorized by statute to present evidence before this body and compel the attendance of witnesses against whom he may institute contempt proceedings if they refuse to testify.[5] The prosecuting attorney must leave the room before the jurors begin the expression of their views or before a poll is taken. The courts have decreed, however, that the mere presence of the prosecuting attorney in the room during the deliberation is "not sufficient to sustain a plea in abatement."[6] Since 1902 the official court stenographer of the county may take shorthand notes of the testimony and furnish a transcript to the prosecuting attorney at his request. This reporter, like the prosecuting attorney and his assistants, is required to retire from the jury room before the grand jury begins its deliberations.[7]

At least twelve of the fifteen jurors must concur in finding and indictment.[8] Indictments found by the grand jury are presented by the foreman to the court and are filed with the clerk of courts.[9]

---

1. *Ohio Const. 1851,* Art. I, sec. 10.
2. G. C. sec. 13436-2.
3. *Ibid.,* sec. 13436-5.
4. *Ibid.,* sec. 13436-16.
5. [Footnote missing].
6. See *State of Ohio* v. *William Stichtenoth,* 8 N. P., n. s., 297-339.
7. G. C. sec. 13436-8.
8. *Ibid.,* sec. 13436-17.
9. *Ibid.,* sec. 13436-21.

No grand juror or officer of the court is permitted to disclose that a person has been indicted before such indictment is filed and the case is docketed.[10] Any incarcerated person charged with an indictable offense who has not been indicted during the term of court at which he is held to answer is discharged.[11]

Since 1869 it has been the duty of the grand jury to visit the county jail once at each term of court at which they may be in attendance, examine its state and condition and acquire into the discipline and treatment of prisoners, and return a written report to the court.[12]

The majority of contemporary opinions holds that the grand jury, although still defended as a safeguard against oppressive prosecution, seems to be of little usefulness in the administration of modern criminal justice. It is argued that the grand jury not only delays the prosecution of criminal offenses but makes it impossible to place responsibility for neglect of duty, and is, in many instances a rubber stamp for the opinions of the county prosecuting attorney.

The grand jury keeps no permanent records. For clerk's jury books, see entries 119, 122; for subpoenas and venires, see entries 120, 123; for jury commissioners' record, see entry; 303 for sheriff's record of subpoenas, see entry 323.

---

10. *Ibid.,* sec. 13436-15.
11. *Ibid.,*sec. 13436-23.
12. *Ibid.,*sec. 13436-20.

PETIT JURY

The petit jury like the grand jury, had its origin in England during the reign of Henry II.[1] The right of trial by jury, guaranteed by the federal constitution, was included in each of the Ohio constitutions. At any trial, in any court, for the violation of a statute of the state of Ohio, or any ordinance of any municipality, except in cases where the penalty involved does not exceed a fine of fifty dollars, the accused is entitled to a trial by jury.[2]

---

1. Adams, *op. cit.,* 116.
2. G. C. sec. 13443.

Except in the method of selecting prospective jurors, the petit jury has remained unchanged for over 134 years. At each session of court the jury commissioners[3] select not less than fifty nor more than seventy-five names for jury service. A venire is issued to the county sheriff for persons whose names are so drawn to appear on the day fixed for the trial.[4] From persons so summoned a jury of twelve is empaneled. The county prosecuting attorney and the defense council may, in capital cases, peremptory challenged six of the jurors. In other cases, four peremptory challenges are allowed.[5] Other challenges, alternately made, may be made for reasons prescribed by statute.[6]

When the case is submitted, the jury may decide the question before it in court, or retire to deliberate. Upon retiring, the jury members must be kept together at a convenient place by an officer of the court until they agree upon a verdict or are discharged by the court. The court may permit them to separate at night.[7] If the jurors disagree as to testimony, or desire to be further instructed on the law in the case, they may request the officer in charge to conduct them to the court for additional information.[8] In civil actions a jury renders a written verdict upon the conclusion of three fourths or more of its members. This verdict is signed by each juror concurring therein.[9]

Under the criminal code adopted in 1929 the accused may waive his right to a jury trial in favor of a trial by a judge. This procedure, although criticized by some, is considered by others to be a logical step in the administration of criminal justice in a modern state.

---

3. See p. 124.
4. G. C. sec. 13443-1.
5. *Ibid.*, secs. 13443-4, 13443-6.
6. *Ibid.*, sec. 13443-8.
7. *Ibid.*, sec. 11420-3.
8. *Ibid.*, sec. 11420-6.
9. *Ibid.*, sec. 11420-9.

The office of prosecuting attorney, unlike those of the sheriff and the coroner, is one of the relatively newer agencies in the administration of criminal justice. Established in America by the English during the colonial period, it offers a striking difference in the development of American criminal procedure as contrasted with English procedure where criminal prosecutions were usually instituted by private persons. As developed in recent years, the office of the prosecuting attorney has become one of the state's most important agencies and its defense against modern crime.

The act of the Northwest Territory placed the responsibility for criminal prosecutions upon the attorney general, who, in turn, appointed and commissioned persons to prosecute cases in their respective counties.

While the acts of the Northwest Territory outlined the local institutions for the newer states, the constitution of Ohio contained no provisions for a prosecutor, leaving the creation of the office to the discretion of the legislature. In 1803, during the first session of the legislature, an act was passed authorizing the supreme court to appoint in each county an attorney to prosecute cases in behalf of the state.[1] Two years later, the appointing power was vested in the court of common pleas.[2] The office remained an appointive one until 1833 when the electorate of the county was directed to choose a prosecuting attorney in each county for a two-year term.[3] The act of 1852 left the office elective and the term unchanged, but in 1881 the term of office was set at three years, and in 1906 it was reduced to two years, and in 1936 increased to four years.[4]

Under the present system the prosecuting attorney is elected for a four-year term.[5] He is required to get bond of not less than one thousand dollars conditioned for the faithful performance of the duties of his office. If the office becomes vacant the court of common pleas is authorized to appoint a successor.[6]

The county prosecuting attorney is authorized to appoint clerks, assistants, stenographers and to fix their salaries subject to the approval of the county commissioners.

---

1. *Laws of Ohio,* I, 50.
2. *Ibid.,* III, 47.
3. *Ibid.,* XXXI, 13-14; Chase, *op. cit.,* III, 1935.
4. *Laws of Ohio,* LXXVIII, 260; XCVIII, 271-272; XCVI, pt. ii, 184.
5. G. C. sec. 2909.
6. *Ibid.,* sec. 2909.

Since 1911 he has been authorized to appoint a secret service agent or officer whose duty it is to aid him in the collection of evidence to be used in the trial of criminal cases and in matters of a criminal nature. The compensation of such an officer is determined by the court of common pleas.[7]

Most important among the duties of the prosecuting attorney are those connected with criminal prosecutions. Differing little from those of the earlier days of the office, these duties include the prosecution on behalf of the state of all complaints, suits, and controversies in which the state is a party, and such other suits, matters, and controversies as he is directed by law to prosecute within or without his county, in the probate court, court of common pleas, and court of appeals. In conjunction with the attorney general, he prosecutes cases in the supreme court which originated in his county.[8]

In felony cases, when a complaint is made to the prosecuting attorney, he is required to examine the evidence and determine if it is sufficient for prosecution. If he decides in the affirmative, he prepares the evidence for presentation to the grand jury.[9] If this body returns an indictment the prosecutor prepares to present the evidence in trial court. The common pleas court may appoint an attorney to assist the prosecuting attorney in criminal cases.[10]

In the case of conviction, the prosecutor causes execution to be issued for the fines or costs and pays into the county treasury all money so received.[11] Without reference to the grand jury, the county prosecutor may initiate prosecutions and misdemeanor cases in the court of common pleas by information.[12] After prosecution is inaugurated, he may eliminate the case without trial by means of the *nolle prosequi.* Although he is prohibited from enlisting the *nolle prosequi* without leave of the court on good cause shown, his requests are usually granted.[13] After prosecution has begun, it remains with the prosecuting attorney whether the case shall be pressed and steps taken that will lead to conviction.

---

7. *Ibid.,* secs. 2914, 2915-1.
8. *Ibid.,* sec. 2916.
9. See p. 126.
10. G. C. sec. 2818.
11. *Ibid.,* sec. 2916.
12. *Ibid.,* sec. 13437-34.
13. *Ibid.,* sec. 13437-32.

Besides prosecution in criminal cases, the prosecuting attorney also acts in civil matters. He may bring suit in the name of the state when he is convinced that public money is being misapplied or is being illegally withheld or withdrawn from the county treasury. Moreover he may bring suit against persons violating the obligations of contracts which the county is a party, or when county property is being used or occupied illegally.[14]

In addition to these, other duties have been prescribed by statute. On the request of the judge having jurisdiction over juvenile cases, he must prosecute individuals for committing crimes against children.[15] Furthermore, when directed by the court of common pleas, he must prosecute persons for keeping a house of prostitution.[16] At the instance of the secretary of state, he must prosecute any officer who refuses to furnish gratuitously statistical information for the use of that office.[17]

The prosecuting attorney has also served in the advisory capacity since 1906.[18] He acts as an advisor to all county boards and officials and to township officers who may require his opinion in writing on matters connected with their official duties.[19] In addition to this, he prepares official bonds for all county officers.[20]

The prosecuting attorney is required to make an annual report to the county commissioners stating the number of criminal prosecutions completed, the name or names of the party or parties to each, and the amount collected in fines and cost, and the amount forfeited.[21] Moreover, on the demand of the attorney general he must make an annual report on forms provided by the state on all criminal actions prosecuted by indictments in his county.[22]

Only current records of the prosecuting attorney's office were located.

---

14. *Ibid.,* sec. 2921.
15. *Ibid.,* sec. 1664.
16. G. C. secs. 6212-5, 6212-7.
17. *Ibid.,* sec. 174.
18. *Laws of Ohio,* XCVIII, 160-161.
19. *Ibid.,* LXXVIII, 120; G. C. sec. 2917.
20. G. C. sec. 2920.
21. *Laws of Ohio,* LXXVIII, 120; G. C. sec. 2926.
22. G. C. sec. 2926; *Laws of Ohio,* XC, 225.

304. PROBATION RECORDS
1933—. 1 file box.

Case records of persons placed on probation by the court of common pleas, showing name of probationer, date, case number, offense, sentence, and term of probation. Also contains reports of probationer to prosecuting attorney, showing date of report, occupation, and signature of probationer. Arranged alphabetically by names of probationers. No index. Typed on printed forms. 12 x 12 x 18. Prosecuting attorney's office, Phillips Building.

305. ALIMONY AND SUPPORT RECORDS
1933—. 2 file boxes.

Record of alimony and support payments made and paid to claimants, showing name of claimant and payer, date, and amount. Arranged alphabetically by names of claimants. No index. Handwritten and typed on printed forms. 12 x 12 x 18. Prosecuting attorney's office, Phillips Building.

306. RECEIPTS [Alimony]
1924—. 9 volumes.

Carbon copies of receipts for money received and paid out in alimony and support cases, showing from whom received, date, amount, and case number; or whom paid, date, amount, and case number. Arranged chronologically by dates of receipts. No index. Handwritten on printed forms. Average 160 pages. 15 x 11 x 1.25. 6 volumes, 1924-1933, County Courthouse, basement, middle storeroom; 3 volumes, 1934—, Prosecuting attorney's office, Phillips Building.

The office of coroner, next to that of sheriff the oldest county office in America, had its inception in England during the latter part of the twelfth century when the coroner kept a record of the activities in the county, especially regarding the administration of criminal justice. At the end of the thirteenth century it was his duty to make inquests whenever there was a sudden death in the shire, and the results were recorded in the coroner's roles and presented to the justices when they made their eyre.[1]

This office, transplanted to America during the colonial period, was continued by the state, and was adopted by the territory of which the state of Ohio was then a part. An ordinance of the Northwest Territory published in 1788 authorized the governor to appoint a coroner in each county within the territory. This act, together with a supplementary act of 1795 adopted from the Massachusetts Code, fixed the power and duties of the coroner. He was empowered to do any act which, by previous legislation had been delegated to the sheriff, and was given the ancient duty of English coroners in holding the preliminary investigations for the bodies of all persons found within his county, and were believed to have died by violence or casualty.[2]

The Ohio Constitution of 1802 continued the historic office, making it elected for a two-year term.[3] A statute of 1805 defined the duties and authority of the coroner which, in the main were comparable with those prescribed in the territorial code, except that he was denied the privilege of concurrent jurisdiction with the sheriff.[4] The act further provided that the coroner should receive his remuneration from fees, and that if the office of sheriff was to become vacant the coroner was to execute temporarily the duties of the sheriff.[5] The latter provision remained active until its abrogation in 1887.[6]

The constitution of 1851 and the constitutional amendments of 1912 left the duties of the coroner unchanged and it was not until recent years when he became an aid in the scientific detection of crime that laws have been passed which materially affected his office. By the legislative act of 1921 the coroner was made official custodian of the morgue in counties where a morgue is maintained.

---

1. Pollock and Maitland, *op. cit.,* I, 519, 571; II, 641.
2. Pease, *op, cit.,* 24-25, 272-275.
3. *Ohio Const., 1802,* Art. IV, sec. 1.
4. *Laws of Ohio,* III, 156-161.
5. *Ibid.,* III, 158-161.
6. *Ibid.,* LXXXIV, 208-210.

The same act provided that only licensed physicians were eligible to the office in counties having a population of 100,000 or more,[7] and in 1937 such restriction was extended to all counties.[8]

The corner is required to draw up and subscribe his findings of facts in inquest and autopsies and to report them to the clerk of courts. This record contains a detailed description of the body over which the inquest has been held and the statement of the coroner's findings as to the cause of death.[9] He is required also to return to the probate court an inventory of articles of property found on or about the body and to preserve such property until the proper distribution may be made.[10] All records are open to public inspection.[11]

In 1936 the tenure of office of the coroner was extended from two to four years.

307. CORONER'S RECORD

1883-1914. 5 volumes.

Record of coroner's inquest in accidental, sudden, or homicidal deaths, showing date, name of decedent, inventory of effects found on body, and findings as to cause of death. Arranged chronologically by dates of entry. No index. 1883-1896, handwritten; 1896-1914, handwritten on printed forms. Average 366 pages. 14 x 9 x 2. Auditor's vault.

For clerk of courts' record, see entries 155, 156.

308. CORNER'S REPORTS

1917—. 2 file boxes. (labeled by years).

Coroner's duplicate copies of reports to the clerk of courts concerning inquest and autopsies, showing date of inquest or autopsy, name of decedent, place of death, cause, report of findings, fees charged, and date filed. Arranged chronologically by dates of filing. No index. Handwritten on printed forms. 10 x 5 x 14. Clerk of courts' vault.

For clerk of courts' copies, see entry 155.

---

7. *Ibid.*, CIX, 543-544.
8. *Ibid.*, CXVII, 43.
9. G. C. secs. 2856, 2857.
10. *Ibid.*, sec. 2859.
11. *Ibid.*, sec. 2856-2.
12. *Ibid.*, sec. 2823.

The office of sheriff antedates the Norman Conquest. This official was enjoying great power and importance centuries ago, and was probably brought into the English system after a model which existed in Roman law. The name comes from the Saxon "shire-reeve" softened to "shireve," "shyrife," and finally to "sheriff." In ancient times he received his commission directly from the king and specifically represented the sovereign. Originally, the sheriff in England was a judicial as well as a ministerial officer. He once held court in the shire and exercised no inconsiderable jurisdiction. By the time of Lord Coke (1560-1634), the functions of the English sheriff had become standardized under three general heads: (1) to serve process by which a suit was begun; (2) to execute the decrees of the court; (3) to act as conservator of peace within the county.[1]

The office appeared in America in modified form among the earliest colonial institutions, being created in Virginia in 1634, and in Massachusetts in 1654. The ancient office was continued by the states created after independence.[2] The office assumed a new significance in the latter part of the eighteenth century when a flood of colonists swept across the ineffective Allegheny barrier to establish homes in the Northwest Territory organized by Congress in 1787. In the remote West the pioneers, far removed from the orderly legal processes of courts of the East, were subjected to the machinations of lawless element prevalent in every new community.

In 1792 the governor and judges of the territory adopted an act providing for the appointment by the governor of a sheriff in each county and defining his duties.[3] This pioneer law clearly established three of the four major duties of the sheriff as they remain today, namely: attendance upon the court; execution of writs, warrants, and the like; and policing and the arrest of criminals.

When Ohio entered the Union as a state in 1803, the office of sheriff was continued by constitutional provision, and was made elected for a two-year term.[4] Since that time relatively few changes have been made in the structural organization of the office.[4]

---

1. Adams, *op. cit.,* 17-19; William A. Morris, "The Office of Sheriff in the Anglo-Saxon Period," *English Historical Review,* XXXI, (1915), 20-40; Raymond Moley, *The Sheriff and the Coroner* (New York, 1926. *The Missouri Crime Survey,* pt. ii,). 59-60.
2. For a comparative study of the sheriff in England and the Chesapeake colonies, see Cyrus Harreld Karraker, *The Seventeenth-Century Sheriff* . . . (Chapel Hill, 1930).
3. Pease, *op. cit.,* 8.
4. *Ohio Const. 1802,* Art. IV, sec. 1.

Since that time relatively few changes have been made in the structural organization of the office. When a new county was erected the associate judges appointed a day on which the qualified voters met at the temporary seat of justice and elected a sheriff who served until the next general election.[5] Although the constitution of 1851 did not specifically provide for this office, it did declare that no person should be eligible to the office for more than four in any period of six years.[6] No county officer was to have a longer term than three years,[7] but the matter of removal from office was left to legislative action.[8] This limitation upon the consecutive terms which a sheriff might serve remained in force until 1933, when it was repealed by an amendment authorizing any county to adopt a charter form of government. The term of office remained at two years until 1936 when it was extended to four years.[9] The sheriff received his remuneration from fees until 1906 when a definite salary was specified by the legislature.[10] The salary for each sheriff was based upon the population of his county according to the last federal census next proceeding his election.[11] In 1931, due to the increasing complexity of the duties of the office, the sheriff was authorized to appoint, with the consent of the court of common pleas, one or more deputies. These men, like their superior, were required to give bonds for the faithful performance of the duties of their office, and the sheriff was made responsible for there neglect of duty or misconduct in office.[12]

The present organization of the office may be briefly summarized: the sheriff is elected for a four-year term,[13] can hold no other elective office at the same time, and may not practice law while in office.[14]

---

5. A. E. Gwynne, *A Practical Treaties on the Law of Sheriff and Coroner with Forms and References to the Statutes of Ohio, Indiana, and Kentucky* (Cincinnati, 1849), 3.
6. *Ohio Const. 1851,* Art, X, sec. 3.
7. *Ibid.,* Art. X, sec. 2.
8. *Ibid.,* Art. X, sec. 6.
9. *Laws of Ohio,* CXVI, pt. ii, 184.
10. *Ibid.,* III, 49-51; XXXIII, 18; XXXV, 53; LII, 86.
11. *Ibid.,* XCVIII, 89.
12. *Ibid.,* XXIX, 410.
13. G. C. sec. 2823.
14. *Ibid.,* secs. 11, 1706, 2565, 2783, 2910.

He is required to give bond, the cost of which is paid by the county commissioners[15] who are also required to provide an office for the sheriff at the county seat, equipment, supplies, and other essentials of the office.[16] The commissioners also appropriate funds for the expenses incurred by the sheriff in carrying out the various duties of his office.[17] The sheriff may appoint a deputy or deputies, but all appointees must be endorsed by the local judge of the common pleas court, be electors of the county, and are not permitted to be a justice of peace or mayor.[18] Deputies are also forbidden to practice law while in office.[19] The sheriff fixes the salaries of the deputies, subject to the budget limitations of the county commissioners,[20] and shares with his deputies certain civil and criminal liabilities.[21] The salary of the sheriff, based on a graded scale according to population with a $6,000 per year maximum is $2,475.[22] The office may be vacated by failure to give proper bond, nonacceptance, or death.[23] Vacancies in the office are filled by the county commissioners.[24]

The sheriff may be removed for various financial defalcations,[25] for willfully refusing or neglecting his duty in criminal cases,[26] for malfeasance in office,[27] or for permitting the lynching of a person in his custody.[28] In the latter case the governor conducts the hearing and may remove the sheriff. If for some reason the sheriff is unable to serve a court order the judge of the common pleas court is authorized to make a temporary appointment for the post.[29]

---

15. *Ibid.*, sec. 2824.
16. *Ibid.*, sec. 2832.
17. *Ibid.*, sec. 2997.
18. *Ibid.*, secs. 1706, 2830.
19. *Ibid.*, sec. 1706.
20. *Ibid.*, sec. 2981.
21. Willis A. Estrich, ed., *Ohio Jurisprudence* (Rochester, 1934), XXXVI, 660-672, 399-701.
22. G. C. secs. 2994, 2996, 2997; Estrich, XXXVI, 704-705; Ohio Auditor of State, *Annual Report,* 1937, 376.
23. G. C. secs. 2827, 12196.
24. *Ibid.*, sec. 2828.
25. *Ibid.*, secs. 3036, 3049.
26. *Ibid.*, secs. 12850, 12851.
27. *Ohio Const, 1851* (Amendment, 1912), Art. II, sec. 38.
28. *Laws of Ohio,* CI, 109.
29. G. C. sec. 2828.

The retiring sheriff is required to deliver to his successor all moneys, papers, books, and the like, as well as the custody of all prisoners.[30]

Aside from his power to appoint deputies, the sheriff has other special powers which are largely the products of historical development. From earliest years the sheriff has been empowered to call to his aid such persons as he deemed necessary to perform his lawful duty in the apprehension of criminals.[31] Thus the *posse comitatus* was at his disposal as it is today.[32]

The specific duties of the sheriff were and are prescribed by statute and maybe classified under four main divisions: (1) attendance upon the courts; (2) executions of summons warrants processes, and other writs; (3) control and responsibility in the care of the jail and courthouse; (4) policing and the arrest of criminals.

The territorial law of 1792 required the sheriff to attend upon the court of common pleas and the court of appeals during their sessions,[33] and this requirement has been carried over into the laws of Ohio;[34] the present duties of the sheriff in this respect being survivals from the provisions of this act. He is required to attend the county court of common pleas,[35] the appellate court,[36] and the probate court if required by the judge of that division.[37] The sheriff may adjourn the court of common pleas from day to day upon failure of the judge to appear at regularly scheduled sessions.[38]

The duty of sheriff to execute all warrants, writs, and processes directed to him by the proper and lawful authority has also been operating since the territorial period.[39] At present he executes every summons, order, or other process, and makes return thereof as required by law.[40]

---

30. *Ibid.*, secs. 2842, 2843.
31. *Laws of Ohio,* III, 156-158; XXIX, 112-113.
32. G. C. Sec. 2828.
33. Pease, *op, cit.,* 8.
34. *Laws of Ohio,* III, 156-158; XXIX, 112; LXXXII, 26.
35. G. C. sec. 2833.
36. *Ibid.*, secs. 1530, 2833.
37. *Ibid.*, sec. 2833.
38. *Ibid.*, sec. 2855.
39. Pease, *op. cit.,* 8; *Laws of Ohio,* III, 156-158; XXIX, 112; LXXXII, 26.
40. G. C. sec. 2834.

He executes processes from the probate, juvenile, common and pleas, and appellate courts. Although the jury commission has supplanted the clerk of courts in the matter of selecting names of prospective jurors from the jury wheel, the sheriff's duties in this respect remain much as they were in the earlier years of his office. He also executes warrants issued by the governor of the state,[41] and serves writs and subpoenas issued by various state officers and boards.[42] In other words, the sheriff serves all the papers which concerned the county as a unit of government and some for state as well.

As early as 1805 the sheriff was made official custodian of the county jail.[43] Although the early statutes directed the county commissioners to provide dungeons for the incarceration of prisoners, the act of 1847 directed the sheriff to exercise reasonable care for the preservation of the life, health, and welfare of those committed to his care. He was and is authorized to transport prisoners to other counties for safekeeping.[44] Under the direction and control of the county commissioners the sheriff is also given charge of the courthouse.[45]

The sheriff has had extensive and important police powers since 1792 when the territorial act authorized him to keep and preserve the peace, and suppress affrays, routs, riots, unlawful assemblies, and insurrections; to apprehend, and confine in jail all felons and traitors; and to return persons who, having committed a crime in his county, had taken refuge in another.[46] During the legislative session of 1805 the general assembly passed an act defining the duties of the sheriff which were in all respects similar to the provisions inherited from the territorial code.[47] In the same year the sheriff was designated as the county's executioner, and was bound to carry out sentences of death by hanging when imposed by the courts upon those convicted of murder.[48] Public executions, the general rule during the earlier years, were abolished in 1844.[49]

---

41. *Ibid.,* sec. 118.
42. *Ibid.,* secs. 285, 346, 2709, *et el.*
43. *Laws of Ohio,* III, 157.
44. *Ibid.,* III, 157; XXIX, 112-113; XCIII, 131. For general provisions as to jail duties see G. C. secs. 3157-3176. *Passim.*
45. G. C. sec. 2833.
46. Pease, *op, cit.,* 8.
47. *Laws of Ohio,* III, 156-158.
48. Chase, *op. cit.,* 97-101, 142-143.
49. *Laws of Ohio,* XLII, 71.

In 1886 the sheriff's duties in this respect were delegated to the warden of the Ohio penitentiary.[50]

An act of 1831, repealing the act of 1805 redefined the duties of the sheriff as a conservator of peace in his county,[51] and his present duties in this respect are survivals from the provisions of this act.[52] Although the sheriff is still regarded as the chief peace officer in the county, many of his earlier duties in this respect have been abolished by the development of other agencies of law enforcement, notably the highway patrol. On the other hand, the powers of the sheriff to suppress affrays, riots, and unlawful assemblies became especially important in times of strike or threatened riots. On a properly issued warrant he may arrest any person charged with the probability of doing injury to another person or the property or of another.[53] Moreover, since 1921 the sheriff has forwarded to the bureau of criminal identification all fingerprints of persons arrested for a felony,[54] and since 1913 has been authorized to arrest any person violating his parole.[55]

The present police powers of the sheriff are quite comprehensive. His jurisdiction is coextensive with the county, including all municipalities and townships, and he is the chief law enforcement officer of the county. In municipalities the sheriff and mayor stand on equality as law enforcement officers so far as state laws are concerned, and neither is permitted to cast the burden of action upon the other.[56]

The sheriff has possessed and still possesses many powers and duties which are miscellaneous in nature. As in England the sheriff, during the earlier years of his office, was required to notify the electors of his county of the time and place of holding elections. He was enjoined to furnish ballot boxes at the expense of the county, hold special elections when so directed by the governor, and deliver the poll books to the secretary of state.[57] Since 1891 these duties have been taken over by the board of elections.[58]

---

50. *Ibid.,* LXXXIII, 145.
51. *Ibid.,* XXIX, 112-113.
52. *Ibid.,* LXXXII, 26.
53. G. C. sec. 13428-1.
54. *Laws of Ohio,* CX, 5; CIX, 584.
55. *Ibid.,* CIII, 404.
56. Estrich, XXXVI, 645. For the most important police powers see G. C. secs, 2833, 3345, 4112, 12811.
57. *Laws of Ohio,* II, 88-90; III, 331-332. See also pp. LXII, LXIII
58. See pp. 215, 216

The sheriff also has many heterogeneous powers and duties regarding elections,[59] executive orders of the secretary of agriculture,[60] fish and game laws,[61] probation officers,[62] military census,[63] traffic rules and regulations,[64] funds and deposits in court,[65] shanty boats,[66] and executive orders of the governor.[67]

The multiplicate duties of the sheriff have made it necessary to require many records of the business of the office to be kept. The present practice of keeping a foreign execution docket began in 1838.[68] Since 1842 the sheriff has kept a cashbook,[69] and since 1843 a jail register.[70] Indexes, direct and reverse, to the foreign execution docket was prescribed by the legislature in 1925.[71] Since 1843 he has been required annually to transmit the jail register, in certified copies, to the clerk of courts, the county auditor, and the secretary of state.[72] 1850 he has been required, on the first Monday of September in each year, to submit to the county commissioners a certified statement of all fines and costs collected during the year, and the amount of fees collected and paid to the clerk of courts of common pleas.[73]

---

59. G. C. secs. 4785-124, 4829.
60. *Ibid.,* sec. 1110.
61. *Ibid.,* secs. 1434, 1441, 1444, 1451.
62. *Ibid.,* sec. 1639-19.
63. *Ibid.,* sec. 5188-5.
64. *Ibid.,* sec. 7251-1.
65. *Ibid.,* sec. 11900.
66. *Ibid.,* sec. 13403-1.
67. *Ibid.,* sec. 118.
68. *Laws of Ohio,* XXXVI, 18; LVII, 6; LXXXIV, 208-209.
69. *Ibid.,* XL, 25; LXV, 115; LXXXIV, 208; LXXXVI, 239.
70. *Ibid.,* XLI, 74.
71. *Ibid.,* CXI, 31. These indexes were initiated in Ross County in 1840, thus antedating by eighty-five years the statute requiring them.
72. *Ibid.,* XLI, 74.
73. G. C. sec. 2844;

Thus the modern sheriff keeps the following records: (1) a cashbook which is a record of all moneys handled; (2) a foreign summons docket which is a record of all summonses from counties other than his own; (3) a foreign execution docket which is a record of executions from counties other than his own; (4) a service record which includes all probate and divorce papers served: (5) an execution register which records all executions handled; (6) an accrued fee record which lists fees received; (7) a commission register which records the commissions of all special deputies; (8) a jail register which records all prisoners brought in, the charge, how long detained, and when released.[74] By statute the sheriff is also required to make an annual financial report to the county commissioners.[75]

---

74. G. C. secs. 2837, 2839, 2979, 3045, 3046.
75. *Ibid.,* sec. 2844. See entry 10.

Dockets

309. SHERIFF'S APPEARANCE DOCKET, PROBATE COURT
1895-1911. 3 volumes.

Sheriff's docket of cases filed in probate court, showing case number, title of case, kind of writ, date of filing, on whom served, how served, date and where returnable, mileage, amount of fees, and date sheriff's fees were paid. Arranged chronologically by dates of filing. Indexed alphabetically by names of plaintiffs or petitioners. Handwritten. Average 430 pages. 16 x 12 x 3. Sheriff's main office.

310. SHERIFF'S APPEARANCE DOCKET
1885-1911. 8 volumes.

Sheriff's docket of cases filed in common pleas court, showing case number, title of case, kind of writ, date of filing, on whom served, how served, date and where returnable, mileage, amount of fees, and date sheriff's fees were paid. Arranged chronologically by dates of filing. Indexed alphabetically by names of plaintiffs or petitioners. Handwritten. Average 400 pages. 16 x 12 x 3. 5 volumes, 1885-1894, Clerk of courts' vault; 3 volumes, 1895-1911, Sheriff's main office.

311. HOME EXECUTION DOCKET
1859—. 9 volumes. (1-9).
Sheriff's record of executions to satisfy judgments issued by Ross County courts, showing volume and page numbers of Execution Docket, entry 102, names of litigants, amount of judgment, costs, date writ filed, notation of service, and record of sale. Arranged chronologically by dates of filing. Indexed alphabetically by names of plaintiffs. Handwritten. Average 380 pages. 16 x 11 x 3. 3 volumes, 1859-1894, Clerk of courts' vault; 6 volumes, 1895—, Sheriff's main office.

312. FOREIGN EXECUTION DOCKET
1840—. 7 volumes. (1, 1-6).
Sheriff's record of executions to satisfy judgments issued by other than Ross County courts, showing names of litigants, names of court and county, date of filing, date returnable, amount of judgment, interest, cost, and date of settlement. Arranged chronologically by dates of filing. Indexed alphabetically by names of plaintiffs; also separate index, entry 313. 1840-1930, handwritten; 1930—, typed. Average 350 pages. 16 x 11 x 3. 3 volumes, 1840-1881, Clerk of courts' vault; 4 volumes, 1881—, Sheriff's main office.

313. INDEX, FOREIGN EXECUTION DOCKET
1840—. 1 volume.
Direct and reverse index to Foreign Execution Docket, entry 312, showing names of plaintiff and defendant, volume and page numbers of docket, kind of action, and kind of writ. Arranged alphabetically, direct, by names of plaintiffs, and reverse, by names of defendants. Handwritten. 600 pages. 18 x 12 x 4.5. Sheriff's main office.

314. FOREIGN SUMMONS DOCKET
1881—. 7 volumes. (3-9).
Sheriff's record of summonses issued by courts other than Ross County courts, showing names of county and court, names of litigants, case number, kind of action, dates writs received and served, date returnable, sheriff's fees, amount deposited for sheriff's fees, and copy of return endorsed on writ. Arranged chronologically by dates received. Indexed alphabetically by names of plaintiffs. Handwritten on printed forms. Average 440 pages. 16 x 11 x 3.5. 1 volume, 1881-1894, Clerk of courts' vault; 6 volumes, 1895—, Sheriff's main office.

315. SHERIFF'S DOCKET

1860-1880. 10 volumes. (labeled by years).

Sheriff's record of court cases and court orders, showing date, names of litigants, case number, kind of action, kind of writ, notation of sheriff's return, sheriff's fees and cost. Arranged chronologically by dates of entry. Indexed alphabetically by names of plaintiffs. Handwritten. Average 380 pages. 16 x 11 x 3. Clerk of courts' vault.

316. ORDER OF SALE AND PARTITION DOCKET

1872-1911. 4 volumes. (labeled by years).

Sheriff's record of orders of sale and partition and foreclosure proceedings, showing date, names of litigants, case number, dates writs issued and returned, names of appraisers, amount of appraisal, dates advertised for sale, date of sale, to whom sold, amount of sale, and date deed delivered. Arranged chronologically by dates of entry. Indexed alphabetically by names of plaintiffs. Handwritten on printed forms. Average 490 pages. 16 x 11 x 3.25. 1 volume, 1872-1888, Clerk of courts' vault; 3 volumes, 1888-1911, Sheriff's main office.

For record of sales, see entry 322.

Fiscal Accounts

317. CASH BOOK

1859—. 10 volumes. (4-13). Prior records missing.

Record of receipts and disbursements: receipts, showing from whom received, date, for what, in what matter, case number, and amount; disbursements, showing dates, to whom paid, for what, in what matter, case number, and amount. Arranged chronologically by dates of entry. Indexed alphabetically by names of payees or payers. Handwritten. Average 400 pages. 16 x 11 x 3. 1 volume, 1859-1868, Auditor's vault; 9 volumes, 1869—, Sheriff's main office.

318. SHERIFFS FEE RECORD

1852-1869. 2 volumes. Title varies: Sheriff's Ledger.

Record of fees due sheriff's office, showing to whom charged, for what, case number, amount, and date paid. Arranged chronologically by dates of payments. No index. Handwritten. Average 200 pages. 15 x 8 x 1.5. Clerk of courts' vault.

319. RECORD OF ACCRUED FEES

1907—. 7 volumes. (labeled by years).

Sheriff's record of fees accrued, showing dates, case number, in what matter, to whom charged, total fees, for what, date paid, and by whom paid. Arranged chronologically by dates of payment. No index. Handwritten. Average 340 pages. 18 x 15 x 3. Sheriff's main office.

320. SHERIFF'S BOARD BILL, JAIL

1895-1905. 1 volume.

Sheriff's account of boarding prisoners in county jail, showing names of prisoners, number of days fed, total amount due, date of commitment, and date of release. Arranged alphabetically by the names of prisoners. No index. Handwritten. 280 pages. 16 x 14 x 2. Sheriff's main office.

321. RECORD OF CHECKS ISSUED

1924—. 6 volumes.

Stubs of checks issued by sheriff's office, showing to whom issued, for what, date, amount, and check number. Arranged numerically by check numbers. No index. Handwritten on printed forms. Average 150 pages. 5 x 11 x 1.25. Sheriff's main office.

Miscellaneous

322. RECORD OF SHERIFF'S SALES

1895—. 9 volumes.

Record of sales of property on order of court to satisfy judgments and partition proceedings, showing names of litigants, kind of action, description of property to be sold, amount of appraisal, date of sale, and amount of sale. Indexed alphabetically by names of plaintiffs. Handwritten on printed forms. Average 280 pages. 18 x 12 x 2. Sheriff's main office.

For orders of sale, 1872-1911, see entry 316.

323. JURY AND WITNESS BOOK

1895-1908. 2 volumes.

Sheriff's record of subpoenas served for witnesses and jurors, showing term of court, date of subpoena, date served, on whom served, how served, number of miles, total fees, and date returned. Arranged chronologically under each court term. No index. Handwritten. Average 480 pages. 16 x 11 x 3.5. Sheriff's main office.

For other records, see entries 118-123, 303.

324. JAIL REGISTER

1881—. 7 volumes. (3, 3-8).

Sheriff's record of commitments to county jail, showing name of prisoner, date committed, by what authority committed, what charge, date discharged, authority of discharge, nativity, color, sex, height, complexion, age, and remarks. Arranged chronologically by dates of commitment. No index. 1881-1930, handwritten; 1930—, typed. Average 397 pages. 17 x 12.5 x 3. Sheriff's main office.

325. RECORD OF LEGAL ADVERTISING

1861—. 14 volumes. (labeled by years).

Clipped copies of legal advertisements published in Ross County newspapers including advertisements of sheriff's sales of property on order of court, showing name of purchaser of property, date, and amount of sale. Arranged chronologically by dates of sale. No index. Handwritten notations on printed copies. Average 200 pages. 15 x 12 x 3. 12 volumes, 1861-1912, Clerk of courts' vault; 2 volumes, 1921—, Sheriff's main office.

The county dog warden, appointed by and responsible to the county commissioners, has as his duty the enforcement of the provisions of the General Code relative to licensing dogs, the impounding and destruction of unlicensed dogs, and the payment of compensation for damages to livestock inflicted by dogs. This officer, like other county officials, is required to give bond conditioned for the faithful performance of the duties of his office. This bond, in the sum of not less than $500 nor more than $2,000, is filed with the county auditor. His compensation and tenure, like that of his deputies, is determined by the county commissioners.[1]

In Ross County the duties of dog warden were performed by the sheriff from 1917 to 1927 as provided by statute.[2] In 1927 an act authorized the commissioners to appoint a county dog warden under which act the Ross County dog warden was appointed on September 1, 1927.[3]

The warden is required to make a record of all dogs owned, kept, or harbored in his county; to patrol the county; and to seize and impound dogs more than three months of age found not wearing a valid registration tag. The latter provisions do not apply, however, to dogs kept in a regularly licensed kennel. Moreover, he is required to make weekly written reports to the county commissioners of all dogs seized, impounded, redeemed, and destroyed. Then, too, he is required to report all claims for damages to livestock inflicted by dogs.

The dog warden and his deputies have, in the performance of their legal duties, the same "police powers" as are conferred by statute upon sheriff's and police. They may summon the assistance of bystanders in performing their duties, serve writs and other legal processes issued by any court in the county with reference to enforcing the provisions of the laws relating to dogs.[4]

---

1. G. C. sec. 5652-7.
2. *Laws of Ohio,* CVII, 535.
3. *Ibid.,* CXII, 348; Commissioners' Journal, volume Q, p. 147.
4. G. C. sec. 5652-7.

326. ANIMAL CLAIMS

1931—. 1 file box.

Copies of claims filed for compensation for animals killed or injured by dogs, showing name of claimant, kind of animal, number, valuation, amount of claim, and date. Arranged chronologically by dates of claims. No index. Handwritten on printed forms. 10 x 5 x 14. Commissioners' office.

For commissioners' record, see entry 23.

327. NOTICES [of Dogs Impounded]

1928—. 2 file boxes.

Copies of notices posted by dog warden of dogs impounded, showing date, description of dog, where found, date on which dog will be destroyed if not claimed, tag fee, and costs paid. Arranged chronologically by dates of notices. No index. Handwritten on printed forms. 10 x 5 x 14. Commissioners' office.

For reports to commissioners', see entry 11.

The first Ohio constitution, adopted in 1802, did not provide for the office of county auditor and it was not until 1820 that the general assembly by a joint resolution appointed an auditor in each county for a one-year term.[1] In 1821 the office became elective and the term was fixed at one year.[2] In 1831 the term was set at two years, and 1877 at three years, and 1906 reduced to two years, and in 1919 extended to four years.[3]

The county auditor is required to take oath and give bond for faithful performance of the duties of his office; to preserve all copies of entries, surveys, extracts, and other documents transmitted to his office from the state auditor; and to transfer to his successor all books, records, maps, and other papers pertaining to his office.[4] With the approval of the county commissioners he is authorized to appoint deputies, for whose official acts he and his sureties are held liable; the record of these appointments which has been required to be filed with the county treasurer since 1869[5] was not located in the inventory of the Ross County treasurer's office. If the office of county auditor falls vacant the county commissioners are authorized to appoint a successor.[6]

The first auditor in each county was required to list all lands in his county subject to taxation. From this list and one submitted to him by the county commissioners and one from the state auditor the county auditor was directed to make a tax duplicate to be kept in a book for that purpose, and to give a copy of the list to the tax collector.[7] The auditor was also directed to compile from the treasurer's duplicate a list of lands on which taxes were delinquent, and if such lands were sold for taxes to grant a deed to purchaser.[8]

Subsequent legislation expanded and itemized the duties of the auditor regarding taxation; with modifications to meet modern requirements these duties have contained much as they were during the earlier years of his office.

---

1. *Laws of Ohio,* XVIII, 71.
2. *Ibid.,* XIX, 116.
3. *Ibid.,* XXIX, 280; LXXIV, 381; XCVIII, 271; CVIII, pt. ii, 1294.
4. *Ibid.,* XIX, 116; R. S. 1033; G. C. secs. 2559, 2582.
5. *Laws of Ohio,* LV, 20; LXVI, 35; G. C. sec. 2563.
6. *Laws of Ohio,* XXIX, 280-291; LXVII, 103.
7. *Ibid.,* XVIII, 79.
8. *Ibid.,* XVIII, 82; XIX, 115.

During the 1840s the office of county assessor was abolished and provision was made for township assessors whose duty it was to list all taxable property and make a return to the auditor.[9] Since 1874 the auditor is required by statute to keep a book in which he lists additions to and deductions from the amount of tax assessment.[10] In 1915 he was made chief assessing officer of the county.[11]

The county auditor has served as a member and the secretary of the county budget commission since its beginning in 1911, his duties including keeping full and accurate records of the proceedings of that body. For the purpose of adjusting the tax rates and fixing the amount to be levied each year the commissioners are governed by the amount of taxable property as shown on the auditor's tax list for the current year. He submits to the commissioners the annual tax budget given him by each taxing authority of each subdivision, together with an estimate of any state levy prepared by the state auditor, and such other information as the budget commission may request or the state tax commission require.[12]

Tax settlements had been made annually until 1859 when the auditor was required to make semiannual settlement with the treasurer to ascertain the amount of taxes the treasurer is to stand charged.[13] Since 1904 liquor, cigarette, and inheritance taxes have constituted separate funds. All other taxes are credited to the general fund.[14]

Since 1831 the county auditor has kept an account current with the county treasurer showing the payments of money into the treasury, listing the dates, by whom paid, and to which fund. On receiving the treasurer's daily statement the auditor enters on his account current the amount shown as a charge to the treasurer.[15] Another important function of the county auditor is the approval before payment of bills and other claims against the county.

---

9. *Ibid.*, XXXIX, 22-25. See also p. XXXVII
10. *Laws of Ohio,* LXXI, 30.
11. *Ibid.*, CVI, 246.
12. G. C. sec. 5625-19; *Laws of Ohio,* CXII, 402.
13. G. C. sec. 2596; *Laws of Ohio* ,LVI, 132; LXXVIII, 226.
14. *Laws of Ohio,* XCVII, 457.
15. *Ibid.*, XXIX, 280-291; LXVII, 103.

Since 1831 he is authorized to issue, on presentation of the proper voucher, all warrants on the county treasurer for moneys payable from the county treasury; and to preserve all warrants, showing the number, date of issue, amount for which drawn, in whose favor, and from which fund.[16] County money due the state is paid on warrant of the state auditor. Since 1904 a bill or voucher for payment from any fund controlled by the county commissioners or board of county infirmary directors is filed with the county auditor and entered in a book for that purpose at least five days before its approval for payment by the commissioners, and when approved the date is entered opposite the claim.[17]

Besides approving bills and claims against the county, the auditor in 1835 was given the duty of certifying all moneys, except collections on the tax duplicate, into the county treasury, specifying by whom paid and the fund to which such payment is credited. Such moneys he charges to the treasurer and keeps a duplicate copy of the statement in his office. Since 1835 all costs collected in penitentiary cases which have been or are to be paid to the state have been certified into the treasury as belonging to the state.[18]

In 1902 the legislature provided for a system of uniform accounting in auditing of all public offices, and for the annual examination of their finances, under the direction of a bureau of inspection in the office of the state auditor.[19] Since 1904 the county auditor has been required to report to the commissioners on the state of county finances; on the first business day of each month he prepares in duplicate a statement of the county finances for the proceeding month, compare it with the treasurer's balance, and submits it to the commissioners to post one copy of it in the auditor's office for thirty days for public inspection.[20]

During the development of the office, additional duties in great diversity have been delegated to the county auditor. Since 1833 he has been authorized to discharge prisoners jailed for nonpayment of any fine or amercement due the county when in his opinion payment is not collectible.[21] In 1838 an act was passed making him county superintendent of schools.

---

16. G. C. sec. 2570; R. S. 1024; *Laws of Ohio,* XXIX, 280-291; LXVII, 103.
17. *Laws of Ohio,* XCVII, 25; CVIII, pt. i, 272.
18. *Ibid.,* XXXIII, 44; LXVII, 103.
19. *Ibid.,* XCV, 511-515.
20. *Ibid.,* XCVII, 457.
21. G. C. sec. 2576; *Laws of Ohio,* XXXI, 18; LXVII, 103.

He was relieved of this duty in 1848 when a county superintendent of schools was authorized in each county.[22] Since 1846 he has served as a sealer of weights and measures, is responsible for the preservation of the copies of the original standards delivered to his office, and enforces in his county all state laws regulating weights and measures.[23] In 1861 he was authorized to report to the state auditor statistics concerning the deaf, dumb, blind, insane, and idiots in his county, with the names and addresses of their parents or guardians.[24] Eight years later, in 1869, he was authorized to report to the same officer statistics concerning livestock in his county as returned to his office by assessors, and an abstract of the funded indebtedness of his county, and of each township, city, village, and school district.[25] Since 1827 he has been authorized to issue licenses to traveling public shows and exhibitions, although municipal authorities may impose an additional license.[26] In 1862 he was authorized to issue peddlers' licenses to persons who filed a statement of stock in trade and conformity with the law requiring the listing of such stock for taxation, and since 1917 he issued dogs licenses.[27] The auditor has issued licenses to wholesale and retail dealers in cigarettes since 1893,[28] in brewers' wort and malt since 1933,[29] and cosmetic licenses from August 1, 1933 to June 30, 1936.[30]

From 1821 to 1933 the county auditor of Ross County served as clerk to the county commissioners; his duties included keeping an accurate record of their proceedings and preserving all documents, books, records, maps, and papers which were required to be filed in his office.[31] Since 1850 he has been official custodian of the reports submitted to the commissioners by the prosecuting attorney, clerk of courts, sheriff, and treasurer; these reports are recorded by the auditor in books kept specifically for the purpose.[32]

---

22. See p. 221.
23. G. C. sec. 2615; *Laws of Ohio,* XIIV, 55; LVIII, 78; CI, 234.
24. *Laws of Ohio,* LVIII, 40.
25. G. C. sec. 2604.
26. *Laws of Ohio,* XXIX, 116; G. C. secs. 6374, 6375.
27. *Laws of Ohio,* LIX, 57; LXXIX, 96; CVII, 534.
28. G. C. sec. 5894-5.
29. *Ibid.,* sec. 5545-5. See also p. XL.
30. *Laws of Ohio,* CXV, 649; CXV, pt. ii, 83; CXVI, pt. ii, 323.
31. G. C. sec. 2536; *Laws of Ohio,* XIX, 147; Commissioners' Journal, volume S, p. 3.
32. G. C. sec. 2504; R. S. 886; *Laws of Ohio,* XLVIII, 66.

The volume record has apparently not been kept in Ross County but the original reports from 1871 to date were listed.[33]

The county auditor is a member of the county board of revision established in 1825, secretary of the budget commission, and serves as a trustee and the secretary of the board of trustees of the sinking fund established in 1919.[34]

---

33. See entry 10.
34. See pp. 208, 209, 213.

Property Transfers
(See also entries 44-76)

328. TRANSFERS

1847-1869, 1877-1914. 24 volumes. 1826-1842, 1910— also in Auditor's Duplicate, entry 346; 1923— also in Auditor's Tax List, entry 342.

Record of real estate transfers, showing date, taxing district, name of grantor and grantee, volume and page number of Deed Record, entry 49, location and description tract, lot number, acreage, consideration, and fee. One volume for the city of Chillicothe is undated. 1847-1869, 1877-1906, arranged alphabetically by names of grantors and chronologically thereunder; 1907-1914, arranged alphabetically by names of taxing districts, alphabetically thereunder by names of grantors, and chronologically thereunder by dates of transfers. No index. Handwritten. Average 260 pages. 14 x 9.5 x 2. 20 volumes, 1847-1869, 1877-1888, 1907-1914, no date, Auditor's vault; 4 volumes, 1889-1906, Basement, middle storeroom.

329. AUDITOR'S DEEDS

1861—. 2 volumes. Last entry 1929.

Record of auditor's deeds to tracts of land sold for delinquent taxes, showing name of owner, date tract sold, description of tract, total tax and penalty due, amount tract sold for, date of deed, names of grantee and grantor, and signature of auditor as grantor. Arranged alphabetically by names of grantee and chronologically thereunder by dates of deeds. No index. Handwritten. Average 250 pages. 18 x 12 x 2. Auditor's vault.

330. [Auditor's] INDEX TO FILES

1844—. 1 volume.

Index to unbound records in commissioners' and auditor's office, showing file box number and date of records. Index serves in whole or in part: [Financial] Reports, entry 7; [Infirmary Directors] Reports, entry 8; [Infirmary Superintendent's] Records, entry 9; [Road] Records, entry 15; Contracts, entry 17; Bids, entry 18; Estimates and Specifications, entry 19; [Animal] Claims, entry 23; Blind Relief Records, entry 26; Deeds and Titles, entry 331; [Tax] Levies, entry 335; Assessments [Highways and Streets], entry 351; Property Valuation, entry 371; [Inheritance tax] Findings, entry 384; Budgets, entry 388; Soldiers' Relief, entry 402; Vouchers Cancelled, entry 414; Warrants, entry 418; Court Warrants [Redeemed], entry 419; School Warrants, entry 420; Cancelled Warrants [Blind Pensions], entry 421; Cancelled Warrants [Mothers' Pensions], entry 422; Dog Tax Applications, entry 424; Statements [Of Fees], entry 432; Cigarette and Liquor Returns, entry 433; Cigarette Returns, entry 434; Statements [Of Fines], entry 435; Reports [To state auditor], entry 437; Balance Sheets, entry 438; Auditor's Financial Reports, entry 439; [Indebtedness] Reports, entry 440; [Interest] Statements, entry 441; [Bank] Entry 442; [School Clerks'] Bonds, entry 446; [Official] Bonds, entry 447; Redeemed Bonds [Infirmary, Roads, Bridges], entry 450; Military and War Records, entry 453; School Reports, entry 456; [School] Enumeration Reports, entry 457; Enumeration, Deaf, Dumb and Blind entry 458, Arranged alphabetically by record titles. Typed. 180 pages. 13 x 10.5 x 1.5. Auditor's vault.

331. DEEDS AND TITLES

1842-1902. 5 file boxes. (5, 158, 161, 420, 497).

Copies of deeds and abstracts of titles to lands to be used for free turnpikes and improved roads, showing date filed. Arranged chronologically by dates of filing. 1842-1843, no index; for index, 1844-1902, see entry 330. Handwritten on printed forms. 10 x 5 x 14. Auditor's vault.

Maps and Plats

(See also entries 77-81, 583-588)

332. PLAT BOOK

1872—. 1 volume. (96 plats).

Plats of Chillicothe additions, subdivisions, and allotments, showing streets, alleys, lot dimensions and area, and street and alley widths; plats of Kingston and Bainbridge villages, showing additions and subdivisions. Prepared by county engineer. Arranged buy subdivisions. No index. Hand drawn. Scales vary: 1 inch equals 65 feet, 165 feet, 4 poles, or 20 poles. 24 pages. 24 x 36 x 1.25. Auditor's vault.

333. ATLAS, ROSS COUNTY

1875. 1 volume.

Illustrated atlas and historical sketch of Ross County, showing each township and town with boundaries of land and names of owners shown on township maps; streets, alleys, lots, and names of owners shown on town maps except that of Chillicothe. Compiled from surveys and official records by Huston T. Gould. Published by H. T. Gould and Company, Columbus, Ohio. Indexed alphabetically by names of townships, towns, and views. Printed. Scales vary: 1 inch equals 20 rods 2.25 inch equals 1 mile, for townships; 1 inch equals 20 rods to 1 inch equals 330 rods, for towns and villages. 92 pages. 26 x 18 x 1.25. Auditor's vault.

334. MAPS

1925, 1930. 1 volume.

Maps of Chillicothe, showing original area, all streets, alleys, lots, public buildings, manufacturing and mercantile buildings, water facilities, and fire department data; mileage chart showing distance to any part of city from station No. 1. Maps are colored to denote type of building such as yellow indicates frame buildings; red, brick buildings; blue, stone buildings; gray, metal construction; and brown, fireproof construction. Maps corrected to 1930. Printed by Sanborn Map Company, New York. Indexed alphabetically by names the streets and buildings. Lithograph. Scales vary: 1 inch equals from 50 feet to 900 feet. 38 pages. 28 x 22 x 1.25. Auditor's vault.

Tax Records
(See also entries 466-496)

Levies and Appraisements

335. [Tax] LEVIES

1864—. 10 file boxes. (125, 127, 336, 491, 547, 631, 717, 802, 887).

Copies of tax levies made yearly for each taxing district, showing property valuation, amount of funds required, and tax rate. Arranged chronologically by years. For index, see entry 330. 1864-1921, handwritten on printed forms; 1922—, typed on printed forms. 10 x 5 x 14. Auditor's vault.

For record of tax levies, 1858-1874, see entry 463; 1892-1811, see entry 336.

336. RECORD OF TAX LEVIES

1892-1911. 1 volume.

Record of tax levies for each taxing district, showing amount of funds required by each taxing district as certified by finance officials, property valuation of each taxing district, and tax rate for each district each year. Arranged chronologically under tabs by years and alphabetically thereunder by names of taxing districts. No index. Handwritten. 500 pages. 18 x 12 x 4. Auditor's vault.

For prior and subsequent records, see entries 335, 463.

337. LAND APPRAISEMENT

1856. 17 volumes. 16 subtitled by names of townships, 1 subtitled Chillicothe.

Record of valuation of real estate for taxing purposes, as listed by district assessors, showing name of owner, entry and survey numbers, original quantity, watercourse, lot number, range, township, and section numbers, total acreage, number of acres arable, grass, wood, and uncultivated land, land valuation, building valuation, and total valuation. Arranged alphabetically by names of property owners. No index. Handwritten. Average 42 pages. 12 x 8 x .25. Auditor's vault.

338. REVALUATION RECORD
1859, 1870. 19 volumes. (1 labeled 1859). 16 subtitled by names of townships, 2 subtitled Chillicothe.

Record of revaluation of lands and town lots in Ross County made by district assessors, subsequently equalized by county and state boards of equalization, showing name of owner, entry and survey numbers, original proprietor, watercourse, township, range, and section numbers, name of municipality, acreage, number of acres arable, grass, wood, and uncultivated land, building, assessors' valuation, and valuation as fixed by county and state boards of equalization. Arranged alphabetically by names of property owners. No index. Handwritten. 1 volume, 572 pages. 14 x 8.5 x 4; 18 volumes, average 54 pages. 20 x 12 x .25. Basement, middle storeroom.

339. LAND APPRAISAL RECORD
1870, 1880, 1890, 1900. 8 volumes.

Record of decennial appraisals of real estate, showing name of taxing district, name of owner, description of tract, acreage, valuation of land and buildings, total valuation, valuation as fixed by county and state board of equalization. Arranged alphabetically by names of taxing districts and alphabetically thereunder by names of property owners. No index. Handwritten. Average 450 pages. 18 x 12 x 3.5. Basement, middle storeroom.

340. REAPPRAISEMENT RECORD
1910, 1925. 27 volumes.

Reappraisal valuation as returned by land appraisers, showing name of taxing district, name of owner, survey and entry numbers, township, range, and section numbers, acreage, description of tract, valuation by appraisers, county auditor, board of revision, and tax commissioners, description and valuation of buildings, and total valuation of land and buildings. Arranged alphabetically by names of taxing districts and alphabetically thereunder by names of property owners. No index. Handwritten. 3 volumes, average 500 pages. 18 x 12 x 4; 24 volumes, average 300 pages. 12 x 8.5 x 2.5. 3 volumes, 1910, Auditor's vault; 24 volumes, 1925, Basement, middle storeroom.

341. RAILROAD APPRAISAL RECORD

1878-1910. 1 volume. Last entry 1900; law repealed 1910.

Record of appraisal of Springfield, Jackson, and Pomeroy Railroad property in Ross County, as returned by board of appraisers, showing track mileage, equipment, real estate and buildings, with valuation of each, and total valuation each year. Arranged chronologically by years. No index. Handwritten. 250 pages. 12 x 8 x 1.5. Auditor's vault.

Tax Lists

342. AUDITOR'S TAX LISTS

1923—. 28 volumes.

List of real and tangible and intangible personal property as listed for taxation, showing name of taxing district, name and address of owner, property valuation, delinquencies, general tax, penalties, amount of December half tax due, and amount of June half tax due. Also contains transfers, entry 328. Arranged alphabetically under tabs by names of taxing districts and alphabetically thereunder by names of taxpayers. No index. Typed. Average 540 pages. 18 x 12 x 4. Auditor's vault.

343. PERSONAL PROPERTY TAX LIST

1930—. 6 volumes.

List of tangible personal property as listed for taxation, showing name of taxing district, name and address of property owner, kind of property, valuation, delinquencies, and penalties. Arranged alphabetically by names of taxing districts and alphabetically thereunder by names of property owners. No index. Typed. Average 600 pages. 15 x 10 x 3. Auditor's office, in safe.

344. BUILDINGS, SCIOTO TOWNSHIP

1843. 1 volume.

Auditor's list of all buildings, mills, and manufacturing established in Scioto Township for taxing purposes, showing name of owner, description of building, location, use, and valuation. Arranged alphabetically by the names of owners. No index. Handwritten. 28 pages. 12 x 8 x .25. Auditor's vault.

Tax Duplicates (See also entries 466-476).

345. LAND DUPLICATE

1801, 1809. 5 volumes,

Auditor's duplicate listing real estate for taxing purposes, showing name of owner, what rate as 1st, 2nd, or 3rd, for whom entered, for whom surveyed, for whom patented, watercourse, what county, entry and survey numbers, township, entry date, transferred to whom, amount of tax, interest, and total due. Two volumes, 1801, list nonresident owners; one volume, 1801, list resident owners. These were records under the territorial government of the Northwest Territory. Arranged alphabetically by names of property owners. No index. Handwritten. Average 80 pages. 12 x 8 x 1. Auditor's vault.

For tax duplicates, 1820—, see entry 346.

346. AUDITOR'S DUPLICATE

1820-1822, 1826-1859, 1871, 1873—. 215 volumes. (labeled by years).

Auditor's duplicate taxes assessed on real property, showing name of taxing district, name and address of property owner, survey and entry numbers, township, range, and section numbers, watercourse, building and land valuation, total valuation, general tax, special tax, delinquencies, and total charge to county treasurer. Records for the following dates also show: 1820-1822, resident proprietor, nonresident proprietor, original proprietor, state and road taxes, and total; 1874—, name of town, lot number, foot frontage, description of tract, acreage, general, special, and road taxes, delinquencies, penalties, and total; 1831-1841 contains in the back of each volume a list of lawyers and physicians, showing amount of income, amount of income tax assessed, and record of payment; 1826-1932 contains duplicate of personal property, showing name and address of property owner, valuation of property, kind of property, amount of tax, delinquencies, and total tax. Also contains: Transfers, 1826-1842, 1915—, entry 328; Abstract of Tax Duplicate, 1830-1859, 1866, 1871, 1873-1882, entry 361; Additions, 1929—, entry 363; Settlement Record, 1854-1859, 1866, 1871, entry 386; Appointment Ledger, 1827-1859, 1863, 1871, entry 389. Arranged alphabetically by names of taxing districts and alphabetically thereunder by names of property owners. 1820-1910, handwritten; 1911—, typed. 1820-1822, 320 pages. 11.5 x 9 x 2.5; 1826-1873, average 480 pages. 16 x 12 x 4; 1874—, average 500 pages. 18 x 13 x 4. Auditor's vault. For prior records, see entry 345; for record of delinquencies, 1823-1850, see entry 376.

347. SPECIAL DUPLICATE [Turnpike and Township House]
1888-1894. 1 volume.

Duplicate of special assessments for free turnpike improvements in Deerfield and Concord Townships, and for the purchase of site, and the erecting of a township house in Austin precinct, showing name of taxing district, name of property owner, original quantity, entry and survey numbers, watercourses, original proprietor, acreage, land and building valuation, personal property valuation, total value, and amount of tax. Arranged alphabetically by the names of taxing districts and alphabetically thereunder by names of property owners. No index. Handwritten. 190 pages. 18 x 12 x 1.25. Auditor's vault.

348. SPECIAL DUPLICATE [Turnpike]
1887-1889. 3 volumes.

Duplicate of special assessments for free turnpike improvements in Deerfield Township and in Clarksburg, showing name of taxing district, name of owner, original quantity, entry and survey numbers, watercourses, original proprietor, acreage, land and building valuation, total valuation, road tax, delinquencies, and total due. Arranged alphabetically by names of taxing districts and alphabetically thereunder by names of property owners. No index. Handwritten. Average 56 pages. 18 x 12 x .25. Basement, middle storeroom.

349. ROAD IMPROVEMENT DUPLICATE
1870-1881. 5 volumes.

Duplicate of special assessments for road improvements, showing names of improvement project and property owner, original quantity, entry and survey number, watercourses, original proprietor, township, range, and section numbers acreage, estimated cost of improvement, amount of assessment, and date paid. Arranged alphabetically by names of improvement projects and alphabetically thereunder by names of property owners. No index. Handwritten. Average 280 pages. 16 x 11 x 2. Auditor's vault.

350. RECORD OF ROAD TAX
1870-1872. 1 volume.

Record of tax levied for road improvements, showing name of property owner, township, original quantity, entry and survey numbers, watercourses, range and section numbers, original proprietor, acreage, what road, and amount of tax. Arranged alphabetically by names of property owners. No index. Handwritten. 440 pages. 12 x 8 x 3. Auditor's vault.

351. ASSESSMENTS [Highways and Streets]
1902-1920. 4 file boxes. (3, 128, 476, 477).
Auditor's copies of special assessment statements for construction of highways and streets, showing dates, taxing district, improvement, name of property owner, description of tract or lot, amount of assessment, amount of each installment, and date due. Arranged chronologically by years. For index, see entry 330. Handwritten on printed forms. 10 x 5 x 14. Auditor's vault.

352. SPRINKLING DUPLICATE
1906-1913. 1 volume.
Duplicate of street sprinkling assessments for city of Chillicothe, showing name of property owner, lot number, feet frontage, and amount of assessment. Arranged alphabetically by names of property owners and chronologically thereunder. No index. Handwritten. 175 pages. 22 x 12.5 x 1.25. Basement, middle storeroom.

353. PAVING DUPLICATE
1907-1917. 1 volume.
Duplicate of special assessments for paving the streets and sidewalks in Frankfort Village, showing name of property owner, lot number, feet frontage, and amount of assessment. Arranged alphabetically by names of property owners and chronologically thereunder. No index. Handwritten. 182 pages. 22 x 12.5 x 1.25. Basement, middle storeroom.

354. STREET IMPROVEMENT DUPLICATE, CHILLICOTHE
1899-1915. 2 volumes.
Duplicate of special assessments for street improvements for city of Chillicothe, showing name of street, name of property owner, lot number, feet frontage, and amount of assessment. Arranged alphabetically under tabs by names of streets and alphabetically thereunder the names of property owners. No index. Handwritten. Average 240 pages. 22 x 12.5 x 2. Basement, middle storeroom.

355. CHILLICOTHE SEWER DUPLICATE
1899-1913. 1 volume.
Duplicate of sewer assessments for city of Chillicothe, showing name of lot owner, lot number, feet frontage, what part of lot, property valuation, direct and district assessments, and total amount due. Arranged alphabetically by names of property owners. No index. Handwritten. 180 pages. 22 x 12.5 x 1. Basement, middle storeroom.

356. SEWER DUPLICATE, CHILLICOTHE

1905-1914. 1 volume.

Duplicate of special assessments for sewer construction, showing name of sewer project, name of property owner, lot number, feet frontage, and total assessment. Arranged alphabetically under tabs by names of sewer projects and alphabetically thereunder by names of property owners. No index. Handwritten. 260 pages. 22 x 12.5 x 2. Basement, middle storeroom.

357. SPECIAL DUPLICATE [Partition and Ditch]

1908-1913. 1 volume.

Duplicate of special assessments covering costs in line fence viewing and other costs in partition fence cases; also a special assessments for township ditches in Huntington Township, showing name of property owner and amount of assessment. Arranged alphabetically by names of townships and alphabetically thereunder buy names of property owners. No index. Handwritten. 72 pages. 20 x 12 x .5. Auditor's vault.

358. CLASSIFIED TAX DUPLICATE

1933—. 2 volumes.

Duplicate of classified property taxes (intangibles classified according to productiveness), showing names of taxing district and property owner, kind of property, number of items, valuation, and amount of tax. Arranged alphabetically by names of taxing districts and alphabetically thereunder the names of property owners. No index. Typed. Average 450 pages. 15 x 10 x 3.5. Auditor's office, in safe.

359. TAX DUPLICATE, LIQUOR TRAFFIC

1883-1904, 1906-1915. 5 volumes.

Duplicate of liquor tax assessments, showing date, name of dealer, business location, owner of property, description of real estate on which business is located, amount unpaid on previous assessment, and amount of assessment. Arranged alphabetically by names of dealers and chronologically thereunder by dates of entry.No index. Average 80 pages. 20 x 18 x 1. 4 volumes, 1883-1904, Auditor's vault; 1 volume, 1906-1915, Basement, middle storeroom.

For other liquor tax records, see entry 433.

360. CIGARETTE DUPLICATE

1883-1909. 2 volumes.

Duplicate of cigarette traffic assessments, showing name of person assessed (licensee), date of assessment, date paid, name of owner of premises on which business is located, and description and location of premises. Arranged chronologically by years and alphabetically thereunder by names of licensees. No index. Handwritten. Average 96 pages. 18 x 12 x 1. Auditor's vault.

For other cigarette tax records, see entries 365, 427, 433.

Abstracts of Duplicates

361. ABSTRACT OF TAX DUPLICATE

1900-1910. 1 volume. 1830-1882 in Auditor's Duplicate, entry 346; 1911— in Record of Abstracts and Settlements, entry 387.

Auditor's abstract of real and personal property valuation for taxation in each taxing district, showing date, amount of property and value in each taxing district, tax rate levied for each fund, amount of tax assessed for each fund, and total amount assessed. Arranged alphabetically by names of taxing districts and chronologically thereunder by years. No index. Handwritten on printed forms. 96 pages. 22 x 17 x 1. Basement, middle storeroom.

For other real property abstracts, see entry 362; personal property abstracts, see entry 463.

362. ABSTRACT OF REAL PROPERTY

1914-1927. 238 Volumes. (labeled by years). Subtitled by names of taxing districts.

Auditor's record of real estate as listed for taxation, showing to whom assessed, description of tract or lot, number of acres arable, meadow, woodland, and cultivated land, total acreage, number of acres oil, coal, or other mineral land, land and building valuation, and total valuation. There is 1 volume for each taxing district, each year. Arranged alphabetically by names of property owners. No index. Handwritten. Average 180 pages. 18 x 12 x 1.25. Basement, middle storeroom.

For related records, see entries 361, 387.

Additions and Deductions (See also entries 477, 478)

363. ADDITIONS
1874-1928. 14 volumes. (labeled by years). 1929— in Auditor's Duplicate, entry 346.

Auditor's record of additions to tax duplicate by reason of error on previous duplicate, new buildings, or property improvements, showing name of property owner, to whom charged, taxing district, and amount of addition. Alphabetically arranged under tabs by names of taxing districts and alphabetically thereunder by names of property owners. No index. 1874-1922, handwritten; 1921-1928, typed. Average 155 pages. 14.5 x 12 x 1.25. 11 volumes, 1874-1922, Auditor's vault; 2 volumes. 1923-1926, Basement, rear storeroom; 1 volume, 1927-1928, Basement, middle storeroom.

364. DEDUCTION ORDERS
1885-1898. 1 volume.

Copies of tax deductions orders to county treasurer, showing dates, to whom allowed, reason for deduction, and amount of deduction. Arranged chronologically by dates of orders. No index. Handwritten on printed form. 100 pages. 12 x 8.5 x 1. Auditor's vault.

365. ADDITIONS, INHERITANCE, AND CIGARETTES
1917-1922. 6 volumes.

Record of additions to inheritance and cigarette tax duplicates, by reason of error on previous duplicates, or interest on delinquent assessments, showing date, name of taxpayer, which tax duplicate, and amount of tax. Arranged chronologically by dates of entry. No index. Handwritten. Average 100 pages. 14 x 10 x 1. Basement, rear storeroom.

For inheritance tax records, see entries 251-253, 384, 396; for cigarette tax records, see entries 360, or 27, 433.

Exemptions and Omissions

366. [Property Tax] EXEMPTIONS, CHILLICOTHE
1926. 1 volume.

Property tax exempt for 1926 and city of Chillicothe, such as churches, schools, cemeteries, hospitals, city and county property, and canal land, showing name of owner, and description and valuation of property. Arranged alphabetically by names of owners. No index. Handwritten and typed on printed forms. 60 pages. 12 x 10 x .5. Auditor's vault.

For subsequent records, see entry 367.

367. AUDITOR'S LIST, EXEMPT REAL AND PERSONAL PROPERTY
1929—. 1 volume.

Record of tax exempt property in Ross County, showing names of taxing district and owner, kind of property, location, description, and valuation of property. Arranged alphabetically by names of taxing districts and alphabetically thereunder by names of property owners. No index. Typed. 200 pages. (loose-leaf) 15 x 10 x 2. Auditor's office, in safe

For prior record of Chillicothe, see entry 366.

368. TAX OMISSIONS
1885-1891. 1 volume.

Auditor's record of taxes omitted from regular duplicate through error, showing name of property owner, taxing district, year, property valuation, text, penalty, total due, and date paid. Arranged alphabetically by names of taxing districts and alphabetically thereunder by names of property owners. No index. Handwritten. 80 pages. 18 x 14 x .5. Auditor's vault.

Tax Returns

369. ASSESSOR'S RETURNS, PERSONAL PROPERTY
1916-1929. 328 volumes. (labeled by years). Subtitled by names of taxing districts.

Returns of personal property assessments by township, ward, and district assessors, showing name and address of owner, itemized list as to kind of property, valuation of each item, and total valuation. Arranged alphabetically by names of personal property owners. No index. Handwritten on printed forms. Average 44 pages. 16 x 10.5 x .25. 211 volumes, 1916-1924, Basement, middle storeroom; 117 volumes, 1925-1929, Basement, front storeroom.

For subsequent records, see entry 370.

370. PERSONAL TAX RETURNS

1919—. 588 volumes. (labeled by years). Subtitled by names that taxing districts.

Returns of personal property as listed by owners for taxation, showing an itemized list of property and valuation. Returns of each taxing district are bound separately. Arranged alphabetically by names of property owners. No index. Handwritten on printed forms. Volumes vary from 150 pages 14 x 9 x 1 to 800 pages 14 x 9 x 5. 202 volumes, 1919-1924, Basement, middle storeroom; 230 volumes, 1925-1931, front storeroom; 145 volumes, 1932—, Auditor's vault.

For assessor's returns, see entry 369.

371. PROPERTY VALUATIONS

1874-1912. 9 file boxes. (6, 123, 168, 271, 294, 302, 347, 349, 365).

Auditor's copies of property returns and valuations for taxation of corporations, banks, and railroads, showing date, taxing district in which property is located, description of property, and valuation of property. Arranged chronologically by dates of returns. For index, see entry 330. Handwritten on printed forms. 10 x 5 x 14. Auditor's vault.

372. CORPORATION RETURNS

1888-1903. 1 volume.

Record of property valuation returns of incorporated companies doing business in Ross County, showing date, name of corporation, name of agent, home office, property valuation, and amount of tax. Arranged alphabetically by names of corporations and chronologically thereunder by years. No index. Handwritten. 208 pages. 12 x 10 x 2. Auditor's vault.

Refunds and Remitters

373. REFUNDER RECORD

1879-1888. 3 volumes.

Auditor's record of refunds on free toll road tax, in accordance with state law of 1878, showing name, taxing district, and amount of refund. Alphabetically arranged by names of payees. No index. Handwritten. Average 170 pages. 12 x 8 x 1.25. Auditor's vault.

For treasurer's record, see entry 479.

374. REFUNDER ORDER

1900-1917. 2 volumes.

Auditor's copies of orders on county treasurer to refund taxes erroneously charged and paid and readjustment of property values, showing date, name of property owner, tax duplicate on which charged, taxing district, amount of refund, reason for refund, and order number. Arranged chronologically by dates of orders and numerically by consecutive order numbers. No index. Handwritten on printed forms. Average 120 pages. 12 x 8.5 x 1. Auditor's vault.

For record of remitters, see entry 375.

375. REMITTERS [for Tax Deductions]

1917-1931. 3 volumes.

Auditor's record of remitter orders on county treasurer for deduction of taxes on real estate, by reason of error, or loss or damage to buildings, showing dates, order number, what duplicate, to whom, taxing district, and amount. Arranged chronologically by dates of orders and numerically by consecutive order numbers. No index. Handwritten on printed forms. Average 170 pages. 9 x 4 x 1.25. Auditor's vault.

For record of refund orders, see entry 374.

Delinquent Taxes (See also entries 487-492)

376. DELINQUENT RECORD

1823-1850. 1 volume.

Record of lands on which taxes are delinquent, showing names of taxing district and resident proprietor, name of nonresident proprietor, entry and survey numbers, original proprietor, original quantity, watercourse, range, township, and section numbers, acreage, number of years delinquent, amount of tax, penalty, and total due; also contains copies of treasurer's certificates of delinquency and copies of auditor's notice of sale, showing name of owner, original quantity, entry number, watercourse, acreage, valuation, taxes, penalty, interest due, to whom sold, amount sold for, if redeemed, and date. Also contains Delinquent List, entry 377. Arranged alphabetically by names of taxing districts, alphabetically thereunder by names of delinquent taxpayers, and chronologically thereunder. No index. Handwritten. 440 pages. 14 x 9 x 3.5. Auditor's vault.

For subsequent records, see entries 346, 379.

377. DELINQUENT LIST

1851-1874, 1879-1884. 30 volumes. (labeled by years), 1823-1850 in Delinquent Record, entry 376.

List of lands on which taxes are delinquent, showing names of taxing districts and owner, original quantity, entry number, watercourse, original proprietor, lot, township, and section numbers, acreage, valuation, tax, penalty, total due, and remarks. Arranged alphabetically by names of taxing districts and alphabetically thereunder by names of delinquent taxpayers. No index. Handwritten. Average 100 pages. 12 x 9 x 1. Auditor's vault.

378. DELINQUENT PERSONAL DUPLICATE

1906-1927. 14 volumes. (labeled by years).

Duplicate of delinquent personal taxes, showing names of taxing district and delinquent taxpayer, number of years delinquent, property valuation, dog tax, penalty, total due, and dates paid. Arranged alphabetically by names of taxing districts and alphabetically thereunder by names of delinquent taxpayers. No index. 1906-1916, 1924-1927, typed; 1917-1923, handwritten. Average 275 pages. 12.5 x 12 x 2. 6 volumes, 1906-1916, 1924, Auditor's vault; 7 volumes, 1917-1923, Basement, rear storeroom; 1 volume, 1925-1927, Basement, middle storeroom.

379. DELINQUENT TAX SALES

1851-1913 9 volumes.

Record of lands and lots returned by county treasurer as delinquent and listed to be sold for taxes due, showing names of taxing district and owner, acreage, entry and survey numbers, original quantity, original proprietor, watercourse, township, range, and section numbers, valuation of property, number of years delinquent, tax penalty, interest, and total due; also record of sales of lands for taxes due and unpaid, showing to whom sold, purchase price, cost of sale, charges due, total due, balance to owner, and date of redemption; also record of auditor's deeds to land sold for taxes due. Arranged alphabetically by names of taxing districts and alphabetically thereunder by names of delinquent taxpayers. Handwritten. Average 380 pages. 16 x 11 x 3. Auditor's vault.

For prior records, see entry 376.

380. FORFEITED LAND SALES

1910. 1 volume.

Auditor's record for 1910 of sales of land forfeited for unpaid taxes and assessments, showing date of sale, name of owner, description of property, quantity of land, valuation, to whom sold, amount of tax, penalties, interest due, amount sold for, and balance due owner. Arranged chronologically by dates of sales. Indexed alphabetically by names of property owners. Handwritten. 172 pages. 17 x 14 x 1.25. Basement, middle storeroom.

For prior subsequent records, see entry 381.

381. FORFEITED LAND RECORD

1882-1914. 1 volume.

Record of lands forfeited for nonpayment of taxes, showing names of taxing district and owner, township, original quantity, entry and survey numbers, valuation, number of years delinquent, tax, penalties, total due, date of sale, and when redeemed. Arranged alphabetically by names of taxing districts and alphabetically thereunder by names of owners. No index. Handwritten. 640 pages. 16 x 11 x 4.5. Auditor's vault.

For additional records, see entry 380.

382. RECORD OF SETTLEMENT OF DELINQUENT TAXES

1923—. 1 volume.

Record of delinquent tax payments, showing names of taxing district and property owner, description and quantity of land, land and building valuation, total valuation, amount of tax and penalty, and date paid. Arranged alphabetically by names of taxing districts, alphabetically thereunder by names of property owners, and chronologically thereunder by dates of payments. No index. Handwritten. 600 pages. 18 x 12 x 4. Auditor's vault.

383. DELINQUENT TAX CERTIFICATES

1925-1931. 2 volumes.

Duplicate certificates of redemption of lands forfeited or sold for taxes due and unpaid, showing date, name of delinquent owner, description of tract, amount of tax and penalty, interest due, and date paid. Arranged chronologically by dates of certificates, and also arranged numerically by consecutive certificate numbers. No index. Handwritten on printed forms. Average 108 pages. 8.5 x 6.5 x 1. Basement, middle storeroom.

Inheritance Tax (See also entries 251-253, 365, 496)

384. [Inheritance Tax] FINDINGS
1920—. 4 file boxes. (545, 596, 766, 930).

Auditor's copies of inheritance tax findings as certified by probate judge, showing date, name of estate, name of administrator or executor, valuation, amount of tax assessed, and to whom charged. Arranged chronologically by dates of findings. For index, see entry 330. Typed on printed forms. 10 x 5 x 14. Auditor's vault.

Settlements
(See also entering 505)

385. [Auditor's School Settlement] RECORD
1838-1915. 7 volumes. 1916— in Record of Abstracts and Settlements, entry 387.

Record of apportionments of school funds and settlements with the various school treasurers in county, showing date, name of school district, and amount; also abstracts of enumeration of unmarried youth between the ages of five and twenty-one years, showing date and total number of boys and girls for each district. Arranged alphabetically by names of school districts and chronologically thereunder. No index. Handwritten. Average 640 pages. 16 x 11 x 4. Auditor's vault.

386. SETTLEMENT RECORD
1914—. 3 volumes. 1854-1973 in Auditor's Duplicate, entry 346.

Auditor's record of settlements with various subdivisions of Ross County, showing receipts from all sources, amount due each fund, total amount due, and date of settlement. Arranged chronologically by dates of settlements and alphabetically thereunder by names of subdivisions. No index. Handwritten. Average 400 pages. 15 x 10 x 3.25. 2 volumes, 1914-1930, Auditor's vault; 1 volume, 1931—, Auditor's office.

387. RECORD OF ABSTRACTS AND SETTLEMENTS
1911—. 1 volume.

Auditor's abstract of tax duplicates, showing tax rate for each taxing district, state, county, township, and local levies, school levy under General Code section 7575, city or village levy, miscellaneous levy, total levy, acreage and valuation of land outside of municipalities, real estate valuation in municipalities, personal property valuation outside municipalities, personal property valuation of municipalities, total valuation, total tax levied, recapitalization of taxes distributed, February settlement sheet, general statement of treasurer's accounts, August settlement sheet, detailed statement of collateral inheritance tax collected by treasurer, and cigarette traffic tax settlement sheet. Also contains: Abstract of Tax Duplicate, entry 361; [Auditor's School Settlement] Record, 1916—, entry 385. Arranged chronologically under tabs by years and alphabetically thereunder by namcs of taxing districts. No index. Handwritten on printed forms. 292 pages. 24 x 16 x 2.5. Auditor's vault.

For other real property abstracts, see entry 362; for personal property abstracts, see entry 463.

Fiscal Accounts

Budgets and Appropriations

388. BUDGETS

1911—. 10 file boxes. (334, 346, 446, 487, 488, 492, 515, 543, 704, 821).

Copies of budgets for each taxing district, showing for each year the valuation, tax rate, amount of revenue by district tax, and amount allowed to each of the various funds. Arranged chronologically by years, for index, see entry 330. 1911-1921, Handwritten on printed forms; 1922—,typed on printed forms. 10 x 5 x 14. Auditor's vault.

389. APPROPRIATION LEDGER

1837-1846, 1874-1889. 3 volumes. 1827-1873 also in Auditor's Duplicate, entry 346.

Auditor's record of apportionment of funds to the various taxing districts in the county, showing amount due each fund in each district and date of settlement. Arranged alphabetically by names of taxing districts, alphabetically thereunder by names of funds, and chronologically thereunder by dates of settlement. No index. Handwritten. Average 280 pages. 18 x 12 x 2.25. Auditor's vault.

For subsequent records, see entry 390.

390. APPORTIONMENT OF TOWN AND TOWNSHIP FUNDS
1890—. 3 volumes.
Auditor's record of semiannual apportionment of funds due to township and municipalities, showing name of subdivision, amount due each fund, total due, date paid, order number, and to whom paid. Arranged alphabetically by names of subdivisions. No index. 1890-1932, handwritten; 1924—, typed. Average 310 pages. 18 x 12 x 2.5. Auditor's vault.
For prior records, see entry 389.

391. APPROPRIATION LEDGER
1913—. 10 volumes. (labeled by years).
Auditor's record of the various county funds, showing date, amount appropriated, and encumbered unexpected balance; also itemized expenditures, showing date, name of payee, for what, warrant number, and amount authorized. Arranged alphabetically under tabs by names of funds and chronologically thereunder. No index. Handwritten. Average 240 pages. 18 x 24 x 2. Auditor's vault.

General Accounts

392. JOURNAL
1855-1961. 1 volume.
Record of accounts with various taxing districts of county, showing date, amount due each district, and amount paid treasurer of taxing district. Arranged alphabetically by names the taxing districts and chronologically thereunder by dates of entry. No index. Handwritten. 400 pages. 12 x 8 x 3.25. Auditor's vault.

393. AUDITOR'S FUND RECORD
1892-1905. 3 volumes. (1-3).
Record of receipts and expenditures, showing date, order number, name of payer or payee, for what, amount, annual credit or debit to each fund, and balance in each fund. Arranged chronologically by dates of entry. No index. Handwritten. Average 320 pages. 20 x 16 x 2.5. Auditor's vault.

394. LEDGER
1853-1858, 1868-1874, 1910—. 4 volumes.
Auditor's daily record of receipts from all sources and of expenditures of county funds, showing credit, debit, and balance. Arranged under tabs by funds and chronologically thereunder. No index. Handwritten. Average 515 pages. 11 x 11.5

x 4. 2 volumes, 1853-1858, 1868-1874, Auditor's vault; 2 volumes, 1910—, Auditor's office.

395. AUDITOR'S RECEIPT BOOK
1867-1887. 4 volumes.

County treasurer's receipts issued to county auditor for money paid into treasury, showing dates, by whom paid, for what amount, and treasurer's stamp and signature. Arranged chronologically by dates of receipts. No index. Handwritten on printed forms. Average 250 pages. 8.5 x 7 x 2. Auditor's vault.

396. PAY-IN ORDERS
1926—. 18 volumes.

Auditor stub of pay-in orders, showing order number, what account, what fund, and date. Arranged chronologically by dates of entry and also numerically by consecutive order numbers. No index. Handwritten on printed forms. Average 125 pages. 7 x 3.5 x 1. Auditor's vault.

Special Accounts

397. FUNDED DEBT RECORD
1857-1872. 1 volume.

Record of the funded debt of Ross County, showing schedule of different bond issues, date and number of issue, date of maturity, names of purchasers, dates and amount of interest payments, and record of redemption. Arranged chronologically by dates of issue. No index. Handwritten. 270 pages. 12 x 8 x 2.25. Auditor's vault.

398. SINKING FUND RECORD
1923—. 1 volume.

Record of funds encumbered for payment of bonds and interest, showing receipts and disbursements of the sinking fund. Arranged alphabetically by names of county, township, and school divisions and alphabetically thereunder by names of bonds issues. No index. Handwritten. 280 pages. 20 x 14 x 2.25. Auditor's vault.

399. BOUNTY CLAIMS

1864-1867. 1 volume.

Record of Union soldiers' bounty claims, showing name, township, amount of claim, and record of payment. Arranged alphabetically by names of townships and chronologically thereunder. No index. Handwritten. 310 pages. 12 x 8 x 2.25. Auditor's vault.

400. WAR FUND

1861-1865. 1 volume.

Record of allotments by Union soldiers from Ross County to the dependents or assigns, showing company, name of soldier, name of assign or dependent, rank, amount of allotment, and amount advanced by Ross County to the fund. Arranged by companies and alphabetically thereunder by names of soldiers. No index. Handwritten. 290 pages. 18 x 12 x 2. Auditor's vault.

401. SOLDIERS' RELIEF

1887-1914. 5 volumes.

Record of disbursements of soldiers' relief fund, showing township or ward, name of payee (soldier, sailor, or widow of soldier or sailor), to whom paid, amount allowed, and remarks. Arranged by township or wards and alphabetically thereunder by names of payees. No index. Handwritten. Average 290 pages. 14 x 9 x 2.25. Auditor's vault.

402. SOLDIERS' RELIEF

1886-1922. 7 file boxes. (129, 417, 483, 484, 495, 607, 743).

Auditor's monthly account of disbursements of soldiers' relief fund, showing name, name of recipient, amount, company, regiment, and rank. Arranged chronologically by dates of entry. For index, see entry 330. Handwritten on printed forms. 10 x 5 x 14. Auditor's vault.

403. ACCOUNTS [Justice of Peace Transcripts]

1865-1867. 1 volume.

Record of accounts allowed for transcripts of justice of peace courts, showing date, an itemized account of cost and fees in each case, voucher number, and date paid. Arranged chronologically by dates of entry. No index. Handwritten. 400 pages. 12 x 8 x 3. Auditor's vault.

404. TIME BOOK
1855-1858. 1 volume.

Record of laborers' time on new courthouse building, showing name, date, number of days worked each week, rate for day, total per week, and date paid. Arranged chronologically. No index. Handwritten. 210 pages. 15 x 9 x 1.5. Auditor's vault.

405. RECORD OF ACCOUNTS
1867-1885. 1 volume.

Record of accounts with contractors, showing project or job, amount of bid, date, extra allowance, payments to contractor on account, for what, amount, and warrant number. Arranged chronologically by dates of entry. Indexed alphabetically names of contractors. Handwritten. 360 pages. 18 x 12 x 2. Auditor's vault.

406. RECORD OF ESTIMATES
1916—. 2 volumes.

Record of estimates on contracts let by county commissioners, showing date, contract number, what construction, name and address of contractor, volume and page number of Commissioners' Journal, entry 2, bids received, award record, estimates paid on account, and recapitalization of funds. Arranged chronologically by dates of entry. Indexed alphabetically by names of contractors. Handwritten on printed forms. Average 400 pages. 16 x 11 x 3. Auditor's vault.

407. LEDGER [Bridge Funds]
1902-1903. 1 volume.

Ledger of bridge funds, showing credit and debit to fund with name of bridge, name of contractor, date, and amount paid on account. Arranged chronologically by dates of entry. Indexed alphabetically by names of bridges or creditors. Handwritten. 460 pages. 16 x 12 x 3.5. Auditor's vault.

408. RECORD OF FEES
1907—. 5 volumes.

Record of fees collected, showing date, from whom, for what service, and amount. Arranged chronologically by dates of entry. No index. Handwritten. Average 240 pages. 16 x 11 x 2. 4 volumes, 1907-1931, Auditor's vault; 1 volume, 1932—, Auditor's office.

409. FEES
1904-1911. 1 volume.

Record of fees turned in by county officials, showing what office, for what service, amount, date, credit, and what fund. Arranged chronologically by dates of entry. No index. Handwritten. 380 pages. 16 x 11 x 3.5. Auditor's vault.

For statement of fees, see entry 432.

Bills and Orders

410. DUE BILLS
1855-1857. 1 volume.

Copies of due bills issued for labor performed on new county courthouse, showing name of payee, amount, date issued, and date paid. Arranged chronologically by dates of issue. No index. Handwritten on printed forms. 110 pages. 12 x 8 x 1. Auditor's vault.

411. AUDITOR'S DOCKET, BILLS FILED, INFIRMARY
1904-1932. 1 volume. 1933— in Auditor's Docket, Commissioners' Bills, entry 412.

Record of infirmary bills filed, showing date of entry, date of bill, consecutive number, name of creditor, for what, amount, date filed, date approved, amount approved, date paid, warrant number, and remarks. Arranged chronologically by dates of entry, and also numerically by consecutive bill numbers. No index. Handwritten. 600 pages. 18 x 12 x 4.5. Basement, middle storeroom.

For bills filed with infirmary directors, 1841-1874, see entry 462.

412. AUDITOR'S DOCKET, COMMISSIONERS' BILLS
1923—. 3 volumes.

Auditor's record of bills filed against the county commissioners, showing name of creditor, for what, amount of bill, date filed, date approved, amount approved, date paid, and warrant number. Also contains: Docket of Bills Filed, entry 21; Auditor's Docket, Bills Filed, Infirmary, 1933—, entry 411. Arranged chronologically by dates of filing. No index. 1923-1933, handwritten; 1933—, typed. Average 320 pages. 18 x 14 x 3. 2 volumes, 1923-1932, Auditor's vault; 1 volume, 1932—, Auditor's office.

413. RECORD OF ORDERS

1841-1891. 11 volumes.

Record of orders drawn on county treasurer, showing date, to whom, or what, what fund, order number, and amount of order. Arranged chronologically by dates of entry, and also numerically by consecutive ordered numbers. No index. Handwritten. Average 380 pages. 18 x 12 x 4. Auditor's vault.

For subsequent records, see entries 393, 415.

Vouchers and Warrants

414. VOUCHERS CANCELLED

1843—. 478 file boxes. (4, 5, 7, 8, 12, 13, 15-77, 143, 145-149, 153, 159, 162-165, 171-174, 190-194, 207, 208, 230, 239-244, 248, 249, 253, 257, 260, 261, 266, 267, 269, 273-279, 281, 290-292, 296, 297, 300, 301, 303-309, 311, 314, 316-330, 337-344, 346, 351, 357-360, 372, 376, 378, 381-391, 393, 395, 397-399, 403-406, 408-411, 414, 416, 439, 440, 442-444, 449-453, 455, 456, 461, 472-479, 480, 487, 488, 490-494, 497-499, 501-503, 507, 508, 510, 512-514, 516, 519, 520, 522-524, 527-529, 532-534, 536, 538, 547, 548, 551-558, 560, 562, 564, 565, 567, 568, 570, 574-578, 580-584, 586-589, 591, 593, 595-597, 599-604, 607-611, 614-616, 618-628, 633-637, 639-642, 644-647, 649-653, 662-664, 667, 673-679, 691-698, 702-710, 720-724, 730-732, 734, 735, 740, 741, 747, 758-765, 763-767, 774, 775, 791-795, 800, 801, 809-815, 819-823, 826-831, 834-839, 845, 849-860, 865-870, 874-876, 880-885, 894-897, 900-903, 905-909, 912, 913, 915-917, 921, 925-932, 935-940, 946, 947, 954-957, 961-965, 970, 971, 974, 976, 977, 983).

Vouchers issued by various county officials who are authorized to issue vouchers in payment of bills and claims against Ross County, showing date, voucher number, name of payee, for what, and amount. Arranged chronologically by dates of entry. For index, see entry 330. Handwritten on printed forms. 10 x 5 x 14. Auditor's vault.

415. AUDITOR'S JOURNAL OF WARRANTS ISSUED AND PAYMENTS INTO TREASURY

1905—. 14 volumes. (2-15).

Auditor's record of warrants issued (in front half of each volume), showing date, name of payee, for what, warrants number, and credited to county treasury, debit what fund; also record of payments into county treasury (in back half of each volume), showing date, name of payer, for what, pay-in order number, amount debited county treasury, and what fund credited. Arranged chronologically by dates of entry, and also numerically by consecutive warrant numbers. No index. Handwritten. Average 480 pages. 20 x 14 x 3.5. 9 volumes, 1909-1933, Auditor's vault; 3 volumes, 1933—, Auditor's office.

For prior record of orders on the treasury, see entries 393, 413.

416. WARRANT REGISTER
1920—. 2 volumes.

Auditor's record of warrants issued, showing dates, to whom, amount, and for what. Arranged under tabs by names of funds and chronologically thereunder by dates of entry. No index. Handwritten. Average 225 pages. 18 x 15 x 2. Auditor's office.

417. COURT WARRANTS
1904—. 6 volumes. (1-6).

Auditor's record of court warrants issued, showing date, name of payee, warrant number, what court, and for what. Arranged chronologically by dates of entry, and also numerically by consecutive warrant numbers. No index. Handwritten. Average 280 pages. 18 x 12 x 2.25. 5 volumes, 1904-1932, Auditor's vault; 1 volume, 1933—, Auditor's office.

418. WARRANTS
1849—. 136 file boxes. (14, 78-116, 211-229, 259, 270, 285, 370, 395, 400, 407, 423, 425, 434, 441, 445, 500, 505, 507, 514, 515, 525, 535, 537, 539, 543-546, 563, 566, 569, 579, 585, 592-594, 605, 617, 629, 638, 648, 655-661, 669, 670, 682-584, 699, 713-715, 725, 736, 744, 745, 770-773, 817, 832, 833, 841, 862, 878, 886, 898, 899, 910, 924, 942, 953, 968, 978).

Warrants on county treasurer issued by county auditor for payment of bills and claims for county funds, which have been cancelled and returned to auditor's office, showing date, name of payee, and warrant number; also soldiers' relief, 1886—. Also contains: Cancelled warrants [Mothers' Pensions], 1913-1932, 1936—, entry 422. Arranged chronologically by dates of issue. For index, see entry 330. Handwritten on printed forms. 10 x 5 x 14. Auditor's vault.

419. COURT WARRANTS [Redeemed]
1904—. 32 file boxes. (13, 181-185, 285, 299, 312, 350, 373, 378, 435-438, 458, 526, 550, 590, 643, 665, 690, 726, 742, 780, 808, 868, 891, 918, 952, 981).

Warrants on county treasurer issued by county auditor for payments of witnesses, jury, and court fees, which have been cancelled and returned to auditor's office, showing date, name of payee, warrant number, what court, and for what. Arranged chronologically. For index, see entry 330. Handwritten on printed forms. 10 x 5 x 14. Auditor's vault.

420. SCHOOL WARRANTS
1862-1920. 31 file boxes. (10, 109, 186, 199, 203, 209, 282, 283, 287, 288, 318, 320, 332, 333, 345, 355, 377, 379, 380, 401, 402, 412, 413, 421, 422, 447, 448, 454, 459, 481, 482).

Original warrants issued for payment of bills and claims approved by board of education, showing date, warrant number, school district, name of payee, amount, for what, what fund, signature of clerk of board of education, counter signature of auditor, and date redeemed by treasurer. Arranged chronologically by dates redeemed. For index, see entry 330. Handwritten on printed forms. 10 x 5 x 14. Auditor's vault.

421. CANCELLED WARRANTS [Blind Pensions]
1933-1935. 3 file boxes. (949, 960, 979). 1898-1932, 1936— in Warrants, entry 418.

Blind pension warrants, showing date, name of recipient, amount, and date paid. Arranged chronologically by dates issued. For index, see entry 330. Handwritten on printed forms. 10 x 5 x 14. Basement, rear storeroom.

422. CANCELLED WARRANTS [Mothers' Pensions]
1933-1935. 6 file boxes. (943, 948, 958, 966, 975, 982). 1913-1932, 1936— in Warrants, entry 418.

Warrants issued on mothers' pension fund, showing date, name of recipient, amount, and date paid. Arranged chronologically by dates of issue. For index, see entry 330. Handwritten on printed forms. Average 200 pages. 16 x 5 x 1.5. 92 volumes, 1874—, Auditor's vault; 19 volumes, 1930-1935, Basement, middle storeroom.

Licenses

424. DOG TAG APPLICATIONS

1919—. 2 cardboard boxes, 5 file boxes. (840, 889, 904, 931, 972).

Applications for dog tag licenses, showing application and tag numbers, amount of tag fee, age, color, breed, and sex of dog, and signature and address of applicant. No orderly arrangement. 1919-1932, no index; for index, 1933—, see entry 330. Handwritten on printed forms. Cardboard boxes, 16 x 14 x 10; file boxes, 10 x 5 x 14. 2 cardboard boxes, 1919-1932, Basement, middle storeroom; 5 file boxes, 1933—, Auditor's vault.

425. DOG LICENSE AND KENNEL REGISTER

1918—. 7 volumes.

Auditor's record of dog and kennel licenses issued, showing tag number, name and address of applicant, age, color, kind of hair, and breed of dogs, number of dogs kept, and registration fee. Arranged numerically by consecutive license numbers. No index. Typed. Average 210 pages. 18 x 12 x 1.5. 6 volumes, 1918-1935, Auditor's vault; 1 volume, 1935—, Auditor's office.

426. AUTO LICENSE APPLICATIONS

1924-1927. 14 file boxes.

Original copies of applications by motor vehicle owners for licenses, showing date, license number, name of applicant, make of vehicle, style, horse-power, and model. Arranged chronologically by dates of applications. No index. Type on printed forms. 10 x 4.5 x 14. Basement, middle storeroom.

427. CIGARETTE LICENSE RECORD

1921—. 4 volumes.

Record of licenses issued to traffic in cigarette, showing date, name of licensee, business location, name of owner of building, description of property where business is conducted, and amount of fee. Arranged chronologically by dates of issue. No index. Typed. Average 140 pages. 15 x 10 x 1. 3 volumes, 1921-1931, Auditor's vault; 1 volume, 1932—, Auditor's office.

For other cigarette tax records, see entries 360, 433, 434.

428. COSMETIC LICENSE RECORD

1933-1934. 1 volume.

Record of licenses issued to dealers in cosmetics, showing date of license, name and address of licensee, and amount of fee. Arranged chronologically by dates of licenses. No index. Typed. 160 pages. 12 x 10 x 1.25. Auditor's vault.

429. BEVERAGE LICENSE RECORD

1933—. 1 volume. Last entry 1934.

Record of licenses issued to dealers in nonintoxicating beverages, showing date issued, name of licensee, business location, and amount of fee. Arranged chronologically by dates of issue. No index. Typed. 200 pages. 12 x 10 x 1.5. Auditor's vault.

430. VENDORS' LICENSE RECORD

1935—. 4 file boxes. (labeled by years).

Auditor's copies of applications for vendors' licenses, showing name of retail dealer, business location, kind of business, and date license was issued. Arranged chronologically by dates of issue. No index. Typed on printed forms. 10 x 5 x 14. Auditor's vault.

Reports

431. AUDITOR'S STATEMENT OF MOTOR VEHICLE TAXES

1925-1935. 2 volumes.

Auditor's daily and monthly reports of motor vehicle license fees collected, showing date, registration district, type of vehicle, and amount of fee. Arranged chronologically by dates of reports. No index. Typed. Average 670 pages. 15 x 17 x 5. Basement, middle storeroom.

432. STATEMENTS [of Fees]

1911-1923. 3 file boxes. (200, 297, 420).

Copies of auditor's monthly statement of fees collected by various county officials, showing date, amount, and for what service. Arranged chronologically by dates of statements. For index, see entry 330. 1911-1914, handwritten on printed forms; 1915-1923, types on printed forms. 10 x 5 x 14. Auditor's vault.

For related records, see entry 409.

433. CIGARETTE AND LIQUOR RETURNS
1900-1920. 10 file boxes. (231, 232, 293, 313, 335, 362, 364, 391, 394, 518).

Copies of auditor's reports of liquor traffic license fees, showing date, number of licenses issued, and amount of fees collected. Also contains cigarette returns, entry 434. Arranged chronologically by dates or reports. For index, see entry 330. Handwritten on printed forms. 10 x 5 x 14. Auditor's vault.

For other cigarette tax records, see entries 360, 365, 427; for other liquor tax records, see entry 359.

434. CIGARETTE RETURNS
1921—. 4 file boxes. (798, 807, 890, 922). 1900-1920 in Cigarette and Liquor Returns, entry 433.

Copies of auditor's reports of cigarette traffic license fees, showing date, number of licenses issued, and amount of fees collected. Arranged chronologically by dates of reports. For index, see entry 330. Typed on printed forms. 10 x 5 x 14. Auditor's vault.

For license record, see entry 427.

435. STATEMENTS [of Fines]
1917—. 3 file boxes. (491, 513, 737, 879).

Auditor's copies of statements from justices of piece of fines assessed and collected in justices courts of Ross County, showing dates, what case, and amount. Arranged chronologically by dates of statements. For index, see entry 330. Typed on printed forms. 10 x 5 x 14. Auditor's vault.

436. EXAMINATION REPORTS
1909—. 6 volumes.

Auditor's record of state examiners reports of the condition of county, township, and school accounts, showing date, and balance in each account. Arranged alphabetically by names of officers and departments and chronologically thereunder by dates of reports. No index. Typed. Average 140 pages. 14 x 11 x 1. Auditor's vault.

437. REPORTS [to State Auditor]
1907—. 3 file boxes. (458, 701, 914).

Copies of county auditor's reports to state auditor, showing date, receipts, expenditures, and balance of each county fund. Arranged chronologically by dates of reports. For index, see entry 330. 1907-1914, handwritten on printed forms; 1915—, typed on printed forms. 10 x 5 x 14. Auditor's vault.

438. BALANCE SHEETS
1908—. 21 file boxes. (128, 353, 356, 365, 367, 369, 415, 424, 457, 460, 509, 521, 541, 549, 598, 618, 622, 630, 666, 919, 967).

Copies of treasurer's daily balance sheets, showing date, receipts, disbursements, and balance of each county fund. Arranged chronologically by dates of sheets. For index, see entry 330. 1908-1926, handwritten on printed forms; 1926—, typed on printed forms. 10 x 5 x 14. Auditor's vault.

439. AUDITOR'S FINANCIAL REPORT
1910—. 7 file boxes. (2, 128, 352, 459, 471, 511, 941).

Copies of auditor's monthly and semiannual reports, showing date, total receipts from all sources, total disbursements, amount of receipts into and disbursements for each fund, and balance of each fund. Arranged chronologically by dates of reports. For index, see entry 330. 1910-1914, handwritten on printed forms; 1915—, typed on printed forms. 10 x 5 x 14. Auditor's vault.

440. [Indebtedness] REPORTS
1873—. 12 file boxes. (9, 37, 92, 141, 205, 272, 382, 401, 559, 716, 841, 929).

Original indebtedness reports submitted by township and municipal finance officials to county auditor, showing date and detailed, itemized account of indebtedness of the subdivision. Arranged chronologically by dates or reports. For index, see entry 330. 1873-1924, handwritten on printed forms; 1925—, typed on printed forms. 10 x 5 x 14. Auditor's vault.

441. [Interest] STATEMENTS
1925—. 3 file boxes. (542, 612, 654).

Statements by depositories of county funds of interest earned on county funds on deposit, showing date, name of depository, and amount of interest. Arranged chronologically by dates of statements. For index, see entry 330. Typed on printed forms. 10 x 5 x 14. Auditor's vault.

442. [Bank] STATEMENTS

1913—. 6 file boxes. (366, 417, 485, 489, 490, 534).

Copies of monthly statements to auditor from depositories (banks) of county funds, showing date, deposits, withdrawals, and balance. Arranged chronologically by dates of statements. For index, see entry 330. Typed on printed forms. 10 x 5 x 14. Auditor's vault.

443. SCHOOL SETTLEMENT FUND

1903—. 6 volumes.

Statement of settlements with school treasurers, showing date, source, and amount of collection; also distribution statement. Arranged chronologically by dates of statements. Indexed alphabetically by names of school districts. Handwritten on printed forms. Average 460 pages. 18 x 12 x 3.5. 4 volumes, 1903-1925, Basement, middle storeroom; 1 volume, 1926-1931, Auditor's vault; 1 volume. 1932—, Auditor's office.

444. [REPORT TO SCHOOL COMMISSIONER]

1850-1854. In Miscellaneous Records, entry 28.

Copies of the county auditor's statistical and financial reports to the state school commissioner, showing number of school districts, number of schools in each district, enumeration, enrollment, source of receipts, and itemized account of disbursements.

Bonds

Official Bonds (See also entries 463, 514-516).

445. RECORD OF OFFICIAL BONDS

1916—. 1 volume.

Auditor's record of surety bonds filed by elected county officials, showing name of official, what office, amount of bond, bonding company or names of sureties, and date of approval. Arranged chronologically by dates of approval. Indexed alphabetically by names of officials. Typed. 500 pages. 20 x 15 x 4. Auditor's office, in safe.

446. [School Clerks'] BONDS

1907—. 6 file boxes. (284, 313, 336, 559, 737, 872). 48 bonds.

Copies of surety bonds of township school clerk-treasurers, showing date, amount of bond, names of sureties, and what district. Arranged chronologically by dates of bonds. For index, see entry 330. 1907-1920, handwritten on printed forms; 1921—, typed on printed forms. 10 x 5 x 14. 6 file boxes, 1907-1931, Auditor's vault; 48 bonds (loose), 1932—, Auditor's office, in safe.

447. [Official] BONDS

1881-1917, 1932—, 7 file boxes. (280, 327, 439, 561, 634, 784, 888). 1 pigeonhole.

Copies of surety bonds of various elected county officials, showing date, amount of bond, what office, names of sureties and approval of county commissioners. Arranged chronologically by dates of bonds. For index, see entry 330. 1881-1917, handwritten on printed forms; 1932—, typed on printed forms. 10 x 5 x 14. 7 file boxes, 1881-1917, Auditor's vault; 1 pigeonhole, 1932—, Auditor's office, in safe.

Debenture Bonds (See also entry 462)

448. REDEEMED BONDS [Improvements]

1853-1898. Estimated 1,650 bonds in 22 bundles.

County bonds which have been authorized by county commissioners and issued to finance new county buildings, free turnpike, road improvements, and new bridges, showing amount of bond, series, for what purpose issued, rates of interest, and date redeemed. No orderly arrangement. No index. Handwritten on printed form. Sizes of bundles vary. Basement, middle storeroom.

449. REDEEMED BONDS [Railroad]

1868-1881. Estimated 900 bonds in 9 bundles.

Railroad bonds issued under state statute authorizing such issuance by counties, showing amount of bond, series, for what railroad project, and date redeemed. No orderly arrangement. No index. Handwritten on printed forms. Sizes of bundles vary. Basement, middle storeroom.

450. REDEEMED BONDS [Infirmary, Roads, Bridges]

1890-1921. 11 file boxes. (154-157, -258, 268, 291, 356, 431, 432, 482).

County bonds authorized by county commissioners and issued to finance erection of new county infirmary building, road improvements, and bridge bond refunding issues, showing amount of bond, series, for what purpose issued, rate of interest, and date redeemed. Arranged numerically by bond numbers. For index, see entry 330. Handwritten on printed forms. 10 x 5 x 14. Auditor's vault.

451. RECORD OF BONDS
1920—. 1 volume.
Auditor's record of bonds issued by authority of county commissioners to finance various county improvements as roads, bridges, and buildings, showing date of issue, for what, total amount issued, interest rate, maturity day, and to whom sold. Arranged chronologically by dates of issue. Indexed alphabetically by names of bond issues. Typed. 500 pages. 20 x 15 x 4. Auditor's office, in safe.

Enumeration Records

452. [Militia] ENROLLMENT
1864. 1 volume.
Enrollment for 1864 of male residents of Ross County between the ages of eighteen and forty-five years for military duty, showing name, age, residence and remarks. Arranged alphabetically by names of township or towns and alphabetically thereunder by names of enrollees. No index. Handwritten. 180 pages. 16 x 12 x 1.25. Basement, middle storeroom.

453. MILITARY AND WAR RECORDS
1861-1865. 3 file boxes. (255, 256, 286)
Enumeration of male residents of Ross County between the age of eighteen and forty-five years for military purposes as returned by township and district assessors; also record of moneys paid into Ross County war fund for relief of dependents of soldiers and sailors, showing date, name of payee, and amount; also record of enrollments of Ross County soldiers, showing company, regiment, rank, and year of enumeration. Enumeration record, arranged chronologically by years, and record of receipts, by dates of payment. For index, see entry 330. Handwritten on printed forms. 10 x 5 x 14. Auditor's vault.

For other records, see entries 454, 455.

454. ENUMERATION OF SOLDIERS AND SAILORS
1900—. 25 volumes.

Enumeration of Ross County soldiers and sailors (living) for 1900 who served in the Mexican, Civil, and Spanish-American wars, and the Philippine Insurrection, showing name, what branch of service, what war, company, regiment, battery, or vessel, rank, and address. Arranged alphabetically by names of townships, towns, and wards, and alphabetically thereunder by names of soldiers and sailors. No index. Handwritten. Average 65 pages. 10 x 10 x .5. Basement, middle storeroom.

For related records, see entries 453, 455.

455. QUADRENNIAL ENUMERATION
1903. 2 volumes.

Enumeration record for 1903 of male inhabitants of Ross County as returned by township and ward assessors, showing name, color, occupation, whether freeholder, and address. Arranged alphabetically by names of townships, and wards and alphabetically thereunder by names of inhabitants. No index. Handwritten. Average 320 pages. 8 x 12 x 2.5. Auditor's vault.

For other records of enumeration, see entries 453, 454.

456. SCHOOL REPORTS
1867-1906. 9 file boxes. (144, 150, 176, 254, 295, 371, 391, 419, 462).

Reports by township and district assessors of enumeration of school age youth; also description of school property, showing date, name of district, name and age of youth, name of parent or guardian, description and location of school building, and inventory of furnishings and equipment. Arranged chronologically by dates of reports. For index, see entry 330. Handwritten on printed forms. 10 x 5 x 14. Auditor's vault.

For subsequent school enumeration records, see entry 457.

457. [School] ENUMERATION REPORTS
1907—. 11 file boxes. (124, 295, 336, 354, 462, 495, 423, 606, 681, 777, 846).

Copies of enumeration reports of school age youths, by district, showing age, number of males, number of females, total for each district, and date of report. Arranged chronologically. For index, see entry 330. Handwritten on printed forms. 10 x 5 x 14. Auditor's vault.

For prior records, see entry 456.

458. ENUMERATION, DEAF, DUMB AND BLIND
1906-1910. 2 file boxes. (8, 371).
Original reports to auditor by township and ward assessors of number of deaf, dumb, and blind persons, showing date, subdivision or ward, name and address, age, name of parent or guardian, and date filed. Arranged chronologically by dates of filing. For index, see entry 330. Handwritten on printed forms. 10 x 5 x 14. Auditor's vault.

Miscellaneous

459. UNCLAIMED ACCOUNTS
1872-1888. 1 volume. Discontinued.
Auditor's record of unclaimed money due from county funds such as court costs and witness fees, showing for what, to whom due, amount, order number, and date paid. Arranged chronologically by dates of payments. No index. Handwritten. 208 pages. 16 x 12 x 1.5. Auditor's vault.

460. RECORD OF AUTO AND TRUCK OWNERS, ROSS COUNTY
1925. 1 volume.
Auditor's list of automobiles and trucks owned in Ross County, showing name and address of owner, type of vehicle, and year. Arranged alphabetically by names of townships and municipalities and alphabetically thereunder by names of owners. No index. Typed. 200 pages. 14 x 12 x 1.5. Basement, middle storeroom.

461. MILITARY CERTIFICATES
1862-1865. 1 volume.
Auditor's record of certificates issued on Ross County military fund, showing date, certificate number, to whom issued, and amount. Arranged numerically by consecutive certificate numbers. No index. AHandwritten. 180 pages. 12 x 8 x 1.25. Auditor's vault.

462. MISCELLANEOUS [Papers]
1841-1874. Estimated 250 bundles in 1 box.
Miscellaneous original papers including bills filed with infirmary directors, redeemed county road and bridge bonds, monthly financial reports of various county officials to the county commissioner, and statistical financial reports of town and city boards of education to county auditor. No orderly arrangement. No index.

Bundles average 9 x 4 x 2.5; wooden box, 14 x 20 x 26. Basement, middle storeroom.

For other infirmary bill records, see entry 411; road and bridge bonds, entry 448, 450; county officials' reports to commissioners, entry 10.

463. DAY BOOK

1858-1874. 1 volume.

Record of miscellaneous items such as tax levies for townships, municipals and school districts, special levies, copies of township trustees and school board certifications of funds required for operating subdivision for ensuing year, receipts and expenditures of various county funds, abstracts of personal property as listed for taxation, copies of bonds filed by elected county officials, county commissioners' report to common pleas court, and contractor's bond on construction of county infirmary, showing dates, amounts, and other pertinent data. Arranged chronologically by dates of entry. No index. Handwritten. 522 pages. 18 x 12 x 3.5. Auditor's vault.

For other records of tax levies, see entries 335, 336, 464; fiscal accounts, entries 388-409; abstracts a personal property taxes, entry 361,387; official bonds, entries 445,447; commissioners' reports, entry 7.

464. MISCELLANEOUS RECORD

1871-1891. 1 volume.

Record of miscellaneous items including tax levies for various taxing districts, levies for school purposes, copies of correspondence from state auditor, contract agreements and bonds of contractors on county infirmary construction, annual financial statement of county commissioners, inspector's report of condition of county treasury, and clipped copies of legal advertising applying to different items recorded, showing date, and other pertinent data. Arranged chronologically by dates of entry. No index. Handwritten. 500 pages. 18 x 12 x 4. Auditor's vault.

For other records of tax levies, see entries 335, 336, 464; reports on condition of county treasury, entry 285, 436.

Weights and Measures

465. [Sealer's] RECORD

1924—. 3 volumes. Prior records missing.

Record of tests and examinations of scales and measures made by deputy sealer of weights and measures, showing date, name of vendor, type of scale or weighting device, type of measure, finding, kind of business, and address. Arrange the chronologically. No index. Handwritten. Average 180 pages. 16 x 14 x 1.25. Auditor's vault.

The office of county treasurer was established by an act of the Northwest Territory in 1792 and continued by the state of Ohio.[1] Although the constitution of 1802 made no provision for the office of county treasurer, it was created by the legislative act of 1803.[2] The treasurer, appointed by the associate judges in 1803 and by the county commissioners in 1804, was required to take an oath and give bond for the faithful performance of the duties of his office, and was subject to removal by the appointing power.[3] The treasurer remained an appointive official until 1827 when the office became an elective one by popular vote in the county.[4] Although it did not specifically create the office, the constitution of 1851 stated that no person shall hold the office of treasurer for more than four years in any six. This provision was repealed in 1933 by an amendment authorizing any county to adopt a charter form of government.[5] Interpreting the constitutional provision, the legislatures fixed the term of office at two years in 1859.[6] The term of office continued at two years until 1936 when it was extended to four years.[7] Until 1906 the county treasurer received his remuneration from fees; since that date his salary has been determined by law according to the population of the county.[8] In 1937 the Ross County treasurer's salary was $3,300.[9]

The duties of the treasurer were defined by statute in the earlier period and specified in detailed by the acts of 1827 and 1831 repealing previous acts. The provisions of the latter act, all those subject to amendment and repeal, furnish the basis for subsequent legislation and laid the basis for the present duties of the treasurer, which do not differ greatly from those prescribed by the earlier statutes.

In 1803 the treasurer was given his present duty of giving public notice of the tax duplicate.

---

1. Pease, *op. cit.,* 68-69.
2. *Laws of Ohio,* I, 97.
3. *Ibid.,* I, 97-98; II, 154.
4. *Ibid.,* XXV, 25-32.
5. *Ohio Const. 1851,* Art, X, sec. 3 (Amendment, 1933).
6. *Laws of Ohio,* LVI, 105.
7. *Ibid.,* CXVI, pt. ii, 184.
8. *Ibid.,* XCVIII, 89.
9. Ohio Auditor of State, *Annual Report,* 1937, 366.

On receiving from the county auditor a duplicate of the taxes assessed upon the property of the county, the treasurer prepares and posts notices in three places in each township including the place in which elections are held; and inserts the notice for six consecutive weeks in the newspaper having the largest circulation in the county.[10] He receives money in payment of taxes levied for the county, for the state, and for other purposes, and gives the payer a receipt.[11] In the earlier years of the office the treasurer was required to give announcement of the time he would be in the respective townships of the county and in his office at the seat of justice to receive tax collections. Since 1858 the treasurer has been authorized to prescribe the semiannual payment of taxes for assessments levied upon real estate or upon delinquent real estate taxes or assignments.[12] Moreover, since 1908, the commissioners have been authorized to extend the time for paying taxes for not more than thirty days after the time fixed by law.[13]

After each semiannual collection of taxes, the treasurer is required to report to the auditor showing the amount of taxes received in each taxing district in the county since the last settlement. Since 1904 the semiannual settlements have been made under the heads of liquor, cigarette, inheritance, delinquent personal, road, and general taxes. The treasurer keeps his accounts in books which enable him to compile such reports.[14]

After the taxes are collected and immediately after each settlement with the county auditor, the county treasurer, upon the presentation of the proper warrant from the auditor, pays to the township treasurer, city or village treasurer, the treasurer of the school district, or treasurer of any "legally constituted board authorized by law to receive the funds or proceeds of any special tax levy," or other officer delegated with authority to receive such funds, all money in the treasury belonging to such boards and subdivisions.[15] In addition, after the treasurer has made each settlement with the county auditor, he is required to pay to the state treasurer, on warrant from the state auditor, "the full amount of all sums" found by the latter to belong to the state.[16]

---

10. *Laws of Ohio,* I, 98; XXIX, 291; LII, 124.
11. G. C. sec. 2650; *Laws of Ohio,* XXIX, 292; LXXVI, 70; LXXXV, 327.
12. *Laws of Ohio,* V, 32; LVI, 101.
13. *Ibid.,* XCIX, 435; CXIV, 730; CXV, pt. ii, 226.
14. G. C. sec. 2643; *Laws of Ohio,* XXIX, 296; XCVII, 458.
15. G. C. sec. 2689; R. S. 1122; *Laws of Ohio,* LVI, 101.
16. *Laws of Ohio,* LVI, 101; CXIV, 732.

Another function of the county treasurer, which had its inception in the earlier years of the office, is the collection of delinquent taxes. It was and is his duty to assess a penalty on the tax duplicate with nonpayment of taxes - which penalty when collected, is paid to the treasurer's fund. If the treasurer is unable to collect the delinquent taxes, he is authorized to apply to the clerk of court of common pleas who serves notice to show cause why such taxes were not paid. The court may enter a rule against the delinquent taxpayer for the payment and cost and enforce it by attachment.[17]

During the last decade provision has been made for the installment payments of delinquent taxes without interest or penalty. In 1931 it was provided that delinquent taxes, assessments, and penalties charged on the tax duplicate against any entry of real estate might be paid in installments during five consecutive semiannual taxpaying periods "whether such real estate had been certified as delinquent or not."[18] The Whittemore Act, passed as an emergency measure in 1933, provided for the collection in installments, without interest or penalty, of delinquent real estate assessments. Anyone electing to pay such delinquent real property taxes and assessments in installments pursuant to this act may, at any installment period, pay the entire unpaid balance, in which event no interest shall be charged or collected on the amount so paid. In 1934 the benefits of the act were extended to include delinquent personal and classified taxes.[19] With slight alteration the law was re-enacted in 1935 and again in 1936.[20] An act was passed providing for the settlement of taxes delinquent prior to 1936 without interest or penalty in one payment or in ten annual installments in February 1937 and re-enacted in February 1938.[21]

The county treasurer has charge of the funds collected by taxes, and also other funds belonging to the county. Although earlier acts made provision for storage vaults in the county treasury for county deposits, the commissioners have been authorized, since 1894, to receive sealed bids for the deposit of county funds; and the banks or trust companies offering the highest rates of interest are selected as the county depositories.[22]

---

17. G. C. sec. 2660; *Laws of Ohio,* LVVI, 175; XCIX, 435.
18. G. C. sec. 2672; *Laws of Ohio,* CXIV, 827.
19. *Laws of Ohio,* CXV, 161-164; CXV, pt. ii, 230, 332.
20. *Ibid.,* CXVI, 199, 468; CXVI, pt. ii, 14-21.
21. *Ibid.,* CXVII, 32, 832.
22. *Ibid.,* XCI, 403; CII, 59; CXV, pt. ii, 215.

The treasurer is required to keep an account current with the county auditor - a practice which originated in 1831. Each day the treasurer makes a statement to the county auditor for the previous day's business showing the amount of taxes received on auditor's drafts, the amount received from other sources, together with the amount of money deposited in the depository, the total amount paid out by check and by cash, and the balance in the treasury.[23]

The treasurer, as well as the sheriff, the prosecuting attorney, and the clerk of courts, has been required since 1850 to report annually to the county commissioners.[24] Since 1874 the county auditor and county commissioners have been required to make a thorough examination of all books, vouchers, accounts, moneys, bonds, securities, and other property in the treasury at least every six months.[25] Besides being under the supervision of the county commissioners and county auditor, the treasurer is subject to the supervision of the state auditor. In 1902 an act was passed providing for a uniform system of accounting and auditing of all public offices in the state, under the direction of a bureau of inspection in the office of the state auditor, and for the annual examination of finances of all public offices.[26]

The treasurer is a member of the budget commission, the county board of revision, and serves as a trustee of the sinking fund.[27] Since the early days of the office the treasurer has been the official custodian of the bonds furnished to the state by the county auditor, county commissioners, and other officials. Since 1869 he has been required to record and preserve a record of the deputies appointed and removed by the county auditor,[28] but such record was not found in Ross County.

Like other county officials, the treasurer is required at the expiration of his term to turn over to his successor all books, papers, moneys, and records appertaining to his office.[29]

---

23. G. C. sec. 2642; *Laws of Ohio,* XCVII, 457.
24. G. C. sec. 2504.
25. *Ibid.,* sec. 2699; R. S. 1129; *Laws of Ohio,* LXXI, 137.
26. G. C. sec. 2641; *Laws of Ohio,* CXIV, 728; R. S. 1084.
27. G. C. secs. 5625-19, 2976-18, 5580. See also pp, 207, 208, 212.
28. G. C. sec. 2563; *Laws of Ohio,* LXVI, 35.
29. G. C. sec. 2639.

Tax Records
(See also entries 335-384)

Tax Duplicates and Assessments (See also entries 345-360)

466. TREASURER'S TAX DUPLICATE
1826—. 508 volumes. (labeled by years).
Treasurer's duplicate of taxes assessed, showing names of property owner and taxing district, survey and section numbers, range, township, acreage, lot number, land value, building value, total value, general tax, special tax, delinquencies and penalties, total amount due, amount paid, and date paid; prior to 1920, also shows entry number, watercourse, original quantity, and original proprietor. Also contains Additions and Deductions, 1931—, entry 477. 1826-1919, arranged alphabetically by names of taxing districts and alphabetically thereunder by names of property owners; 1920—, arranged alphabetically by names of property owners (each taxing district in a separate volume). No index. 1826-1920, handwritten; 1921—, typed. 196 volumes, 1826-1919, average 493 pages 18 x 14.25 x 4; 1920—, average 100 pages 18 x 15 x 1. 81 volumes, 1826-1872, Basement, rear storeroom; 115 volumes, 1873-1919, Basement, middle storeroom; 321 volumes, 1920—, Treasurer's vault.

For delinquent duplicate, see entry 487; for record of collections, see entries 493, 494.

467. TREASURER'S PERSONAL PROPERTY DUPLICATE
1897-1931. 35 volumes. (labeled by years).
Duplicate taxes assessed on personal (chattel) property, showing name of property owner and taxing district, property valuation, amount of tax, special tax, delinquencies and penalties, total amount due, amount paid, and date paid. Arranged alphabetically by names of taxing districts and alphabetically thereunder by names of property owners. No index. Handwritten. Average 450 pages. 18 x 12 x 4.25. Basement, rear storeroom.

For subsequent records, see entry 468; for record of collections, see entries 493, 494.

458. PERSONAL AND CLASSIFIED DUPLICATE
1932—. 5 volumes. Initiated 1932.
Duplicate taxes assessed on chattels and intangibles, showing names of property owners and taxing district, value of chattels, value of intangibles, amount of tax, special tax, delinquencies and penalties, and total amount due. Arranged

alphabetically by names of taxing districts and alphabetically thereunder by names of property owners. No index. Handwritten. Average 600 pages. 18 x 14 x 4.5. Treasurer's vault.

For prior chattel duplicate, see entry 467.

469. SPECIAL ASSESSMENT DUPLICATE [Boulevard Lights]
1928-1930. 1 volume.

Tax duplicate a special assessments for boulevard lights in Chillicothe, showing name of property owner, lot number, feet frontage, yearly assessment, and date paid. Arranged alphabetically by names of lot owners. No index. Handwritten. 200 pages. 12.5 x 22 x 1.5. Basement, middle storeroom.

470. SPECIAL ASSESSMENT DUPLICATE [Street Sprinkling]
1906-1931. 4 volumes.

Tax duplicate of special assessments for street sprinkling in Chillicothe, showing name of property owner, lot number, feet frontage, yearly assessment, and date paid. Arranged alphabetically by names of lots owners. No index. Handwritten. Average 200 pages. 12.5 x 22 x 1.5. Basement, middle storeroom.

471. SPECIAL ASSESSMENT DUPLICATE [Sewer Construction]
1905-1914, 1928—. 3 volumes.

Tax duplicate of special assessment for sewer construction in Chillicothe, showing name of property owner, lot number, feet frontage, annual assessment, and date paid. Arranged alphabetically by names of property owners. No index. Handwritten. Average 204 pages. 12.5 x 22 x 1.5. 2 volumes, 1905-1914, 1928-1931, Basement, middle storeroom; 1 volume, 1932—, Treasurer's vault.

472. SPECIAL ASSESSMENT DUPLICATE [Streets, Frankfort]
1905-1924. 2 volumes.

Tax duplicate of special assessments for street improvements of Frankfort corporation, showing name of property owner, lot number, feet frontage, annual assessment, and date paid. Arranged alphabetically by names of lot owners. No index. Handwritten. Average 160 pages. 12.5 x 22 x 1. Basement, middle storeroom.

473. SPECIAL ASSESSMENT DUPLICATE [Street Cleaning]
1923-1931. 1 volume.

Tax duplicate of special assessments for street cleaning in Chillicothe, showing name of lot owner, lot number, feet frontage, annual assessment, and date paid. Arranged alphabetically by names of lot owners. No index. Handwritten. 208 pages. 12.5 x 22 x 1.5. Basement, middle storeroom.

474. SPECIAL ASSESSMENT DUPLICATE, MISCELLANEOUS
1913-1931. 2 volumes.

Tax duplicate of special assessments including Kingston village street grading, paving, and oil sprinkling of streets; Green Township I. C. H. No. 361, Section N, paving; Twin Township I. C. H. No. 258, Section H-I, paving; Bainbridge village oil sprinkling of streets; Clarksburg village oil sprinkling of streets; Jefferson Township I. C. H. No. 364, Section M, paving; Scioto Township I. C. H. No. 5, Section O, paving; Clarksburg village street lighting; and Bainbridge village street paving; showing name of subdivision, name of lot owner or landowner, lot number, acreage, feet frontage, annual assessment, and date paid. Arranged by subdivisions and alphabetically thereunder by names of property owners. No index. Handwritten. Average 200 pages. 12.5 x 22 x 1.5. Basement, middle storeroom.

475. TREASURER'S LIQUOR DUPLICATE
1897-1904, 1907-1917. 4 volumes.

Duplicate of liquor traffic license tax, showing name of licensee, date, location of business, owner of real estate on which business is located, and license fee. Arranged chronologically by dates of licenses. No index. Handwritten on printed forms. Average 160 pages. 18 x 16 x 1.25. Basement, rear storeroom.

476. TREASURER'S CIGARETTE DUPLICATE
1923—. 3 volumes.

Record of cigarette traffic license tax, showing name of licensee, date, location of business, owner of building in which business is conducted, and amount of tax. Arranged chronologically by dates of licenses. No index. Handwritten. 150 pages. 12 x 14 x 1.25. Treasurer's office.

Additions and Deductions (See also entries 363-365)

477. ADDITIONS AND DEDUCTIONS
1909—. 22 volumes. (labeled by years). 1931— also in Treasurer's Tax Duplicate, entry 466.

Record of additions to tax duplicate, showing names of taxpayer and taxing district and amount of addition by reason of error on previous duplicate, new buildings, or improvements to property; also record of deductions from tax duplicate, showing names of taxpayer and taxing district and amount of deduction by reason of error on previous duplicate, buildings destroyed, or other depreciation of property value. Record of additions in front half of each volume; of deductions in back half of each volume. Arranged alphabetically by names of taxing districts and alphabetically thereunder by names of taxpayers. No index. Handwritten. Average 190 pages. 18 x 12 x 1.5. 3 volumes, 1909-1912, Auditor's vault; 16 volumes, 1913-1926, Basement, rear storeroom; 3 volumes, 1927-1930, Treasurer's vault.

478. ADDITIONS TO INHERITANCE AND CIGARETTE DUPLICATE
1919-1925. 7 volumes. (labeled by years).

Record of additions to inheritance and cigarette tax charges, showing name of estate or cigarette dealer, reason for addition, amount added, and date paid. Arranged chronologically by dates of payments. No index. Handwritten on printed forms. Average 100 pages. 10 x 12 x 1. Treasurer's vault.

Refunds and Allowances

479. FREE ROAD TAX REFUND
1880-1888. 9 volumes.

Refunder orders from county auditor on over-assessments for free turnpike, showing to whom due, amount of refund, description of real estate, acreage, valuation, personal property valuation, and total property valuation. Arranged chronologically by names of taxing districts and alphabetically thereunder by names of property owners. No index. Handwritten. Average 190 pages. 18 x 14 x 1.5. Basement, middle storeroom.

For auditor's record, see entry 373.

480. ROAD RECEIPTS REDEEMED
1891-1899. 1 volume.
Record of taxes worked out by labor on public roads, showing name of taxpayer, taxing district, amount of tax allowed to be worked out, number of hours worked, and amount credited. Alphabetically arranged by names of taxing districts and alphabetically thereunder by names of taxpayers. No index. Handwritten. 360 pages. 20 x 12 x 3. Treasurer's vault.

Tax Stamps

481. EXCISE TAX, COSMETICS
1933-1934. 1 volume. Discontinued; law repealed.
Record of cosmetic tax stamps sold, showing name of retailer, business location, and date and amount of sale. Arranged chronologically by dates of sale. No index. Handwritten. 200 pages. 10 x 8 x 1.25. Treasurer's vault.

482. EXCISE TAX, BEVERAGES, BREWERS' WORT AND MALT
1933—. 1 volume.
Record of excise tax stamps sold on beverages and brewers' wort, and malt tax, showing name of dealer, business location, date, and amount. Arranged chronologically by dates of entry. No index. Handwritten. 200 pages. 18 x 11 x 1.25. Treasure's vault.

483. CIGARETTE TAX STAMP RECORD
1931-1935. 1 volume.
Record of cigarette excise tax stamps sold, showing name of purchaser, date, and number sold. Arranged chronologically by dates of sale. No index. Handwritten on printed forms. 285 pages. 12 x 8 x 2. Treasurer's vault.

484. DAILY INVENTORY AND SALES RECORD OF SALES OF TAX STAMPS
1935—. 1 volume.
Record of daily inventory of sales tax stamps, showing dates, number of each denomination on hand, and number received; also daily record of stamps sold, showing date, name of vendor, license number, and amount of sale. Arranged chronologically by dates of inventory. No index. Handwritten on printed forms. 600 pages. 18 x 14.5 x 4.5. Treasurer's vault.

Tax Receipts

485. TAX RECEIPTS

1911—. 608 volumes. (labeled by years). Subtitled by names of taxing districts.

Official individual tax receipt stubs, showing receipt number, name of taxpayer, taxing district, amount paid, and date. Arranged numerically by consecutive receipt numbers. No index. Handwritten on printed forms. Average 260 pages. 18 x 12 x 2. 260 volumes, 1911-1923, Basement, rear storeroom; 234 volumes, 1924-1932, Basement, middle storeroom; 114 volumes,1933—, Treasurer's vault.

486. CIGARETTE TAX PAYMENT RECORDS

1931—. 2 volumes.

Cigarette tax receipt stubs, showing name of licensee, date, amount paid, and license number. Arranged numerically by license numbers. No index. Handwritten on printed forms. Average 200 pages. 16 x 9 x 2. Treasurer's vault.

Delinquent Taxes (See also entries 376-383)

487. TREASURER'S DELINQUENT LAND DUPLICATE

1898-1932. 9 volumes.

Record of delinquent land tax, showing name of landowner, taxing district, location and description of tract or lot, valuation of land and of buildings, total valuation, amount delinquent, penalty, and total amount due. Arranged alphabetically by names of taxing districts and alphabetically thereunder by names of property owners. No index. Handwritten. Average 240 pages. 17 x 14 x 2. Treasurer's vault.

Subsequent records, see entry 466; for cumulative duplicates, see entry 488.

488. TREASURER'S CUMULATIVE DUPLICATE

1932—. 1 volume. Initiated 1932.

Record of accumulated delinquencies, showing name of property owner, taxing district, number of years delinquent, description and location of property, personal property valuation, land and building valuation, total tax due, penalties, interest, and total due. Arranged alphabetically under tabs by names of taxing districts and alphabetically thereunder by names of property owners. No index. Handwritten on printed forms. 500 pages. 12 x 14 x 4. Treasurer's vault.

For other delinquent duplicates, see entry 487.

489. TREASURER'S DELINQUENT PERSONAL DUPLICATE
1873-1874, 1900—. 17 volumes. Title varies: Duplicate Delinquent Chattel Tax, 1873-1884, 2 volumes.

Record of delinquent taxes on personal property, showing name of property owner, taxing district, valuation of property, number of years delinquent, total amount of tax due, penalty, and total amount due. Arranged alphabetically by names of taxing districts and alphabetically thereunder by names of delinquent taxpayers. No index. Handwritten. 1873-1884, average 400 pages 18 x 12 x 3; 1909—, average 120 pages 12 x 16 x 1. Treasurer's office.

490. TREASURER'S JOURNAL OF THE DELINQUENT CERTIFICATES
1917-1927. 4 volumes.

Delinquent land tax certificates, showing name of owner, taxing district, certificate number, number of years delinquent, amount delinquent, penalty, interest, and total due. Arranged alphabetically by names of taxing districts and alphabetically thereunder by names of taxpayers. No index. 1917-1920, handwritten on printed forms; 1921-1927, typed on printed forms. Average 340 pages 18 x 14 x 2.25. Basement, middle storeroom.

For subsequent delinquent certificates, see entry 491.

491. TREASURER'S QUADRENNIAL [and Triennial] LAND CERTIFICATES
1928—. 1 volume.

Record of land taxes certified delinquent (every four years, 1928-1930, and every three years, 1931—), showing names of owners, taxing district, description of tract, acreage, lot number, number of years delinquent, amount of delinquency, penalty, interest, and total amount due. Arranged alphabetically under tabs by names of taxing districts and alphabetically thereunder by names of landowners. No index. Handwritten on printed forms. 480 pages. 17 x 14 x 3.5. Treasurer's vault.

For journal of delinquent certificates, see entry 490.

492. TREASURER'S UNDERTAKINGS [Installment Payments, Delinquent Taxes]
1933—. 5 volumes.

Record of installment payments of delinquent taxes, showing name of taxpayer, description of property, taxing district, property valuation, amount of arrears, and amount of each installment. Arranged alphabetically under tabs by names of taxing districts and alphabetically thereunder by names of taxpayers. No index. Handwritten on printed forms. Average 200 pages. 12 x 16 x 2.25. Treasurer's vault.

Tax Collections

493. JOURNAL [Tax Collections]
1865-1898. 6 volumes.

Daily record of tax collections, showing date, names of taxpayer and taxing district, and amount. Arranged chronologically by dates of entry. No index. Handwritten. Average 400 pages. 14 x 10 x 3.5. Basement, rear storeroom.

For subsequent records, see entry 494; for record of assessments, see entries 466, 467.

494. RECAPITULATION OF TAXES COLLECTED
1898—. 14 volumes. Title varies: Record of Tax Collections, 1898-1927, 12 volumes.

Record of taxes collected in each taxing district, showing date, amount for each district, and total for county. Arranged chronologically by dates of entry. No index. Handwritten. Average 1898-1927, 650 pages 15 x 11 x 4.5; 1928—, 250 pages 18 x 11 x 2. Treasurer's vault.

For journal of tax collections, 1865-1898, see entry 493; for record of assessments, see entries 466, 467.

495. RECORD OF LIQUOR TRAFFIC TAX COLLECTION AND DISTRIBUTION
1902. 1 volume.

Record of liquor license fees, showing name of payer, date, and amount of payment; also record of apportionments to state, county, and various subdivisions, showing to which political division, date, and amount of payment. Arranged alphabetically under tabs by names of political divisions and chronologically thereunder by dates of payments. No index. Handwritten on printed forms. 66 pages. 14 x 20 x .5. Basement, middle storeroom.

Inheritance Tax (See also entries 251-253, 365, 384)

496. INHERITANCE TAX RECORD
1920—. 3 volumes.

Treasurer's record of inheritance taxes as certified by probate court, showing names of decedent, heirs-at-large, legatees, devisees, amount of tax, and date paid. Arranged chronologically by dates of payment. No index. Handwritten on printed forms. Average 280 pages. 14 x 14 x 2.

Fiscal Accounts

Cashbooks and Ledgers

497. TREASURER'S CASH BOOK
1845-1851. 45 volumes. (labeled by years).

Treasurer's itemized daily record of receipts and expenditures, showing names of payer and payee, date, amount, and for what purpose. Arranged chronologically by dates of entry. No index. Handwritten. Average 480 pages. 16 x 10 x 3. 23 volumes, 1845-1851, 1862-1904, Basement, rear storeroom; 22 volumes, 1905—, Treasurer's vault.

498. DAILY CASH BALANCE
1893—. 7 volumes.

Daily record of cash balance, showing date, amount of receipts and disbursements, and balance. Arranged chronologically by dates of entry. No index. Handwritten. 480 pages. 18 x 11 x 3.5. 2 volumes, 1893-1904, Auditor's vault; 5 volumes, 1905—, Treasurer's vault.

499. JOURNAL, PAYMENTS INTO TREASURY
1914—. 15 volumes. (labeled by years).

Record of payments into treasury, showing date, by whom, for what, to what fund, and amount. Arranged chronologically by dates of payment. No index. Handwritten. Average 340 pages. 18 x 12 x 2.5. 10 volumes, 1914-1929, Basement, middle storeroom; 5 volumes, 1930—, Treasurer's vault.

500. AUDITOR'S RECEIPT BOOK
1887-1896. 1 volume.

Treasurer's record and auditor's receipts for money paid into county treasury from sources other than taxes, showing by whom paid in, for what, what fund, amount, and date paid. Arranged chronologically by dates of payments. No index. Handwritten. 340 pages. 14 x 10 x 2.5. Treasurer's vault.

501. TREASURER'S LEDGER
1844-1867, 1905. 12 volumes.
Record of credits and debits to county, township, corporation, and school funds, showing date, source of receipts, by whom paid in, for what, to whom paid out, order number, and amount. Arranged chronologically by dates of entry. No index. Handwritten. Average 400 pages. 16 x 13 x 3. 3 volumes, 1844-1867, Auditor's vault; 9 volumes, 1905—, Treasurer's vault.

502. [Fund] LEDGER
1844-1868. 3 volumes.
Account with bridge, township, school, infirmary, corporation, railroad bond, railroad bond interest, tax redemption, forfeited land, peddlers' licenses, state war military relief, and military commutation funds, showing date, itemized receipts to the various funds, and itemized expenditures of funds. Arranged chronologically by dates of entry. Indexed alphabetically by names of funds. Handwritten. Average 420 pages. 18 x 12 x 3.25. Auditor's vault.

503. TREASURER'S GENERAL FUND RECORD
1867-1877, 1892-1896, 1921—. 6 volumes.
Daily itemized account of county general fund, showing date, credit and debit, by whom paid in, amount, for what, to whom paid out, warrant or ordered number, for what, and amount. Arranged chronologically by dates of entry. No index. Handwritten. Average 600 pages. 20.5 x 16.5 x 4.5. 1 volume, 1867-1877, Auditor's vault; 5 volumes, 1892-1896, 1921—, Treasurer's vault.

504. TREASURER'S ACCOUNT, SCHOOL FUNDS
1916—. 4 volumes.
Account with school funds, showing receipts and disbursements to various funds, date, and amount. Arranged chronologically by dates of entry. No index. Handwritten. Average 280 pages. 16 x 20 x 2. Treasurer's vault.

505. SETTLEMENT SHEETS

1881—. 3 volumes.

Treasurer's detailed statement of receipts into treasury, showing date, amount, and source of receipts; also record of semiannual settlements with the various subdivisions of Ross County, showing date, subdivision, and amount. Arranged chronologically by February and August settlement dates. No index. Handwritten on printed forms. Average 110 pages. 11.5 x 16 x 1. 2 volumes, 1881-1922, Basement, middle storeroom; 1 volume, 1923—, Treasurer's vault.

For auditor's settlement records, see entry 385-387.

506. IN ACCOUNT WITH CHILLICOTHE

1856-1867, 1870-1889. 4 volumes. Title varies: Day Book, 1856-1867, 1 volume.

Treasurer's record of receipts and expenditures of funds in account with city of Chillicothe: receipts, showing date, amount, and what fund; expenditures, showing date, to whom paid, for what, amount, what fund, and voucher number. Arranged chronologically by dates of entry. No index. Handwritten. Average 500 pages. 18 x 1 x 4. Treasurer's vault.

507. SUNDRY FUNDS

1868-1888. 3 volumes.

Treasurer's account with state, war, and military relief, railroad bond interest, indigent relief, and public road funds, showing what fund, date, and amount. Arranged under marginal indentations by funds and chronologically thereunder by dates of entry. No index. Handwritten. Average 250 pages. 16 x 14 x 2. Treasurer's vault.

508. RECEIPTS

1859-1869. 1 volume.

Record of fines and costs paid into county treasury by clerk of courts and fees on licenses issued by clerk of courts, showing name of payer, for what, and amount and date paid. Arranged chronologically by dates of payments. No index. Handwritten. 208 pages. 8 x 8 x 1.5. Auditor's vault.

509. RECORD OF FEES

1815-1819. 1 volume.

Record of fees received from licenses issued for the operation of taverns and other retail businesses, showing date, name of licensee, for what business, location of business, amount, and date paid. Arranged chronologically by dates of entry. No index. Handwritten. 208 pages. 8 x 8 x 1.5. Auditor's vault.

Warrants

510. DAY BOOK
1853-1858. 1 volume.

Daily record of warrants cashed, showing name of payee, date, amount, and for what. Arranged chronologically by dates of entry. Handwritten. 544 pages. 12 x 8 x 3.5. Auditor's vault.

511. FLOATING ORDERS
1896-1903. 1 volume.

Record of warrants unpaid for lack of funds, warrants being cashed by banks and held pending redemption by county, showing warrant number, date, name of payee, and amount. Arranged numerically by warrant numbers and also arranged chronologically by dates of warrants. No index. Handwritten. 270 pages. 14 x 10 x 2. Treasurer's vault.

512. TREASURER'S JOURNAL OF WARRANTS REDEEMED
1904—. 7 volumes. (1-7).

Record of warrants redeemed, showing warrant number, name of payee, for what, what fund, and amount. Arranged numerically by warrant numbers. No index. Handwritten. Average 550 pages. 18 x 12 x 4.25. 3 volumes, 1919-1929, 1931-1935, Basement, middle storeroom; 4 volumes, 1904-1918, 1929-1931, 1935—, Treasurer's vault.

513. COURT WARRANTS REDEEMED
1919—. 2 volumes. (1, 2).

Record of warrants redeemed in payment of witness, juror, and court fees, showing date, name of payee, warrant number, what court, for what, and amount. Arranged numerically by warrant numbers and also arranged chronologically by dates of warrants. No index. Handwritten. Average 360 pages. 20 x 13 x 3. 1 volume, 1919-1930, Basement, rear storeroom; 1 volume, 1931—, Treasurer's office.

Official Bonds

(See also entries 445-447, 463)

514. RECORD OF OFFICIAL BONDS

1885—. 3 volumes.

Record of bonds filed by elected county officials, showing date, amount, names of sureties, and approval by county commissioners. Arranged chronologically by dates of filing. No index. Handwritten on printed forms. Average 420 pages. 18 x 12 x 3. Treasurer's vault.

515. OFFICIAL BONDS

1887—. 2 file boxes.

Original bonds filed by elected county officials, showing date, what office, name of official, amount of bond, names of sureties or name of bonding company and approval by county commissioners. Arranged alphabetically by names of the officials and chronologically thereunder by dates of bonds. No index. 1887-1921, handwritten on printed forms; 1922—, typed on printed forms. 10 x 5 x 14. Treasurer's vault.

516. BONDS, TOWNSHIP CLERK-TREASURER

1924—. 2 file boxes.

Original bonds filed by township clerk-treasurers, showing date, name of official, amount of bond, names of sureties, and approval by township trustees. Arranged alphabetically by names of officials and chronologically thereunder by dates of bonds. No index. Handwritten on printed forms. 10 x 5 x 14. Treasurer's vault.

A budget commission was established in Ross County in 1911 under the provisions of the act of that year which authorized the establishment of a budget commission in each county to be composed of the county auditor, the mayor of the largest municipality, and the prosecuting attorney.[1] It was not until after the World War, when county expenditures steadily increased, that the importance of improved methods of finance were forcibly brought to the attention of the legislature. This new need was met in 1927 by the establishment of a budget commission in each county. This commission, consisting of the county auditor, the county treasurer, and the prosecuting attorney, receives and examines the annual budget of the county, municipal, township, and school authorities, with an estimate of the total amount to be raised for stated purposes in each subdivision.[2] If the total amount exceeds the sum authorized to be raised, the commission adjusts the amount to be raised and may change and revise the estimates. The commission may reduce all items in the budget, but it is prohibited from increasing the total of any budget or any item.

The adjusted budget is certified to the taxing authority in each subdivision. If the work of the commission is satisfactory, each taxing authority by ordinance or resolution authorize the necessary tax levies and certifies them to the county auditor. On the other hand, the taxing authority in any subdivision may appeal, through its fiscal officer, from the decision of the budget commission to the state tax commission of Ohio, which is empowered to adjust the estimates of revenues and balances in fixing the tax rate.[3]

The county auditor, as secretary to the commission, is required to keep a full and accurate record of the proceedings of the commission.[4]

---

1. *Laws of Ohio,* CII, 271.
2. *Ibid.,* CXII, 399.
3. G. C. secs. 5625-25, 5625-28.
4. *Ibid.,* sec. 5626-19.

517. RECORD AND JOURNAL [Budget commission]
1911—. 3 volumes.

Minutes of the meetings of the budget commission, showing date, record of proceedings, and amount of budget for each taxing district. Arranged chronologically by dates of meetings. Indexed alphabetically by names of taxing districts. 1911-1925, handwritten; 1926—, typed. Average 380 pages. 16 x 11 x 3. Auditor's vault.

The county board of revision, the object of which was to correct some of the defects and inequities of tax assessments, was established by the legislature in 1825. The first board of revision, or equalization as it was sometimes called, was composed of the county commissioners, the county auditor, and the assessor. The board was authorized to meet at the seat of justice on the first Monday in June annually "to hear and determine the complaint of any owner of property listed and valued by the assessor . . . and shall correct any list or valuation made by the assessor, either by adding to or deducting from his valuation"[1] The act of 1831, repealing the act of 1825, left the duties and personnel of the board unchanged.[2]

In 1859 the legislature made provision for two county boards of equalization. One board, composed of the county auditor and the county commissioners, was directed to meet annually for the purpose of equalizing real and personal property, and moneys and credits in the county. The other board, composed of the county auditor, the county surveyor, and the county commissioners, was authorized to meet sexennially for the same purpose.[3]

The act of 1863, amending the act of 1859, left to the personnel and duties of the annual county board unchanged. The second county board, although continuing without alteration in composition or duties, was directed to meet decennially, rather than sexennially.[4] The legislative act of 1868, amending the act of 1863, left the membership of the annual and special boards, as well as their duties, practically unchanged.[5]

The annual and special boards of equalization were abolished, when, in 1913, the tax commission of Ohio was given the task of supervising the assessment of real and personal property in the state.[6] Under this arrangement each county constituted a district. In each district containing less than 60,000 inhabitants, by which stipulation Ross County was included, there was to be appointed by the governor one state tax commissioner. In all other districts their were appointed, in the same manner, two state deputy tax commissioners. In each district there was appointed a district board of complaints.

---

1. *Laws of Ohio,* XXIII, 64.
2. *Ibid.,* XXIX, 278.
3. *Ibid.,* LVI, 193-194.
4. *Laws of Ohio,* LX, 57, 59.
5. *Ibid.,* LXV, 168-170.
6. See also 99. 168-170.

This board, appointed by the state tax commission with the consent of the governor, took over the duties and powers formerly vested in the boards of equalization. The county auditor, made secretary to the board of complaints, was required to present at each meeting in person or by deputy, and keep an accurate record of their proceedings to be kept in a book for that purpose.[7] Moreover, the board was directed to take full minutes of all evidence given before it and might have such evidence taken in shorthand and extended into typewritten form. The auditor was required to preserve in his office separate records of all minutes and documentary evidence offered in each complaint.[8]

This arrangement, after being in operation for two years, was abrogated by the legislature in 1915. In that year the county auditor, under the supervision of the tax commission of Ohio, became the chief assessing officer in the county. The county treasurer, the county prosecuting attorney, the probate judge and the president of the county commissioners were to serve as a board for the purpose of appointing three members to constitute a board of revision. Again the county auditor was made secretary of the board and was directed to keep a record of their proceedings and to preserve in his office a separate record of all minutes and documentary evidence offered in each complaint.[9]

Under the present system, inaugurated in 1917, the county treasurer, the county auditor, and the president of the county commissioners constituted a board of revision. This board organizes annually, on the second Monday in June, by electing a chairman for the ensuing year. The county auditor serves as secretary to the board.[10] The county board of revision may, with the consent and approval of the tax commission of Ohio, employ experts, clerks, and other employees.[11]

The duties of the board, not differing in detail from those prescribed in 1825, include the hearing of all complaints relating to valuation or assessment of both real and personal property as it appears upon a tax duplicate of the "then current year." The board is authorized to investigate all complaints and may increase or decrease any valuation or correct any assessment complained of, or may order a reassessment of the original assessing official.[12]

---

7. *Laws of Ohio,* CIII, 791.
8. *Ibid.,* CIII, 794.
9. *Ibid.,* CVI, 254-258.
10. G. C. sec. 5580.
11. G. C. sec. 5587.
12. *Ibid.,* sec. 5597.

However, no valuation is increased without giving notice to the person in whose name the property affected is listed.[13] The board of revision, in all respects, is governor by the laws relating to the valuation of real property and makes no change of any valuation except in accordance with such laws.[14]

On the second Monday in June, annually, the county auditor lays before the board of revision the statements and returns of assessments of any personal property for the current year, and the board proceeds to review the returns. On the first Monday in July, annually, the auditor lays before the board the returns of assessments of any real property for the current year. The board of revision reviews the assessments and certifies its action to the county auditor who corrects the tax list and duplicate according to the additions and deductions ordered by the board. The auditor is prohibited by statute from making up his tax list and duplicate, until the board has completed its work and has submitted to him all returns late before it with revisions.[15] But in the event the tax duplicate has been delivered to the county treasurer, the auditor is required to certify such corrections to him and enter such corrections in his tax duplicate.[16]

In its investigations the board may examine, under oath, persons as to their or others' real property. In the event witnesses fail to appear or refuse to testify, the board through its chairman is authorized to make a complaint in writing to the probate judge, who, by statute, is directed to institute proceedings against them.[17] The decisions of the board of subject to appeal to the tax commission of Ohio, within thirty days after a decision is served.[18]

The secretary of the board is required to keep "an accurate record of the proceedings of the board in a book to be kept for that purpose."[19] The county auditor, as in 1913, is required to preserve in his office separate records of all minutes and documentary evidence offered in each complaint.[20] The records of the board are open to the inspection of the public.[21]

---

13. *Ibid.*, sec. 5599.
14. *Ibid.*, sec. 5596.
15. *Ibid.*, sec. 5605.
16. *Ibid.*, sec. 5602.
17. *Ibid.*, sec. 5596.
18. *Ibid.*, sec. 5610.
19. *Ibid.*, sec. 5592.
20. G. C. sec. 5603.
21. *Ibid.*, sec. 5591.

518. [MINUTES, CITY BOARD OF EQUALIZATION]
1879-1891. 1 volume.

Minutes of meetings of special board of equalization (city of Chillicothe), showing date of meeting, and amounts in readjustment of city property valuations for taxation purposes. Arranged chronologically by dates of meetings. No index. Handwritten. 400 pages. 16 x 11 x 3. Auditor's vault.

519. [MINUTES, CITY BOARD OF REVIEW]
1890-1912. 2 volumes.

Minutes of meetings of city (Chillicothe) board of review, showing date of meeting, and amounts in readjustment of property valuations for taxation purposes; and also contains record of re-appraisements on order of county auditor. Arranged chronologically by dates of meetings. No index. Handwritten. Average 600 pages. 18 x 12 x 4.5. Auditors' vault.

520. [MINUTES, COUNTY BOARD OF REVISION]
1849-1853, 1859—. 6 volumes.

Minutes of meetings of county board of revision and of district board of complaints, showing date of meeting, and amounts and readjustment of land values for taxation purposes. Arranged chronologically by dates of meetings. No index. 1849-1853, 1859-1922, handwritten; 1923—, typed. 3 volumes, average 100 pages. 14 x 9 x 1; 3 volumes, average 400 pages. 18 x 12 x 3. Auditor's vault.

521. [MINUTES, COUNTY BOARD OF REVIEW]
1903-1904. 1 volume.

Record of meetings of the county board of review, showing date of meeting, and decisions of the board in readjustment of property valuations for taxation purposes. Arranged chronologically by dates of meetings. No index. Handwritten. 270 pages. 14 x 9 x 2. Auditor's vault.

522. COMPLAINTS [to City Board of Review]
1906. 1 file box.

Copies of complaints filed with the city board of review asking readjustment of property valuations for taxation purposes, showing date, name of property owner, what property, and reason for complaint. No orderly arrangement. No index. Handwritten on printed forms. 10 x 4.5 x 14. Basement, middle storeroom.

The board of trustees of the sinking fund, composed of the prosecuting attorney, auditor, and treasurer, was organized in 1919 in Ross County and in each county owing a bonded debt. The county prosecuting attorney serves as president of the board and the auditor as secretary. It is the duty of the trustees to provide for the payment of all bonds issued by the county and interest returning thereon.[1]

From 1919 all bonds issued by the county were required to be recorded in the office of the trustees of the sinking fund, and to bear a stamp containing the words "recorded in the office of the sinking fund trustees" and be signed by the secretary before they became valid in the hands of any purchaser. In 1921 the act was amended to allow such recording and authenticating to be performed by the county treasurer and in 1935 such provisions were abrogated by the legislature.[2]

On or before the first Monday in May of each year, the trustees certify to the county commissioners the rate of tax necessary to provide a sinking fund both for the payment at maturity of bonds heretofore issued by the county and the payment of interest on bonded indebtedness. The amount certified by the trustees is set forth without diminution in the annual budget of the commissioners.[3] Then, after each semiannual settlement of taxes and assessments, the county auditor reports to the trustees the amount of money in the treasury of the county charge to the credit of the sinking fund. Money is drawn from the county treasury for investment or disbursement by the issuance of a voucher signed by all the members of the board and directed to the county auditor. The trustees are directed, by statute, to invest all money subject to their control in United States bonds, Ohio bonds, or bonds of a municipal corporation, school district, township, or county in the state.

The board members are required to keep "a full and complete record of their transactions, a complete record of the funded debt of the county specifying the dates, purposes, amounts, numbers, maturities, and rates and maturities of interest and installments thereof, and were payable, and an account exhibiting the amount held in the sinking fund for the payment thereof."[4]

---

1. G. C. secs. 2976-18, 2976-19.
2. *Laws of Ohio,* CIX, 16; CXVI, 442.
3. G. C. sec. 2976-26.
4. *Ibid.,* sec. 2976-24.

The meeting of the trustees are open to the public. All questions relating to the purchase or sale of securities or the payment of bonds or interest are decided by yay or nay vote, which is recorded in their journal.

523. [MINUTES, SINKING FUND TRUSTEES]
1919—. 1 volume.
Minutes of meetings of the board of trustees of the sinking fund, showing date and proceedings; also record of bonds issued, showing for what purpose, number and amount of each bond, interest rate, and total issue. Arranged chronologically by dates of meetings. No index. Typed. 300 pages. 18 x 12 x 2.25. Auditor's vault.

(State Deputy Supervisors of Elections)

The responsibility for supervising and conducting elections in the county is delegated to the state deputy supervisors of elections - the county board of elections. This board, created by the legislature in 1891 and consisting of four qualified voters in the county, is appointed for a four-year term by the secretary of state, who, by virtue of his office, is the chief election official of the state.[1] On the first day of March in the even-numbered years, the secretary of the state appoints two board members, one of whom is from the political party which polled the highest number of votes in the state for the office of governor at the last proceeding state election, and the other from the political party which polled the next highest vote at such election.[2] The board members may be removed by the secretary of state for the neglect of duty, malfeasance, misfeasance in office, for willful violation of the election laws or for other good and significant causes.[3] The compensation of the members is determined on the basis of population of the county and is paid by the county.[4] Similarly the expenses of the county board are paid from the county treasury, "in pursuance of appropriations by the county commissioners," in the same manner as other expenses are paid.[5]

The persons so appointed by the secretary, meeting five days after their appointment, select one of their members as chairman and a resident elector of the county who is not a member of the board as clerk.[6] The board is vested with authority to establish, define, and provide election precincts; fix places of registration; provide for the purchase, preservation, and maintenance of voting booths, ballot boxes, books, maps, flags, blanks, cards of instructions, and other equipment used in registration; and to issue rules, regulations, and instructions not inconsistent with the law or contrary to the rules and regulations as established by the chief election official.[7]

---

1. *Laws of Ohio,* LXXXVIII, 449.
2. G. C. sec. 4785-8. For the method of appointment when the term of each of the four members of the board expires on the same date see G. C. sec. 4785-8a.
3. G. C. sec. 4785-11.
4. *Ibid.,* sec. 4785-18.
5. *Ibid.,* sec. 4785-20.
6. *Ibid.,* sec. 4785-10.
7. G. C. sec. 4785-13.

Besides providing places of voting and equipment, the board is authorized to appoint a clerk and other officers of elections. On or before the first day of September before each November election the board by a majority vote is authorized, after careful examination and investigation as to the qualifications, to appoint for each precinct six "competent persons, four as judges and two as clerks, who shall constitute the election officers of such precinct." Not more than two of the judges and one of the clerks, states the law, "shall be members of the same political party." Precinct election officers, appointed for a one-year term, may be removed by the board for neglected duty, malfeasance, or misconduct in office.[8]

The county board of elections is authorized to receive and examine nominating petitions and to certify their sufficiency and validity. They received the election returns, canvas the returns, then make abstracts therefrom and transmit them to the proper authorities. They issue certificates of elections on forms prescribed by the secretary of state and report annually to the same official, on forms prescribed by him, the number of voters registered, elections held, votes cast, appropriations received, expenditures made, and such other information as the secretary of state may require. Moreover, the board prepares and submits to the proper authorities a budget estimating the cost of elections for the ensuing year.[9]

Finally the board is empowered to investigate irregularities, non-performance of duty, or violation of election laws by election officials. For the purpose of conducting investigations they may administer oaths, issue subpoenas, summon witnesses, and compel the presentation of books, papers, and records in connects with any investigation and report the facts to the prosecuting attorney.[10]

The secretary of state, in 1930, ruled that the members of various board of elections were to be considered as state officers. This ruling had reference to appointments made under section 4785-8a of the General Code.[11]

The clerk of the board is required to keep a record of the proceedings of the board and of all moneys received and expended, and to file and preserve in his office all records of the board.

---

8. *Ibid.,* sec. 4785-25.
9. *Ibid.,* sec. 4785-13.
10. *Ibid.,* sec. 4785-13.
11. See George C. Trautwein, ed., *Supplement to Page's Annotated General Code 1926-1935* (Cincinnati, 1935), note on p. 688.

Poll lists and tally sheets are to be preserved for two years, ballots for thirty days. These records are open to the inspection of the public under the regulations established by the board.[12]

---

12. G. C. secs. 4785-14, 4785-147.

Journal

524. JOURNAL

1908—. 3 volumes.

Minutes of meetings of board of elections, showing date, proceedings, record of candidacy, and of fees paid to board of elections by candidates. Arranged chronologically by dates of meetings. No index. Handwritten. Average 320 pages. 16 x 11 x 2.5. Board of elections record room.

Records of Electors

525. REGISTRY OF MALE ELECTORS (Chillicothe)

1916-1920. 51 volumes. (labeled by years). Subtitled by names of wards. Record of registration of male electors and city of Chillicothe, showing registration number, name, age, residence, occupation, term of residence in state, county, and precinct, citizenship, personal description, date registered, and signature of registrants. No index. Handwritten. Average 100 pages. 10.5 x 14 x .5. Basement, rear storeroom.

For subsequent records, see entries 527, 528.

526. REGISTRY OF WOMEN ELECTORS (Chillicothe)

1916-1920. 47 volumes. (labeled by years). Subtitled by names of wards. Record of the registration of women collectors in city of Chillicothe, showing registration number, name, age, residence, occupation, term of residence in state, county and precinct, citizenship, marital status, personal description, date registered, and signature of registrant. Arranged alphabetically by names of registrants. No index. Handwritten. Average 100 pages. 10.5 x 14 x .5. Basement, rear storeroom.

Subsequent records, see entries 527, 528.

527. REGISTRATION LIST, DEMOCRAT (Chillicothe)
1920-1928. 120 volumes. (labeled by years). Subtitled by names of wards and precincts.

List of Democrat electors who have been certified to precinct officials, showing registration number, name, age, residence, and previous voting record. Arranged alphabetically by the names of electors. No index. Handwritten. Average 100 pages. 10.5 x 14 x .5. Basement, rear storeroom.

For prior records, see entries 525, 526; for subsequent records, see entry 529.

528. REGISTRATION LIST, REPUBLICAN (Chillicothe)
1920-1928. 120 volumes. (labeled by years). Subtitle by names of wards and precincts.

List of Republican electors who have been certified to precinct officials, showing registration number, name, age, residents, and previous voting record. Arranged alphabetically by names of electors. No index. Handwritten. Average 100 pages. 10.5 x 14 x .5. Basement, rear storeroom.

For prior records, see entries 525, 526; or subsequent records, see entry 529.

529. REGISTRATION RECORDS
1930—. 25 file drawers. Subtitle by names of wards and precincts.

Card record of the registration of voters in city of Chillicothe, showing name, address, ward, and precinct of elector; also signature of registrant. Arranged by precincts and alphabetically thereunder by names of registrants. No index. Typed on printed forms. 3 x 24 x 28. Board of elections record room.

For prior records, see entries 525-528.

530. PRECINCT POLL LISTS (Chillicothe)
1930—. 100 volumes. (labeled by years). Subtitled by names of wards and precincts.

List of all registered electors as certified to the precinct officials, showing date of election, name, address, date registered, and date transferred. Arranged chronologically by dates of elections and alphabetically thereunder by names of electors. No index. Typed. Average 90 pages. 16 x 12 x .5. 50 volumes, 1930-1932, Basement, rear storeroom; 50 volumes, 1933—, Board of elections record room.

Poll Books and Tally Sheets
(See also entries 138-142)

531. POLL BOOKS AND TALLY SHEETS
1923—. 689 volumes. (labeled by years). Subtitle by names of townships, wards, and precinct.

Poll books used in general elections, showing names and address of electors casting ballots; also tally sheets, showing a summary of votes cast and number of votes cast for each candidate and for each proposal. Arranged alphabetically by names of electors. No index. Handwritten on printed forms. Average 28 pages. 26 x 16 x .25. 477 volumes, 1923-1931, Basement, rear storeroom; 212 volumes, 1932—, Board of elections record room.

532. POLL BOOKS AND TALLY SHEETS
1923—. 521 volumes. (labeled by years). Subtitle by names of townships, wards, and precincts.

Precinct poll books used in primary elections (Republican and Democrat), showing names of electors voting each party ticket; also tally sheets, showing a summary of votes cast and number of votes received by each candidate. Arranged alphabetically by names of electors. No index. Handwritten. Average 22 pages. 26 x 16 x .25. 351 volumes, 1923-1931, Basement, rear storeroom; 170 volumes, 1932—, Board of elections record room.

533. ABSTRACT OF VOTES
1912—. 49 volumes.

Complete summary of votes cast in each precinct at each general election, primary, or special election, showing total number of votes received by each candidate or for each proposal. Arranged by names of offices and alphabetically thereunder by names of candidates. No index. Handwritten. Average 12 pages. 26 x 18 x .25. 42 volumes, 1912-1932, Basement, rear storeroom; 7 volumes, 1933—, Board of elections record room.

Fiscal Accounts

534. LEDGER

1914—. 2 volumes.

Record of expenses in connection with the operation of the board of elections, showing name of creditor, amount, for what, and date. Also contains Payroll, Precinct Officials, entry 535. Arranged chronologically by dates of entry. No index. Handwritten. Average 280 pages. 16 x 10 x 2. Board of elections record room.

535. PAYROLL, PRECINCT OFFICIALS

1889-1913. 1 volume. 1914— in Ledger, entry 534.

Payroll record of precinct officials, showing date, name, what party, duty, ward or township, precinct, number of days, and amount due. Arranged chronologically by dates of payrolls. No index. Handwritten. 250 pages. 18 x 15 x 2. Basement, rear storeroom.

536. VOUCHERS

1918—. 6 volumes.

Stubs of vouchers issued to precinct election officials and for other election expenses, showing name of payee, voucher number, date, amount, and for what service. Arranged numerically by consecutive voucher numbers. No index. Handwritten on printed forms. Average 100 pages. 20 x 4 x 1. 4 volumes, 1818-1929, Basement, rear storeroom; 2 volumes, 1930—, Board of elections record room.

537. RECEIPTS

1916—. 2 volumes.

Official receipt stubs for candidates' filing fee, showing receipt number, name of candidate, for what office filed, and amount of fee. Arranged numerically by consecutive receipt numbers. No index. Handwritten on printed forms. Average 180 pages. 13 x 3.5 x 1.25. 1 volume, 1916-1929, Basement, rear storeroom; 1 volume, 1930—, Board of elections record room.

The county board of education, a modern administrative and supervisory agency developed during the last two decades, supplanted the smaller educational units, which, established during the early period of Ohio history, became ineffective and unable to meet the modern requirements as demanded by rural communities.

During the earlier period of Ohio history, educational administration, because of the newness of the state, the sparseness of the population, and the undeveloped means of transportation was, by necessity, local in character. For fourteen years after the accession of Ohio to statehood, though the constitution stated that means of education should be encouraged by the general assembly no legislation was enacted for public schools.[1] It was not until 1817 that the legislature authorized six or more people to form associations to build school houses and to be incorporated for educational purposes.[2]

The first permanent law for the organization of schools in Ohio was passed in 1821. Under the provisions of this act, the electors of the township were authorized to vote on the proposition of dividing the townships into school districts. If the proposal carried, there were to be elected three school commissioners, who, in turn, were authorized to select a clerk and a collector who should act as a treasurer. They were instructed also, to levy taxes for the support of schools and to hire teachers.[3]

As education began to advance in the early years of the nineteenth century, some kind of state control was needed. Accordingly, in 1837, the office of state superintendent of schools was established.[4] A year later an act was passed making the county auditor also the county superintendent of schools; and in each township the clerk became superintendent of the smaller unit. The county superintendent was made responsible to the state superintendent in all educational affairs. In the same year each incorporated city, town, or borough not regulated by a charter was made a separate school district. The voters in each division were authorized to elect three directors.[5]

---

1. *Ohio Const. 1802,* Art. VIII, secs. 3, 25, 27.
2. *Laws of Ohio,* XV, 107.
3. *Laws of Ohio,* XIX, 52.
4. *Ibid.,* XXXV, 82.
5. *Ibid.,* XXXVI, 21.

The effectiveness of this organization, however, was destroyed in 1840, when the legislature abolished the office of state superintendent and the secretary of state took over his functions of tabulating and transmitting school statistics.[6] Seven years later, twenty-five counties exclusive of Ross were allowed to have county superintendents,[7] and in 1848 the provisions of the previous act were extended to Ross and all other counties in the state.[8]

Although marked changes were made in the curricula of the schools, the history of education in Ohio from 1850 to the early part of the twentieth century was largely one of the gradual transference of power from districts to townships, and from townships to county in the interest of a better system of education. It was not, however, until within the last three decades that the county became the unit for educational administration.[9]

Although the county superintendent was known as early as 1838, the first permanent law for the establishment of a county board of education was enacted in 1914. Under this act the school districts were classified, and provision was made for a county school district, exclusive of the territory embraced in any city or village having a population of three thousand or more desiring exemption. The county district was to be under the supervision of five board members elected by the presidents of the village and rural school boards, the members were to hold office for one, two, three, four, and five years respectively, and each year thereafter one member was to be selected to serve a five-year term.[10]

The county board of education was authorized to change school district lines; afford transportation for children living more than two miles from a schoolhouse; appoint a county superintendent; and certify annually to the county auditor the number of teachers and superintendents employed, their salaries, and the amount apportioned to each school district for the payment of salaries of the county and district superintendents. The county superintendent, acting as secretary of the board, was required to keep in a book provided for the purpose of a full record of the proceedings of the board properly indexed. Each motion, together with the name of the person making it and the vote thereon, was to be entered on the record.[11]

---

6. *Ibid.,* XXXVIII, 130.
7. *Ibid.,* XLV, 32.
8. *Ibid.,* XLVI, 86.
9. *Ibid.,* LXX, 195, 242; XCVII, 354.
10. *Ibid.,* CIV, 133.
11. *Ibid.,* CIV, 133; CVIII, pt. i, 704

The county was divided into administrative divisions containing one or more villages or rural school districts. Each district was to be under the supervision of a district superintendent, who was required to visit the schools in his charge, direct and assist teachers in the performance of their duties, and classify and control promotion of pupils. Moreover, he was required to report annually to the county superintendent on matters under his charge, and assemble teachers for the purpose of conferring on curricular matters, discipline, and school management.[12]

Significant changes were made by the act of 1921, under which the board members became elective by popular vote. They were authorized to appoint one or more assistant county superintendents for a term of three years. Ross County, however, has no assistant. The board was authorized to publish, with the advice and consent of the county superintendent, a minimum course of study to serve as a guide to local board members. The same act abolished the office of district superintendent.[13]

The county organization has placed the rural schools on a plane of equality with the city schools. The consolidation of the smaller units has eliminated the small, ill-equipped schools, and provides under one roof facilities and instruction suited to the needs of the rural children under the supervision of educational specialist.

All records of the board of education are located in the office of the county superintendent of schools. With the exception of the minutes of the board of education, which date from the establishment of the board, only comparatively recent records are kept.

---

12. *Ibid.,* CIV, 133-145.
13. G. C. secs. 4728-1, 4729; *Laws of Ohio,* CIV, 242.

538. [MINUTES, BOARD OF EDUCATION]
1914—. 3 volumes.
Minutes of meetings of the county board of education, showing date, proceedings, and a record of receipts and expenditures. Arranged chronologically by dates of meetings. No index. Average 300 pages. 16 x 11 x 2.5.

539. ANNUAL FINANCIAL REPORTS [Schools]
1932—. 7 reports.
Copies of annual reports to state department of education by the county superintendent of schools, showing name of township and school, and receipts and

expenditures of the school fund. Arranged alphabetically by names of townships and alphabetically thereunder by names of schools. No index. Typed on printed forums. (No. 36). Average 35 pages. 10 x 8 x .25.

540. STATISTICAL REPORTS [Schools]
1929—. 10 reports.
Copies of annual statistical reports to state department of education by the county superintendent of schools, showing names of township and school, enrollment, average attendance, and promotion records. Arranged alphabetically by names of townships and alphabetically thereunder by names of schools. No index. Typed on printed forms. (No. 6). Average 40 pages. 10 x 8 x .25.

541. CERTIFIED STATISTICAL REPORTS [Schools]
1934—. 5 reports.
Copies of certified statistical reports to state department of education which have been certified by county superintendent of schools, showing names of township and school, complete record of attendance, and promotions; also notarization. Arranged alphabetically by names of townships and alphabetically thereunder by names of schools. No index. Typed on printed forms. (sf. 4). Average 36 pages. 10 x 8 x .25.

542. HIGH SCHOOL PRINCIPALS' REPORTS
1930—. 6 file boxes.
Copies of monthly and annual reports to county superintendent of schools from high school principals, showing names of township and school, date, enrollment, attendance, and promotions. Arranged alphabetically by names of schools and chronologically thereunder by dates of reports. No index. Handwritten on printed forms. (No. 21). 10 x 10 x 20.

543. TEACHERS' REPORTS
1922—. 24 file boxes.
Copies of monthly and annual reports to county superintendent of schools by grade-school teachers, showing name of school, date, name of pupil, date of birth, names of parents, addresses, grade, age, days present, grade in each subject, average grade, and promotion record. Arranged alphabetically by name of schools and chronologically thereunder by dates of reports. No index. Handwritten on printed forms. 10 x 10 x 20.

The general health district, or county health department is one of the recent developments in county health administration. An act of the legislature in 1919 provided that townships and municipalities in each county, exclusive of any city with 25,000 or more population, should constitute a general health district; cities with 25,000 or more population a municipal health district; and municipalities of not less then 10,000 nor more than 25,000 population, and maintaining a board of health meeting the qualifications of the legislative act, were authorized after examination by the state health department to continue operation as separate health districts.[1]

An amendment in December 1919 made each city a health district; the townships and villages in each county were combined into a general health district; and a city and general health district might combine for administrative purposes,[2] The mayor of each municipality not constituting a city health district, and the chairman of the trustees of each township, are authorized to meet at the seat of justice and by selecting a chairman and a secretary organize a district advisory council which selects and appoints a district board of health composed of five members, one of whom must be a physician, who serves without compensation.[3]

Within thirty days after their appointment the members of the district board of health - the county board of health - organized by appointing one of their members president and the other president *pro tempore.* The board is authorized to appoint as district health commissioner a licensed physician who serves as secretary to the board. This official is designated deputy state registrar of vital statistics and is required to report monthly to the state registrar of vital statistics.[4]

On recommendation of the district health commissioner the board appoints a full-time public health nurse, a clerk, and such additional public health nurses, physicians, and others as may be necessary for the proper conduct of its work. The board studies the prevalence of disease, especially communicable diseases, provides treatment for venereal diseases, and is authorized to make any and all regulations it deems necessary for the prevention or restriction of disease, and the prevention, abolition, or suppression of nuisances.

---

1. *Laws of Ohio,* CVIII, pt. i, 238.
2. *Ibid.,* CVIII, pt. ii, 1085.
3. *Ibid.,* CVIII, pt. ii, 1082.
4. G. C. sec. 1261-32; *Laws of Ohio,* CVIII, pt. i, 238-242.

It provides for inspection of public charitable, benevolent, correctional, and penal institutions; and may provide for inspection of dairies, stores, restaurants, hotels, and other places where food is manufactured, handled, stored, sold, or offered for sale. The board is authorized to carry on necessary laboratory tests by establishing a laboratory or contracting with existing laboratories, and all state institutions supported in whole or in part by public funds must furnish such laboratory service to a county board of health under the terms agreed upon.[5]

The health department is financed by public taxation. The district board of health annually estimates in itemized form the amount needed for the fiscal year, and these estimates are certified to the county auditor and submitted by him to the county budget commissioners who may reduce any item but cannot increase any item or the aggregate of all items. The total amount fixed by the commissioners is apportioned by the county health department on the basis of taxable valuation in the townships and municipalities composing the district.[6]

All records are located in the office of the county board of health, welfare department.

---

5. *Laws of Ohio,* CVIII, pt. ii, 1088, 1089.
6. *Laws of Ohio,* CVIII, pt. ii, 1091.

Journals and Reports

544. JOURNAL [District Board of Health]
1914—. 4 volumes.

Minutes of meetings of Ross County district health board, showing date and record of proceedings. Arranged chronologically by dates of meetings. No index. Handwritten. Average 220 pages. 16 x 11 x 2.

545. SANITATION REPORTS
1921—. 8 file boxes.

Reports of sanitation officer, showing date of inspection, findings, and recommendations made. Arranged chronologically by dates of inspection. No index. 1921-1929, handwritten on printed forms; 1929—, Typed on printed forms. 12 x 14 x 26.

546. REPORTS, VISITING NURSES

1923—. 7 file boxes. Subtitled by subjects.

Reports of visiting nurses, showing date, number of calls made, reports on case under care, record of visits to public schools, and examination of pupils. Arranged chronologically by dates of reports. No index. Typed on printed forms. 12 x 14 x 26.

547. REPORTS [Tuberculosis]

1915—. 2 file boxes. 1 subtitled County Commissioners, 1 subtitled State Board.

Copies of department reports to county commissioners and to state board of health on tuberculosis cases and measures for control, showing date and number of cases treated. Arranged chronologically by dates of reports. No index. 1915-1920, handwritten on printed forms; 1921—, typed on printed forms. 12 x 14 x 26.

548. REPORTS

1924—. 4 file boxes. Subtitle by contained subjects.

Copies of reports to state department by Ross County district board. Reports cover vital statistics, child health, physical examinations, correction of defects, drinking water examinations, tuberculosis, and contagious and venereal diseases. Arranged by subjects and chronologically thereunder. No index. Typed on printed forms. 12 x 14 x 26.

Vital Statistics

*Births and Death*s (See also entries 265-267)

549. RECORD OF BIRTHS

1908—. 64 volumes. (labeled by years).

Record of births in Ross County as reported by physicians and midwives, showing name of parents, date of birth, residence, sex, color, and name of child. Also contains Birth Records (Chillicothe), entry 550. Arranged alphabetically by surnames and chronologically thereunder. No index. Handwritten. Average 450 pages. 8.5 x 12 x 3.25.

550. BIRTH RECORDS (Chillicothe)

1897-1907. 1 volume. 1908— in Record of Births, entry 549.

Record of birth for the city at Chillicothe, showing names of parents, address, date of birth, sex, and color of child. Evidently this record was kept by the city health commissioner. Arranged chronologically by dates of births. No index. Handwritten. 500 pages. 18 x 12 x 4.

551. RECORD OF DEATHS

1908—. 30 volumes.

Record of deaths as reported to county board of health, showing name, age, sex, color of decedent, residence, and cause of death. Arranged alphabetically by surnames and chronologically thereunder. No index. Handwritten. Average 450 pages. 8.5 x 12 x 4.

Immunizations

552. IMMUNIZATION RECORDS [For School Pupils]

1926—. 5 volumes.

Record of vaccinations of school children against smallpox and diphtheria, showing date, name and age of child, what school, and name of physician. Arranged chronologically by dates of entry. No index. Average 180 pages. 12 x 14 x 1.25.

Fiscal Accounts

553. LEDGER

1912—. 3 volumes. (1-3).

Record of appropriations and expenditures of county board of health, showing date, and itemized record of appropriations and expenditures. Arranged chronologically by dates of entry. No index. Handwritten. Average 280 pages. 15 x 10 x 2.

The Mount Logan Sanatorium District, composed of Ross, Fayette, Pike, Highland, and Scioto Counties, was organized in July 1, 1915.[1] Later Jackson County was added to the district. The district board purchased from Rufus Marzluff a tract of land located on the crest of Carlisle Hill overlooking the city of Chillicothe from the southwest. Construction plans were approved in May of 1916, and in July of the same year contracts amounting to $50,000 were let for the erection of the buildings. The sanatorium was open for the admission of patients, July 1, 1918.

Accommodations are provided for sixty patients and although it is a public institution for the care of those who are unable to pay for treatment, paying patients are admitted.[2] Admissions from the various counties are provided according to the population of the county. Each of the counties of the district bears a share of the expense proportionated to the number of its patients admitted.

The sanatorium is administered by a board of trustees composed of residence of the sanatorium district.[2]

All records are located in the office of the sanatorium.

---

1. *Scioto Gazette,* October 4, 1915.
2. Records in the office of Walter H. Hartung, Director, State Department of Health.
3. *Laws of Ohio,* C, 87.

554. REGISTRATION JOURNAL

1918—. 2 volumes.

Records of admittance to hospital, showing name, what county, address, age, and name of nearest relative. Arranged alphabetically by names of patients and chronologically thereunder. No index. Handwritten. Average 17 x 14 x 3.

555. INDEX TO CASE RECORDS

1918—. 2 file boxes.

Index to Case Records, Active, entry 556, and Case Records, Closed, entry 557, showing name of patient, X-ray number, and section of file in which case record is filed. Arranged alphabetically by names of patients. Typed on printed forms. 6 x 6 x 16.

556. CASE RECORDS, ACTIVE

1931—. 4 file boxes.

Records of cases receiving treatment, showing name of patient, X-ray number, from what county, address, sex, age, family history, and technical data of case. Arranged numerically by X-ray numbers. For index, see entry 555. Typed on printed forms. 12 x 14 x 26.

557. CASE RECORDS, CLOSED

1918—. 12 File boxes.

Records of cases closed by discharge from hospital as cured, or because progress of disease was arrested, or by death, showing name of patient, X-ray number, county, address, sex, age, family history, and technical data of case. Arranged numerically by X-ray numbers. For index, see entry 555. Types on printed forms. 12 x 14 x 26.

558. LEDGER

1918—. 3 volumes.

Record of receipts and expenditures, showing date, source of receipts, and itemized account of expenditures. Arranged chronologically by dates of entry. No index. Handwritten. Average 320 pages. 18 x 12 x 2.25.

The Ross County poorhouse, now called the county home, was established in 1818 under the provisions of the legislative act of 1816. In April 1818 a site was purchased from James Dunlap and notice of bids for furnishing material and erecting the poorhouse was published in July of the same year. Contracts totaling $3,700 were let during the following year and in April 1820 the building was accepted from the contractors.[1]

Construction of the present three-story brick and stone county home building were started in 1872[2] and occupied the following year.[3] The institution, in addition to caring for indigent adults and orphan children, was used from 1900 to 1914 by the welfare department to house unwed mothers. In 1914 children and unwed mothers were provided for outside of the infirmary.[4] The building has been unaltered since its construction sixty-five years ago, except for the installation of a water system and an electrical light and power plant.

By the provisions of the legislative act of 1816, the county commissioners were authorized to build a "poor house," and to appoint annually seven persons to constitute a board of directors. This board, a corporate body, was authorized to make such rules and regulations as were necessary for the management of the institution, and to appoint a superintendent. This officer was directed to receive only persons who had the required order from the township trustees. He was directed to keep a book listing the name and age of every person received, together with the date of admission.[5] The board of directors, or a committee of that body, was required to visit the "poor house"monthly to examine the condition of the paupers and to make a report on such matter as the food, clothing, and treatment of the inmates. Moreover, they were required to inspect the books and accounts of the superintendent. Annually the board was required to report to the county commissioners the "state of the institution" with a full and correct account of all their proceedings, contracts, and disbursements; and the expense of establishing and supporting the institution were to be paid on the order of the county commissioners out of the money in the treasury not otherwise appropriated.[6]

---

1. Order Book, 1809-1819, 1819-1827, *passim.*
2. Commissioners' Journal, volume B, pp. 202, 212, 255, 256, 262, 265, 267, 275, 295, 296.
3. Henry Holcomb Bennett, *State Centennial History of Ohio and Ross County* (Madison, 1902), 99.
4. Commissioners' Journal, volume M, p. 12. See also entries 561, 562.
5. *Laws of Ohio,* XIV, 447.
6. *Ibid.,* XIV, 499.

By the legislative act of 1831, the membership of the board was reduced to three. This board, like its predecessor, was authorized to appoint a superintendent. It was his duty, upon the order of the board, to discharge from the poor house any person who had been admitted because of illness when he had sufficiently recovered.[7] Moreover, the directors were authorized to remove paupers to their legal place of residence.[8] Besides this, any pauper rejected by the board of directors could be turned over to the township overseers to be cared for by contracting with the lowest bidder.[9]

In 1850 the name county poorhouse was changed to that of county infirmary.[10] Fifteen years later, in 1865, the board of infirmary directors, consisting of three resident electors, was to be elected by the voters of the county for a three-year term. The board was still authorized to appoint a superintendent, and was still required to make inspection visits, and report their findings to the county commissioners.[11]

Although reports have been required in previous years, it was not until the decade of the seventies that the legislature enacted measures looking forward to some business-like management of this ancient institution. Accordingly, in 1872, an act was passed which required each infirmary director, as well as the superintendent, to give bond conditioned for the faithful performance of the duties of his office.[12] Under this act the directors were required to report semi-annually to the county commissioners the condition of the infirmary, the number of inmates, and such other information as the county commissioners believed proper. Furthermore, the board of directors was required to file a full account "of all moneys received and paid out, together with the vouchers . . . from whence received, to whom and for what paid out" with the county commissioners, who, after examining it, entered the report in the minutes of their proceedings. This report, as well as the vouchers, was filed in the auditor's office, it was to be "safely preserved" by that officer.[13]

---

7. *Laws of Ohio,* XXIX, 319.
8. *Ibid.,* XXIX, 319.
9. *Ibid.,* XXIX, 321-322.
10. *Ibid.,* XLVIII, 62.
11. *Ibid.,* LXII, 24-25.
12. *Ibid.,* LXIX, 120-121.
13. *Ibid.,* LXIX, 121-122. See entry 8.

The county infirmary served also as a place for the confinement of children, the mentally ill, and persons afflicted with epilepsy. Although the state assumed responsibility for the mentally ill in the early years of the nineteenth century, it was not until 1898 that it was made unlawful to confine adult insane and epileptics in the county home.[14] Previously, in 1884, the legislature prohibited the housing of children in the county infirmary who were eligible to the county children's home or to some other charitable institution unless separated from adults.[15] However exceptions were made in the case of insane, idiotic, and epileptic children.[16] The latter provision is still effective in Ohio.[17]

By an act of May 31, 1911, effective January 1, 1913, the board of infirmary directors was abolished and the powers formerly exercised by this body was transferred to the county commissioners and the infirmary superintendent.[17] The superintendent is still required to keep a record of the inmates, as prescribed by statute, and to report annually to the county commissioners. This report, the acceptance of which is evidenced by an entry in the commissioners' journal, is filed with the county auditor and by him preserved.[18] In 1919 the name county infirmary was changed to that of county home.[19]

The county commissioners still make provision for the establishment and maintenance of the county home, appoint a superintendent, and make regular inspection visits. The superintendent is appointed from a list of names of persons eligible under civil service regulations.[20] The superintendent is authorized to appoint a matron and other employees.[21] Moreover, since 1882, they have been authorized to appoint an infirmary physician, who, like the superintendent, is required by statute to report to the county commissioners. This report, made quarterly, includes such information as the nature and extent of medical services rendered, to whom, and the character of the disease treated.[22]

---

14. *Laws of Ohio,* XCIII, 274.
15. *Ibid.,* LXXXI, 92.
16. *Ibid.,* CIII, 890.
17. G. C. sec. 3091.
17. *Laws of Ohio,* CII, 433. [sic]
18. G. C. sec. 2535. See entry 9.
19. *Laws of Ohio,* CVIII, pt. i, 68.
20. Ohio Attorney General, *Opinions,* III, 2021.
21. G. C. sec. 2522.
22. *Ibid.,* sec. 2546; *Laws of Ohio,* LXXIII, 233; LXXIX, 90; CII, 436; CVIII, pt. i, 269.

Although there is some relation between the old age pension system and the county home the newer form of aid is merely supplementary to the institution. As always the county home cares for those whose condition is such that they cannot be satisfactory cared for except in an institution.[23] Since the inauguration of aid for the aged there has been a slight reduction in the population of the Ross County home which is now approximately 75. The social aid programs have resulted in no reduction in the cost of operating county homes. Despite the decline in population of the Ross County home the per capita cost of operation has increased 69 percent since 1934.[24]

All records are in the office of the superintendent of the county home.

---

23. *The Reorganization of County Government in Ohio* . . . , 132, 135.
24. Ohio Auditor of State, *Comparative Statistics, Counties of Ohio* (Columbus, 1934-1937), *passim.*

559. [Infirmary Directors'] RECORD
August 20, 1912-December 31, 1912. 1 volume.
Minutes of meetings of the board of infirmary directors, showing date, all orders, resolutions, and transactions including record of expenditures and receipts. Arranged chronologically by dates of meetings. No index. Handwritten. 300 pages. 14 x 9 x 2. Auditor's vault.

For other records, see entries 4, 25.

560. INFIRMARY RECORD
1842-1884. 1 volume.
Record of cases cared for outside the home and of inmates of county home, showing date of admittance, name, age, sex, birth date, physical condition, date discharged, date bound out, and to whom. Arranged alphabetically by names of dependents and chronologically thereunder by dates of admittance. No index. Handwritten. 360 pages. 18 x 14 x 3.

For subsequent records, see entries 561, 562.

561. SUPERINTENDENT'S RECORD OF INDIGENT PERSONS
1900—. 1 volume.

Record of births at county home, showing date, name of mother, and color, sex, and name of child, pages 1-16; also record of deaths at county home, 1900-1914, showing name and age of decedent, cause of death, and from what township admitted, page 17-40; also superintendent's record of inmates, showing name, date of admittance township, sex, color, birthday, physical condition, date discharged, and reason for discharge, page 41-482. Arranged chronologically by dates of entry. Indexed alphabetically by names of inmates. Handwritten on printed forms. 560 pages. 20 x 14 x 4.5.

For prior records, see entry 560.

562. RECORD OF CHILDREN
1900-1914. 1 volume.

Superintendent's record of dependent children who were cared for at the county home, showing name of child, names of parents, age, sex, color, and physical condition of child, date of admittance, birth date (if known), date of indenture, to whom bound out, residence, taken on trial, by whom, residence, date discharge, reason of discharge, date of death, and remarks. Arranged chronologically by dates of admittance. No index. Handwritten. 400 pages. 18 x 12 x 3.

For subsequent records, see entries 566-572.

563. DAILY MOVEMENT OF POPULATION
1828—. 98 volumes.

Daily record of population at county home from which monthly reports to the state welfare board are compiled by the superintendent, showing names of inmates, number registered, admitted, number discharge, and number of deaths. Arranged alphabetically by names of inmates. No index. Handwritten. Average 80 pages. 7 x 10 x .5.

564. ANNUAL REPORTS

1930—. 1 file box.

Copies of superintendent's annual reports to state welfare department, showing date, number of persons under care at beginning of year, number admitted during year, number discharged, number of deaths, and number in care of institution at end of year. Arranged chronologically by dates or reports. No index. Handwritten on printed forms. 13 x 11 x 3.5.

565. LEDGER

1891—. 3 volumes.

Superintendent's record of receipts and expenditures of institution, showing date, source of receipts, and itemized account of expenditures. Arranged chronologically by dates of entry. No index. Handwritten. Average 370 pages. 18 x 11 x 3.

Although the legislature made provision for the institutional care of the county's indigent as early as 1816, it was not until after the middle of the nineteenth century, when hundreds of Ohio children were left homeless by the scourge of civil war, that the legislature enacted measures for the care of dependent children. Previous to this time the Ohio statutes relative to the care of children had been taken from the territorial code which authorized the overseers of the poor, and later the trustees of the "poor house," to apprentice the children of the indigent, boys under twenty-one and girls under eighteen years of age.[1] The fact that this system was not only inhuman, but entirely unsatisfactory, is evidenced by the innumerable advertisements for run away apprentices appearing in the press.

In 1865 the legislature authorized the county commissioners to receive request for orphans' asylums and, when funds accumulated in sufficient quantities, to construct such a home, and appoint a board of directors consisting of six persons who were given the task of managing the institution, subject to the rules and regulations of the county commissioners. This board, electing a president and a treasurer from its own number, was required annually to make a report of the receipts and disbursements of the asylum, together with the number of orphans received into and discharged from the institution. This report was to be published by the commissioners in the newspaper having a general circulation.[2]

A year later, in 1866, the commissioners were authorized, when in their judgment the best interest of the wards of the county would be served, to establish children's homes, and to provide by means of taxation, funds to be used for the purchase of a site, to construct buildings, and to maintain such charitable institutions.[3] Then, in 1876, an act was passed which repealed all previous legislation and established the present duties of the county commissioners, trustees, superintendent, and matron in respect to children's homes. The act authorized the county commissioners to appoint a board of trustees and a superintendent of each children's home.[4]

---

1. Pease, *op. cit.,* 219; *Laws of Ohio,* III, 276; VIII, 223-224; XXIX, 318.
2. *Laws of Ohio,* LXII, 97.
3. *Ibid.,* LXIII, 45.
4. *Ibid.,* LXXIII, 64.

Prior to 1914 the dependent and neglected children in Ross County were cared for at the county infirmary. From May 1914 to the spring of 1924, many dependent children were sent to the Cleveland Protestant Orphan Asylum in Cleveland, Ohio, but the majority were placed in private homes in Ross County. Early in 1924 Colonel Richard Enderlin, a public spirited altruistic citizen of Ross County, championed the movement to establish a separate home for the care of children. He offered to deed without cost to the county a tract of land one and a half acres in extent on which stood a brick house, located on the north side of Western Avenue in Chillicothe, which offer the county commissioners promptly voted to accept.[5]

By May of 1924 the structure had been remodeled to suit its new requirements, and all modern conveniences were installed. Since that time, the dependent children of Ross County have been cared for at their new quarters until its capacity of 30 was exceeded. It still remains necessary, therefore, to place the overflow into private homes for care, the institution acting as a receiving home for the children who are thus placed. All crippled and mentally deficient children, however, are retained in the home.

The board of trustees consists of five members appointed for a five-year term. The trustees, besides appointing a superintendent, hold monthly meetings at which time they examine all accounts presented for payment, examine into the condition of the property and the manner of care offered to the wards. Annually, or oftener, they are required to file with the state board of charities a detailed account giving the whereabouts of each child and the physical condition of each ward under their care.[6]

The superintendent, operating under the rules and regulations of the trustees, has entire charge and control of the home and its wards. He may appoint a matron, assistant matron, and other necessary employees, subject to the approval of the board of trustees. It is the duty of such employees to care for the inmates in the home, direct their employment, and give suitable physical, mental, and moral training. Under the direction of the superintendent, the matron has general management and supervision of the household duties of the home.

---

5. Commissioners' Journal, volume O, p. 559.
6. G. C. sec. 3082-1.

The matron, like other employees, receives such salaries as the trustees may direct and maybe removed by the superintendent or at the pleasure of a majority of the trustees.[7]

The county children's home serves as a refuge for children under eighteen years of age who have resided in the county one year and who are, in the opinion of the trustees, eligible to admission by reason of orphanage, abandonment, or neglect by parents, or the inability of parents to provide for them.[8] Children are admitted to the home on order of the juvenile court or upon order of a majority of the board of trustees. Since 1876 each child committed to the children's home must be accompanied by a statement of the facts setting forth his name, his age, his birthplace, and his condition. These facts, recorded by the superintendent in a book kept for that purpose are confidential and open to inspection only at the discretion of the board of trustees.[9] All wards of the children's home who have been committed to the institution by the juvenile court because of abandonment, neglect, or dependency, or who have been voluntarily surrendered by their parents are under the exclusive jurisdiction, guardianship, and control of the trustees until they have become of lawful age.[10]

The county commissioners may, subject to the approval of the board of state charities, after an opportunity has been given to the electorate to demand a referendum on the proposition, abandon the children's home. If the home is discontinued, they may sell the site and buildings and use the funds for care of neglected and dependent children, providing that the wards in the children's home who are placed in foster homes and those who are under the guardianship of the trustees are legally committed to the guardianship of the board of state charities.[11]

All records are located in the office of superintendent of the children's home.

---

7. *Ibid.,* sec. 3085.
8. *Ibid.,* sec. 3089.
9. *Ibid.,* sec. 3089; *Laws of Ohio,* LXXIII, 64; LXXXII, 196; XCIX, 187; CIII, 889.
10. G. C. sec. 3093.
11. *Laws of Ohio,* CIX, 533.

Case Records
(See also entry 562)

566. REGISTRATION RECORDS
1924—. 10 file boxes. (labeled by contained letters of the alphabet)
Record of admittance to home, showing name of child, names of parents, date of birth (if known), age, sex, color, and date of admittance. Arranged alphabetically by names of children. No index. Typed on printed forms. 6 x 9 x 20.

567. CASE RECORDS
1924—. 6 file boxes. (labeled by contained letters of the alphabet).
Case records of each child admitted to the home, showing name of child, parentage, date of birth, age, color, sex, defects, education, court proceedings (if any), and progress sheet. All records of each case in individual folder. Arranged alphabetically by names of children. No index. Typed on printed forms. 12 x 12 x 26.

568. PLACEMENT RECORDS
1924—. 8 file boxes. (labeled by years).
Record of children placed in private homes, showing dates, name of child, name and address of person taking child, report of investigation of home in which child is placed, and progress report. Arranged chronologically by years and alphabetically thereunder by names of children. No index. Typed on printed forms. 6 x 9 x 20.

569. ADOPTION RECORDS
1924—. 1 file box.
Record of adoptions of children in custody of the children's home, showing name of child, names of foster parents, notation of court proceedings and orders, and date of adoption. Arranged chronologically by years and alphabetically there under by names of children. No index. Typed on printed forms. 6 x 9 x 20.

Reports

570. MONTHLY REPORTS
1924—. 151 reports in 1 file box.
Duplicate copies of superintendent's monthly reports to state welfare department, showing date, number of children admitted during past thirty days, number placed in homes, number discharged, number of deaths, and total number under care of home. Arranged chronologically by dates and reports. No index. Typed on printed forms. 12 x 12 x 26.

571. ANNUAL REPORTS
1924—. 12 reports in 1 file box.
Duplicate copies of superintendent's annual reports to state welfare department, showing date, number of children admitted during past year, number placed in homes, number of adoptions, number discharged, number of deaths, and total number cared for during the year. Arranged chronologically by dates are reports. No index. Typed on printed forms. 12 x 12 x 26.

Fiscal Accounts

572. JOURNAL
1924—. 2 volumes.
Record of expenditures pertaining to the operation of the institution, showing daily expense account, for what, to whom due, amount, date, and what fund. Arranged chronologically by dates of entry. No index. Handwritten. Average 280 pages. 18 x 12 x 2.25.

The board of county visitors, an agency for the examination and inspection of county institutions supported wholly or in part by county municipal taxation, was created by an act of the general assembly in 1882. Under this act, the judge of the court of common pleas was authorized to appoint five persons, three of whom were to be women, who were to visit periodically such county institutions as the county infirmary, county jail, municipal prisons, and children's home, and file annually a report of their proceedings and recommendations for the changes with the clerk of courts, and forward a copy to the state Board of charities. The members, appointed for an indefinite period, were to serve without compensation.[1]

By the act of 1892 the personnel of the board was increased to six persons, three of whom were to be women, and not more than three to have the same political affiliations. Furthermore the act made it the duty of the probate judge, whenever proceedings were instituted in his court to commit a child under sixteen years of age to the boys' industrial home or to girls' industrial home, to have notice given to the board of such proceedings; and it was made the duty of the board of visitors to attend the meeting of the court, as a body or as a committee, to protect the interest of the child.[2]

While the provisions of the act of 1892 were amended by the acts of 1898 and 1900, these acts did not, in the main, affect the duties of the board.[3] The latter act, however, made the board a continuous body with two members serving for one year, two members serving for two years, and two members serving for three years. In addition to this, the board was allowed a minimum expense schedule for their services.[4] Six years later the board was authorized to recommend to the county commissioners measurers for the more economical administration of county institutions. Their report, together with their recommendations, was to be filed each year with a judge of the probate court and with the county prosecuting attorney.[5]

---

1. *Laws of Ohio,* LXXXIX, 107.
2. *Ibid.,* LXXXIX, 161.
3. *Ibid.,* XXCIII, 57; XCIV, 70.
4. *Ibid.,* XCIV, 70.
5. *Ibid.,* XCVIII, 29.

In 1913 the power of appointment of board members was transferred to the probate judge. Under this act the juvenile judge, like the probate judge under the act of 1892, was authorized to notify the visitors when any proceedings were instituted in his court for the commitment of any child to a state institution for correction.[6] The practice of annually filing reports of the board with the probate judge, prosecuting attorney, and state board of charities has been continued.[7]

Although the statute requires reports from the board of county visitors, none was found in Ross County.

---

6. *Ibid.,* CIII, 173-174, 888.
7. G. C. sec. 2976.

The soldiers' relief commission was established by an act of the legislature passed May 19, 1886, entitled "An act to provide for the relief of indigent Union soldiers, sailors and marines, and the indigent wives, widows and minor children of indigent or deceased Union soldiers, sailors and marines." Under provisions of this act the commissioners of each county were authorized to levy a specific tax for the purpose of creating a fund for the relief of such beneficiaries; and the judge of the court of common pleas was authorized to appoint three county residents, at least two of whom were honorably discharged Union soldiers, to serve for a term of three years as members of the commission, which was organized by the selection of a chairman and secretary and was known as the soldiers' relief commission.[1]

An amendment passed on March 4, 1887, provided that councilmen of city wards, as well as a board of trustees of the townships, certified to the soldiers' relief commission names of those requiring and entitled to aid under this act.[2]

By an act of the legislature, passed April 28, 1890 the soldiers' relief commission was required to appoint annually a committee of three in each township and a committee of three in each ward in any city in the county, whose duty it was to receive all applications for aid and to certify them to the soldiers' relief commission.[3]

Sections 2930 and 2933-4 of the General Code were amended, March 6, 1917, to provide for the appointment to each county commission of one member who is the wife, widow, son or daughter of an honorably discharged soldier, sailor, or marine of the Civil War or of the Spanish-American War, the other two members to be honorably discharged soldiers, sailors, or marines of the United States; and for the appointment to each township and ward committee of a wife or widow of a soldier, sailor, or marine of the United States.[4] Two years later, in 1919, the provisions of the act was extended to include indigent veterans of the World War or to indigent parents, wives, widows, or minor children of such veterans.[5]

---

1. *Laws of Ohio,* LXXXIII, 232.
2. *Ibid.,* LXXXIV, 100.
3. *Ibid.,* LXXXVII, 352.
4. *Ibid.,* CVII, 27.
5. *Ibid.,* CVIII, pt. i, 633.

Section 2930 and 2934 of the General Code were amended on April 6, 1929 to provide for the appointment by the court that common pleas in each county of a soldiers' relief commission, to consist of three members, one to be the wife, widow, son, or daughter of an honorably discharge soldier, sailor, or marine of the Civil War, of the Spanish-American War, or of the World War, the other two members to be honorably discharged soldiers, sailors, or marines of the United States, one of whom should, if possible, be a member of the Spanish-American War Veterans, the other a member of the American Legion.[6]

The soldiers' relief commission in Ross County keeps no permanent records. For county commissioners records, see entry 2; for auditor's records, see entries 401, 402.

6. *Ibid.*, CXIII, 466.

SOLDIERS' BURIAL COMMISSION

In 1884 the legislature made provisions for a soldiers' burial commission in each county, to consist of three persons in each township appointed by the county commissioners, which was directed to defray the expense incurred in the interment of any honorably discharged Union soldier, sailor, or marine who died in poverty. The commission, serving at the pleasure of the appointing power, was required to report to the county commissioners the name, rank, and command of the decedent, which report was transcribed by the county commissioners in a book kept for that purpose.[1] The original act, amended in 1891, extended the provisions of the act to include the interment of the wives or widows of Union soldiers.[2] In 1893 the act was again amended to provide for the interment of mothers of Union soldiers, sailors, or marines, and army nurses.[3] In 1908 the personnel of the commission was reduced to two.[4]

1. *Ibid.*, LXXXI, 146-147.
2. *Ibid.*, LXXXVIII, 330-331.
3. *Ibid.*, XC, 177.
4. *Ibid.*, XCIX, 99.

Under the present law which became effective in 1921 the county commissioners are authorized to appoint two suitable persons in each township and ward in the county, who are directed to contract with the undertaker selected by the family or friends of the deceased, and to direct the burial in a respectable manner of the body of any honorably discharge soldier, sailor, or marine having at any time served in the army or navy of the United States, or the mother, wife, or widow of any soldier, sailor, or marine for that of any war nurse who served at any time in the army of the United States who died in poverty.[5]

The burial commission is instructed to enforce all laws relative to the burial of indigent veterans, investigate the financial status of the descendant's family, and reports its findings to the county commissioners, together with the name, rank, and command to which the deceased belonged, date of death, place of burial, occupation while living, and an itemized statement of the cost of burial.[6]

Upon receiving this report of the burial commission, the county commissioners transcribe the information in the book kept for that purpose, and certify the expense to the county auditor who draws his warrant for payment to the person or persons specified by the county commissioners.[7]

The amount contributed by the county for the burial of an indigent veteran set by the legislature at $35 in 1884 was increased to $75 in 1908, and to $100 in 1921.[8] Since 1908 each member of the burial commission has been allowed $1 for each service performed.[9]

No permanent records are kept by the soldiers' burial commission. For county commissioners records, see entries 2, 13.

---

5. G. C. sec. 2950; *Laws of Ohio,* CVIII, pt. i, 34; CIIX, 211.
6. *Laws of Ohio,* XCIX, 100.
7. *Ibid.,* XCIX, 101.
8. *Ibid.,* LXXXI, 146-147; XCIX, 99; CIX, 212; G. C. sec. 2951.
9. *Laws of Ohio,* XCIX, 99; G. C. sec. 2951.

Provision for the relief of the indigent was made in 1805, but it was not until 1898 that the legislature provided separate relief for the indigent blind. The act authorized the township trustees to certify to the county commissioners an amount not to exceed $100 per person per annum for such relief, the certification to be made a record listing the name of the beneficiary and the amount required; and directed the county commissioners to levy on the townships to the amount certified, this amount to be paid into the county treasury and thence to the township treasurer to be used for blind relief.[1]

Six years later, in 1904, certification authority was transferred from the township trustees to the probate judge, who was required to register the name and address of beneficiaries and to issue to each a certificate giving his name, address, and the amount to be drawn. Persons eligible for relief were blind males over twenty-one and blind females over eighteen years of age, without property or means of support. Not less than two county citizens, one a physician selected by the court, were required to testify that the applicant had been a resident of the state for five years and a resident of the county for one year immediately proceeding the filing of an application for relief as a condition for granting aid.[2]

The act of 1904 was declared unconstitutional for the reason that it required spending for a private purpose public funds raised by taxation.[3] Hence, in 1908, an act was passed authorizing the county commissioners to levy a stipulated tax to create a fund for relief of the needy blind, the maximum benefit not to exceed $150 per person per annum to be paid quarterly; and authorizing the probate judge to appoint a blind relief commission consisting of three members to serve for three-year term, directed to meet annually in the office of the county commissioners to examine applications recorded in order of their receipt in a book furnished by the county commissioners. This record was required to be kept open for public inspection.[4]

---

1. *Laws of Ohio,* XCIII, 270.
2. *Ibid.,* XCVII, 392-394.
3. *Auditor of Lucas County* v. *The State, Ohio State Reports,* LXXV, 114-137.
4. *Laws of Ohio,* XCIX, 56-58.

The blind relief commission was abolished by the legislature in 1913 and its powers and duties were transferred to the county commissioners who were authorized, on evidence furnished by a registered physician or surgeon that the applicant for blind relief might have such disability benefited or removed by medical or surgical treatment, and with the written consent of the patient, to expend all or part of a year's relief allowance for this purpose.[5]

Six years later, in 1919, this allows for blind relief was raised to $200 per person per annum, and the county commissioners were authorized to appoint such clerks as they might deem necessary to investigate applications and to serve at the pleasure of the county commissioners.[6]

In 1927 the maximum benefit for blind relief was increased to $400 per person per annum, but in the event of both a husband and wife being blind and both receiving relief, the total maximum benefit for the two was fixed at $600 per annum.[7]

In April 1936 the state accepted the provisions of the federal social security act approved August 14, 1935, providing federal grants for state aid to the blind, and the legislature designated the Ohio commission for the blind as the administration agency in the state, and the county commissioners were made the administration agency in the county. The county commissioners were directed to appropriate from the general fund of the county a some sufficient when supplemented by federal and state grants to provide for the blind a subsistence "compatible with decency and health," and if they failed to make such appropriations the attorney general was directed to bring *mandamus* proceedings against them.

The act of 1936 provides that those entitled to blind relief are persons not less than eighteen nor more than sixty-five years old, who have lost their sight while residents of the state, and who have resided in the state for a period of five years in the nine years immediately preceding application, the last year of which period shall have been continuous. Applications for blind relief are filed with the county commissioners who are required by statute to list such claims in their order of application in books kept for that purpose.

---

5. *Ibid.,* CIII, 60.
6. *Ibid.,* CVIII, pt. i, 521-422.
7. *Ibid.,* CXII, 109.

At least ten days prior to action on a claim the applicant files a dualy certified statement, including a certificate from a registered physician "skilled in diseases of the eye" stating to what extent the applicant's vision is impaired, and written evidence from two reputable citizens that they know the applicant to be blind and that "he has the qualifications to entitle him to relief asked." The county commissioners may allow the examining physician a fee not to exceed five dollars, and may employ an additional physician to examine the applicant. If after such inquiry the county commissioners are satisfied that the applicant is entitled to relief, they are directed by statute to issue an order for such sum as the board finds necessary, not to exceed the maximum fixed in 1927, such sum to be paid monthly from the fund created for that purpose. The ruling of 1913 concerning medical and surgical treatment for applicants remains in effect. Persons whose qualifications are denied by the county commissioners may appeal to the state commission for the blind which on its own motion may revise any decision of the county commissioners. Both the Ohio commission for the blind and the county commissioners have power to issue subpoena, compel presentation of papers, and examine witnesses.

At least once a year, oftener if directed by the Ohio commission for the blind, the county commissioners must examine the qualifications, disabilities, and needs of all persons on the list of the blind, and may increase or decrease the amount of relief according to the budgetary requirements within the limits fixed by law. If the county commissioners remove a name from the list of the blind they are required to notify the county auditor and the Ohio commission for the blind as to their action.[8]

In Ross County the clerk of the county commissioners has immediate supervision of blind relief, while investigations are made by the relief case workers.

All records are located in the county commissioners' office.

---

8. *Laws of Ohio,* CXVI, pt. ii, 195-200.

573. JOURNAL, BLIND RELIEF

1935—. 1 volume.

Record of proceedings regarding blind relief, showing name of client, date of application, investigation report, medical examination report, amount of award, and date granted. Arranged chronologically by dates of grants. Index alphabetically by names of clients. Typed. 400 pages. 16 x 11 x 3.

For original papers, see entries 574, 575; for records of payments, see entry 262.

574. APPLICATIONS

1935—. 1 file box.

Applications for blind relief, showing name and address of applicant, date, and number of dependents. Arranged chronologically by dates of applications. No index. Handwritten on printed forms. 10 x 18 x 24.

For other applications, see entry 26, 575; for journal, see entry 573; for record of payments, see entry 262.

575. DENIALS

1935—. 1 file box.

Applications for blind relief which have been denied, showing date and notations of reason for refusal. Arranged chronologically by dates of denials. No index. Handwritten on printed forms. 10 x 12 x 18.

For other applications, see entries 26, 574; for journal, see entry 573; for record of payments, see entry 262.

Old age pensions, although well known in Europe at the end of the nineteenth and beginning of the twentieth century and in a few American States during the same period, were not provided for in Ohio until recently.[1] In 1933 an "Old Age Pension" law, proposed by initiative petition, was voted upon at the general election of that year, providing for the granting of aid to the aged in Ohio under certain conditions. The law was adopted by a majority of the electors voting thereon.[2] The act, as amended in 1936, provides, among other things that any person sixty-five years of age or upward (unless confined in any penal or correction institution or the state hospital) who is a citizen of the United States, who has resided in Ohio not less than five years during the nine prior to making application for aid, and who has resided for one year in the county wherein application for aid is made is eligible to receive a pension, providing his income from all and every source does not exceed $360 per year.[3] Moreover the applicant must be unable to support himself, and have no husband, wife, child, or other person who is legally responsible for his support, and found by the division of aid for the aged able to support him. In addition to this, the net value of all real and personal property of the unmarried applicant, less all encumbrances and liens, must not exceed $3,000; if the applicant is married the net value of the property of husband and wife shall not exceed $4,000. It may be required that such property, as a condition precedent to payment of aid, be transferred to the division of aid for the aged in trust. This provision does not however, prohibit the applicant or his wife from occupying such property during their lifetime.[4] An amendment to this act in 1937 eliminated the transfer of property as a possible condition precedent to granting aid, leaving the transfer optional. The amended act further states that any property, either real or personal, which has heretofore been conveyed to the division in trust could be recovered to the grantor by the division.[5]

---

1. Arthur Lyon Cross, *A Shorter History of England and Greater Britain* (New York, 1925), 746-747; J. Salwyn Schapiro, *Modern and Contemporary European History 1815-1928* (New York, 1931), 347, 396, 790.
2. *Laws of Ohio,* CXV, pt. ii, 431-439.
3. *Ibid.,* CXVI, pt. ii, 86-88, 216-221.
4. *Ibid.,* CXV, pt. ii, 431-439.
5. G. C. Sec. 1359-6.

For the purpose of administering the old age pension law there was created in 1933 in the state department of public welfare a division of aid for the aged. The chief of the division of aid for the aged, appointed by the director of public welfare with the approval of the governor, is authorized to appoint all necessary assistants, clerks, stenographers, and other employees and fix their salaries, subject to the approval of the director of public welfare.[6]

In each county the commissioners constituted a board for administering the act. However, if the commissioners by a majority vote declined to serve in such capacity, the chief of the division of aid for the aged is authorized, with the consent of the director of public welfare, to appoint a board consisting of three or five members, who, like the county commissioners, serve without compensation. The local boards are required to keep such records and make such reports as the division may prescribe, and are also authorized to employ, subject to the approval of the division, such investigators, clerks, and other employees as are necessary for performance of their duties.[7]

In 1937 the chief of the division was directed to appoint an advisory board in each county consisting of five citizens of such county. The members of the board, appointed for two years, are required to take an oath of office before entering upon their duties. This board succeeded to the duties formerly performed by the county commissioners.[8]

Applications for relief were made annually to the local board but an act of the legislature in 1937, reorganizing the division of aid for the aged, omitted the provision for annual reapplication.[9] Each applicant is thoroughly investigated. In its investigations the local board is not bound by common law or statutory rules of evidence, but is authorized to make inquiries in such a manner as seems "best calculated to conform to substantial justice." For the purpose of its investigations, each county board has the power to compel the attendance and testimony of witnesses. Decisions of the local boards may be appealed to the division.[10]

---

6. *Laws of Ohio,* CXV, pt. ii, 431-439.
7. *Laws of Ohio,* CXV, pt. ii, 431-439.
8. G. C. sec. 1359-12.
9. *Ibid.,* 1359-14.
10. *Laws of Ohio,* CXV, pt. ii, 431-439.

After the applicants have been investigated by the board, "certificates of aid" are granted to persons entitled to relief in conformity with the provisions of the law. Each certificate, bearing the applicant's name and the pension allowed, as well as the records pertaining to the investigation, is forwarded to the division, which may approve, modify, or reject the certificate and findings of the board.[11]

Under the provisions of this act the state became the general guardian of public and private welfare. The pension system relieves the increasing burden placed upon county homes, which, even under the most favorable conditions, are poor substitutes for homes. In February 1934 the general assembly made its first appropriation for old age pensions covering the last half of the calendar year 1934.[12] The total cost to the state and federal government for old age pensions and the administration of old age pension system in Ohio since its inauguration has been $99,509,315.43. The cost to the state of Ohio for the year 1937 exclusive federal grants was $14,993,155.56.[13]

All records are located in the main office of the board of aid for the aged, 63 West Second Street.

576. CASE RECORDS

1934—. 12 file boxes. (labeled by months).

Complete record of each case in which an award of aid for the aged had been made, showing copy of application, certificate of award, property inventory, insurance record, and investigator's quarterly report. Each case is contained in a separate folder, showing certificate number. Each file box contains records for the month specified for the years coverage. Arranged numerically by certificate numbers. For index, see entry 577. Typed on printed forms, except applications, which are handwritten on printed forms. 12 x 14 x 26.

577. INDEX TO CASE RECORDS

1934—. 1 file box.

Index to Case Records, entry 576, showing name of recipient, month certificate of award was issued, and certificate number. Arranged chronologically by months and alphabetically thereunder by names of recipients. Typed on printed forms. 4 x 5.5 x 26.

578. CASE RECORDS, CLOSED

1935—. 3 file box.

Applications and complete records of cases which have been closed by death, denial, or withdrawal, showing copy of application, certificate of award, property inventory, insurance record, and investigator's quarterly report. Each case is contained in a separate folder, showing certificate number. Arranged alphabetically by names of clients. No index. Typed on printed forms, except applications, which are handwritten on printed forms. 14 x 26 x 12.

579. APPLICATIONS

Current, 1 file box.

Copies of applications for aid, showing name of applicant, address, financial status, and case history. Original applications have been forwarded to state office for approval and when returned will be filed with active cases or with closed cases. Arranged alphabetically by names of applicants. No index. Handwritten on printed forms. 14 x 26 x 12.

580. [Investigator's] REPORTS

1934—. 2 file boxes.

Monthly reports by investigators, showing date, number of cases investigated, miles traveled, and other data pertaining to investigations. Arranged chronologically by dates of reports. No index. Typed on printed forms. 14 x 26 x 12.

Aid to dependent children, although provided for by the Ohio legislature in 1913 in the form of mothers' pensions, assumed a new significance, when, in April 1936, the Ohio legislature accepted the provisions of the federal social security act. With the acceptance of the act, the sections of the General Code[1] relative to mothers' pensions were repealed

The administration of the act in the state is delegated to the department of public welfare through the division of charities. In the administration of the act, the department was authorized to prescribe forms, certificates, reports, records, and accounts to be kept by the local departments.

The administration of the act in the counties is delegated to the juvenile judge or to the judge of the court of domestic relations, excepting in counties in which by charter or by law the powers were vested in or imposed upon "a county department, board, commission, or officer other than the juvenile judge." In Ross County the juvenile judge[2] performs this function. When he serves in the capacity of county administrator, the judge is directed to utilize the services of the employees of the court exercising juvenile jurisdiction. In the performance of his duties the judge is authorized to compel the attendance of witnesses and the production of books, and may institute contempt proceedings against persons refusing to testify. Except for this, powers conferred upon a judge are administrative powers only.

Those entitled to aid under the act include, among others, a child residing in the state less than sixteen years of age who has been deprived of parental support or care by reason of death, continued absence of a parent, or mental or physical incapacity of a parent. However, a child more than sixteen but less than eighteen years of age may receive aid at the discretion of the county administrator.

Applications for aid is made to the court by the parent or a relative, with whom the child must be living. Before aid is granted, a careful examination of the home is made by the employees of the courts. If the child is found to be eligible, the court may grant such amount as is deemed proper. The amount of aid payable to any child is determined on the basis of actual needs "and shall be sufficient to provide support and care requisite for health and decency." In the event aid is granted, the home of such a child must be visited four times during each year. Each month the county auditor issues warrants upon the county treasurer for the payment of warrants certified by the court.

---

1. G. C. sec. 1683-2 - 1683-10.
2. See p. 118.

The decision of the juvenile judge are subject to abrogation or modification by the department of public welfare. Any person attempting to receive aid on behalf of any child not entitled to such aid is deemed guilty of a misdemeanor and upon conviction may be punished by fine or imprisonment or both.

Under authority of section 1639-18 of the General Code the juvenile judge appoints a visitor to investigate cases applying for or receiving aid for dependent children.[3]

Aid to dependent children is financed by federal, state, and local funds. The county commissioners are required to include in the annual tax budget an amount not less than that computed to yield a levy of fifteen one-hundreds of 1 mill on each dollar of the general tax list of the county. If the commissioners failed to comply with the provisions of the act relative to appropriations, the state department of public welfare is directed to request the attorney general to institute *mandamus* proceedings against them.[4]

All records of aid to dependent children are in the juvenile court office.

---

3. *Laws of Ohio,* CXVII, 525.
4. G. C. secs. 1359-31 - 1359-45; *Laws of Ohio,* CXVI, pt. ii, 188-195.

581. RECORD OF DEPENDENT CHILDREN

July 1, 1936—. 8 file boxes.

Records names, ages, and residence of dependent children, and mothers' names. Arranged alphabetically by names of clients. No index. Typed on printed forms. 8 x 10 x 20.

582. RECORD OF AID TO DEPENDENT CHILDREN

July 1, 1936—. 2 file boxes.

Record of aid to mothers of dependent children, showing name of mother, number of children, names and ages of children, amount of award, and case history. Each case in separate folder. Arranged alphabetically by names of mothers. No index. Typed on printed forms. 12 x 14 x 26.

For prior records, see entry 300.

The office of county surveyor, another English institution transplanted to America during the colonial period, became an important office in frontier Ohio where land titles and boundary lines were often in dispute. The office is purely a creation of statue, there being no constitutional provisions for its establishment.

The first act of the general assembly pertaining to the surveyor was passed during the first legislative session of 1803. Under this act the court of common pleas was authorized to appoint a person well qualified to act as county surveyor. He received his commission from the governor, was required to give bond conditioned for the faithful performance of the duties of his office, and was directed to survey all lands which were sold or were to be sold for taxes, and was authorized to appoint chainmen or markers whose function it was to establish corners. The surveys made by the surveyor or his deputies were the only ones to be accepted as legal evidence in any court of law of equity. For remuneration, the surveyor was permitted to retain all fees collected by him and the operation of his office.[1]

Although it made no fundamental change in the duties of the surveyor, the act of 1816 fixed his term of office at five years; authorized him to appoint deputies, and made him responsible for their official acts; and made him liable to removal by the court for negligence or incompetency, and liable to suit by persons believing themselves damaged by his negligence or that of his deputies.[2] A year later, in 1817, provision was made for the appointment of a successor in the event the office became vacant because of death, resignation, or removal.[3]

The act of 1831 consolidated the previous acts, redefined the duties of the surveyor, increased the amount of his bond, and authorized him, when directed by the county commissioners, to procure from the surveyor general's office a "certified plat, together with the field notes of corners, and bearing trees to each section, quarter section, lot, or original survey in his county, and cause the same to be preserved in a book by him provided for that purpose; which shall be deposited in the county auditor's office, for the use of the landholders in the county." It provided further, that the surveyor shall keep "a fair and accurate record of all official surveys made by himself or by his deputies," in a suitable book to be kept by him for that purpose, and that he should number his surveys progressively.

---

1. *Laws of Ohio,* I, 90-93.
2. *Ibid.,* XIV, 424-431.
3. *Ibid.,* XV, 64.

More significant, however, was the fact that the office was made elective for a three-year term by the act of 1831. The term remained at three years until 1906 when it was reduced to a two-year period; and by the act of 1927 effective with the term of the surveyor elected in 1928, the term was increased to four years.[4]

During the years of the development of the office other duties have been delegated to the surveyor. In 1842 he was given the duty of ascertaining and reporting trespassing on public lands.[5] Later, in 1854, he was given the same powers as the justice of the peace to take acknowledgments of and certify deeds, mortgages, powers of attorney, and other instruments affecting real estate, to administer oaths, and to take and certify affidavits.[6] In 1867 he was given authority, when directed by the county commissioners, to transcribe any and all dilapidated maps, records of plats, and field notes of survey of other counties.[7] Similarly, in 1881, he was authorized to procure from any office in the state a certified plat together with the field notes of corners, quarter sections, lots, or original surveys and place them in a book provided for that purpose. Certified copies from his book were to be taken as *prima facie* evidence.[8]

With the increase in modern means of transportation, there developed a growing need for more efficient methods of road construction and maintenance. Accordingly, in 1906, the surveyor was directed to act, whenever the services of an engineer was required, in the capacity of an engineer with respect to roads, turnpikes, bridges, or ditches, except in cities of the first grade.[9] He was directed by statue to perform all duties in his county which would be done by a civil engineer or surveyor, to prepare all plans, specifications, and estimates of cost, and to submit forms for contracts for the construction and repair of all bridges, culverts, roads, draws, ditches, and other public improvements (except buildings) over which the county commissioners had authority. At the same time, he was made responsible for the inspection of all public improvements, and was directed to keep a complete list of all estimates and bids received for such work, as well as of contracts awarded for improvements.[10]

---

4. *Ibid.,* XXIX, 399; XVIII, 245-247; CXII, 179.
5. *Ibid.,* XL, 57.
6. *Ibid.,* LII, 70.
7. *Ibid.,* LXIV, 216-217; LXXVIII, 285.
8. *Ibid.,* XXIX, 399; LXXVIII, 285.
9. *Ibid.,* XCVIII, 245-247.
10. *Ibid.,* XCVIII, 245-247.

Similarly, another measure enacted in 1919 increased the duties of the surveyor regarding road construction and road maintenance. Under this act the surveyor was authorized to designate one of his deputies as maintenance engineer. This engineer, under the direction of the surveyor, was to have charge of all "road maintenance and repair work" in his county. Furthermore, when authorized by the county commissioners, the surveyor was to appoint a maintenance supervisor or supervisors to have charge of the maintenance of improved highways within a district or districts established by the commissioners or the surveyor, and containing not less than ten miles of improved county roads.[11] In 1923 the surveyor was delegated to assist the county planning commission wherever such commission was established.[12]

Thus the general responsibility of planning and directing county road construction is vested, by statute, in the county surveyor. Because of this increased responsibility placed on this office there has been an attempt to raise the general qualifications of those seeking election to it. In 1935, an act was passed changing the title of the office to that of "county engineer,' and eligibility to the office was restricted to "*a registered professional engineer and registered surveyor licensed to practice in the state of Ohio.*"[13] This act was amended in 1936 to permit the incumbent to continue in office upon re-election, regardless of lack of these qualifications.[14]

All records are located in the engineer's drafting and record room.

---

11. *Ibid.,* CVIII, pt. ii, 497.
12. *Ibid.,* CX, 312.
13. *Ibid.,* CXVI, 283.
14. *Ibid.,* CXVI, pt. ii, 152.

Surveys and Plats
(See also entry 77-81, 332-334)

583. VIRGINIA MILITARY SURVEYS
1793-1866. 1 volume.

Record of surveys of tracts of land in that part of Ross County which was in the Virginia Military District, showing sketch of tract with landmarks, boundaries, watercourses, survey number, and description of tract. Arranged numerically by consecutive survey numbers. For index, see entry 584. Handwritten and hand drawn. 370 pages. 18 x 14 x 3.

584. INDEX TO VIRGINIA MILITARY SURVEYS
1793-1866. 1 volume.

Index to Virginia Military surveys, entry 583, showing survey number, name of survey, name of party ordering survey, volume and page numbers of record, and date of survey. Arranged numerically by consecutive survey numbers. Handwritten. 340 pages. 16 x 11 x 2.5.

585. SURVEYOR'S RECORD
1808—. 6 volumes. (labeled by years). Title varies: Record of Surveys, 1808-1887. 5 volumes.

Record of surveys made by county surveyor, showings sketch of tracts with boundary lines and landmarks, name of landowners, description of tracts surveyed, area, date of survey, and copy of surveyor's affidavits of survey. Arranged chronologically by date of survey. Indexed alphabetically by names of landowners; also separate index to surveys of Congressional Lands, entry 586. Handwritten and hand drawn. Average 435 pages. 16 x 11 x 3.25.

586. INDEX TO SECTIONAL LANDS
1808—. 1 volume.

Index to surveys of sectional lands (Congressional Lands) in Surveyor's Record, entry 585, showing name of surveyor, name of party ordering survey, date of survey, area surveyed, and volume and page numbers of record. Arranged alphabetically by names of townships and numerically thereunder by section numbers. Handwritten. 380 pages. 18 x 13 x 3.

587. SURVEYOR'S PLAT RECORD
1803—. 7 volumes.

Record of surveys made, showing plats, date of recording, and date pertaining to survey. Prepared by county engineer. Arranged chronologically by dates of recordings. No index. Handwritten and hand drawn. Scales vary. Average 100 pages. 20 x 30 x 2.

588. [TOWNSHIP BOUNDARY SURVEYS]
1804-1821. In Road Record, entry 589.

Copies of petitions of residents to change township lines or to establish new townships, and surveyor's record, showing new boundary lines and landmarks.

Roads, Bridges, and Culverts
(See also entries 14-19)

589. ROAD RECORD
1799-1913. 7 volumes. (A-G).

Record of all roads in Ross County which were established or vacated by order of county commissioners with copies of petitions to establish or vacate roads, showing signatures of petitioners and date filed; also survey records of all roads as authorized; surveyor's record of bridges, 1804-1821. Also contains [Township Boundary Surveys], 1804-1821, entry 588. Arranged chronologically by dates petitions filed. For index, see entry 590. Handwritten. 1 volume, 362 pages. 12 x 8 x 2; 6 volumes, average 600 pages. 18 x 12 x 4.5.

For commissioners' records, see entry 14; for road papers, see entry 15.

590. INDEX TO ROAD RECORD
1799-1913. 1 volume.

Index to Road Record, entry 589, showing names of roads and of principal petitioners, date road established, date vacated, and volume letter and page number of record. Arranged alphabetically by names of roads. Handwritten. 280 pages. 16 x 11 x 2.

591. SURVEYOR'S ROAD AND SECTION RECORD

1914—. 1 volume. Initiated 1914.

Surveyor's identification data of roads and sections of roads, showing road number, name of road, class, townships and corporations through which road passes, number of miles in each subdivision, place of beginning, place of termination, and total miles. Arranged numerically by road numbers. No index. Typed. 280 pages. 15 x 20 x 2.25.

592. STATE HIGHWAY ESTIMATES

1918—. 2 file boxes.

Copies of engineer's estimate on construction or repair of state roads in Ross County, showing date of estimate, itemized estimated cost of labor and materials, and date of filing. Arranged chronologically by dates of filing. No index. Typed on printed forms. 12 x 10 x 22.

593. ROAD ESTIMATES

1924—. 2 file boxes.

Copies of engineer's estimates on construction or repair of county and township roads, showing date of estimate, itemized estimated cost of labor and materials, and date of filing. Arranged chronologically by dates of filing. No index. Typed on printed forms. 12 x 10 x 22.

594. BRIDGE AND CULVERT ESTIMATES

1916—. 1 file box.

Copies of engineer's estimates on construction or repair of bridges and culverts, showing date of estimate, itemized estimated cost of labor and materials, and date of filing. Arranged chronologically by dates of filing. No index. 1916-1919, handwritten on printed forms; 1919—, typed on printed forms. 12 x 10 x 22.

595. CONTRACT RECORD

1914—. 6 volumes.

Surveyor's record of contracts, showing date, for what construction or contract number, township or subdivision, name of contractor, volume letter and page number of [Commissioners'] Journal, entry 2, estimate of engineer, amount of bid accepted, record of bids received, and payments on account as per estimate. Arranged chronologically by dates are recording. Indexed numerically by contract numbers. 1914-1920, handwritten on printed forms; 1921—, typed on printed forms. Average 430 pages. 16 x 11 x 3.5.

Fiscal Accounts

596. SURVEYOR'S RECORD OF FEES

1892—. 8 volumes.

Record of fees for services by engineer's department, showing date, for what service, to whom charged, amount, and date paid. Arranged alphabetically by names of payers and chronologically thereunder. No index. Handwritten. Average 240 pages. 15 x 10 x 2.

597. PAYROLLS, GAS TAX

1928—. 3 file boxes. (labeled by years).

Record of expenditures of gasoline funds for highway maintenance payrolls, showing date, names of employees, time of each, name of township, and total for each payroll. Arranged alphabetically by names of townships and chronologically thereunder by dates of payrolls. Typed on printed form. 12 x 10 x 22.

598. PAYROLLS, FORCE ACCOUNT

1921—. 8 file boxes. (labeled by years).

Record of payrolls on county and township roads and bridges, showing date, names of employees, time for each, and total for each payroll. Arranged alphabetically by names of townships and chronologically thereunder by dates of payrolls. No index. Typed on printed forms. 10 x 8 x 22.

599. TIME BOOKS

1925—. 372 volumes. (labeled by years), Subtitled by names of foreman.

Road foreman's record of time worked by employees on county road jobs, showing date, names of employees, days worked each week, rate per hour, and total due. Arranged chronologically by dates of entry. No index. Handwritten on printed forms. Average 150 pages. 9 x 6 x 1.

Miscellaneous

600. ANNUAL INVENTORY, TOWNSHIPS
1921—. 2 volumes.

County engineer's annual inventory of township road maintenance equipment, showing date, number of items, and valuation of each. Arranged alphabetically under tabs by names of townships and chronologically thereunder by years. No index. Typed on printed on forms. Average 200 pages. 18 x 15 x 1.5.

601. ANNUAL INVENTORY, COUNTY
1917—. 2 volumes.

County engineer's annual inventory of county machinery and equipment, showing date, number of items, and valuation for each. Arranged chronologically under tabs indicating years. No index. 1917-1920, handwritten; 1921—, typed. Average 120 pages. 18 x 15 x 1.

The legislature at its 1914 session, following the disastrous floods of the previous year, made provision for the establishment of conservancy districts in Ohio the objects of which were to prevent floods, to protect cities, villages, farms, and highways from inundation. This act, authorized by constitutional amendment of 1912,[1] was upheld by the courts as a valid exercise of the police power of the state.[2] The conservancy districts, according to the act, may be established not only to prevent floods but to regulate streams, reclaim overflowed lands, provide irrigation, regulate the flow of streams, or divert water courses.

The court of common pleas of any county in the state or any judge in vacation is authorized, after a petition signed either by five hundred freeholders or by a majority of freeholders has been filed with the clerk of courts, to establish a conservancy district which might be within or without the county or where the court is located. The court, after conducting hearings on the petition as to the purpose of the district, may declare the district organized and give it a corporate name. The clerk of court, within thirty days after the district has been declared a corporation by the court, transmits to the secretary of state, and to the county recorder in each county having lands in the district, copies of the finding in the decree of the court incorporating the district which, according to statute is considered a political subdivision.

Within thirty days after the decree of incorporation the court is authorized to appoint three persons, at least two of whom are freeholders in the district, to serve as a board of directors of the district to serve three, five, and seven years respectively. After the expiration of their terms the tenure of the office is five years. The board of directors, after taking an oath that they "will not be interested directly or indirectly in any contract let by the district," organized by selecting one of their members as president and some person, not a member of the board, as secretary. The board is authorized to employ a chief engineer who may be an individual, co-partnership, or corporation; an attorney; and such other engineers and attorneys as may be necessary for carrying on the work. The board may provide for their compensation, which, with all other necessary expenditures, shall be taken as part of the cost of improvement.

---

1. *Ohio Const, 1851,* Art II, sec. 3.
2. *County of Miami* v. *Dayton, Ohio State Reports*, XCII, 223-234, 236.

While the chief engineer prepares plans and specifications of work, all contracts which exceed $1,000 are let by competitive bidding.

The board or its agents, is authorized to enter upon lands within or without the conservancy district for the purpose of making surveys. They are authorized to exercise the right of eminent domain; condemn property, after appraisal, for the use of the district; make regulations to protect their work by prescribing the method of building roads, bridges, or fences; to remove bridges, cemeteries, or other structures impeding their work; and to cooperate with federal government, with persons, railways, corporation, the state government of Ohio or other states, for assistance for drainage, conservancy, or other improvements.

To finance such improvements the board is authorized to levy upon the property of the district a tax not to exceed three-tenths of a mill on the assessed valuation. This tax is certified to the county auditor, and to the various treasurers of the counties within the district and is used to pay the expenses of organization, surveys, and plans. The commission is authorized further to borrow money at a rate not to exceed six percent per annum and levy assessments for a bond fund.[3]

The board is required to "keep in a well-bound book a record of all its proceedings, minutes of all meetings, certificates, contracts, bonds given by employees and all corporate acts, which shall be open to the inspection of all owners of property in the district, as well as to all other interested parties." The secretary, who may serve also as treasurer, is designated as the "custodian of the records of the district and its corporate seal."[4]

Ross County is the Scioto-Sandusky conservancy district, which embraces seventeen counties and has headquarters in Columbus where the records are located. These records will be listed in the forthcoming *Inventory of the County Archives of Ohio,* No. 25, *Franklin County.*

3. *Laws of Ohio,* CIV, 13-64.
4. *Laws of Ohio,* CIV, 18.

A cattle show held near Chillicothe on November 8, 1819, aroused the interest which led to the organization of the first agricultural society in Ross County in 1821. A fair was held in October of that year and for a number of years thereafter then abandoned.[1]

A second agricultural society was formed in 1833 and fairs were held for a number of years. Out of this organization grew the Ohio Importing Company with the purpose of importing blooded cattle from England.

A third Ross County agriculture society was organized in August 17, 1846 under the provisions of the legislative act of that year.[2] The society purchased a tract of land and erected numerous buildings for fair purposes. The organization eventually dissolved because of financial difficulties. Another society was organized in 1870 and fairs were conducted for a number of years. A fair held in 1900 was the last attempt by the society.[3]

County agriculture societies in Ohio were provided for by statute as early as 1846. On February 28 of that year the legislature passed an act authorizing the forming of such societies and making provisions for their aid by the counties.[4] On February 15, 1853, the legislature declared such societies to be bodies corporate and politic, capable of suing and being sued, and capable of holding in fee simple such real estate as they might purchase for sites whereon to hold fairs, the same to be paid by the county commissioners.[5]

By act of the legislature passed February 20, 1861, county agriculture societies were required to report annually to the state board of agriculture, and to send a delegate to meet with the state board at Columbus once each year.[6] In 1883 the legislature provided for the organization of district or county agricultural societies. The act making this provisions stipulated that when thirty or more persons, residents of any county or district embracing two counties, organized themselves into an agricultural society, under the rules and regulations of the state board of agriculture, the county might aid such society with a grant not to exceed $400 per year.[7]

---

1. Bennett, *op. cit., 138.*
2. *Ohio Department of Agriculture, Annual Report,* 1936, 37.
3. Bennett, *op. cit.,* 138. 139.
4. *Laws of Ohio,* XLIV, 70.
5. *Ibid.,* LI, 333.
6. *Ibid.,* LVIII, 22.
7. *Ibid., LXXX, 142.*

By an act of April 21, 1896, provision was made for representation in a county society of thirty or more residents of any county or district embracing two or more counties.[8] In 1900 the legislature extended the amount of county aid to $800 per year.[9] Later, on May 6, 1902, the legislature passed an act authorizing thirty or more residents of the county or of a district embracing one or more counties, to organize themselves into an agricultural society.[10]

On April 17, 1919, the legislature provided for the organization of county and independent agricultural societies, the payment of class premiums; defined the duties of persons competing for premiums; prescribed the publication of treasurers' accounts and the list of awards by societies; designated conditions of membership in a county agricultural society; authorized the society to elect a board of directors consisting of eight members, and prescribed their term of office and the manner of their election. The act for the stipulated how such societies might obtain state aid, and authorized the county commissioners to insure all buildings belonging to agricultural societies.[11]

The legislature of 1921 passed an act stipulating that the total amount of county aid to county agriculture societies should equal one hundred percent of the amount paid by the society in regular class premiums but not to exceed $800.[12] By act of March 27, 1925, the county commissioners were authorized to purchase or lease, for a term of not less than twenty years, real estate whereon to hold fairs under the management of county agriculture societies, and to erect thereon suitable buildings.[13] On March 10, 1927, the legislature authorized the county commissioners to appropriate annually on the request of the agricultural society and a sum not less than $1,500 nor more than $2,000 from the general fund for the purpose of "encouraging agricultural fairs."[14]

---

8. *Ibid.,* XCII, 205.
9. *Ibid.,* XXCIV, 395.
10. *Ibid.,* XCV, 403.
11. *Ibid.,* CVIII, pt. i, 381-385.
12. *Ibid.,* CIX. 240.
13. *Ibid.,* CXI, 238.
14. *Ibid.,* CXII, 84.

The most recent legislation affecting agricultural societies was that of March 19, 1935. This act provides that where no duly organized county agricultural society existed, and when no fairs were held by a duly organized county agricultural society which had held an annual exposition for three years previous to January 1, 1933, the county commissioners should, on the request of an independent society, appropriate annually from the general fund a sum not more $2,000 nor less than $500 for the encouragement of independent agricultural fairs.[15]

No records for the agricultural society were located in Ross County.

---

15. *Laws of Ohio,* CXVI, 47.

In 1914 the federal government passed an act providing for co-operative agricultural extension service between the state agricultural colleges and the United States Department of Agriculture. The purpose of the extension service was to give instructions and practical demonstrations in agriculture and home economics to persons not attending college, and to give such information through field demonstrations, publications, and other means. The funds for such work were to be supplied in part by the federal government and part by the state.[1]

A year following the federal legislation, the Ohio legislature accepted the provisions of the act by providing that when twenty or more residents of the county organized themselves into a "farmers' institute society for the purpose of teaching better methods of farming, stock raising, fruit culture and business connected with agriculture," accepted a constitution and bylaws conforming to the rules and regulations prescribed by the trustees of the Ohio State University, and elected proper officers, the institute could be a corporate body. The Ohio State University was required to furnish speakers for their annual meeting. At the close of the session the trustees were authorized to publish the lectures in pamphlet or book form.

Besides maintaining an institute, the society was authorized to maintain a county experiment farm. Furthermore the county commissioners were authorized to select a county agent subject to the approval of the dean of the college of agriculture of the Ohio State University. The first agent in Ross County was appointed in 1918.[2] It is the duty of the agent to inspect and study the agricultural conditions in his county, distribute agriculture literature, co-operate with United States Department of Agricultural and the college of agriculture of the Ohio State University. In the event the commissioners failed to make such an appointment, the electorate could require them to do so on a referendum vote.[3]

In 1929 the original legislation was amended so as to authorize the trustees of the Ohio State University to employ home demonstration agents and boys' and girls' club agents and such other employees as they deem necessary. At present Ross County has an assistant county agent but does not have either a home demonstration agent or a club agent.

---

1. *United States Statutes at Large,* XXXVIII, pt. i, 372-374.
2. From records on file in the Agricultural Extension Service Office, Ohio State University.
3. *Laws of Ohio,* CVI, 356-359.

The county extension agent was given the additional duty of carrying the teachings of the college of agriculture of the Ohio State University in agricultural and home economics to the residents of his county through personal visits, bulletins, and practical demonstrations. Furthermore it was his duty to render educational service not only in relation to agricultural production, but also in relation to economic problems including marketing, distribution, and utilization of farming products.[4]

The initial legislation contained a clause which required the county commissioners to appropriate annually one thousand dollars if they wished to obtain the services of an agricultural agent. This amount was to be matched by the state. Under the present system the commissioners are empowered to levy a tax and to appropriate money from the proceeds thereof or from the general fund of the county an amount not to in excess of three thousand dollars for each agent to be paid into the county treasury to the credit of the agricultural extension fund. Amounts in excess must have the unanimous consent of the commissioners.[5]

All records are in the office of the agricultural extension agent.

---

4. *Ibid.,* CXIII, 82-83.
5. *Ibid.,* CXIII, 82-83.

Crops, Conservation, and Extension Records

602. INDEX FILES

1933—. 4 file boxes. One subtitled AAA Records, Wheat; 1 subtitled AAA Records, Corn-hog; 2 subtitled Conservation Records.

Card index to AAA Records, entry 603. and Conservation Records, entry 604, showing name of farm operator, township, year, type of project under which working, and contract number. Arranged by type of projects and alphabetically thereunder by names of farmers. Typed. 4 x 6 x 25.

603. AAA RECORDS

1933-1936. 16 file boxes. 12 subtitled Corn- hog Records; 4 subtitled Wheat Records.

Records of individual farmers operating their farms under the provisions and regulations of the federal agricultural adjustment act, showing crop title, name of farmer, and amount of reduction in produce. There are approximately 400 wheat records and 1,175 corn-hog records. Arranged by crop titles and alphabetically thereunder by names of farmers. For index the entry 602. Typed on printed forms. 12 x 13 x 26.

604. CONSERVATION RECORDS

1936—. 25 file boxes. Subtitled by names of subjects.

Record of farmers engaging in agricultural conservation under the federal program, showing name of farmer, type of work, and amount of reduction in produce. Arranged by type of work and alphabetically thereunder by names of farmers. For index, see entry 602. Typed on printed forms. 12 x 13 x 26.

605. 4-H CLUB ENROLLMENT RECORDS

1925—. 5 file boxes. Subtitled by type of club or activity.

Record of registration and membership of 4-H clubs in Ross County, showing type of club or activity, name of member, work records, and accomplishments of each boy or girl. Arranged by types of clubs or activities and alphabetically thereunder by names of members. No index. Typed on printed forms. 12 x 13 x 26.

606. 4-H CLUB ADVISORS' RECORDS

1925—. 8 file boxes. Subtitle by types of clubs or activities.

4-H club advisors' and leaders' records of progress and accomplishments, showing type of club or activity, name of member, date of record, and individual and collective progress records of project activities. Arranged chronologically and thereunder by types of clubs or activities, and alphabetically thereunder by names of members. No index. Typed on printed forms. 12 x 13 x 26

607. EXTENSION WORK RECORDS

1930—. 22 file boxes. Subtitled by names of townships and subjects.

Record of all extension work activities supervised by county agent, showing date, type of work, and names of farm operators. Arranged chronologically by years, thereunder by types of work, and alphabetically thereunder by names of farm owners. No index. Typed on printed forms. 12 x 13 x 26.

Reports and Correspondence

608. MONTHLY AND ANNUAL REPORTS
1924—. 1 file box.
Copies of county agent's reports to the state department of agriculture, showing date, activities, progress, and finances of the program. Arranged chronologically by dates of reports. No index. Typed on printed forms. 12 x 13 x 26.

609. NARRATIVE REPORTS
1930—. 1 file box.
Copies of county agent's narrative reports to Ohio State University extension department covering extension work activities, showing date, text, and signature of agent. Arranged chronologically by dates or reports. No index. Typed on printed forms. 12 x 13 x 26.

610. 4-H CLUB REPORTS
1925—. 2 file boxes.
Copies of county agent's monthly and annual reports to Ohio State University extension department on 4-H club activities in Ross County. Arranged chronologically by dates of reports. No index. Typed on printed forms. 12 x 13 x 26.

611. COUNTY AGENT'S REPORTS
1931—. 3 file boxes.
Copies of county agent's reports, showing summation of daily activities and connection with county agricultural agent's office; also monthly and annual reports to Ohio State University extension department and United States Department of Agriculture. Arranged chronologically by dates of reports. No index. Typed on printed forms. 12 x 13 x 26.

612. CORRESPONDENCE
1933—. 2 file boxes.
Original copies of letters sent to Ross County agricultural agent and carbon copies of outgoing letters. Arranged chronologically by dates of letters. No index. Typed. 12 x 13 x 26.

Documentary Sources

Acts of the General Assembly, 1803-1938 (117 volumes, published annually under state authority).

Baldwin, William Edward, ed., *Throckmorton's Ohio Code* (certified edn.; Cleveland, 1936).

Carter, Clarence Edwin, ed. and comp., *The Territorial Papers of the United States* (4 volumes, Washington, 1934, in progress). Volumes II and III of this monumental work treat of the Northwest Territory.

Chase, Salmon P., comp., *The Statutes of Ohio and of the Northwestern Territory, 1788-1833* (3 volumes, Cincinnati, 1833-1835).

Commissioners' Journal [Ross County], 1841—. 22 volumes. This journal, as well as other records listed under the various offices included in the inventory, constitutes the most important source material on the history of Ross County.

Curwen, Maskell E., comp., *Public Statutes at Large of the State of Ohio* (3 volumes, Cincinnati, 1853-1854).

Estrich, Willis A., ed., *Ohio Jurisprudence* (43 volumes, Rochester, 1928-1938). Henry P. Farnham was editor in chief, 1928-1929.

Hammond, Charles, and others, eds., *Reports of Cases Argued and Determined in the Supreme Court of Ohio in Bank . . .* (20 volumes, Cincinnati, 1824-1852).

Howe, Henry, comp., *Historical Collections of Ohio . . .* (2 volumes, Norwalk, 1896). Contains much valuable material.

Laning, Jay. F., *Revised Statutes of the State of Ohio* (3 volumes, Norwalk, 1905).

Laws of the Territory of the United States Northwest of the River Ohio (3 volumes, Philadelphia and Cincinnati, 1792-1796).

McCook, G. W., and others, ed., *Reports of Cases Argued and Determined in the Supreme Court of Ohio . . .* (132 volumes, Cincinnati 1852—).

Ohio Attorney General, *Opinions,* 1846— (69 volumes, published under state authority). Title varies: *Annual Report.*

Ohio Auditor of State, *Annual Report,* 1836-1937 (73 volumes, published under state authority).

Ohio Department of Agriculture, *Annual Report,* 1846-1935 (81 volumes, published under state authority).

Ohio Secretary of State, *Annual Report,* 1836-1936 (89 volumes, published under state authority). Some volumes titled: *Ohio Statistics.*

__________, Commission Register, 1858-1938 (3 volumes). Manuscript volumes in the office of the secretary of state.

__________, *Ohio Fifteenth Federal Census*, *1930* (Columbus, 1931).

Ohio Tax Commission, *Financing State and Local Government in Ohio, 1900-1932* (mimeographed, Columbus, 1934).

Page, William H., ed., *Page's Ohio General Code, Annotated* . . . (lifetime edn.; 12 volumes, Cincinnati, c 1937-1939).

Pease, Theodore Calvin, comp., *The Laws of the Northwest Territory, 1788-1800 (Illinois State Bar Association Law Series,* Springfield, 1925, I).

The Reorganization of County Government in Ohio: Report of the Governor's Commission on County Government (n. p. December 1934). An excellent analysis of the merits and defects of present-day county government as administered in Ohio.

Sayler, J. R., comp., *The Statutes of the State of Ohio* (4 volumes, Cincinnati, 1876).

Shepherd, Vinton R., ed., *The Ohio NISI PRIUS REPORTS* (32 volumes, n. s., Columbus and Cincinnati, 1894-1934). Cases decided by the common pleas, probate, and municipal courts of the state of Ohio.

Smith, J. V., rep., *Official Reports of the Debates and Proceedings of the Ohio State Convention . . . held at Columbus Commencing May 6, 1850, and at Cincinnati, Commencing December 2, 1850* (Columbus 1851).

Trautwein, George c., ed., *Page's Ohio Cumulative Code Service* (22 volumes, Cincinnati, 1927-1938).

__________, *Supplement to Page's Annotated General Code 1926-1935* (Cincinnati, 1935).

United States Statutes at Large, 1789-1937 (51 volumes, United States Government Printing Office).

Bibliography and Memoirs

Burnet [Jacob], *Notes on Early Settlement of the North-Western Territory* (Cincinnati, 1847). An interesting contribution by a Cincinnati pioneer.

Finley, Isaac J., and Putnam, Rufus, *Pioneer Record and Reminiscences of the Early Settlers and Settlement of Ross County, Ohio* (Cincinnati, 1871). Contains much valuable information, but is inaccurate in detail. Based upon the observations and visits to places and persons discussed.

Strickland W. P., ed., *Autobiography of Rev. James B. Finley; or, Pioneer Life in the West* (Cincinnati, 1859). Contains significant observations of a circuit rider.

Secondary Sources

Adams, George Burton, *Constitutional History of England* (New York, 1921). A standard work.

Amer, Francis J., *The Development of the Judicial System in Ohio from 1787 to 1932* (Johns Hopkins University, Baltimore, 1932. *Institute of Law Bulletin* no. 8). This well-documented study treats the evolution of the judicial system in Ohio.

Baker, Ray Stannard, *Woodrow Wilson Life and Letters: Youth 1856-1890* (New York, 1927). Although containing the natural bias expected in an official biography, this is the first sketch of the World War president that can be considered as of serious historical importance. The author had access to all of Wilson's papers.

Bates, Sanford, *Prisons and Beyond* (New York, 1937). This volume, written by the former director of United States prisons, emphasizes the values of correctional treatment of offenders confined in penal institutions.

Bennett, Henry Holcomb, *State Centennial History of Ohio and Ross County* (Madison, 1902). Interesting but incomplete.

Bond, Beverley W., Jr., *The Civilization of the Old Northwest: A Study of Political, Social, and Economic Development, 1788-1812* (New York, 1934). An excellent study in which the author develops the thesis that the Northwest was a laboratory in which the American colonial system was developed.

Chaddock, Robert E., *Ohio Before 1850: A Study of the Early Influence of Pennsylvania and Southern Populations in Ohio* (Columbia University, *Studies* XXXI, no. 2, New York, 1908). A critical study of the political and social contributions made to Ohio by emigeants from Virginia and Pennsylvania.

Channing, Edward, *A History of the United States* (6 volumes, New York, 1905-1925). A monumental work, but with the advance and historical scholarship the author's work becomes more inadequate as an authoritative treatment.

Cross, Arthur Lyon, *A Shorter History of England and Greater Britain* (New York, 1925). A standard textbook, but too sharp in outline.

Downes, Randolph Chandler *Frontier Ohio, 1788-1803 (Ohio Historical Collections,* III, Columbus, 1935). One of the most satisfactory treatments of Ohio frontier– well- documented.

Evans, Lyle S., *A Standard History of Ross County, Ohio* (2 volumes, Chicago and New York, 1917). Although undocumented and uncritical this volume contains much valuable information difficult to obtain elsewhere.

Fess, Simon D., ed., *Ohio Reference Library* (4 volumes, Chicago and New York, 1937). A popular and uncritical work edited by a former United States senator.

Gregory, William M., and Guitteau, William B., *History and Geography of Ohio* (Boston, 1922). Especially important for junior and senior high-school classes.

Gwynne, A. E., *A Practical Treatise on the Law of Sheriff and Coroner with Forms and References to the Statues of Ohio, Indiana, and Kentucky* (Cincinnati, 1849).

Hanna, Charles A., *The Scotch Irish; or the Scot in North Britain, North Ireland and North America* (2 volumes, New York and London, 1902). A poorly organized and unbalanced study, overburdened with excessive quotations, in which the author unsuccessfully presents the thesis that the majority of prominent men in early America were of Scotch-Irish extraction.

Heiges, R. E., *The Office of Sheriff in the Rural Counties of Ohio* (Findlay, 1933). This volume has the usual limitations of a doctoral dissertation.

Hodge, Frederick Webb, ed., *Handbook of America Indians North of Mexico* (Bureau of American Ethnology, *Bulletin* XXX, pt. ii, Washington, 1912). A standard work.

Karraker, Cyrus Harreld, *The Seventeenth-Century Sheriff: A Comparative Study of the Sheriff in England and the Chesapeake Colonies, 1607-1689* (Chapel Hill, 1930). Although interesting, this volume does not supersede the earlier studies made of that office.

Kennedy, Aileen Elizabeth, *The Ohio Poor Law and Its Administration* (Sophonisba P. Breckinridge, ed., *Social Service Monographs* no. 22,University of Chicago Press, Chicago, 1934). A biting criticism of the administration of poor relief in Ohio to 1932.

McCarty, Dwight G., *The Territorial Governors of the Old Northwest: A Study in Territorial Administration* (Iowa City, 1910). A well-documented study of the development of territorial government and administration in the old Northwest.

Mills, William C., *Archaeological Atlas of Ohio* (Columbus 1914). Contains maps showing the location of Ohio mounds, villages, and other remains.

Moley, Raymond, *The Sheriff and the Coroner* (New York, 1926. *The Missouri Crime Survey,* pt. ii). This study treats the present-day aspects of the office of the sheriff and of the coroner.

Ohio Study of Local School Units, *A Study of the Public Schools of Ross County* . . . (mimeographed, Columbus, 1937). An extensive study of the organization and operation of the schools of Ross County - contains variable statistical charts and tables.

Peattie, Roderick, *Geography of Ohio, Geological Survey of Ohio,* series iv, *Bulletin* XXVII, (Columbus, 1923). A study prepared for teachers in primary, secondary, and normal schools. Contains valuable maps, charts, and tables.

Peters, W. E., *Ohio Lands and Their Subdivision* (2d edn.; Athens, 1918). An important study of early land surveys.

Pollock, Sir Frederick, and Maitland, Frederic William, *The History of English Law Before the Time of Edward I* (2 volumes, Cambridge, 1895). A standard work.

Renick, L. W., and others, *Che-le-co-the, Glimpses of Yesterday* (Chillicothe, 1896). An interesting but uncritical narrative, prepared as a souvenir of the hundreth anniversary of the founding of Chillicothe.

Roseboom, Eugene Holloway, and Weisenberger, Francis Phelps, *A History of Ohio* (New York, 1934). The most satisfying history of Ohio– scholarly and impartial.

Schapiro J. Salwyn, *Modern and Contemporary European History 1815-1928* (revised edn., New York, 1931). A standard textbook. Especially good on the intellectual and social history of the period.

Sherman, C. E., *Original Ohio Land Subdivisions* (Ohio Co-operative Topographical Survey, *Final Report* III, Columbus 1923). An excellent study of original land surveys in Ohio, with maps.

Sutherland, Edwin H., *Principles of Criminology* (Chicago, 1934). An excellent study.

Van Waters, Miriam, *Youth in Conflict* (New York, 1925). An excellent study of the causes of delinquency written by the referee in juvenile court, Los Angeles.

Williams Brothers, pub., *History of Ross and Highland Counties, Ohio* (Cleveland, 1880). An incomplete and uncritical history of the subscription type.

Willoughby, W. F., *Principles of Judicial Administration* (Washington, 1929). A critical analysis of the enforcement of the law as it exists in modern society. Excellent for bibliographical annotations.

Articles in Periodicals

Atkinson R. C., "County Home Rule Developments in Ohio," *National Municipal Review,* XXIII (1934). 235.

Atkinson R. C., "Ohio - County Charter Elections," *National Municipal Review,* XXIV (1935), 702-703.

__________, "Ohio - Optional County Legislation," National Municipal Review, XXIV, (1935), 228.

Downes, Randolph Chandler "Evolution of Ohio County Boundaries," *Ohio State Archaeological and Historical Quarterly,* XXXVI, (1927), 340-477.

Dykstra, C. A., "Cleveland's Effort for City-County Consolidation," *National Municipal Review,* VIII (1911), 551-556.

Gates, Charles M., "The Administration of State Archives," *The Pacific Northwest Quarterly,* XXIX (January 1938), no. 1.

Hunter, W. H., "Influence of Pennsylvania on Ohio,"*Ohio State Archaeological and Historical Quarterly,* XII (1903), 287-309.

Kaplan, H. Eliot, "A Personal Program for County Service," *National Municipal review,* XXV (1936), 596-600.

McAlpine, William, "The Origin of Public Education in Ohio," *Ohio State Archaeological and Historical Quarterly,* XXXVIII (1929), 409-447.

Morris, William A., "The Office of Sheriff in the Anglo-Saxon Period," *English Historical Review* XXXI, (1916), 20-40.

Shetrone, Henry C., "Exploration of the Hopewell Group of Prehistoric Earthworks," *Ohio State Archaeological and Historical Quarterly,* XXXV (1926) 5-227

Stone, Donald C., "The Police Attack Crime," *National Municipal Review,* XXIV (1935), 39-41.

Utter, William T., "Saint Tammany in Ohio: A Study in Frontier Politics, *Mississippi Valley Historical Review,* XV (1928-1929), 321-340.

Williams, Samuel W., "The Tammany Society in Ohio," *Ohio State Archaeological and Historical Quarterly,* XXII (1913), 349-370.

Newspapers

Chillicothe *News-Advertiser,* 1931.

The Ohio State Journal, 1840, 1933.

Scioto Gazette, 1915.

ROSTER OF COUNTY OFFICIALS*
1798-1939

Commissioners**

Name	Years
John McLean	1807-1821
William McCleach	18060
(Part of year, resigned)	
Ebenezer Fenimore	1806-1817
(Vice W. McCleach)	
John Mathews	1809-1811
William Wallace	1811-1818
(Resigned)	
Thomas White	1812-1814
Benjamin Turner	1814
(Part of year)	
Presley Morris	1817-1820
David Crouse	1818-1821
George Porter	1820-1822
Thomas Marshall	1821-1836
John Carlisle	1822-1831
Francis Baldwin	1823-1829
Jeriel Root	1829
(Part of year)	
John Crouse, Jr.	1829-1832
Peter Leister	1831-1833
George Will	1832-1834
John Carlisle, Sr.	1833-1835
Thomas Scott	1834-1837
Warner Barnes	1835-1838
Aaron Foster	1836-1839
Martin Dresback	1837-1840
John Carlisle	1838-1847
Isaac Sperry	1839-1841
Nathan Gillilan	1840-1842
John Thompson	1842-1854
James Cutright	1843-1849
James Rowe	1848-1856
D. C. Entrekin	1849-1852
Simon Ratcliff	1852-1855
John M. Wisehart	1856-1857
James Rittenhouse	1855-1856
Jacob May	1856-1858
(Vice J. Rittenhouse)	
George W. Renick	1857-1859
Isaac Stookey	1857-1863
Samuel McAdow	1858-1861
Daniel Karshner	1859-1863
Alexander Ewing	1862-1864
Wm. Carson	1863
(Part of year)	
Satterfield Scott	1863-1866
William Welsh	1864-1867
Lewis W. Sifford	1865-1868
Jacob Shotts	1866-1869
Anton Alberti	1867-1870
Samuel Nichols	1868-1871
Samuel Cline	1869-1872
Wesley Claypool	1870-1873
John Karshner	1871-1874
E. Rockhold	1872-1875
David Shotts	1873-1879
William E. Floyd	1874-1877
David Jones	1874-1875
F. D. Ford	1875-1878
John Gaynor	1877-1883
A. J. Karlhuer	1878-1881

*Compiled from: Ohio Secretary of State *Annual Report*, 1836-1936, some volumes titled *Ohio Statistics:* Ohio Secretary of State, Commission Register, 1858-1938; William Brothers, *History of Ross and Highland Counties, Ohio* (Cleveland, 1880), 67; General Record of Governor's Office, 38 volumes, 1803-1929; [Ross County] Commissioners' Order Books, 1809-1841; Auditor's Record of Orders, 1841-1863.

Commissioners** (continued)

James Strawdor	1879-1882	Thomas O. Miller	1905-1909
Simon R. Dixon	1881-1884	Lee R. Riley	1909-1913
Austin Peeple	1882-1885	Benjamin H. Walker	1909-1911
Conrad H. Runtinger	1883-1892	Schuyler Slager	1909-1915
Taylor Boggs	1884-1887	Joseph I. Vance	1911-1915
John Gaynor	1885-1888	Adam G. Falter	1913-1915
Simon R. Dixon	1887-1890	Samuel S. Steel	1915-1917
John W. Jenkins	1888-1891	Charles B. Gearhart	1915-1917
James C. Crawford	1890-1893	John H. Dailey	1915-1917
(Died in office)		Joseph I. Vance	1917-1919
Benjamin P. Asbury	1891-1894	Adam G. Falter	1917-1919
J. P. Gartner	1892-1895	C. H. Free	1917-1919
Wm. A. Baird	1893-1896	John T. Daily	1919-1921
(Vice J. C. Crawford)		Thad S. Hanson	1919-1929
Simon Holderman	1894-1900	W. J. Haynes	1919-1921
Nelson Purdum	1895-1901	Fred Putnam	1921-1925
John W. Jenkins	1896-1899	Phillip Dunlap	1921-1927
John W. Ott	1899-1902	George J. Heinzelman	1925-1933
Rufus Hosler	1900-1903	John Ott	1927-1932
(Died in office)		(Died in office)	
Henry Grieshimer	1901-1904	Russell McCorkle	1929-1933
Charles B. Gearhart	1903	Walter F. Tinker	1932-1935
Joseph I. Vance		(Vice John Ott)	
(Part of year, vice R. Hosler)		R. Lee Riley	1933—
Morgan Wood	1903-1909	James F. Blain	1933—
Samuel G. Davenport	1904-1909	Edwin H. Martindill	1933—

**The board of county commissioners, with three members each serving a three-year term, was established in 1804 (2 O. L. 150). In 1906 the term of office was changed to two years (98 O. L. 271); in 1920 it was increased to four years, and so remains (108 O. L. pt. ii, 1300).

Recorders*

Winn Winship	1803-1810	Daniel Wilhelm	1882-1885
Angus Lewis Langhan	1810-1812	Joshua R. Wisehart	1885-1889
Humphrey Fullerton	1812-1819	John F. Brown	1889-1895
Samuel Taggert	1819-1838	Lee Des Martin	1895-1901
Arthur O. Lucket	1838-1844	J. Earnest Ratcliff	1901-1907
Josiah L. Hearn	1844-1847	Romulus H. Organ	1907-1911
S. D. Stratton	1847-1850	John Schweitzer	1911-1917
Henry Whissen	1850-1853	Claude B. Schaeffer	1917-1921
William Briggs	1853-1858	George W. Spencer	1921-1925
Stephen O. Hand	1858-1861	Pearl Terwilliger	1925-1927
Squire D. Stratton	1861-1867	John Stitt	1927-1933
Henry Whissen	1867-1870	W. F. Sheely	1933-1937
William Briggs	1870-1876	James W. Vause, Jr.	1937—
Edward Cryder	1876-1882		

*Under the law of 1803, the associate judges of the court of common pleas appointed the recorder for a seven-year term (1 O. L. 136). The office became elective for a three-year term in 1829, a two-year term in 1905, and a four-year term in 1936 (27 O. L. 65; 116 O. L. pt. ii, 184; *Ohio Constitution, 1851*, Art. VII, sec. 2).

Clerks of the Court of Common Pleas**

Thomas Foote	1803—	P. G. Griffin	11879-1880
John McDougal	1809-1811	(Vice E. W. Pearson)	
Humphrey Fullerton	1811-1845	Samuel J. Briggs	1880-1886
Angus L. Fullerton	1845-1855	Charles Reed	1886-1892
A. Hanson	1855-1861	Tiffin Gilmore	1892-1898
James D. Miller	1861-1864	Isaac M. Jordon	1898-1904
Erskine Carson	1864-1867	John C. Staggs	1904-1908
P. G. Griffin	1867-1873	Charles E. Biechler	1908-1913
Samuel Miller	1873-1875	Elmore R. Terry	1913-1917
Frank J. Esker	1875-1877	George J. Heinzellman	1917-1923
E. W. Pearson	1877-1879	Madge West	1923-1933
(Died in office)		Hettie M. Ott	1933—

*Called the prothonotary under the laws of the Northwest Territory and appointed by the governor. Under the Ohio constitution of 1802 the court appointed its own clerk for

Clerks of the Court of Common Pleas* (continued)

a seven-year term (Art. III, sec. 9). The constitution of 1851 made the office elective for a three-year term (Art. IV, sec. 16). Under the constitutional amendment of 1905 the term was changed to two years and to four in 1936 (97 O. L. 641; 116 O. O. pt. ii, 184).

Judges of the Court of Common Pleas**

Judges under the territorial government

Thomas Worthington (President Judge)	1798-1802	Elias Langham	1798-1802
		James Dunlap	1799-1802
James Scott	1798-1802	James Ferguson	1799—
Samuel Finley	1798-1802	William Guthrie	1799-1801
William Patton	1798-1802		

**The president and associate judges under the first constitution were appointed for seven-year terms by joint ballot of both houses of the general assembly (*Ohio Constitution, 1802*, Art. III, sec. 8). The constitution of 1851 made the office elective for five-year periods and required the incumbent to be a resident of the district in which elected (*Ohio Constitution, 1851*, Art. IV, sec. 12). The amendment of 1912 changed the term to six years, required the election of at least one judge for each county, who must be a resident of the county in which elected (Art. IV, sec. 12, as amended Sep. 3, 1912).

President judges under the constitution of 1802 in the districts which included Ross County

Wyllys Silliman (Resigned)	1803-1804	Gustavus Swan (Resigned)	1824-1829
Levin Belt (Vice W. Silliman)	1804-1805	Frederick Grimke (Vice G. Swan)	1829-1835
Robert F. Slaughter (Removed from office)	1805-1807	John H. Keith	1835-1850
		Henry C. Whitman	1850-1852
Levin Belt (Vice R. F. Slaughter)	1807-1810	James L. Bates (Part of year)	1852
John Thompson	1810-1824	John L. Green (Part of year)	1852

Associate judges under the constitution of 1802 in the districts which included Ross County

Name	Years
Reuben Abrams (Resigned)	1803-1805
Felix Renick (Resigned)	1803-1804
William Patton (Resigned)	1803-1804
John Hutt (Vice W. Patton)	Aug 1804-1807
Isaac Cook (Vice F. Renick)	Sep 1804-1809
Isaac Cook	1809-1824
James Armstrong (Vice R. Abrams)	1805-1809
James Armstrong	1809-1824
Thomas Hicks	1807-1817
Joseph Gardner	1817-1824
Presley Morris	1824-1831
James McClintick	1824-1845
John Bailhache	1825-1829
Samuel Swearingen	1830-1832
Isaac Cook	1832-1838
Isaac McCracken	1832-1840
Jacob Bonser	1838-1845
Tilgham Rittenhouse	1840-1846
Owen T. Reeves	1845-1852
Thomas Orr	1846-1852
Joseph Blacker	1847-1850
John Foster	1850-1851
Joshua Robinson	1851-1852

Judges under the constitution of 1851 in District V, subdivision 2, which included Ross County

Name	Years
John L. Green (Resigned)	1852-1857
James L. Bates	1852-1857
Shephard F. Norris	1853-1858
Thomas W. Bartley	1854-1859
James Sloan (Resigned, vice J. L. Green)	1857-1858
Alfred S. Dickey (Vice J. Sloan)	1858-1872
Robert M. Briggs	1859-1864
William H. Safford	1869-1874
Samuel F. Steel (Resigned)	1872-1881
Thomas M. Grey (Resigned)	1874-1876
John N. Van Meter (Part of year, vice T. M. Grey)	1876
Thaddeus A. Minshall (Resigned)	1876-1886
Ace Gregg	1881-1886
James H. Thompson (Vice S. F. Steel)	1881-1882
Henry M. Huggins	1882-1892
William Edgar Evans (Vice T. A. Minshall)	1886-1894
Cyrus Newby	1892-1915
J. C. Douglas	1894-1904
Ace Gregg (Part of year, died in office)	1894

Judges under the constitution of 1851, (continued)

H. B. Maynard (Vice Ace Gregg)	1894-1899	Willis H. Wiggins	1904-1909
		Charles Dresbach	1905-1910
Festus Walters	1895-1905	Frank G. Carpenter	1909-1915
Joseph Hidy	1899-1904	John W. Golsberry	1909-1915
Silvester W. Durflinger	1904-1909	Clarence Curtain	1911-1915

Resident judges under the constitutional amendment of 1912

John W. Goldsberry	1915-1921	Luther B. Yaple	1928-1930
Peter J. Blosser	1921-1928	Wilbur J. McKenzie	1930—

Judges of the Probate Court*

Samuel F. McCoy	1851-1860	Huston T. Robins	1900-1906
Samuel H. Hurst (Resigned)	1860-1862	Horation C. Claypool (Resigned)	1906-1910
William F. Hurst (Part of year, vice S. H. Hurst)	1862	Garrett S. Claypool (Vice H. C. Claypool)	1910-1913
Nicholas Throckmorton	1862-1865	Charles E. Capple	1913-1921
Thomas Welke	1865-1874	Elijah J. Cutright, Sr.	1921-1925
Benjamin F. Stone	1874-1884	Elijah J. Cutright, Jr. (Died in office)	1925-1930
J. L. Throckmorton	1884-1888		
George B. Bitzer	1888-1894	Marshall G. Fenton (Vice E. J. Cutright, Jr.)	1930—
James M. Thomas	1894-1900		

*The probate court, established under the laws of the Northwest Territory in 1788, consisted of a probate judge and two judges of the court of common pleas (Pease, *op. cit.*, 9). Under the constitution of 1802 it lost its identity completely in the court of common pleas. It emerged with its present form and functions, with a single judge serving a four-year term, under the constitution of 1851 (Art. IV, sec. 8).

1798-1939

Prosecuting Attorneys*

Henry Bush	1809-1810	Edward Lewis	1855-1858
Richard Douglas	1810-1811	Charles W. Gilmore	1858-1866
Carlos A. Norton	1811-1812	F. A. Marshall	1866-1867
Richard Douglass	1812-1813	Charles W. Gilmore	1867-1871
Levin Belt	1813-1815	Lawrence T. Neal	1871-1872
William Key Bond	1815-1817	Archibald Mayo	1872-1874
Joseph Sill	1816-1818	William E. Evans	1874-1876
Edward Kind	1819	Albert Douglas, jr.	1876-1880
(Part of year)		George B. Bitzer	1880-1882
Thomas Scott	1819-1820	R. R. Freeman	1882-1885
Samuel Atkinson	1820-1821	Marcus G. Evans	1885-1892
William S. Murphy	1821-1822	Payl Cooke	1892-1897
Samuel Atkinson	1822-1824	Edward U. Weidler	1897-1898
James McDowell	1824-1825	(Died in office)	
Edward King	1825-1829	Archibald Mayo	1898-1899
William Allen	1829-1832	(Vice E. U. Weidler)	
Joseph Sill	1832-1836	Horation C. Claypool	1899-1905
Gustavus Scott	1826-1838	Peter J. Blosser	1905-1911
Thomas T. Scott	1838-1840	Walter W. Boulger	1911-1915
James D. Caldwell	1840-1842	Addison P. Minshall	1915-1919
Robert Bethel	1842-1844	John P. Phillips, Jr.	1919-1923
Joseph Miller	1844-1846	Marshall G. Fenton	1923-1925
Milton L. Clark	1846–1850	Wilbur M. McKenzie	1925-1929
William T. McClintick	1850-1852	Howard Goldsberry	1929-1933
Thomas P. Hurst	1852-1855	Lester S. Reid	1933—

*At first appointed by the supreme court and later (1805) by the court of common pleas, a law passed Jan 23, 1833, made the office of prosecuting attorney elective for a term of two years (31 O. L. 13). In 1881 the term was increased to three years, in 1906 reduced to two, and in 1936 increased to four (78 O. L. 260; 98 O. L. 271; 116 O. L. pt. ii, 184).

Coroners*

Benjamin Urmston	1803-1806	William Roberts	1860-1861
David Boner	1806-1807	John R. Tucker	1861-1863
Thomas Steel	1808-1813	John R. Turner	1863-1864
William Rutledge	1813-1817	Uriah P. Wheaton	1864-1866
Josephus Collet	1817-1818	John R. Tucker	1866-1882
James McClifford	1818-1821	Mathias Bonner	1882-1886
James McCollister	1821-1823	Valentine Kramer	1886-1897
Williiam Rutledge	1823-1834	Hiram Streitenberger	1897-1899
Mathew Gillfillan	1834-1835	George J. Smith, Jr.	1899-1903
James H. King	1835-1836	Frank I. Gibbs	1903-1906
William Creighton	1836	Henry R. Brown	1906-1909
(Part of year)		Harry R. Welch	1909-1911
William G. Mick	1836-1839	Lewis T. Franklin	1911-1915
Pleasant Thurman	1839-1840	J. M. Leslie	1915-1921
John R. Tucker	1840-1854	W. W. Davis	1921-1923
Satterfield Scott	1854-1855	E. C. Robbins	1923-1927
George S. Baker	1855-1857	Albert Fry	1927-1929
Thomas Clemons	1857-1859	Everett C. Robbins	1929-1933
Mathew Armour	1859-1860	Robert E. Oliver	1933—

*Established in 1788, the county coroner was appointed for two-year terms by the territorial governor (Pease, *op. cit.*, 24-25). The Ohio Constitution of 1802 (Art. VI, sec. 1) made the office elective without changing the term which remained at two years until 1936, when it was increased to four years (116 O. L. pt. ii, 184).

Sheriffs**

Jeremiah McLene***	1798-1806	Charles Martin	1837-1841
David Shepherd	1806-1808	James McClintick	1841-1845
William Creighton	1808-1813	Charles Martin	1845-1848
James McClintick	1813-1815	William H. McMillin	1848-1853
James Steel	1815-1818	John R. Anderson	1853-1857
Josephus Collett	1818-1821	Thomas Ghormley	1857-1859
James Clifford	1821-1825	Edward Adams	1859-1866
John Tarlton	1825-1829	D. G. Dunnuck	1866-1867
Charles Martin	1829-1833	John C. McDonald	1867-1869
John Tarlton	1833-1837	John S. Mace	1869-1872

Sheriffs** (continued)

Felix B. Mace	1872-1877	William H. Stoker	1911-1915
Thomas L. Mackey	1877-1879	Alonzo T. Swepston	1915-1919
William L. Tulleys	1879-1884	Alfred D. Immel, Jr.	1919-1923
S. W. Clark	1884-1889	Donald B. Swepston	1923-1925
Joshua R. Wisehart	1889-1891	Alfred D. Immel, Jr.	1925-1929
John H. Blacker	1891-1895	Charles Fox	1929-1931
Hugh W. Warner	1895-1897	T. Ewing Arganbright	1931-1933
Alonzo T. Swepston	1897-1901	(Died in office)	
James A. Devine	1901-1905	Joseph Vincent	1933-1935
Latta Morrison	1905-1909	(Vice T. E. Arganbright)	
J. Henry Swope	1909-1911	Joseph Vincent	1935—

*** (previous page) Commissioned by the governor of the territory October 11, 1798; also served as first sheriff of Ross County under state government.

**Under the territorial government the sheriff was appointed by the governor from the time the office was created in 1792 (Pease, *op. cit.*, 8). Under the first constitution the office was made elective for two-year terms (*Ohio Constitution 1802* Art. VI, sec. 1) and was not changed until 1936, when the term was increased to four years (116 O. L. pt. ii, 184).

Treasurers*

Thomas Van Swearingen	1803-1804	Theodore Spetnagle	1876-1878
(Resigned)		Stanislaus Burkley	1878-1881
William Creighton	1804-[1809]	Rufus Hosler	1881-1886
(Vice T. Van Swearingen)		Nelson Purdum	1886-1890
Moses McClean	1809-1812	Samuel N. Veail	1890-1894
James Ferguson	1812-1828	Frank A. Sosman	1894-1898
Henry Lewis	1828-1854	Luther B. Hurst	1898-1902
Thomas Ghormley	1854-1857	Milton J. Scott	1902-1906
Daniel Dustman	1857-1861	Millard F. Partee	1906-1908
William Rittenhouse	1861-1865	George A. Wooster	1908-1913
S. A. Langdon	1865-1870	John B. Long	1913-1917
William A. Wayland	1870-1875	John H. Kellhofer	1917-1921
David Shotts	1875-1876	Latta Morrison	1921-1924

Treasurers* (continued

Pearl K. Rice	1924-1925	L. G. Thomas	1931-1933
T. Ewing Arganbright	1925-1929	(Vice F. Grubb)	
Oather M. Junk	1929-1931	L. G. Thomas	1933-1937
Frank Grubb	1931	Edward C. Noth	1937—
(Part of year, died in office)			

*Omitted from the constitution of 1802, the office of treasurer was created by legislative act of 1803 (1 O. L. 98). Appointive, by the associate judges in 1803 and, annually, by the county commissioners from 1804 to 1827, when the office became elective for two-year terms (1 O. L. 98; 2 O. L. 154; 25 O. L. 25-32). The constitution of 1851 provided that no person should hold the office for more than four years of any six (Art. X, sec. 3). In 1859 the general assembly made the term two years (56 O. L. 105). In 1936 it was increased to four years, as at present (116 O. L. pt. ii, 184).

Auditors**

David Collins	1820-1823	John A. McCoy	1877-1878
John McClean	1823-1841	Frank J. Esker	1878-1887
William B. Franklin	1841-1857	John A. Somers	1887-1893
William H. Skerrett	1857-1859	P. White Brown	1893-1896
William B. Franklin	1859-1861	Harry S. Adams	1896-1902
E. P. Kendrick	1861-1863	John H. Miller	1902-1905
Samuel Kendrick	1863-1865	Charles H. Pinto	1905-1909
Daniel Dustman	1865-1867	Robert D. Alexander	1909-1915
Samuel Frederick	1867-1869	Walter S. Barrett	1915-1923
Samuel Kendrick	1869-1871	Robert T. Weaver	1923-1927
R. D. McDougall	1871-1873	Fred L. Schlegel	1927-1935
Philip G. Griffin	1873-1877	William H. Herrnstein	1935—
Frank J. Esker	1877		
(Part of year)			

**Office established by legislative act Feb 18, 1820 (18 O. L. 70). At first appointive, it was made elective annually by an act of Feb. 2, 1821, the person elected taking office March 1 each year. (19 O. L. 116). In 1831 the term was set at two years, in 1877 at three years, in 19063 at two years, and in 1919 at four years (29 O. L. 280; 74 O. L. 381; 98 O. L. 271; 108 O. L. pt. ii, 1294).

Infirmary Directors*

Name	Years
James Armstrong	1830
James Minary	1830-1835
Anthony Walke	1830
Henry Johnston	1831-1833
Willis Hicks	1831-1838
James Armstrong	1834-1840
Nicholas Cunningham	1836-1837
Samuel Ewing	1838-1841
Nicholas Cunningham	1839-1841
willis Hicks	1841-186
Martin Dresbach	1842-1848
Daniel Ott	1842-1851
Elijah Huston	1848
John Entrekin	1849
Elijah Johnson	1849
Hezekiah Ingham	1850-1855
Martin Dresbach	1850-1851
Elijah Johnson	1851-1856
Andrew Carlisle	1851-1859
Nathan Hyde	1856-1860
D. H. Cryder	1857-1860
Jacob Thomas	1860
James Dunlap	1861
Sennet Allen	1861-1868
Nathaniel Hillhouse	1861-1862
Joseph Miskimmins	1861-1866
Anthony Hirn	1863-1866
Hugh Savage	1868-1872
Major Dunlap	1867-1870
Jeremiah Goodman	1868-1874
Jacob Grubb	18700-1873
Michael Kirsch	1872-1878
Joseph Smith (Part of year)	1873
James Lenox, Jr.	1873-1879
Joseph Smith	1874-1877
Robert A. Mace	1877-1880
Hiram Pritchard	1878-1881
Martin Rozell (Resigned)	1879-1881
Hanson Greenberry	1880-1883
Rufus Putnam, Jr. (Part of year, vice M. Rozell)	1881
John C. Price	1881-1884
Rufus Putnam	1882-1885
William J. Rodgers	1882-1884
Isaac J. Finley (Died in office)	1883-1884
Charles M. Dunlap	1884-1887
Isaac Lutz (Vice I. J. Finley)	1884-1890
Herman Trieber	1885-1888
Edwin B. Dolohan	1886-1892
Herman Schiller	1889-1895
Job S. Brown	1891-1897
Elwood Hough	1893-1899
George McCorkle	1895-1901
George W. Garrison	1897-1905
William Corcoran	1899-1902
William E. Floyd (Part of year)	1899
Frank Long	1901-1908
Bernard H. Kathe	1902-1905
Alfred Immell	1903-1909
George W. Brown	1904-1909
Joseph Janes	1909-1911
Martin Enderlin	1909-1913
Major Briggs	1909-1913
Alexander S. Babb	1911-1913

Infirmary Directors* (continued)

*This office was created by a legislative act in 1816, authorizing the appointment by the commissioners of seven directors, to have charge of the county infirmary and choose its superintendent (14 O. L. 447-448). By an act of 1831, the membership of the board was reduced to three, and in 1865 the members were made elective for terms of three years (29 O. L. 317; 62 O. L. 24-25). The board was abolished by law in 1913, its powers and duties being transferred to the board of county commissioners and the infirmary superintendent (102 O. L. 433).

Surveyors**

Name	Years	Name	Years
Duncan McArthur (Part of year)	1803	John A. Fulton (Part of year, resigned)	1855
James Denney (Resigned)	1803-1804	William Fulton (Vice J. A. Fulton)	1855-1858
John Evans (Vice J. Denney)	1804-1819	Joseph D. Ogle	1858-1861
		James E. Freeman	1861-1866
Allison C. Looker	1819-1822	James B. Mayberry	1866-1872
Cadwallader Wallace	1822-1824	Alexander W. McCoy	1872-1876
Mathew Bonner	1824-1829	Lorenzo Wesson	1876-1882
E. P. Kendrick	1829-1834	William P. DeLong	188-1885
Hiram A. McNeemar	1834-1836	Phillip Laessle (Died in office)	1885-1891
Thomas J. Timmons	1836-1840		
Henry Stipp (Resigned)	1840-1844	Benjamin H. Walker (Vice P. Laessle)	1891-1898
Nathaniel Massie (Vice H. Stipp)	1844-1849	Augustus W. Jones	1898–1904
		Benjamin H.Walker	1904-1909
Samuel Kendrick	1849-1850	[George] Murray Anderson	1909-1911
Allen C. McArthur	1850-1851	George Murray Anderson	1911-1913
Lewis W. Sifford	1851-1852	Glenn L. Perry	1913-1917
Henry Stipp	1852-1855	George Murray Anderson	1917-1919

**From 1803 to 1831 the surveyor was appointed by the court of common pleas and commissioned by the governor (1 O. L. 90-93). From 1831 to 1906 he was elected for a three-year ter, from 1906 to 1928 for a two-year term, and since 1928 for a four-year term (29 O. L. 399; 98 O. L. 245-247; 112 O. L. 179).

Surveyors* (continued)

Benjamin H. Walker	1919-1923	Benjamin H. Walker	1929-1931
George Bayne	1923-1925	John O. Black	1931-1933
John Schweitzer	1925-1919	John Schweitzer	1933-1935

Engineers**

John Schweitzer	1935—

**An act of 1935 changed the title of surveyor to engineer (116 O. L. 283).

Governmental

All addresses refer to Chillicothe, Ohio, unless otherwise noted

Auditor
2 N Paint St, Suite G
https://auditor.rosscountyohio.gov/

Board of Elections
475 Western Ave. Suite D
https://www.boe.ohio.gov/ross/

Clerk of Courts
2 N. Paint St., Suite B
https://www.rosscountyohio.gov/clerk/index.html

Commissioners
2 North Paint Street, Suite H
https://www.rosscountyohio.gov/commissioners/index.html

Common Pleas # 1
2 North Paint Street
https://www.rosscountycommonpleas.org/judges/courtroom-1.html

Common Pleas # 2
2 North Paint Street
https://www.rosscountycommonpleas.org/judges/courtroom-2.html

Coroner
217 Delano Ave., Suite A
https://www.rosscountyohio.gov/coroner/index.html

Dog Warden
2308 Lick Run Road, Suite B
No Website

Engineer
755 Fairgrounds Road
https://www.rosscountyohio.gov/engineer/index.html

Health Dept.
150 E Second Street
https://rosscountyhealth.org/

Humane Society
2308 Lick Run Road
https://www.rosscountyhumanesociety.org/

Probate-Juvenile Court
2 N. Paint St, Suite A
https://www.rossprobatejuvenile.com/

Prosecutor
33 W Main St, Suite 200
https://rosscountyprosecutor.com/

Recorder
2 North Paint Street, Suite E
https://www.rosscountyohio.gov/recorder/index.html

Sheriff
28 North Paint Street
https://www.rosssheriff.com/

Soil and Water Conservation
475 Western Avenue, Suite H
https://www.rosscountyswcd.org/

Treasurer
2 N Paint St, Suite F
https://www.rosscountyohio.gov/treasurer/index.html

Veterans Service Commission
475 Western Avenue, Suite C
https://www.rosscountyvsc.org/

Non-governmental websites

FamilySearch
https://www.familysearch.org/search/catalog

FamilySearch is a free website with digitized records. Court records located for Ross County include: Auditor, Clerk of Courts, Court of Common Pleas, Court of Quarter Sessions of Peace, Department of Health, Probate Court, Recorder . Other records listed include abstracts of records published by an individual or society.

Ross County Genealogical Society
A chapter of the Ohio Genealogical Society
303 S. Paint St.
P. O. Box 6352
Chillicothe, OH 45601
https://rcgsohio.org/

A very good website. Along with the basic information regarding the society, the site includes links to cemetery records, obituaries and death notices, lineage societies offered by the chapter, plus a library catalog listing the books held by the society. Library hours are listed as well as a map to the library.

Ohio Genealogical Society
611 State Route 97 West
Bellville, OH
ogs.org

The Samuel D. Isaly Library is Ohio's "top repository for Ohio genealogical information." The extensive collection includes: 70,000 volumes arranged by state, county, and subject matter; original 1880 census for all 88 Ohio counties; 250,000 ancestor cards by surname; 4,000 Bible records; over 23,000 high school and college year books; and over 5,000 lineage society applications. OGS offers lineage societies for First Families of Ohio, Settlers & Builders of Ohio, Century Families of Ohio, The Society of Civil War Families of Ohio, and the Society of Families of the Old Northwest Territory. The library also contains over 5,000 family histories.

Heritage Books by Jana Sloan Broglin:

Additions and Corrections to the W.P.A. Inventory of Adams County, Ohio: West Union

Additions and Corrections to the W.P.A. Inventory of Allen County, Ohio: Lima

Additions and Corrections to the W.P.A. Inventory of Ashland County, Ohio: Ashland

Additions and Corrections to the W.P.A. Inventory of Athens County, Ohio: Athens

Additions and Corrections to the W.P.A. Inventory of Belmont County, Ohio: St. Clairsville

Additions and Corrections to the W.P.A. Inventory of Cuyahoga County, Ohio: Cleveland

Additions and Corrections to the W.P.A. Inventory of Fulton County, Ohio: Wauseon

Additions and Corrections to the W.P.A. Inventory of Geauga County, Ohio: Chardon

Additions and Corrections to the W.P.A. Inventory of Hamilton County, Ohio: Cincinnati

Additions and Corrections to the W.P.A. Inventory of Hancock County, Ohio: Findlay

Additions and Corrections to the W.P.A. Inventory of Lake County, Ohio: Painesville

Additions and Corrections to the W.P.A. Inventory of Lorain County, Ohio: Elyria

Additions and Corrections to the W.P.A. Inventory of Lucas County, Ohio: Toledo

Additions and Corrections to the W.P.A. Inventory of Medina County, Ohio: Medina

Additions and Corrections to the W.P.A. Inventory of Montgomery County, Ohio: Dayton

Additions and Corrections to the W.P.A. Inventory of Muskingum County, Ohio: Zanesville

Additions and Corrections to the W.P.A. Inventory of Ross County, Ohio: Chillicothe

Additions and Corrections to the W.P.A. Inventory of Seneca County, Ohio: Tiffin

Additions and Corrections to the W.P.A. Inventory of Trumbull County, Ohio: Warren

Additions and Corrections to the W.P.A. Inventory of Washington County, Ohio: Marietta

Additions and Corrections to the W.P.A. Inventory of Wayne County, Ohio: Wooster

Hookers, Crooks and Kooks, Part I: Hookers

Hookers, Crooks and Kooks, Part II: Crooks and Kooks

Lucas County, Ohio, Index to Deaths, 1867–1908

Mason County, Kentucky Wills and Estates, 1791–1832, Second Edition

www.ingramcontent.com/pod-product-compliance
Lightning Source LLC
LaVergne TN
LVHW010223110826
845148LV00022B/1330

* 9 7 8 0 7 8 8 4 5 2 2 0 8 *